State and Party in
America's New Deal

State and Party in America's New Deal

Kenneth Finegold
and
Theda Skocpol

The University of Wisconsin Press

The University of Wisconsin Press
114 North Murray Street
Madison, Wisconsin 53715

3 Henrietta Street
London WC2E 8LU, England

Printed in the United States of America

Library of Congress Cataloging-in-Publication Data
Finegold, Kenneth, 1957–
    State and party in America's New Deal / Kenneth Finegold
and Theda Skocpol.
    360 p.   cm.
    Includes bibliographical references and index.
    ISBN 0-299-14760-6 (cl.).—ISBN 0-299-14764-9 (pbk.)
    1. United States—Politics and government—1933–1945.
2. Political parties—United States. 3. United States—Economic
policy—1933–1945. 4. New Deal, 1933–1939. 5. United States.
National Recovery Administration. 6. United States. Agricultural
Adjustment Administration. I. Skocpol, Theda. II. Title.
JK271.F48   1995
338.973'009'043—dc20   95-5709

To Martin Shefter,
from whom we keep learning

Contents

Figures

Tables

Preface

This book has been a long time in the making. Back when Ken Finegold was a doctoral candidate and Theda Skocpol was a junior faculty member at Harvard University, we launched a comparative-historical investigation of the roots and effects of the National Recovery Administration (NRA) and the Agricultural Adjustment Administration (AAA). We wanted to address theoretical issues about the role of the state in capitalist society in an empirically concrete way. And both of us were fascinated by the history of the New Deal in the United States.

From our original research, several professional presentations and published articles resulted. Then we found ourselves drawn into debates with many other scholars in political science and historical sociology who, like us, were using studies of New Deal policies as a way to explore theoretical issues. In due course, we decided to deepen our historical analysis and pull together our responses to scholars of other theoretical persuasions in this book. Other challenges intervened in each of our professional and personal lives before this work could be completed. But we kept at it and, at last, here it is.

State and Party in America's New Deal offers a historically grounded analysis of two major governmental interventions into the U.S. economy, but it is not for the most part a work of primary history. We have drawn in detail on past and recent works by historians about the New Deal, the NRA and AAA, and the administrative history of the U.S. government. Our contribution is one of synthesis and theoretically informed analysis.

The book is neither an abstract conceptual manifesto nor an atheoretical narrative. Our purpose is not primarily to criticize alternative approaches or describe past events but to explain actual patterns of political development. Our method is to work back and forth between theories of politics in advanced capitalist democracies and two concrete historical trajectories. Our argument is that the origins, implementation, and consequences of the NRA and AAA can best be explained with a historical institutionalist, state- and party-centered approach. We hope that this analysis of state, party, and public policy in the 1930s will contribute to theoretical debates in the social sciences and also to America's quest for just and realizable policies for the future.

Over the years of working on the project, we have been helped by many people, and we would like to express our thanks. Martin Shefter, to whom this book is dedicated, brought us together, encouraged our efforts, and inspired us by his successful battle to overcome the effects of a horrible accident. Thomas Regan served as research assistant for parts of this project and did a great job. Edwin Amenta, Amy Bridges, Richard Chapman, Albert O. Hirschman, John Ikenberry, Ira Katznelson, Richard Kirkendall, Michael Katz, Ann Shola Orloff, Harvey Rishikof, Robert Spitzer, Richard Valelly, Margaret Weir, and John Witte all gave up helpful comments at various points, as did our graduate students and colleagues at Chicago, Harvard, and Rutgers. As readers for the University of Wisconsin Press, Erwin C. Hargrove and Elizabeth Sanders gave detailed comments that helped us to improve the book. Rosalie Robertson and her predecessors at the Press, Lester Gordon-Massman and Barbara Hanhrahan, were patient and thoughtful editors. We have also benefited from criticisms of earlier versions of our arguments that appeared in the published works of Donald R. Brand, Paul Cammack, G. William Domhoff, Jess Gilbert and Carolyn Howe, Michael Goldfield, Gregory Hooks, Rhonda F. Levine, Steven McClellan, David Plotke, Jill Quadagno, and James T. Young. Finally, we are grateful for the many ways in which our spouses, Elaine K. Swift and Bill Skocpol, have helped during the course of writing this book. We could not do our work without them.

State and Party in
America's New Deal

1

Introduction

New Deal Interventions in Industry and Agriculture

U.S. policymakers today seek industrial competitiveness and agricultural prosperity. Which proposals for achieving these goals will they select? How effectively can these proposals be carried out? What impact will they have on class relations within industry and agriculture? Will these policies serve organized special interests or a broader, unorganized public interest? In many ways, contemporary debates over industrial and agricultural policy are conflicts over the limitations, legacies, and lessons of the two most significant previous experiments in economic intervention by the national government of the United States: the National Recovery Administration and the Agricultural Adjustment Administration.

As our exploration of these two New Deal programs will show, the origins, implementation, and effects of policy proposals are determined not by their abstract merits but by the organization of the national state and party systems. Such historically evolved institutional arrangements profoundly influence political alliances, policy formulation, and the consequences of administrative interventions in the economy. That was true in the 1930s, and it is still true today.

The NRA and the AAA were both created during the "Hundred Days" in 1933 under newly elected president Franklin Delano Roosevelt. Suddenly, these new federal administrative agencies were given sweeping authority to promote economic recovery from the Great Depression. Both the NRA and the AAA were to exercise their planning authority to reduce output and thereby increase prices. Within a few years, the Supreme Court ruled that both the NRA and

3

the AAA were unconstitutional in their original forms. Despite the apparent similarities of timing and purpose, however, the NRA and the AAA came about in different ways and had very different results.

Originally promoted by organized business groups, the National Recovery Administration was an unqualified failure, both economically and politically. It did little to improve economic conditions and may have even retarded recovery. NRA code provisions for particular industries stimulated conflicts between firms of different sizes, regions, and sectors. Capitalists and workers fought over the interpretation and enforcement of the ambiguous promise of protection for labor unions contained in Section 7(a) of the founding statute, the National Industrial Recovery Act. Even before the Supreme Court struck down the NRA in *Schechter Poultry Corporation v. United States*, 1935, it had been abandoned by both the Roosevelt administration and its original business supporters.

The AAA was a qualified success: it contributed to increased agricultural prosperity, and its production control approach has served as the basis for American agricultural policy to this day. Organized farmers had long opposed production control, yet the AAA was enacted instead of proposals advocated by the farm groups. Ironically, the AAA ultimately worked to benefit the large commercial farmers who had originally opposed it. After the Supreme Court struck down the AAA in *United States v. Butler*, 1936, production controls were quickly reformulated and continued.

The following two sections of this introductory chapter present overviews of these two cases of New Deal economic intervention. For the NRA and then the AAA, we lay out the crisis of the 1930s, the alternative solutions that were debated by political actors, the selection of some of these solutions for incorporation into national policy, and the economic and political results. Then we comment on the longer-term significance of these major New Deal efforts at the management of economic recovery. Finally, we pose the analytic questions about the NRA and the AAA that the remaining chapters of this book will address.

The Origins and Failure of the NRA

The NRA was an independent agency set up by the National Industrial Recovery Act (NIRA), which President Roosevelt signed on June 16, 1933. Roosevelt announced the NIRA as perhaps "the most important and far-reaching legislation ever enacted by the American Congress." The goal of the legislation, according to Roosevelt, was "the assurance of a reasonable profit to industry and living wages for labor with the elimination of the piratical methods and practices which have not only harassed honest business but also contributed to the ills of labor."[1] Title I envisaged the pursuit of industrial recovery through the "united action of labor and management under adequate governmental sanctions and supervision." "Codes of fair competition" were to be drawn up to regulate production practices within each industrial sector. Each code was required to include provisions setting minimum wages and maximum hours for workers. Directly or indirectly, the codes would constrain price decisions. Section 7(a) of the NIRA stipulated that the codes would also guarantee employees the right "to organize and bargain collectively through representatives of their own choosing."[2]

In several ways, this act broke with traditions of American industrial policy. First, although the Sherman Antitrust Act (1890), the Clayton Act (1914), and the Federal Trade Commission Act (1914) prevented competing firms from acting together to set prices, the NIRA reversed antitrust policy by encouraging competing firms to cooperate.[3] Title I, Joseph Schumpeter wrote, "as embodied in the codes of fair competition, introduced a type of state-supervised industrial self-government the gist of which, stripped of phraseological mimicry and apart from provisions about labor, was legal recognition and official encouragement, amounting to compulsion, of a modified form of the German cartel which, quite independently, tended to grow out of the activities of trade associations."[4]

Second, before 1933, employers had been largely free to set their own hours and wages. Federal laws limited hours only for maritime and railroad workers and for workers on federal projects, and they did not regulate wages for any workers. State "protective" laws applied mostly to women and had frequently been struck down by the courts. But under the NIRA, wages and hours in all industries would be supervised by the national government.[5]

Third, at key moments in the development of the American labor movement, the federal government had intervened against unions: Grover Cleveland sent the army to end the Pullman Strike of 1894, and Attorney General Harry Daugherty obtained an injunction to stop the railway shop strike of 1922.[6] Section 7(a), in contrast, placed the federal government in support of labor organization.

The Depression and Possible Policy Responses

The context for these extraordinary shifts in federal policy was, of course, the collapse of American industry in the Great Depression.[7] That collapse was truly momentous. The macroeconomic indicators in

Table 1. Macroeconomic indicators, 1929–1936

Year	Money GNP (billion $)	Price Index (1929=100)	Real GNP (billion $)	Unemployment (% civilian labor force)	Money Supply (billion $)[a]	Bank Failures (number)
1929	104.4	100.0	104.4	3.2	26.4	659
1930	91.1	96.4	94.4	8.9	25.4	1352
1931	76.3	86.8	87.8	16.3	23.6	2294
1932	58.5	78.1	74.8	24.1	20.6	1456
1933	56.0	76.9	72.7	25.2	19.4	4004[b]
1934	65.0	81.6	79.5	22.0	21.5	61
1935	65.0	82.5	87.8	20.3	25.5	32
1936	82.7	83.0	99.5	17.0	29.2	72

Sources: Money GNP, price index, real GNP from Lester V. Chandler, *America's Greatest Depression, 1929–1941* (New York: Harper & Row, 1970), pp. 4–7. Unemployment, bank failures from U.S. Department of Commerce, Bureau of the Census, *Historical Statistics of the United States, Colonial Times to 1970*, Bicentennial ed. (Washington, D.C.: U.S. Government Printing Office, 1975), 1:135, 2:1038. Money supply calculated from Milton Friedman and Anna Jacobson Schwartz, *A Monetary History of the United States, 1867–1960* (Princeton: Princeton University Press, 1963), pp. 711–13.
[a] Average of monthly M-1, currency held by public plus demand deposits in commercial banks.
[b] Figure noted in source as not strictly comparable to previous years.

table 1 show the course of the depression from 1929 to 1933. The Gross National Product, measured in current dollars (money GNP), dropped 46 percent. Prices also dropped, though not as severely, declining 23 percent. Real GNP (money GNP adjusted for price changes) is the best measure of aggregate output: this statistic indicates that the economy produced 30 percent less goods and services in 1933 than in 1929. In 1929, unemployment was significantly below the 5 percent level that connotes "full employment" today. Incredibly, by 1933, almost a quarter of the labor force was out of work. Money supply fell by 27 percent. Each of these statistics, computed on an annual basis, worsened in every year from 1929 to 1933 and then improved in every year from 1933 to 1936. Banking failures followed a more distinctive pattern, concentrating in three waves: October to December 1930, including the collapse of the Bank of the United States, at the time the largest failure in American history; March 1931 to January 1932, when the crisis became worldwide as the Austrian Kreditanstalt bank failed and Britain went off the gold standard; and October 1932 until the emergency bank holiday of March 1933.[8] Failures were dramatically reduced after the creation of the Federal Deposit Insurance Corporation and other reforms in 1933, but one-fifth of the nation's banks had already failed.[9]

Table 2. Industrial production, 1929–1936

Year	Textile Mill (million $ value add.)	Petroleum and Coal (million $ value add.)	Lumber and Wood (million $ value add.)	Raw Steel (million short tons)	Motor Vehicles (million factory sales)
1929	2321	829	1322	61.7	4.5
1930	—	—	—	44.6	2.8
1931	1525	432	524	28.6	1.9
1932	—	—	—	15.1	1.1
1933	1342	395	379	25.7	1.6
1934	—	—	—	29.2	2.2
1935	1461	471	542	38.2	3.3
1936	—	—	—	53.5	3.7

Source: U.S. Department of Commerce, Bureau of the Census, Historical Statistics of the United States, Colonial Times to 1970, Bicentennial ed. (Washington, D.C.: U.S. Government Printing Office, 1975), 2:669–80, 2:693, 2:716.

When the industrial economy is disaggregated into sectors, differences in the timing and severity of the Depression are apparent. From 1929 to 1933, declines in real output ranged from 3.4 percent in shoe production to 86.4 percent for locomotives.[10] Michael Bernstein found that "most manufacturing industries experienced movements in employment that coincided with the aggregate cycle," but the date of lowest employment and the speed of recovery varied between sectors.[11] Table 2 shows output statistics for the "Big Six" industries, each among the ten largest in the nation in 1933, placed under the first NRA codes.[12] Each sector traces the general pattern of decline and resurgence, but production of lumber and wood, linked with construction, fell more precipitously than production of textiles or petroleum and coal, and steel manufacturing recovered before sales of the motor vehicles that contained steel.

Data on output, prices, unemployment, money supply, and bank failures measure interrelated aspects of the economic crisis but do not make obvious the causes of the Depression or its solution. More than sixty years of theory and methodology have not produced consensus as to which of these variables (or others) should be regarded as causes and which as effects, why the Depression began when it did, why and when it became so severe, why it endured so long, or what should have been done. Interpretation of this crisis remains instead of touchstone for competing ways of understanding advanced capitalist economies.[13] Each interpretation carries with it a suggested governmental response. Keynesians trace the Depression to the slump of the automobile and construction industries, which began in mid-1929, before the

stock market crash of October 28. These sectors had led the growth of
the 1920s; their decline produced a fatal reduction in investment. The
remedy, Keynesians suggest, would have been increased government
spending to boost aggregate demand.[14] Paul Baran and Paul Sweezy
adopt some of the Keynesian analysis of underinvestment and stagna-
tion but see these phenomena as consequences of the "tendency of monopoly capitalism to create more surplus than it can absorb" and not
as just temporary disruptions. The Depression, in their view, demonstrates that socialism is a more rational economic system.[15] Monetarists
claim that the Federal Reserve's contraction of the money supply made
a normal recession into a catastrophe, particularly during the first
banking panic of 1930. They thus use the Great Depression to argue
for a regime of fixed monetary growth.[16] Charles Kindleberger emphasizes the international dimensions of the Depression: the Smoot-
Hawley Tariff of 1930, he argues, initiated a round of protectionism
that made adjustment through world trade impossible.[17] Bernstein
portrays the Depression as the coincidence of a downturn of the business cycle with a demand shift from durable to nondurable goods. Federal policy, he says, should have promoted a concomitant shift in investment toward the newer and more dynamic nondurable sectors.[18]

Back at the time of the Great Depression, neither the initial response of Republican President Herbert Hoover nor the subsequent
policies adopted by Democratic President Franklin Roosevelt corre-
sponded exactly with the solutions suggested by any of these modern
interpretations. The policies of these leaders developed from the political interplay of interests and institutions, as well as from the nature of
the economic crisis itself, as understood by the experts who advised
them. Hoover did not avoid action, as New Deal demonology would
have it. But his policies were constrained by his limited conception of
legitimate state activity, which in turn reflected the ideology of business interests within the Republican coalition. Hoover's administration was more interventionist than those of Harding and Coolidge, in
which he was also a leading figure. But revisionist claims that his approach either anticipated the New Deal or was superior to it are exag-
gerated.[19] Hoover's initial program for industrial recovery was "voluntaryism": business was asked to avoid wage cuts, labor to refrain
from seeking wage increases, state and local governments to increase
employment through public works, and private charity to prevent the
unemployed from becoming hungry and cold. The national government was to encourage and coordinate these efforts. In mid-1931,
Hoover shifted to a more activist program that included the creation of
the Reconstruction Finance Corporation to expand credit, banking re-

form, and increased federal construction spending. Congress rejected Hoover's proposal for a federal sales tax to balance the budget.[20] As secretary of commerce from 1921 to 1928, Hoover had supervised the formation of trade associations to provide data and establish industry standards, and his administration continued to do so. Hoover, however, would not endorse efforts by business organizations to revise the antitrust laws or relax their enforcement. He also opposed proposals by trade organizations and business peak associations to involve the state in sectoral planning.[21]

Roosevelt's policies, often stimulated by an activist Congress, were more comprehensive and more interventionist.[22] Recovery legislation during the "Hundred Days" of March–June 1933 included the NIRA; the Agricultural Adjustment Act; the Tennessee Valley Authority Act, establishing the TVA; and the Glass-Steagall Act, creating the Federal Deposit Insurance Corporation. During the same period, Roosevelt took the nation off the gold-exchange standard, a move that inflated the economy and insulated it from the harsh punishments the world monetary regime automatically inflicted on nations with overvalued currencies.[23] A series of new acronymic agencies—the Federal Emergency Relief Administration (FERA), the Civil Works Administration (CWA), the Public Works Administration (PWA), the Works Progress Administration (WPA), the Civilian Conservation Corps (CCC), and the National Youth Administration (NYA)—created jobs through public works large and small. During the "Second Hundred Days" of June–August 1935, Congress passed the Wagner Act, establishing the National Labor Relations Board (NLRB); the Public Utilities Holding Company Act; the Banking Act, centralizing the Federal Reserve System; the Social Security Act; and the mild Wealth Tax Act. The last great New Deal measure, the Fair Labor Standards Act of 1938, set minimum wages and maximum hours, though many exceptions were permitted.

Visions of Industrial Recovery

The NRA and the AAA were to contribute to general recovery by adjusting price, production, and employment levels in industry and agriculture. The NRA incorporated several contradictory visions of recovery.[24] Through the NIRA, Robert F. Himmelberg has written, "the business community achieved much of what it had sought during the depression years in its crusade for antitrust liberalization."[25] Some business leaders extended earlier voluntary ideas into proposals for recovery through governmentally enforced business planning. The NRA codes gave industrial sectors the opportunity to enforce coordination through state coercion and persuasion.

Other perspectives competed with business planning within the NRA. One approach sought regulation of employment conditions: maximum hours and minimum wages would reduce unemployment by spreading work. Regulatory views were sometimes combined with a nascent underconsumptionist doctrine, which held that increasingly productive industry would create more goods than could be sold unless mass purchasing power was increased. These responses to the Depression were embodied in Senator Hugo Black's bill for a maximum thirty-hour work week and in Secretary of Labor Frances Perkins's alternative, based on a minimum wage. The Black Bill, unacceptable to the Roosevelt administration, stimulated the administration's formulation of the NIRA as an alternative recovery measure.[26] The NIRA incorporated the regulatory and underconsumptionist approaches with its requirement that NRA codes stipulate minimum wages, maximum hours, and other labor conditions (such as abolition of child labor) and with Section 7(a), empowering unions to bargain for themselves on these issues. Advocates of national planning (most notably Brains Truster Rexford Tugwell) and of the old Wilsonian antimonopolism (most notably Louis Brandeis and Felix Frankfurter) had less influence on the NIRA statute. However, they could potentially shape policy through the provisions for public interest and consumer representation that were soon introduced by Roosevelt and NRA Administrator Hugh S. Johnson.

Neither the initial legislation nor the structures and procedures set up to implement the NIRA determined which of these visions the new industrial policy would fulfill. Business planning through the industrial codes became dominant because there was no preexisting state capacity for industrial policy. Without experts from within the state to write and administer code provisions, the NRA had to rely on business representatives to perform these tasks. Not surprisingly, they did so in their own private interests. Business control was a hollow victory, however, because the same lack of state capacity that allowed business to dominate the NRA made the program an economic and political disaster.

The Effects of the NRA

The National Recovery Administration did not contribute to recovery and probably actually hindered it. Tables 1 and 2 do indicate some recovery after 1933. Prices, output, GNP, and money supply increased; unemployment and bank failures went down. As a careful Brookings Institution report directed by Leverett S. Lyon pointed out in 1935, however, recovery of the U.S. lagged behind that of some other industrialized nations and was disappointing compared with gains after the previous slump of 1920–1921. The NRA, moreover, was "but one of a galaxy of recovery agencies operating simultaneously and with intermingled effects." The Brookings study concluded that "the NRA on the whole retarded recovery," though "to what extent it was detrimental no one can say with much assurance." The increases in profits that capitalists and business planners had hoped would follow upon the stabilization of production and the regulation of competition did not materialize in many sectors. Expectations that the NRA would solve the problem of underconsumption were also unmet. The NRA did raise nominal wages for a minority of workers. But because the NRA also raised prices, it produced no increase in real wages and thus no increase in purchasing power. Prices generally went up before wages, so there was not even a temporary stimulus to consumption.[27]

Other contemporary observers reached similar conclusions. Charles F. Roos, the NRA's former director of research, described the program as "a sincere but ineffective effort to alleviate depression," the main legacy of which was a set of warnings about what not to do in the future. Roos suggested that the NRA's net impact on purchasing power was zero or negative, since any stimulatory effects from wage increases were canceled out by the effects of business uncertainty.[28] At the end of 1933, John Maynard Keynes wrote Roosevelt that although he approved of such social reform provisions as the abolition of child labor and the regulation of hours, the NRA would not provide "any material aid to recovery."[29] Joseph Schumpeter believed that the NRA had had some beneficial effects under the crisis conditions of 1933: he credited the program with strengthening industrial organization and with improving business morale. But Schumpeter also thought that NRA wage increases and the discouragement of price competition retarded the subsequent recovery, resulting in disappointing output and employment levels.[30]

Michael Weinstein's more recent study provides econometric evidence for these pessimistic assessments. NRA price increases, Weinstein suggests, effectively nullified the expansionary effects of gold inflows; the money supply was larger, but it could not purchase more goods. Without the NRA, the gold-induced expansion of the money supply would have increased output 8 percent per year and reduced unemployment 15 percent per year. NRA price increases also pushed up interest rates, which in turn reduced investment. This diminution of real wealth lowered annual GNP an additional 6–11 percent.[31]

The NRA's political failure was even clearer than its economic inadequacy. By 1935, the NRA had lost most of its governmental support. In February, Roosevelt proposed a two-year extension of the expiring program but in a form that adhered more closely to antimonopolistic principles. Even this modified NRA seemed unlikely to win congressional approval. The Supreme Court resolved the issue in May 1935, when its unanimous decision in the "sick chicken" case of *Schechter Poultry Corporation v. United States* declared the NRA unconstitutional as a delegation of congressional authority and as a violation of the limitation of that authority to interstate commerce. Roosevelt loudly expressed outrage at the decision but would not at this time declare war on the Court. He merely asked Congress for a temporary, skeletal NRA to study the results and do what Hoover's Commerce Department had done: encourage voluntary cooperation. One NRA lawyer remembered that "when it was declared unconstitutional, Mr. Roosevelt purported to be quite upset. I think he was secretly relieved to have the Supreme Court do what he would otherwise have had to do himself."[32]

The NRA, as legislated and implemented, had conformed most closely to the vision of business planners. After the NRA, some sectors, including bituminous coal, oil, cotton textiles, trucking, shipping, aviation, and retail trade, continued to plan under government supervision.[33] But before long all branches of industry were placed under the Wagner Act, which strengthened Section 7(a)'s protections for labor organization. All industries were also covered by the Wages and Hours Act of 1938, which was administered by the Department of Labor rather than by easily captured code agencies.

In fact, the collapse of the NRA sundered the early political alliance between Roosevelt and business. Roosevelt survived the break, winning reelection in 1936 with a new coalition in which organized labor was much more important than it had been in 1932. The end of the NRA and the reelection of the president placed most of America's industrial capitalists in what was for them an unusual position. Having lost hegemony over the legitimate means of national governmental authority, America's captains of industry were by the mid-1930s in opposition to much of the federal government and the New Dealers who controlled it. As a result, capitalists had to put up with sweeping new enactments of labor and social legislation that they might previously have been in a position to block.

The Roots and Success of the AAA

The debacle of the NRA might suggest that state intervention in the economy must necessarily fail, its intended beneficiaries overwhelmed by its unintended consequences. New Deal intervention in agriculture, however, was much more of an economic and political success.

The AAA was authorized by the Agricultural Adjustment Act, which Roosevelt signed into law on May 12, 1933. The act aimed to raise prices for "basic agricultural commodities"—raise prices, that is, in relation to the prices farmers paid for industrial goods. The objective was nothing less than to change the overall economic relationship between commercial agriculture and industry in America. This attempt was doubly justified by the Roosevelt administration: as a new line of attack on the long-festering agricultural depression that had left farmers clamoring for government aid throughout the 1920s and as a propitious route to national economic recovery.[34]

As one of the program's key architects and administrators said, "Production control is the great distinction not only between the Triple A and its present critics but between the Triple A and previous farm relief expedients."[35] The AAA was authorized to pay producers of wheat, cotton, corn, hogs, rice, tobacco, and milk to reduce their output. Reduced output would in turn boost prices. Subsidies were financed by a tax on processors, to be passed on to consumers. Higher prices and subsidies would together give producers of each commodity the same purchasing power they had enjoyed during the 1910–1914 base period. This increased purchasing power, it was hoped, would alleviate the problem of underconsumption: more prosperous farmers would be able to buy the unsold products of industry.

Production control was a policy innovation. The farm problem was effectively defined as chronic overproduction, the solution as state intervention to reduce output. For most of the period since the New Deal, American farm policy has been based on production control. Before 1933, federal production controls were neither popular nor passable. Efforts at nongovernmental production controls, sometimes enforced by violence, dated back to the colonial period. But such efforts were inevitably hampered by the free-rider problem: it was in the interest of each farmer to produce as much as he or she profitably could while benefiting from the efforts of others to reduce their own production. The free-rider problem is especially severe in agriculture, since farmers must produce enough to repay fixed loans on land, seed, and machinery. Moreover, agrarian ideology dictated that the farmer produce as much as nature would allow; restriction of production was viewed as subordinating agriculture to industry. Proposals for enforcement of production controls by state governments—of which the most notably was Huey Long's plan to prohibit planting or harvesting cotton for the 1932 season—required interstate cooperation that could not be achieved.[36]

Beginning in the mid-1920s, agricultural economists based primarily in the United States Department of Agriculture (USDA) and the land-grant colleges developed the domestic allotment plan to raise farm prices by production control through the national government. The single most important figure in the origins of the domestic allotment plan was M. L. Wilson, an agricultural economist at Montana State College who revised and enthusiastically promoted the proposal.[37] For all the efforts of Wilson and others, the domestic allotment proposal had never been embraced by the farmers or their organizations. Even after adjustment became government policy, farmers continued to view production control as an unwanted child and strongly preferred legislation that would guarantee them the cost of production.[38]

Policy innovation in agriculture, as in industry, was a response to depression, yet the agricultural depression began earlier and was even more severe than the industrial crisis. The depression in agriculture began not in 1929 but in the latter half of 1920. Agricultural depression was an indirect consequence of the First World War. The impossibility of trade with many prewar suppliers and higher wartime needs increased the demand for American farm products, both at home and among the Allies. Increased demand led to higher farm prices, which led in turn to increased production of most commodities.[39] (See table 3 for the price and production levels of key commodities and the parity ratio, from the prewar years that were the base period for the AAA to 1936, the last year of the original AAA.) The boom did not end with the November 1918 armistice but continued for an additional year and a half. Between July and December 1920, however, prices fell quickly. Among the causes for the sudden collapse were the cutoff of war loans to Europe (which had allowed the Allies to purchase American commodities), the restoration of the railroads to private ownership at higher freight rates, and the deliberately deflationary monetary policy of the Federal Reserve Bank. Prices continued to drop until 1923. The industrial sector also suffered a slump after the First World War, but the depression in agriculture was deeper and more prolonged. One indication of this is that the parity ratio, measuring the relative position of the two sectors, shifted in industry's favor.[40]

Year	Wheat Production (in million bushels)	Wheat Price (in $/ bushels)	Corn Production (in million bushels)	Corn Price (in $/ bushels)	Hogs Production (in million pounds)	Hogs Price (in $/ pound)	Cotton Production (in thousand bales)	Cotton Price (in ¢/ pound)[a]	Cotton Parity Ratio[b]
1910	625	.91	2,853	.52	12,025	8.14	11,609	13.96	107
1911	618	.87	2,475	.68	12,517	6.21	15,694	9.65	96
1912	730	.81	2,948	.55	11,945	6.73	13,703	11.50	98
1913	751	.79	2,273	.70	12,220	7.54	14,153	12.47	101
1914	897	.98	2,524	.71	12,594	7.52	16,112	7.35	94
1915	1,009	.96	2,829	.68	13,935	6.47	11,172	11.22	103
1916	635	1.43	2,425	1.14	13,582	8.37	11,448	17.36	120
1917	620	2.05	2,908	1.46	12,928	13.89	11,284	27.09	119
1918	904	2.05	2,441	1.52	14,792	16.14	12,018	28.88	110
1919	952	2.16	2,679	1.51	13,986	16.39	11,141	35.34	99
1920	843	1.83	3,071	.64	13,533	12.92	13,429	15.89	80
1921	819	1.03	2,928	.52	14,132	7.63	7,945	17.00	87
1922	847	.97	2,707	.73	16,518	8.40	9,755	22.88	89
1923	759	.93	2,875	.81	17,008	6.94	10,140	28.69	89
1924	842	1.25	2,223	1.06	15,388	7.34	13,630	22.91	95
1925	669	1.44	2,798	.70	14,168	10.91	16,105	19.62	91
1926	832	1.22	2,547	.74	14,909	11.79	17,978	12.49	88
1927	875	1.19	2,615	.85	16,340	9.64	12,956	20.20	91
1928	914	1.00	2,666	.84	16,189	8.54	14,477	17.98	91
1929	824	1.04	2,516	.80	15,582	9.42	14,825	16.78	92
1930	887	.67	2,080	.60	15,176	8.84	13,932	9.46	83
1931	942	.39	2,576	.32	16,541	5.73	17,097	5.66	67
1932	756	.38	2,930	.32	16,368	3.34	13,003	6.52	58
1933	552	.74	2,398	.52	16,566	3.53	13,047	10.17	64
1934	526	.85	1,449	.82	12,385	4.14	9,636	12.36	75
1935	628	.83	2,299	.66	10,673	8.65	10,638	11.09	88
1936	630	1.02	1,506	1.04	12,976	9.37	12,399	12.36	92

Source: U.S. Department of Commerce, Bureau of the Census, *Historical Statistics of the United States, Colonial Times to 1970,* Bicentennial ed. (Washington, D.C.: U.S. Government Printing Office, 1975), 1:511, 519, 517, 489.

a One bale = 500 lb. cotton.

b The parity ratio is the ratio of farm prices to farm costs, each computed with the 1910–1914 average set at 100. Hence, a parity ratio above 100 means farm purchasing power is more than in the base period; a ratio below 100 means farm purchasing power is less than the base.

Farm prices rose during the mid-1920s, but the parity ratio remained below that of the prewar "Golden Age," and farmers were pressed by rising taxes and by interest payments on mortgages that had been taken out to finance wartime expansion.[41] Farmers did not seem to think conditions had improved, and they continued to mobilize in support of demands for state intervention in agriculture. The collapse of the world economy after 1929 brought the third phase of what was already a long agricultural crisis. Unemployment and lower wages reduced domestic demand, while high tariff barriers and industrial unemployment abroad reduced the possibility of relief through exports. Once again, industrial prices also dropped, but not as sharply as farm prices. Industrial manufacturers could act to maintain prices by reducing their own production, through trade association agreements or the temporary suspension of factory operations. Farmers could not do the same, since their acreage was determined at planting time and had to allow for the possibility of bad weather. Lower prices might even lead to increased production, as farmers planted more to meet their fixed costs.[42]

President Hoover responded to the depression in agriculture as he responded to the depression in industry, with policies of ideologically constrained innovation. Like his predecessor, Calvin Coolidge, who had twice vetoed the McNary-Haugen bill, Hoover opposed this popular proposal to raise domestic farm prices by dumping, that is, by exporting surplus commodities at lower prices. Instead, Hoover's central initiative was the Agricultural Marketing Act of June 15, 1929, which set up a Federal Farm Board to provide cooperatives with low-interest loans and to establish stabilization corporations that would hold surpluses for future domestic sale.[43] The cooperatives reflected the same associational ideology that Hoover applied to other policy areas: farmers were to be organized from the top down, by centralized agencies of managers and processors. The stabilization corporations could reduce short-term fluctuations, but they could not plan or export surpluses. Many of the agricultural economists who would serve in the AAA participated in the Farm Board, and it set a crucial precedent by identifying overproduction as the source of farm problems. The Farm Board's approach to production control, though, was always voluntary.

The general economic collapse that began late in 1929 made the farm problem worse, as did the Smoot-Hawley Tariff of 1930, which Hoover signed with misgivings. Foreign nations, unable to sell their goods in the U.S. market (and thus to earn dollars to buy U.S. commodities), retaliated by imposing high tariffs on American agricultural products. As demand for farm goods fell, the Farm Board was forced to purchase surpluses of wheat (one-third of the nation's supply) and cotton. These were eventually dumped abroad, just as McNary-Haugen would have done, or donated to the Red Cross. Losses from the program exceeded $300 million.

The New Deal and Agriculture

During the course of the 1932 presidential campaign, Franklin Roosevelt spoke about agriculture only in general terms, listing the goals a farm policy need accomplish. Roosevelt was masterfully effective at making each leader of a major farm organization believe that his ideas were being accepted by the presidential candidate.[44] In retrospect, though, only the domestic allotment plan for production control met all his conditions. After the election, Roosevelt and his advisors were able to use the ties developed with the farm organizations during the campaign to persuade them to accept a policy of production control. The farm organizations, in turn, won the consent of their members for the new direction in farm policy.[45]

As in industry, Roosevelt's policy in agriculture incorporated contradictory approaches. George Peek, coauthor of the McNary-Haugen Plan, was made administrator of the AAA, and the program included marketing provisions. Moreover, to keep the support of farm leaders through the passage of the AAA, Roosevelt gave in to congressional pressure to accept an amendment authorizing inflation of the currency, a nostrum long popular among farmers struggling with debt. But the AAA was placed within the USDA, and Peek was made responsible to Secretary of Agriculture Henry A. Wallace, who, along with his assistant secretary, Rexford Guy Tugwell, was a confirmed believer in production controls. M. L. Wilson became administrator of the Wheat Section and later assistant secretary of agriculture and under secretary.[46]

Internal conflicts were worked out more quickly and more completely in the AAA than they were in the NRA. Production control won. Peek's attempts to use the new agency for marketing programs pitted him against Wallace, Tugwell, and the agricultural economists within the AAA. In December 1933, Peek was forced out of the AAA and replaced with Chester A. Davis, a convert to production control.[47]

The AAA production-control program required the determination of parity targets, processing taxes, benefits rates, production levels, and acreage bases.[48] The same USDA–land-grant college experts who had developed and promulgated proposals for production control were brought into the AAA to carry out these tasks. Connections between the USDA and the land-grant colleges provided the AAA with a source of staffers oriented to professional planning norms rather than to the demands of either farmers or businessmen. The NRA, in contrast, remained conflict-ridden because, unable to draw on a preexisting industrial policy network, it had been forced to rely on businessmen who had never been trained (or given any incentive) to plan in the public interest or for industry as a whole.

Economic and Political Successes

Preexisting capacity for state intervention in the USDA and the land-grant colleges made the AAA an economic and political success. It is difficult to isolate the economic impact of production controls from the effects of other AAA activities and federal programs. Nonetheless, a contemporary Brookings Institution study, similar in format and approach to the critique of the NRA by Lyon and his collaborators, gave the AAA a positive assessment. Edwin G. Nourse, Joseph S. Davis, and John D. Black found that a high proportion of farmers signed up and subsequently complied with the production control contracts and that the program increased farm income in both absolute and relative terms. Table 3 indicates that for each of the four major commodities, production levels dropped and prices increased, while the parity ratio climbed as well. Production control was most effective in decreasing supply and raising prices for cotton and tobacco; supplementary legislation requested by producers of these two crops had subjected production in excess of individual allotments to heavy taxation. Nourse, Davis, and Black credited drought rather than the AAA with most of the reduction in wheat and corn-hog production but speculated that the program would have had a greater impact under more bountiful weather conditions. The Brookings authors tentatively concluded that the AAA had contributed to general recovery by enlarging and accelerating purchasing power and by restoring confidence in the industries closely tied to the rural market, although the magnitude of these effects was less than had been predicted by Roosevelt, Wallace, and other AAA supporters.[49] Keynes said that "A.A.A. is organising for the farmer the advisable measure of restriction which industry long ago organised for itself. Thus, the task which A.A.A. is attempting is necessary though difficult; whereas some part of what N.R.A. seems to be aiming at is not only impracticable but unnecessary."[50] Schumpeter also viewed the AAA more favorably than the NRA, concluding, "Whatever we may think about technique, details, aims professed, or arguments used, the success of the policy in removing a major obstacle from the road of recovery and in reviving shriveled tissues in the economic organization is beyond reasonable doubt."[51]

The AAA's political success was even more striking: a program that was unpopular in 1933 was institutionalized by 1936. Even as the NRA was coming under increasingly vociferous political attacks, the AAA received a favorable congressional review and gained support from farmers and their organizations. In January 1936, a 6-to-3 Supreme Court vote struck down the Agricultural Adjustment Act on the grounds that the processing tax that financed the program was unconstitutional (in *United States v. Butler*, also known as the Hoosac Mills Case). Far from signaling the end of state intervention in agriculture, the decision gave agricultural economists in the AAA Program Planning Division a chance to put into effect proposals they had developed during the first three years of production control. Their recommendations, including reorganization of the AAA along regional rather than commodity lines and subsidies for farmers planting soil-conserving crops, were incorporated into the Soil Conservation and Domestic Allotment Act of 1936. To conform with the Supreme Court ruling, the new program was financed through general revenues. The commodity program was further modified, again in accord with the recommendations of agricultural economists, by the Agricultural Adjustment Act of 1938. This measure established taxes for production above quotas of wheat, cotton, and tobacco and initiated a loan program designed to create an "ever-normal granary" in which surpluses would be stockpiled for times of need. The 1936 act was passed without controversy shortly after the Hoosac Mills decision. The 1938 act aroused more opposition, including that of the Grange, but won congressional approval with the support of the Farm Bureau.[52]

During the same period in which the agricultural economists were able to revise the economic programs they had originated, efforts to extend the New Deal in agriculture to the reform of class relations were defeated. The Farm Bureau expanded its membership and operations, especially in the South, in tandem with the local administration of AAA production controls. The enlarged Farm Bureau linked large-scale producers of corn and cotton, helping to forge the Conservative Coalition between midwestern Republicans and southern Democrats, who represented the two sets of farmers in Congress. From the mid-1930s on, the Farm Bureau became pivotal in defending its own organizational interests and the class interests of commercial farmers. Tenant farmers were denied their share of benefit payments, and AAA lawyers who supported their right to organize were purged.[53] The

Farm Security Administration, created to help poor farmers, was restricted and eventually dismantled.[54] By the end of the Roosevelt administration, conservatives had also crippled efforts by the agricultural economists who had developed and administered production control to expand state intervention to encompass comprehensive planning and social research.[55]

With the breakdown of the NRA, industrial capitalists lost power relative to labor unions. The institutionalization of the AAA, in contrast, allowed commercial farmers to beat back all challenges from the agricultural underclasses.[56] A program that farmers did not want created an enduring governmental niche within the post–New Deal political economy. But that niche was only for some of them.

Consequences for the U.S. Political Economy

These contrasting outcomes were significant not only for the recovery efforts of the early New Deal but also for the long-term development of the American economy and polity. Imagine for a moment that the NRA and the AAA had together fully achieved their declared objectives. If both programs had succeeded—and if their efforts could have been coordinated—the United States might have emerged from the Great Depression as a centralized system of politically managed corporatist capitalism. The state would have been directly involved in planning price and production levels and in allocating income shares to capitalists, farmers, and workers. Commercial farmers and (to a small degree) industrial workers would have made income gains relative to capitalists. Workers would have gained some sort of collective organization but without rupturing in the process their subordinate and cooperative relationship to industrial management. Industrialists, meanwhile, would have enjoyed regularized, minimally competitive relationships with one another under the aegis of government supervision.

Yet instead of a politically managed, centralized capitalist system, the New Deal established the "Broker State," a "government intervening in an adhoc and piecemeal fashion," on behalf of favored groups and sectors.[57] Incapable of national planning in any meaningful sense, the post–New Deal state has been an enlarged and more socially intrusive hodgepodge of separate nexuses of power, a collection of subsystems linking partially autonomous bureaucratic agencies, special support in Congress, and organizations representing well-bounded socioeconomic interests.[58] The Democrats, who had constructed this state, could for a time win elections, but they could not achieve many of their governmental objectives. To be sure, the consequences of the

NRA and AAA helped to establish a Democratic majority, but that majority was relatively narrow and often could not be translated into public policies of economic planning. The failure of the NRA shattered the ideal of overall business coordination in favor of an uneven pattern of government regulation: a few industries achieved special government intervention to help rationalize competition in their own ranks, while most shied away from further "bureaucratic" entanglements. The dream of harmony between corporate management and industrial unions dissolved into ever more bitter conflicts over the NRA's labor provisions. By 1935, these conflicts had fed back into the administrative and representative process of government to produce the National Labor Relations Act (the Wagner Act), sanctioning independent unions. After the New Deal, business could gain industrial "peace" but only through collective bargaining with trade unions independent of direct management control.

The success of the AAA meant that commercial farmers, unlike most industrial capitalists, would continue to be organized by the state for their own collective economic good. Since the New Deal, the national government has intervened in the market to control price and production levels for key commodities. These decisions have been made in the interests of commercial farmers. Agricultural tenants and sharecroppers were denied benefit payments from farm programs. These programs, moreover, encouraged the transformation of tenants and sharecroppers into landless farm laborers.

The policies of the New Deal made the winning coalition of 1932 into what Martin Shefter and Benjamin Ginsberg describe as a "regime," a set of durable political arrangements that determined not only electoral outcomes but also the agenda, resources, and ideology of American politics.[59] The successes and failures of the NRA and the AAA were especially important in creating this regime—and in defining its limits. Industrial labor unions, protected and enlarged by the NRA and then by the Wagner Act, provided votes, money, and organizational resources for the Democrats.[60] Firms that benefited from the prolabor policies and the sector-specific programs that replaced the NRA became Democratic; firms that did not benefit from such policies or that challenged those that did became Republican.[61] The AAA and successor farm programs kept southern cotton, tobacco, and peanut farmers in the Democratic party and converted wheat and dairy farmers in the Upper Midwest from state-level third parties to the Democrats. Farmers in the Corn Belt, who were not brought completely under federal commodity controls until the 1980s, remained Republicans.[62] Farm workers continued to be excluded from both parties.

Overall, these alignments favored the Democrats. Yet the New Deal Democratic majority was relatively short-lived. Continuous Democratic control of Congress ended in 1946; continuous Democratic control of the presidency ended in 1952. The party alignment created by the New Deal then entered a long phase of decay.[63] "The post-1952 resumption of the march toward electoral disaggregation," Walter Dean Burnham suggests, "leads one to suspect the possibility that, in terms of the history of American voting behavior at least, the New Deal might come to be regarded one day as a temporary if massive deviation from a secular trend toward gradual disappearance of the political party in the United States."[64]

What made the New Deal deviation temporary was its dependence on the addition of northern workers to the white voters of the Solid South to form a national Democratic majority, for the white South would be solidly Democratic only as long as its racial domination of the black South was solidly unchallenged.[65] The civil rights revolution triggered long-delayed electoral change in the South. Southern white defections from the New Deal Democratic coalition, in turn, helped Republicans to win five of six presidential elections from 1968 to 1988.[66]

The New Deal Democratic majority, measured over the long run, was actually less robust than that of the Republicans under the pre–New Deal party alignment, "the system of 1896." From 1896 to 1928, the Republicans won seven of nine elections, with an average margin of 9.4 percent of the total popular vote, as table 4 shows. From 1932 to 1964, the years of the New Deal party system, the Democrats also won seven of nine elections but by a lower margin, averaging 6.4 percent better than the Republicans. The Republican advantage from 1896 to 1932 is more striking when splinter third parties are counted towards the major parties' votes (figures in parentheses).

Under the New Deal alignment, moreover, the Democrats were not as successful in making policy as they were in winning elections. Southern Democrats in Congress, responsive to large landowners and the Farm Bureau but not to disorganized (and often disfranchised) farm workers, became the great anomaly of the New Deal party system, necessary to the party's congressional majorities and occupying many of its leadership positions yet hostile to the party's liberal policies. A conservative congressional coalition linking southern Democrats with Republicans was evident by 1937 and became the norm after 1946. When this coalition secured an effective congressional majority, as it has in most sessions since 1946, Democratic presidents were severely constrained: neither Franklin Roosevelt's bargaining nor John Kennedy's charisma could overcome this cross-party alliance.[67]

Table 4. Majority party average electoral margins, 1896–1964 (percentage distribution)[a]

Years	Republican	Democratic	Margin
1896–1928	50.3	40.9	9.4
	(55.2)	(40.9)	(14.3)
1932–1964	45.8	52.5	6.7
	(46.1)	(53.1)	(7.0)

Source: Percentages computed from Congressional Quarterly, Inc., *Congressional Quarterly's Guide to Presidential Elections*, 2d ed. (Washington: Congressional Quarterly, Inc., 1985), pp. 344–61.

[a] These figures sum to less than 100 percent because they are percentages of the total vote, not the two-party vote. The first line for each period does not include other parties. Figures in parentheses include the most important splinter parties with the party with which their candidate had previously been identified. Votes for Theodore Roosevelt (1912, Progressive), Robert La Follette (1924, Progressive), and William Lemke (1936, Union) are added to the Republican totals for those elections; Strom Thurmond (States' Rights) and Henry Wallace (Progressive) are added to the Democratic totals for 1948. Other parties were genuinely independent (Prohibition, Socialist) or received less than 1 percent.

Looking Ahead

To understand the economic and political arrangements that emerged from the New Deal and continued to structure the American political economy, it is necessary to understand the NRA and the AAA. Why did the national government enact recovery programs favored by organized industry and rejected by organized agriculture? Why did the industrial program fail, and why did the agricultural program succeed for commercial agriculture? Why did the NRA stimulate class conflict in industry while the AAA reinforced class domination in agriculture?

Part 1 of this book is devoted to answering these questions. The origins, implementation, and consequences of the NRA and AAA can best be explained, we believe, by a theory that focuses on the ways patterns of party and state organization select among policy alternatives and shape policy outcomes. Our analysis is historical, institutional, and resolutely antifunctionalist: there is no necessary match between situation and response. Advanced capitalist economies are sufficiently complex that crises do not come with obvious solutions attached. Policies change in response to economic conditions but only as those conditions are mediated by state and party organizations. The consequences of these policies are often unintended and are political as well as economic.

In chapter 2, we outline a historical and institutionalist approach that places the states and political parties at the center of analysis. The main variables employed in our analysis of the state are autonomy and capacity. The main variables employed in our analysis of parties are alignments and strategies. This chapter also explores the problems of comparing industry and agriculture and suggests how economic differences between sectors can be incorporated into our institutionally focused approach.

In the remaining three chapters of part 1, we use our theoretical approach to make sense of the origins, implementation, and impact of the NRA and the AAA. Chapter 3 traces the origins of both programs by analyzing the contradictions of the early New Deal Democratic coalition. In each case, a key Democratic constituency was able to elicit federal intervention but not to control the choice among competing interventionist proposals. Workers' representatives backed the Black Bill to regulate hours; farmers' representatives wanted the national government to boost prices without controlling production. Each of these proposals, however, would have violated Roosevelt's sense of what was needed to restore prosperity; the structural constraints of a capitalist economy were thus enforced by the president's own policy preferences. Roosevelt endorsed alternative policies that did not have popular support: the ideas of agricultural economists became the basis for the AAA, and the ideas of business planners became the basis for the NRA.

Chapter 4 explains what happened when the two programs were put into practice. Their contrasting outcomes reflected the very different administrative resources available to the national state in implementing the NRA and the AAA. The NRA collapsed because it was unable to draw on a preexisting administrative elite trained to plan for industries as wholes. It had to rely instead on businessmen concerned only with the interests of their individual firms. The AAA, in contrast, was able to draw on a cohesive network of agricultural economists based in the land-grant colleges and the USDA. These experts effectively carried out the AAA's production control proposals.

Chapter 5 compares the consequences of the NRA and the AAA for class relations in industry and agriculture. Different patterns of implementation combined with different patterns of incorporation into party coalitions to produce different consequences for industrial workers than for agricultural sharecroppers, tenants, and laborers. The failure of the NRA led to a split between business and the Roosevelt administration, which then became more closely allied with trade unions. Labor influence was expanded by urban liberal gains in the congressional elections of 1934. With passage of the Wagner Act in 1935, the national government would continue to encourage (and simultaneously rechannel) union organization under the Wagner Act, which expanded the NRA's labor guarantees. The conservative orientation of agricultural officials in the AAA commodity divisions, however, meant that large commercial farmers would benefit most from renewed farm prosperity. And southern Democrats, who gained crucial positions in Congress as a result of Roosevelt's national electoral majority, used those positions to attack federal efforts to improve conditions among the disfranchised agricultural underclasses.

In part 2 of the book, we enter into critical dialogues with the proponents of alternative theoretical perspectives that have been, or might be, applied to the economic interventions of the New Deal. Chapter 6 examines pluralist and elite theories about the New Deal, chapter 7 considers Marxist approaches, and chapter 8 discusses rational choice arguments. These alternative theoretical frameworks, we argue, cannot make consistent sense of the origins, implementation, and consequences of the NRA and the AAA. But we should not throw away their specific insights. Careful analysis of their strengths and weaknesses in explaining the New Deal in industry and agriculture reinforces the case for our historical and institutional, state- and party-centered explanatory approach. Our approach, we show, can specify conditions under which processes highlighted by alternative theories operate. Part 2 of this book can be useful to teachers and students who want to use concrete, empirical materials to explore theoretical debates that are too often waged in purely rhetorical or metatheoretical terms.

The conclusion (chapter 9) summarizes our analysis of the NRA and the AAA and restates its theoretical implications. This final chapter also sketches the implications of our findings for policy debates today. As in the 1930s, whether new proposals will be enacted, whether they will work, and what the consequences will be will depend on the political institutions of party and state. The failure of the NRA, the most ambitious such effort in American history so far, suggests the electoral and administrative conditions that would be necessary for a contemporary industrial policy to be enacted and successfully implemented. Proposals to move away from the production control approach begun with the AAA, toward either a greater reliance on the free market or a more redistributive version of supply management, face other institutional barriers. Contemporary proposals for reformulation of industrial and agricultural policies typically assume more favorable political and administrative conditions than really exist; their enactment and effective implementation are thus improbable. Proposals that address themselves to the development of state and party organizations are more likely to produce lasting policy change than proposals that are formulated as if institutions did not matter.

Part 1

Explaining the National Recovery Administration and the Agricultural Adjustment Administration

Introduction to Part 1

As parallel programs of state intervention in industry and agriculture, the National Recovery Administration (NRA) and the Agricultural Adjustment Administration (AAA) provide comparative case studies in the politics of advanced capitalism. As chapter 1 demonstrated, the outcomes of the NRA and the AAA have been central to the political and economic development of the United States from the New Deal to the present. A theoretical approach that can explain the NRA and the AAA, therefore, should make sense of fundamental characteristics of the modern U.S. political economy as well. To say that a theory explains the NRA and the AAA is to say that it generates testable predictions about the content and trajectories of these major New Deal industrial and agricultural policies and that these predictions turn out to be accurate.

As we shall see in part 2, rational choice, pluralist, elitist, and Marxist theories—the most commonly accepted ways of analyzing politics in capitalist democracies—often do not generate clear predictions about the NRA and the AAA, or they generate predictions that are inaccurate. In this part of the book, we argue and demonstrate that a theory based on the concepts of state capacity and party alignments best explains the roots and fate of the NRA and the AAA. This state- and party-centered approach, we argue, is the most promising way to analyze the intersections of advanced capitalism and representative democracy in the United States and other nations.

It is worth stressing at the outset that our theoretical approach is state- and party-centered but does not ignore the influence of variables pertaining to the individuals, groups, elites, and classes that are central to the society-centered theories we discuss in part 2. Taken together, "the state" and "the party system" do not explain all interesting political phenomena. But economic patterns and social actors must be situated in relation to the state and political parties if we wish to understand the contrasts between the NRA and the AAA. And this suggests that a theoretical approach that makes state and parties central is likely to be applicable, as well, to other fundamental problems of political development and policy making in the United States and beyond.

2
State, Party, and Policy
A Historical and Institutional Approach

The National Recovery Administration (NRA) and the Agricultural Adjustment Administration (AAA) were similar in purpose, different in result. Similarities between the two programs reflected the circumstances they shared. Both were products of their time period and thus of the experiences of the Great Depression and the memories of World War I. Both were situated within a constitutional system that divided authority among executive, legislative, and judicial branches and guaranteed due process to individuals and corporations whose rights had been violated. Both were situated as well within a capitalist economic system, which they sought to revive through the partial substitution of planning for markets.

Differences between the NRA and the AAA reflected, to some degree, the differences between industry and agriculture as major sectors of the U.S. economy. Even more, however, the critical differences of content and trajectory between the NRA and the AAA occurred as a result of the differential positions of groups within industry and agriculture in relation to the U.S. state and political parties of the 1930s.

This chapter begins with a discussion of the economic and organizational differences between industry and agriculture at that time, showing why such differences are relevant—but insufficient—to an explanation of the NRA and the AAA. Then we proceed to outline our theoretical approach, focusing first on the political party system and then on the administrative and other institutional arrangements of the U.S. state. For each of these discussions, we begin with general conceptual issues and then turn to a more historically grounded analysis of U.S. parties and governmental institutions in the 1920s and 1930s.

Industry and Agriculture

"Comparing apples and oranges" is a cliché for what cannot be compared at all. How then can we compare apples and steel, or oranges and automobiles? We can compare industry as a whole with agriculture as a whole by noting the similarities and differences, economic and organizational, that are most salient to the study of the New Deal policies that are the focus of this book. All such characteristics represent tendencies rather than absolutes. Each major economic sector contains diverse subsectors, and any particular characteristic may fit one subsector better than another.

Sectoral ·Characteristics

Some might argue that either industry or agriculture is inherently more "complex" than the other, but we disagree. Because industry and agriculture are each composed of distinct but interrelated sectors, the structure of agriculture is as complex as the structure of industry. Some subsectors within agriculture compete with one another: in the same way that aluminum and steel manufacturers try to sell to sheet metal users, apple and orange growers compete to meet the demand for fresh fruit and for packaged juice. Some subsectors also produce inputs for other sectors: automobiles require steel, and hogs eat corn. At the micro level, agriculture and industry both demand that producers make complicated decisions despite uncertainty.[1]

Yet in several other ways industry and agriculture *are* different, and we need to keep these differences in mind as we proceed with our analysis of public-policy making. Compared with industry, agriculture is less stable, more competitive, less organized, and more volatile. The economic and political differences between industry and agriculture derive from agriculture's closer relation to nature, which plays a fundamental role in both the production and the consumption of farm commodities.

One reason agriculture is more unstable than industry is that demand for most farm products is inelastic. That is, a 1-percent increase in the price of a typical commodity would reduce consumer demand by less than 1 percent, and a 1-percent decrease in price would increase consumer demand by less than 1 percent.[2] Eighty-five percent of agricultural production is food, a biological necessity that must be consumed daily regardless of price. Demand for all farm produce taken together is less elastic than demand for individual commodities, since consumers can substitute one commodity for another (wheat for corn, or chicken for beef) more readily than they can substitute nonfoods for food. Industrial products, in contrast, include durables such as automobiles and furniture, the purchase of which can be postponed. Even for nondurable industrial products, demand is not as severely inelastic as for food.[3]

The sensitivity of agricultural production to natural variations in weather, plant disease, and insect infestation combines with inelastic demand to generate large fluctuations in farm output.[4] The effort to insulate agricultural production from nature had led to such innovations as refrigeration and hybrid crops by the 1930s and has since given us biotechnology, irradiation, intensive use of pesticides and fertilizers, and the virtual factory production of tomatoes and broiler chickens.[5] Agriculture nonetheless remains more dependent on nature than industry and thus more prone to instability in production and income. When crop production expands, the additional income from increased sales will be more than offset by the drop in price, resulting in an overall loss of income. Conversely, when crop production decreases, the decline in sales volume is more than offset by the rise in price, resulting in increased farm income.

Another consequence of agriculture's dependence on nature is that the supply of most farm commodities is inelastic, especially in the short run.[6] Once planted, a crop cannot be increased in size, though a farmer can decrease output by harvesting only a portion of the yield. Many of the costs of agricultural production, including land, machinery, and family labor, are fixed over a longer period; hired labor and other variable costs tend to be less significant in agriculture than in industry. Supply inelasticity, like demand inelasticity, makes agricultural income more unstable than industrial income. In economic terms, demand shifts along an inelastic supply curve produce little change in output but large variations in price and thus in revenue. During depressions, farmers continue to produce at high levels as demand for farm products drops. The result is that prices and revenue drop more dramatically for agriculture than for industry.[7]

The inability of farmers to curtail production during depression is exacerbated by the structure of American agriculture, which a 1921 textbook described as "anarchy."[8] Despite recent trends toward concentration, farming is still competitive. In contrast, most industrial sectors, including food processing and farm machinery, are oligopolistic.[9] Unable to regulate their collective output to achieve desired price levels, farmers are price takers, not price makers. In the absence of government intervention, farmers can plan only their individual production, and this is always subject to the unpredictable influence of natural events.[10]

American agriculture is competitive because of the limits to large-scale capitalist enterprises based on wage labor. One natural barrier to capitalist accumulation in agriculture is the seasonality of production. Theodore W. Schultz explains that

> a farm is not like a steel mill which can produce a scheduled tonnage, say, during the next week. Agricultural production does not emerge as a flow from day to day or week to week. On the contrary, the product is garnered during a short period, usually once a year. Agricultural production is highly seasonal and typically there are long intervals between "harvests."[11]

Susan Mann argues that seasonality results in the nonidentity of production time and labor time: capitalists need to maintain their workers over the entire year but can only exploit (that is, employ) them for limited periods of time. Long turnover time, perishability, and price fluctuations are other natural barriers to capitalist accumulation in agriculture identified by Mann. All these obstacles are more easily overcome by family farmers, who in hard times can live by producing for subsistence, than by capitalist enterprises, which must produce for profit.[12]

Agricultural competition discourages collective action. "The most striking fact about the political organization of farmers," Mancur Olson says, "is that there has been so little."[13] Olson's theory of collective action suggests that any single farmer, accounting for an infinitesimal share of the market, receives an infinitesimal share of the benefits of organizational activity and so has little incentive to pay the costs of organizing. Yet industrial workers, who face the same free-rider problem, are more readily organized. The authors of *The American Voter* argued that farmers, working in isolation, are outside the social groups that bind members of other occupations and thus less likely to form interest groups.[14] Similar explanations for the relative disorganization of agriculture were offered by Adam Smith, who suggested that "country gentlemen and farmers, dispersed into different parts of the country, cannot so easily combine as merchants and manufacturers," and by Karl Marx, who, observing the physical isolation and economic self-sufficiency of French peasants, concluded that "the great mass of the French nation is formed by simple addition of homologous magnitudes, much as potatoes in a sack form a sack of potatoes."[15]

"The dispersal of the rural workers over large areas," Marx wrote elsewhere, "breaks their power of resistance, while concentration increases that of the urban workers."[16] The disparity in organizational capacity between agricultural and industrial workers is greater than the disparity between agricultural and industrial capitalists. Agricultural workers, strictly defined, are wage laborers employed by large-scale corporate enterprises. Given the natural barriers to capitalist accumulation, this pattern of labor relations has emerged only where an especially exploitable work force is available. In the United States, capitalist farming has been most enduringly successful among growers of specialty crops in California.[17] The perishability of these crops gives workers a potentially strategic location, but this advantage has been more than offset by the effects of migration and of racial and ethnic divisions and by growers' violence against labor organizers, recruitment of off-farm workers, and importation of foreign workers under a series of federal programs.[18] A second type of farm has been the southern plantation, where labor relations took the form of sharecropping or tenancy. Sharecroppers and tenants were disabled by a paternalistic system that left them dependent on the grower for credit and a range of in-kind benefits and by a system of racial oppression and political exclusion that developed in the context of paternalistic class relations.[19] Paternalism of a more literal sort prevails on the third type of American farm, the family farm that is most typical of the Midwest. These farms hire few or no outside workers, depending instead on the unpaid labor of wives and children.[20]

Racial and ethnic barriers have combined with geographic mobility to make the electoral participation of the agricultural underclasses ephemeral or nonexistent. Economic competition and social isolation, together with low levels of collective organization, have made farm owners electorally volatile. *The American Voter* found the farmers of the 1950s to be as loosely connected to the major parties as they were to their own interest groups. Farmers were therefore apt to switch their support from election to election in response to current economic trends.[21] More recent studies suggest that the political behavior of American farmers is no longer unusually changeable. Television and highways have reduced rural isolation, while the rest of the electorate has joined farmers in voting in response to current economic conditions (as in 1980 and 1992), rather than on the basis of enduring party identifications.[22] Earlier elections suggest that the recent pattern, rather than the voting behavior of the 1950s, is the departure from historical norms: late-nineteenth-century agrarian radicalism,[23] the Republican takeover of congress in 1918,[24] and Truman's upset over Dewey in 1948[25] have all been attributed to farmers' special sensitivity to economic fluctuations and federal agricultural policies. Moreover, British and French farmers have also been electorally volatile and weakly linked to their nations' parties.[26]

Sectoral Differences and New Deal Policies

Differences between industry and agriculture were played out in the crises that afflicted both sectors in the early 1930s and in the programs of economic intervention to resolve these crises. The NRA and the AAA thus demonstrate the importance of sectoral differences. The content and trajectories of these public policies also demonstrate, however, that state and party organizations can work to neutralize or reverse economic sectoral differences, producing policy outcomes that contrasting sectoral characteristics would not, in themselves, lead us to expect. The competitive structure and inelastic supply of farm production help explain why the Great Depression was more serious and persistent for agriculture than for industry. During the depression that followed World War I, "agricultural prices fell *first*, fell *fastest*, and fell *farthest*."[27] The pattern was repeated after the stock market crashed in 1929. Agricultural conditions were better during the period in between but, relative to industry, were not as favorable as they had been either before or during the war.[28]

The greater severity of the agricultural depression is consistent with the contrast between the Roosevelt administration's responses to the crises in industry and agriculture: the Agricultural Adjustment Act was a relatively well-thought-out product of campaign strategizing, expert deliberation, and discussions with farm group leaders, whereas the National Industrial Recovery Act was a hastily drafted alternative to Senator Hugo Black's bill mandating a thirty-hour work week.[29] Yet, as American farmers had learned during the 1920s, the federal government does not necessarily respond in proportion to the severity of the problem. A comparison between the disorganization of farmers and the organization of industrial capitalists, who had been mobilized into trade associations under Hoover's associationalist policy, would lead us to expect a more vigorous state response to industrial than to agricultural demands for help.[30]

There are other anomalies as well. Agricultural processors were among the industrial sectors that were oligopolistic and were therefore more easily organized than the competitive farmers with whom the processors dealt.[31] This makes it especially surprising that the administration chose to enact an agricultural recovery program that not only reduced the volume of processing operations but was financed by a processing tax. Yet the efforts of cotton textile and tobacco manufacturers to block or repeal the AAA and its processing tax by congressional action failed. The Supreme Court ultimately granted the processors' wishes in *United States v. Butler* (1936).[32]

The origins of the NRA and the AAA suggest that neither the magnitude of the problem nor the extent to which those affected are organized directly determine state response to capitalist crisis. Both are relevant, but only as they affect the calculations of parties seeking power within the context of particular electoral alignments. Pre–New Deal Republican farm policies subordinated the needs of the farmers to those of northern industry and finance, who were more central to the party's winning coalition. Roosevelt and the Democrats, in contrast, took advantage of northern farmers' sensitivity to economic conditions to overcome their cultural antipathies toward the party of Al Smith, prohibition repeal, and Tammany Hall.

The industrial-agricultural comparison would lead us to expect that the NRA was easier to implement than the AAA. While the complexity of both sectors of the economy meant that neither program would be simple to carry out, competition among farmers, the low level of farm organization, the severity of the agricultural depression, and the uncertainties of nature all posed apparently greater problems for state intervention in agriculture than in industry. The AAA was nonetheless more successful than the NRA. At the implementation stage, sectoral differences favoring industrial over agricultural recovery proved less significant than differences in preexisting state capacities that operated in the opposite direction to favor agriculture. The Department of Commerce offered less to the NRA than the Department of Agriculture did to the AAA, and no system of industrial education and research existed in parallel to the agricultural land-grant colleges. The influence of state-based experts on the AAA was demonstrated both by the ouster of the processors' champion, George Peek (formerly of Moline Plow), as AAA administrator and by the failure of the farmers themselves to get the policy they most wanted, cost of production legislation, instead of the experts' scheme for production control.[33]

Finally, the consequences of the NRA and the AAA for class interests and relationships were as sectoral characteristics might lead us to expect, only more so. The superior capacity of industrial workers for collective action leads us to expect that they would be more likely to benefit from state intervention than workers in agriculture would be. Indeed, in the historical event of the New Deal, the roles of state and party organizations served to amplify these predictable differences in outcomes. The collapse of the NRA due to the absence of prior state capacity allowed its pro-union component, led by Senator Robert Wagner, to survive hostile decisions by the NRA leadership and President Roosevelt. With passage of the National Labor Relations Act in 1935, Wagner's conception of labor relations—collective bargaining with trade unions selected by majority rule—won out over the vision of the NRA's administrators, based on company unions and proportional representation.[34] The agricultural underclasses also had their supporters within the AAA, but they lost out to the officials of the successful cotton program, who enjoyed the support of southern Democrats and, not coincidentally, of Secretary of Agriculture Henry A. Wallace.[35] Though they received less attention than farmers in the presidential campaign, Wagner and other urban liberals were part of Roosevelt's 1932 electoral coalition and gave the president his most consistent support as Congress considered the administration's industrial and agricultural recovery bills.[36] Wagner's wing of the Democratic party became more important after the failure of the NRA cost Roosevelt much of his initial business support and after Section 7(a) of the National Industrial Recovery Act had brought into being a new trade union movement with the ability to mobilize votes and dollars for prolabor candidates.[37] Agricultural workers, often disfranchised by reason of race, nationality, or poverty, could not do the same.

In sum, it is clear that mere discussion of the economic and organizational characteristics of U.S. industry and agriculture in the 1930s is insufficient to explain all we need to know about how and why the New Deal's economic interventions developed as they did. To be sure, the NRA and the AAA must be considered in economic context. But comparison of the two programs cannot stop there. Instead, we should try to understand how the intrinsic characteristics of industry and agriculture interacted with the characteristics of political parties and state agencies as organizations.

Party Alignments and Party Strategies

Asked to do something by members of a particular sector or social class, public officials have several choices. To put it broadly, they can do what they have been asked to do, construct alternatives that they find more acceptable, ignore the demands altogether, or use state power to repress the voters doing the demanding. The organized competition between parties divides blocs of voters and places them in different positions relative to the party in power at a given time. These electoral locations, in turn, help to explain how that party's candidates, as government officials, respond to demands from societal interests. Thus, the secure position of southern cotton planters within the New Deal Democratic party and the contested support of midwestern farmers influenced New Deal agricultural policy. The participation of industrial capitalists in Roosevelt's initial electoral coalition and their gradual replacement by newly mobilized industrial workers also influenced New Deal industrial policy.

E. E. Schattschneider defined a political party as "an organized attempt to get power."[38] In a representative democracy, this means an organization that competes to win elections. "In cases where the government is determined by a formally free ballot and legislation is enacted by vote," Max Weber said, parties "are primarily organizations for the attraction of votes."[39] Joseph Schumpeter noted the similarity of vote-seeking politicians, organized into parties, and the profit-seeking entrepreneurs of the market economy, organized into firms.[40] Upon this analogy Anthony Downs built his spatial model of democracy, within which no single party can manipulate electoral conditions and in which patterns of party support are determined by the distribution of attitudes among individual voters.[41] In the Downsian model, parties are like firms in the equilibrium model of neoclassical economics: no single firm can manipulate market conditions to its own advantage, and market behavior is therefore determined by underlying consumer preferences.

Like the neoclassical models of economics, Downs's model of party politics assumes perfect competition. The political parties of most democracies, however, are not perfectly competitive but oligopolistic.[42] A common measure of industrial concentration is the market share of the top eight firms. By this standard, even such relatively fragmented party systems as those of Italy, Israel, Denmark, and the Netherlands are extremely concentrated.[43] The duopolistic American party system is even further from perfect competition. An economic model based on perfect competition, then, is less relevant to party politics than are models of oligopoly, which emphasize market structures and the strategic interaction among firms.[44] The concepts of *party alignments* and *party strategies*, each of which we discuss below, are of similar importance to the study of oligopolistic politics.

Party Alignments

"What happens in politics," Schattschneider said, "*depends on the way in which people are divided* into factions, parties, groups, classes, etc. The outcome of the game of politics depends on which of a multitude of possible conflicts gains the dominant position."[45] A party alignment is the way in which the people of a particular time and place are divided into parties. As oligopolistic firms, parties can shape their "market" by advertising, which creates artificial demand and product differentiation.[46] In any given society, there are thus many possible ways in which citizens can be organized for electoral competition. That is, there are many feasible party alignments.

Party alignments can be seen as sets of relationships linking the four components of parties distinguished by Weber: "party leaders and their staffs"; "active party members"; "the inactive masses of electors or voters"; and "contributors to party funds."[47] Because the division of voters, contributors, and activists between parties determines who will be in each camp and because internal conflicts affect parties' abilities to compete in elections, the organization of conflicts within parties is inseparable from the organization of conflicts between parties. Party alignments thus encompass patterns of intraparty competition among candidates and factions.

A party's elite, composed of its leaders and their staffs, supplies the party with direction. A party's activists supply it with effort. The party elite and the party activists together constitute the party organization, which seeks to attract support from the mass of voters by appealing to the voters' identification with a class, ethnic group, religion, region, or ideology or with the party itself. To reach target groups with these appeals and to sway voters who would otherwise be undecided, party organizations need money, supplied by contributors.

"It is of crucial importance," Weber said, "for the economic aspect of the distribution of power and for the determination of party policy by what method the party activities are financed."[48] Capitalists can influence elections and policies by providing money to acceptable candidates and parties and denying money to unacceptable ones. Trade unions and other social movements can counter this form of business influence when they too are able to collect and distribute campaign funds or when they can provide volunteer labor as a substitute for cash.[49]

Weber also warned against exaggerating the role of money in party politics.[50] Claus Offe and Helmut Wiesenthal distinguish between organizations that depend on their members' "willingness to pay," and organizations that depend on their members' "willingness to act."[51] Parties are necessarily both: party elites seeking to win elections depend on financial contributors *and* on activists and voters. The extent to which a party draws on each kind of support is affected by the rules of the game, including civil service provisions that regulate the use of patronage to reward party activists, franchise restrictions that determine who can vote, and campaign finance laws that govern monetary contributions. The extent to which a party draws on each kind of support is also affected by the party's strategic choices.

Party Strategies

Much as corporate strategies shape the division of consumers among oligopolistic firms, party strategies shape the division of voters among oligopolistic parties. Richard L. McCormick defines party strategy as

> the combination of official government action and political rhetoric which the leaders adopt in order to gain and maintain the voters' allegiance and to fulfill other commitments upon which party success depends. It includes both style and substance, symbols and policies.[52]

A party strategy can be thought of as a political vision, showing all at once the existing alignment as party leaders conceive it, the alignment that would be most beneficial for the party, and how the one might be transformed into the other. Strategies for electoral transformation can incorporate institutional change, policy making, and what William H. Riker calls "heresthetics," the art of manipulating alternatives.[53]

Parties are constrained in their strategic choices by past strategies and by governing responsibilities.[54] Party strategies are also constrained by commitments to external groups. Where parties are tightly linked to interest groups that provide them with electoral support, as in Great Britain and Japan, party leaders may have little freedom to maneuver. Comparatively loose linkages give American party leaders more strategic flexibility.[55] Yet even in the United States, party coalitions are not completely plastic. The Democratic party of the pre–New Deal years, for example, was a party of southerners and city bosses, and the lags inherent in local organization and individual party identification would have made it impossible, even for Roosevelt, to transform the party overnight.[56]

Electoral Influence and Policy Influence

Demographic cleavages associated with party alignments and perceptual distinctions associated with party strategies together place particular sets of voters in particular locations relative to a particular party.[57] Policy choices reflect these locations, albeit imperfectly. Politicians can use polls and returns to tell fervent supporters from fervent

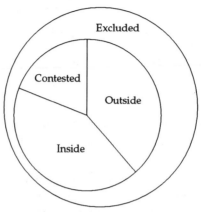

Figure 1. Party alignment and group locations

enemies, and election laws and registration lists to distinguish those who can vote from those who cannot. But there is still room for judgment about who is safe for either side and who can be swayed and about who is likely to turn out and who is likely to stay at home. Successive representatives of the same district from the same party, for example, may understand their constituency in alternate ways.[58]

Figure 1 shows the four possible group locations.[59] *Inside* groups are a party's most faithful supporters. From the perspective of the individual politician, these voters make up the primary constituency.[60] It is not necessary to persuade these voters, only to turn them out. Comparative examples include the position of trade union members in the Swedish Social Democratic Party and the position of Japanese farmers and business executives in the Liberal Democratic Party.[61]

Contested groups are not dependable supporters for any of the parties. In Richard Fenno's terms, these are voters who do not belong to the primary constituency but are necessary for the reelection constituency.[62] Campaign appeals will therefore focus on these marginal voters as the ones most likely to make the difference between victory and defeat. In the 1880s, Democrats and Republicans strove to win voters in the swing states of Indiana, New York, Connecticut, and New Jersey.[63] "Reagan Democrats," variously identified with the South, blue-collar ethnics, or middle-class suburbanites, were seen as occupying a similarly critical position one hundred years later.

Outside groups are the inside groups of the other party or parties. A "realistic" definition of a politician's constituency, Aage R. Clausen argues, omits these voters: "Stated in the baldest terms . . . legislators are expected to represent the subset of constituents who voted for them on the Big Day."[64] The party to whom they do not belong will not win many votes or contributions from them; its best hope is that their electoral participation will be low. The British Labour Party, for example, cannot expect to be financed by British capitalists.[65]

Excluded groups are denied the franchise and do not participate in electoral competition.[66] They may, however, serve as convenient targets for scapegoating or scare tactics. Requirements of property, race, religion, and gender have at various times defined potential American voters as excluded from the electorate. Age and naturalization requirements still exclude some potential voters, if only temporarily. Other rules and restrictions do not exclude particular individuals outright but nonetheless operate to reduce overall turnout, with disproportionate impact on the uneducated and the poor.[67]

The electoral locations of various groups, as determined by the interaction of party alignments with party strategies, affect public policies by determining which interests will be represented, by whom, and at what stages of the policy process. Platform pledges provide one indication of groups' places within a party. These pledges are often specific, and they are often fulfilled.[68] The policy impact of electoral realignments provides further evidence for the significance of electoral locations. During realigning periods, national cleavages dominate the usual local influences on legislative elections and behavior. Parties are unusually cohesive and capable of carrying out programs for nonincremental policy change.[69]

Electoral locations affect public policies, but electoral importance is not quite equivalent to policy influence. Another way of saying this is that governing coalitions and electoral coalitions do not exactly correspond. Contested groups may receive more attention than inside groups during the campaign, but the situation is likely to be reversed after the election, when the direct access of the insiders becomes more important than the strategic position of the contested. A seniority system, moreover, privileges legislators from districts that have given long-time support to the majority party over legislators from districts that have only recently even been contested.[70]

Outside groups will have less influence than inside or contested groups, but they are not necessarily shut out completely. Their influence will reflect the extent to which the structure of government gives electoral minorities opportunities to obstruct or veto potential policy measures. Parliamentary systems offer outside minorities little opportunity to affect policy. When Northern Ireland was under home rule, for example, there were few domestic constraints on the ability of the Unionist party to govern for the Protestant majority and against the Catholic minority.[71]

Under the U.S. constitution, in contrast, opportunities for minority influence abound. Federalism; the separation of powers between legislature, executive, and judiciary; bicameralism; and the frequency with which the legislative process demands extraordinary majorities or unanimous consent all give opposition parties—and, through them, outside groups—some measure of policy influence. Even during the Hundred Days of 1933, Roosevelt often relied on Republican votes to offset Democratic defections. Final passage of both the NIRA and AAA came on party-line votes. But Roosevelt needed the help of northeastern Republican conservatives to block an amendment to the AAA that would have guaranteed farm prices covering cost of production and to prevent the insertion into the NIRA of antitrust restrictions against price fixing. Roosevelt also needed votes from Republican insurgents of the Midwest and West to defeat an anti-union amendment, supported by a majority of southern Democrats, that would have modified the guarantees of NIRA Section 7(a) and protected existing labor-management relations.[72]

People who are excluded from the electorate are more easily excluded from the policy process. Before universal suffrage, European countries frequently denied policy influence to industrial workers.[73] The enfranchised white minority of South Africa was long able to oppress the disfranchised nonwhite majority.[74] As the South African example suggests, excluded groups are not completely powerless. Protests, from fasts and sit-ins to strikes and armed struggle, can give the excluded some influence over public policy. Outside groups that lack formal powers can also use protest effectively. Though the Japanese labor movement's close ties to the Japan Socialist Party reduced its access to the governing Liberal Democrats, unions were still able to affect policy through mass rallies and similar tactics.[75]

Protest, though, is really a last resource. Under favorable conditions, particularly sympathy from political actors removed from the conflict and disruption of central economic or social institutions, protest by the disfranchised can result in reforms, including extension of the right to vote. But under other conditions protest can be met with repression, to which disfranchised groups such as aliens and migrant workers have been particularly vulnerable.[76]

U.S. Party Politics in the 1920s and 1930s

During the 1930s what we now know as "the New Deal party alignment" came into existence. The combination of Democratic strategies and Depression conditions transformed the politics of the 1920s, which in turn had represented a return to the politics of the 1890s. The Republican electoral majority constructed during the 1890s was disrupted by Progressivism, which allowed the Democrats to regain the House in 1910 and split the presidential vote between Theodore Roosevelt and William Howard Taft in 1912, electing Woodrow Wilson as the only Democratic president between Cleveland and FDR. The restoration of the alignment of the 1890s and the Republican majority it produced began with GOP capture of the House and the Senate in 1918. The Republicans held both houses of Congress until 1931 and controlled the White House from 1921 to 1933. The dominant faction of the party, led by Treasury Secretary Andrew Mellon and presidents Warren Harding, Calvin Coolidge, and Herbert Hoover, was close to northeastern industry and finance. These probusiness Republicans were challenged by the insurgent Republicans of the Midwest and West, led by the old Progressives Robert La Follette (who won seventeen percent of the presidential vote as a third-party candidate in 1924), George Norris, and William Borah. In Minnesota, insurgency produced a new Farmer-Labor party, which displaced the Democrats as the main alternative to Republicans in the state.[77]

The Democratic opposition in Congress and in the electoral college was predominantly southern. From 1924 to 1930, for example, about two-thirds of the Democrats in the House were southerners.[78] Southern Democrats controlled the congressional party because they remained dominant at home during a period when the Democrats almost vanished from much of the North. "A party," Maurice Duverger says, "is dominant when it is identified with an epoch; when its doctrines, ideas, methods, its style, so to speak, coincide with those of the epoch."[79] The very phrase "the Solid South" shows how well the region, the party, and the era were fused. As Duverger observed, the factionalism and low turnout of the South were characteristic of nations in which one party was dominant.[80] Like the politicians of dominant parties in Israel and Italy, southern Democrats invoked (and revised) historical memory to delegitimate the opposition. The Republicans were the party of the War between the States and Radical Reconstruction, the Democrats the party of Redemption.[81] Blacks and poor whites, who might have remembered things differently, were denied the votes that might have made their memories paramount.

The rival Democratic faction was composed of New York's Tammany Hall and other big-city organizations, which were particularly influential at the party's presidential nominating conventions. Ethnocultural issues—prohibition, immigration, and the Ku Klux Klan—generated the most bitter conflicts between the two factions. The drys, led by William Jennings Bryan and William McAdoo, appealed to native-born Protestants, while the wets, led by Alfred E. Smith, appealed most to Catholics and to voters of foreign stock. In 1924, neither Smith nor McAdoo could gain the two-thirds vote necessary for the presidential nomination. John W. Davis, nominated on the 103d ballot, went on to win only 29 percent of the popular vote against Coolidge and La Follette.[82]

When Smith did win nomination as the Democratic presidential candidate in 1928, his Catholicism became an even bigger issue than his identification with the forces of repeal. Democratic support increased among urban Catholics but was offset by defections to the Protestant Hoover in the normally Democratic states of the border South; in the first major disruption to the Solid South since Reconstruction, Hoover carried Tennessee, Florida, North Carolina, Texas, and Virginia. The religious cleavage also overwhelmed Smith's efforts to win support among farmers who were unhappy about Republican vetoes of the McNary-Haugen bills for agricultural relief through surplus removal.[83]

The 1932 presidential candidacy of Franklin Roosevelt, an Episcopalian, did not divide Protestants from Catholics so sharply. Yet a restoration of pre-1928 party politics would still have left Roosevelt the candidate of a bitterly divided minority party—if he could win a nomination that required a two-thirds convention vote. From the time of Smith's defeat, Roosevelt and his advisers developed a series of strategies to overcome the obstacles. Roosevelt sought the nomination as the candidate of the South and West. Though he was a wet and these regions were predominantly dry, the Depression had made economic conditions more salient than prohibition. Roosevelt also mitigated the divisive impact of the prohibition question by advocating that prohibition be a matter for state option, a "responsible wet" stance that was more acceptable to the drys than Smith's demand for immediate repeal. Smith, his main rival, retained the support of the northeastern bosses throughout the campaign. Roosevelt's campaign initially emphasized his personal affability but shifted to a more policy-oriented approach after setbacks in the early primaries suggested that a stop-Roosevelt coalition might succeed. Roosevelt won a majority of first-ballot votes at the Democratic convention in Chicago but needed the California-Texas alliance of McAdoo, William Randolph Hearst, and John Nance Garner (who received the vice-presidential spot) to obtain the required two-thirds on the fourth ballot.[84]

Roosevelt offered generalities to suit every philosophy in the course of the general election campaign but stressed farm conditions and a balanced budget. His victory was due less to his positions on the issues than to the depressed economy, for which Hoover was blamed. Roosevelt's trip to California, the major event of the campaign, helped win the West, a swing region since the 1890s. Absent the religious conflicts of 1928, the South was again solidly Democratic. As in the nomination contest, Roosevelt was weakest in his own section of the country, the Northeast. Hoover carried six states: Maine, Vermont, New Hampshire, Connecticut, Pennsylvania, and Delaware. The Democrats and Republicans both depended on northeastern business for financial support and were nearly even in their overall campaign spending.[85]

In 1934 and 1936, Roosevelt was able to hold on to voters whose support he had won in 1932, while adding to them northern white workers who had previously been outside the electorate and northern blacks who had previously been Republicans. In the 1934 congressional elections, the Democrats accomplished the unusual feat of gaining seats in a midterm election. In 1936, Roosevelt was reelected by a landslide, carrying every state but Maine and Vermont; Republicans were reduced to sixteen seats in the Senate and eighty-nine in the House. The Republican effort to win back the agricultural Midwest failed, in part because Roosevelt was willing to back New Deal supporters who ran as Republican or third-party candidates. The South remained solidly Democratic. These components of the Democratic coalition of 1932 held together. Yet the Democrats of 1936, unlike the party of 1932, which had not even mentioned unions in its platform, were to some extent a labor party. Section 7(a) of the NIRA stimulated the growth of a trade union movement that was more militant and more willing to become directly involved on behalf of the Democratic party. The presidential vote for 1936—but not for 1932—shows the class cleavage that made the Democrats the party of the workers; 1936 was also the first presidential election in which northern blacks, mainstays of later Democratic politics, abandoned their traditional allegiance to the Republicans.[86]

The change in the composition of the Democratic majority is demonstrated even more dramatically by the party's finances than by its electorate. Money from the new Labor's Non-Partisan League, itself backed primarily by John L. Lewis's United Mine Workers, compensated in part for the substantial fall in Democratic contributions from business. Contributions from bankers and brokers declined especially precipitously. Manufacturers' contributions to the Democrats rose slightly but amounted to less than one-sixth of what manufacturers gave the Republicans. Labor's contribution in effort is harder to measure than its financial support, but union activity certainly helped Roosevelt to overcome the Republicans' ability to spend 71 percent more than the Democrats.[87]

Reformers had hoped since the Progressive Era for a realignment that would pit a liberal party against a conservative one, and Roosevelt himself occasionally endorsed this goal. Labor's new importance in supplying money, votes, and effort brought the Democrats closer to a purely liberal party. The return of northern Democrats to competitive status also made the party more liberal by reducing southerners to a minority of the congressional party.[88] The congressional reapportionment of 1930, the first since 1910, altered the intraparty balance as well, transferring representation from rural to urban districts: the biggest gainers were Los Angeles, which added six seats, and Detroit, which added four. The shift would have been greater if New York and Illinois had reapportioned; their failure to do so cost New York City and Chicago two seats apiece.[89]

Transformation of the Democrats into an ideologically liberal party, however, required subtraction as well as addition. Most of the anti–New Deal Democrats outside the South were eventually pushed out. New York Representative John O'Connor was the sole victim of Roosevelt's attempt to purge intraparty opponents in the 1938 primaries. A less publicized but more successful effort in 1940 removed three northern "Bourbons" from the Senate. Others were gradually replaced by New Deal Democrats or by Republicans.[90] The South, however, remained a bastion for conservative Democrats. Most of the purge of 1938 was concentrated on southerners, and its targets survived to ally with a Republican party that gained eighty-two seats in the House and seven seats in the Senate, largely in response to the exacerbation of depression conditions during Roosevelt's second term. However, attempts by Republicans and southern Democrats to consolidate the conservative coalition that had formed in Congress into a genuine new party were abandoned by late 1939. Anti-Bourbon Southern politicians, it should be noted, were not necessarily pro–New Deal. Maverick neopopulists Huey Long of Louisiana and Eugene Talmadge of Georgia were as unreliable allies for Roosevelt as the conservative stalwarts, Virginia's Carter Glass and South Carolina's "Cotton Ed" Smith.[91]

The awkward fit between southern Democrats and the rest of their party created "a functional three-party system under the forms of two-party domination of American electoral politics."[92] When Republicans, northern Democrats, and southern Democrats are viewed as three separate parties, the United States looks like less of an exception to the polarization of industrial societies, for class divisions are usually more muted in the South than in other regions.[93] Canada, where elections often result in minority governments, shows what American politics might have looked like if these three parties competed in a parliamentary system. Between 1933 and 1980, Republicans, like Canadian Liberals, would have been the usual party of government. Northern Democrats, like Canadian Conservatives, would have been the usual party of opposition. Southern Democrats would have been in the position of Canada's New Democratic Party (NDP): needed to form minority governments but holding too few seats to lead a government of their own.[94]

Party Politics and Public Policy in the New Deal

The public policies of the Republican 1920s and the Democratic 1930s were related to the respective electoral locations of industrial capitalists, industrial workers, agricultural capitalists, and agricultural workers. The dominant position of northeastern industry and finance within the Republican party meant that the administrations of Harding, Coolidge, and Hoover stood for low taxes, trade associations, opposition to trade unions, and resistance to McNary-Haugenism. The Democrats' replacement of the Republicans as the national majority party during the 1930s produced fundamental change in industrial and agricultural policies. The Republican industrial policy of voluntary associationalism was replaced by the NRA, which gave official sanction to both trade associations and trade unions. Republican agricultural policies of the 1920s had blocked McNary-Haugen and offered instead Hoover's Federal Farm Board, which attempted to solve the farm crisis through marketing. Under Roosevelt, the Democrats also rejected McNary-Haugenism but subordinated domestic marketing to production control as the basis for the AAA. The NRA and the AAA were thus products of the electoral shifts that created a Democratic majority by 1932.[95]

Southerners were the insiders of the New Deal Democratic party, exercising superior influence in the interests of agricultural capitalists. The advantages of southern Democrats included the seniority system and their early support for Roosevelt as presidential nominee, which earned them the important status of "FRBC": for Roosevelt before Chicago.[96] Most industrial capitalists, in contrast, were outside the Democratic coalition by 1936 and thus able to exert less influence on the Roosevelt administration than at the start of the New Deal.

The most hotly contested voters of the New Deal era were farmers from the Midwest and the West.[97] Roosevelt and the Democrats appealed to them on the basis of their economic interests, which had suffered during the long agricultural depression. Republicans appealed instead to their Protestantism and prohibitionism, seeking to mobilize them on the basis of ethnocultural identities as the party had done before 1932. The contested position of northern farmers kept agriculture on the New Deal policy agenda, even after the Supreme Court invalidated the original AAA.

Industrial and agricultural workers were both mobilized for protest during the New Deal, often by Socialists, Communists, or other radicals. The very different results of their protests reflected the different political situations of the two groups. The white primary excluded blacks from the only competitive elections held in the South; many poor southern whites were disfranchised by the poll tax. The economic position of many of the South's sharecroppers, tenant farmers, and farm laborers deteriorated during the 1930s, and their political exclusion was mirrored by their exclusion from the Wagner Act and from much of the New Deal's social welfare legislation. With the help of labor unions and urban party organizations, many potential voters overcame the somewhat less formidable registration requirements of the northern states and moved from exclusion to a location inside the Democratic coalition. Industrial workers made economic gains in their struggles with employers and made political gains with the passage of the Wagner Act.[98]

In this section, we have suggested that the NRA and the AAA developed differently and had different consequences for class conflict in agriculture and industry, in part because agricultural and industrial interests were incorporated into the New Deal Democratic party coalition in different ways. At the same time, however, the differences between the NRA and the AAA were also attributable to contrasts in state capacities for intervention in the two economic sectors. So let us proceed to offer concepts for the consideration of the autonomy and capacity of U.S. state organization in the 1930s.

State Autonomy and Capacity

Electoral locations cannot be translated into policies except through the decisions and actions of state officials; state intermediation thus limits electoral determinism. One way the role of the state can limit the importance of electoral locations is that highly developed state organizations can be sources of policy initiatives that compete with—and are formulated independently from—the proposals of groups within the governing party. Corporate liberals who supported Roosevelt in 1932 saw their vision of business planning embodied in the NRA. But farmers, who were numerically more important to the Democratic electoral coalition, were not able to gain enactment of surplus-marketing or cost-of-production legislation. The preference's of farmers were bypassed by public officials in the USDA and the land-grant colleges. These resourceful and well-situated officials and policy intellectuals offered a plan for production controls that displaced the demands of farm organizations.

A second way state intermediation limits electoral determinism is that the implementation of new policies depends on the organizational capacities available to government. The agricultural economists of the USDA and the land-grant colleges were able to realize the plans of the AAA. The NRA, without access to comparable expertise, could not be implemented so successfully.

Which policies are chosen and how they are implemented have consequences for the future electoral positions of different groups. Thus, a third way state intermediation limits electoral determinism is that policies shaped by the state alter patterns of party politics. Party alignments are not just manifestations of social cleavages, exogenous to the policy process, but products of the ongoing interaction of social groups, state organizations, and public policies. The consequences of the NRA and the AAA transformed the coalition that had elected Roosevelt in 1932. The failure of the NRA pushed most industrial capitalists outside the Democratic coalition and placed industrial workers inside it. Yet the influence of industrial workers within the New Deal Democratic party remained secondary to the influence of the South's landowners, who were both strengthened and enriched by the success of the AAA. As for the agricultural underclasses, they became even weaker and poorer than they had been before Roosevelt attained the presidency.

Components of "Stateness"

To explain the NRA and the AAA, therefore, it is necessary to understand the New Deal state as well as the New Deal party system. Max Weber defined the state as a continuous organization with compulsory membership, territorial authority, and a monopoly of the legitimate use of force.[99] Like other Weberian concepts, the state is an ideal type that serves to organize analysis, not a description of any actual governmental apparatus. It is thus possible to identify variations in "stateness": in a single polity over time, between contemporary nation-states, and between different policy arenas within a single nation-state.[100] The two components of stateness with the most direct impact on programs of sectoral intervention such as the NRA and the AAA are *state autonomy* and *state capacity*.

S. N. Eisenstadt defines autonomy as the extent to which social subsystems "can develop goals more or less independently of the main system and other subsystems, and then can pursue them more or less effectively."[101] It follows that state autonomy can be defined as the extent to which the operational goals of public officials are formulated independently from the goals of external actors. By this definition, autonomy is a variable quality of a state. Inherent in the Weberian definition of the state is not the achievement of autonomy but the potential for it.[102] Whoever controls the state may be able to pursue independently formulated goals—if they can convert legitimate, coercive authority over the population residing within geographic boundaries into actual, usable resources and if they do in fact have goals of their own.

The definition of state autonomy presented here is a negative one, telling us only that state goals are not formed outside the state. This definition does not equate autonomous policy making with good policy making. As David Wilsford puts it, "There is of course no guarantee that a strong state, operating with maximum autonomy, will make the right decisions."[103] Moreover, under this definition, by just what kinds of internal processes state goals are constructed and acted on and with what kinds of results remain open questions. State goals may be determined by the preferences of public officials as private individuals.[104] Particular agencies or departments may act to maintain their own independence, not only from society but also from the rest of the state.[105] State institutions may act in the interests of the state as a whole, working to maintain the state's abilities to carry out its basic activities of making war and extracting revenue in the face of external challenges and internal resistance.[106] Institutional interests may coincide with the national or public interest, at least as the national interest is viewed by policymakers.[107] A state that is autonomous from capitalists, finally, may nonetheless serve capitalists' interest in continued accumulation rather than any genuinely inclusive public interest.[108] Which of these models fits best is an empirical question, to be explored, along with the very extent of autonomy, by applying them to a particular state or portions of it.[109]

State capacity can be defined as the extent to which state goals, however determined, can actually be carried out. Like state autonomy, state capacity is a variable quality. In employing the concept of capacity, we are not assuming that any given set of institutions actually has

it. To avoid tautology, it is also important that we not use policy success as evidence of capacity or policy failure as evidence of its absence.
The most easily available indicators of capacity are measures of organizational resources such as budget allocations, number of employees,
and percentage of discretionary officials holding relevant educational
credentials. Resources, however, are only "administrative stock"; capacity also requires the abilities to attract, absorb, manage, and pur-
posefully employ resources.[110]

State capacity is necessary if governmental organizations are to
implement official goals, but the existence of sufficient capacity is always problematic. Decisions made by governments cannot always be
carried through; there is no law guaranteeing that governmental authorities will attempt only those interventions that they really can ex-
ecute. State capacity is particularly problematic when policies call for
increased government intervention in the economy. Such policies require that state officials confront the actual or potential opposition of
powerful social groups or that they face recalcitrant socioeconomic
conditions. Governments that have—or can quickly assemble—their
own knowledgeable administrative organizations are better able to
carry through interventionist policies than are governments that must
rely on extragovernmental experts and organizations.

The U.S. State and Economic Administration

By limiting and dividing governmental authority and by denying the
state any claim to sovereignty, the constitutional system of the United
States tends to deprive national bureaucratic organizations of either
autonomy or capacity.[111] State autonomy and state capacity are nevertheless found together in exceptionally "strong" areas of an otherwise
"weak" state. Generalizations about the weakness of the American national state do not, for example, fit the U.S. foreign policy apparatus.[112]
Such areas are characterized by persistent traditions of independent
and effective action. These traditions originate in the circumstances of
particularly critical periods. They are then reproduced through recruitment, training, and operating practices that imbue state administrators
with both the will to intervene and an understanding of what to do.
Administrative traditions also provide one solution to a standard organizational problem: how to ensure "field behavior consistent with
headquarters directives and suggestions."[113]

For historical reasons specified below, the U.S. national state in the
early 1930s had greater capacity to intervene autonomously in the economic affairs of agriculture than in those of industry. The comparison

demonstrates the superiority of a genetic approach to the state, in which state organizations continue to reflect their origins, over a functional approach suggesting the certainty of successful state adaptation to necessity.[114] As Ezra Suleiman says, "A state is dependent on structures that have a past."[115] Why, then, did the AAA succeed while the NRA failed? Because the extensive preexisting capacity for intervention in agriculture contrasted with the lack of such capacity in industry. The formation of state-based expertise in the U.S. Department of Agriculture and the land-grant colleges, first in the natural sciences and then in agricultural economics, made U.S. agricultural policy a strong area within a weak state. In the absence of any such tradition, U.S. industrial policy reflected the more general pattern by which the organizations of the American national state are neither autonomous nor capacious. Both the National Industrial Recovery Act and the Agricultural Adjustment Act pledged the early New Deal to grandiose objectives and granted broad interventionist authority to the government. But given the state capacities actually at hand, it explicably turned out that the NIRA promised the truly impossible, whereas the Adjustment Act set its sights, in part, on attainable grounds.

Writing in 1939, Joseph Schumpeter underlined the absence of a previously entrenched "skilled civil service," and "experienced bureaucracy" in New Deal America: "As a rule . . . reforming governments enjoy at least the advantage of having that indispensable tool ready at hand—in most historical instances it grew up along with the tendencies which they represent. . . . In this country a new bureaucracy had suddenly to be created."[116] Never was this more true than when it came to implementing the NIRA's program of industrial regulation. As Schumpeter's observation suggests, the National Recovery Administration can best be understood by focusing on prior historical development of the U.S. state.

During the nineteenth century, the U.S. national polity was, as Stephen Skowronek has put it, "a state of courts and parties"—one that functioned remarkably well in an expanding, decentralized capitalist economy.[117] A potent judicial system regulated and defended property rights, while locally rooted and highly competitive mass political parties handed out divisible economic benefits to meet their patronage requirements. The parties knit together the various levels and branches of government and placed severe limitations on the expansion of any bureaucratic administration or civil service composed of positions outside the electoral-patronage system. The way was finally opened for the construction of autonomous national administrative systems—civil and military alike—but only after the electoral realignment of 1896 sharply unbalanced the parties in many formerly competitive states and created a national imbalance strongly in favor of the Republicans. Even so, administrative development came slowly, unevenly, and in ways imperfectly under central executive coordination and control. Presidents from Theodore Roosevelt onward took the lead, along with groups of professionals, in promoting federal administrative growth and bureaucratization. Yet Congress resisted many of the efforts at administrative expansion and, at each step, contested the executive branch for control of newly created federal agencies.

One might suppose that World War I would have suddenly enhanced the U.S. national government's capacities for economic administration. In the historical experience of late medieval and early modern Europe, war was the great state builder, as monarchs assembled officials to help them wrest men and goods from reluctant local authorities and resistant peasant communities. But America's first—somewhat limited—involvement in a modern international war came only *after* the emergence of a national capitalist economy in which corporations had taken the lead in the development of bureaucracy and in the employment of trained experts. Existing federal bureaucracies were not prepared to mobilize human resources and coordinate the industrial economy for war, so emergency agencies were thrown together for the occasion, mostly staffed by professional experts and "businesscrats" temporarily recruited from the corporate capitalist sector.[118] The major agency for industrial mobilization, the War Industries Board (WIB), was headed by freewheeling financier Bernard Baruch, who used business-executives-turned-government-officials to hound corporations into a semblance of cooperation in support of the war effort.[119] Because America's involvement in World War I was relatively brief and because the task was to orchestrate a profitable overall expansion of production, the WIB's very tenuous ability to coordinate economic flows, control prices, and manage the interface between the military and industry was never made as glaringly apparent as it might have been. And once the "emergency" of war had passed, Congress quickly dismantled agencies such as the WIB, leaving the U.S. national state in many ways as administratively weak as before the war and leaving corporations on their own to pursue profitable growth, intramural control of their labor forces, and whatever industry-wide cooperation they could achieve without violating antitrust laws.

During their unbroken national ascendancy in the 1920s, Republican administrations showed little inclination to extend the reach of bureaucratic state power. Instead, a distinctive way of extending government influence—an antibureaucratic strategy of state building particularly well suited to the existing political and ideological circumstances—was ingeniously pursued by Secretary of Commerce Herbert Hoover, using his own initially relatively humble department, "the smallest and newest of the federal departments," as a center of operations.[120] Starting from a puny administrative base did not matter to Hoover because, as Ellis Hawley explains, he envisaged the Commerce Department as the core of an "associative state" that would "function through promotional conferences, expert inquiries, and cooperating committees, not through public enterprise, legal coercion, or arbitrary controls."[121] The personnel and budgets of the component units of the Commerce Department expanded steadily under Hoover. But the more significant form of growth was through the spread of "adhocracy" rather than bureaucracy, for Hoover used many government officials as facilitators of cooperation within and among powerful private groups, especially business trade associations.[122] Indeed, Hoover's strategy of state building was very congenial to American capitalists, not only because his Commerce Department did many useful things for them but even more because it splendidly accommodated "business groups desirous of governmental services but reluctant to give up their own autonomy."[123] Given the enormous barriers in the way of centralized administrative development, Herbert Hoover had, it seemed, hit upon the perfect formula for modern government in America.

With the crash of 1929, followed by the deepening depression and the advent of the Democrats, Hoover's ideal of the associative state and the trappings of power linked to it were inevitably swept aside. If for no other than the obvious reasons of adversary politics, the National Recovery Administration was *not* (either by the terms of the NIRA or by Roosevelt's decision) put into the Department of Commerce. The early New Deal's major venture into industrial regulation was instead launched as an independent agency, with its head directly responsible to the president.

Politics aside, there would have been little administrative advantage to be gained in placing the NRA within Commerce. Without Hoover and his "adhocracy"—his network of cooperative private associations—the Commerce Department was still, as it had been before Hoover, disunified and decentralized.[124] For while the Department of Commerce as a whole had grown during Hoover's tenure as secretary (1921–1928) by over three thousand employees (a 50-percent increase) and had nearly doubled its annual appropriations,[125] the supervisory center of the department, the Office of the Secretary of Commerce, had not expanded commensurately. In fact, from 1920 to 1929 the office had actually declined in personnel.[126] Moreover, the near collapse of foreign exports in the early days of the Depression undercut the major thrust of the Bureau of Foreign and Domestic Commerce, the one departmental agency that had grown the most (by 552 percent in expenditures and by 436 percent in personnel) during the 1920s.[127]

All in all, the Commerce Department had relatively little to contribute to the formulation and administration of regulatory codes for domestic industries—certainly much less than one might imagine at first glance, considering the strategic position of the department in the 1920s. One participant in the early New Deal recalled that

> the Commerce Department then had very little to do. . . . In the thirties, the Commerce Department was a very moribund place. The Secretary did not have Roosevelt's confidence. The NRA was the big thing, with all the big shots in America walking up and down the four hundredth corridor. The NRA was where the action was as far as the press was concerned.[128]

U.S. State Capacity in Agriculture

Unlike the NRA and uniquely among the major emergency agencies of the early New Deal, the AAA was placed inside an existing federal department—the United States Department of Agriculture—and under the authority of its secretary, rather than under a special administrator reporting directly to the president. Secretary of Agriculture Wallace actively coordinated AAA activities with established USDA programs, and the AAA benefited in numerous concrete ways from its embeddedness in the department. One of the most important connections, Van Perkins notes,

> was that between the AAA and the Bureau of Agricultural Economics [BAE], which performed a considerable amount of statistical and analytical work for the AAA. . . . The records that had been compiled over the years by the BAE's Division of Crop and Livestock Estimates were indispensable for all control programs because, without those statistics, it would have been impossible to determine base production, allotments, and benefits. There were some instances of friction between the AAA and the older organizations; more common, however, and rather remarkable, was the sense of accommodation and cooperation which existed.[129]

In addition to resources of information, the AAA also drew key trained personnel from other parts of the USDA, especially from among present and previous employees of the Bureau of Agricultural

Economics.[130] Moreover, the federally supervised Extension Service, tied to the USDA since the Smith-Lever Act of 1914, provided both personnel for the AAA and a ready-made field administration for organizing local groups of farmers to implement AAA programs. Without the Extension Service, the AAA in 1933 would have faced the almost impossible task of assembling a field administration from scratch in a matter of weeks.[131]

Just as we linked the difficulties of the NRA to the historically explicable absence of relevant administrative strength in the U.S. national state, our explanation for the AAA's better performance looks back historically from the vantage point of the USDA's special administrative contributions. In general, as shown above, the civil administrative capacities of the U.S. national state in the 1930s were weak and poorly coordinated. But the historical development of different parts of the federal government had been uneven, and at the coming of the Great Depression, the U.S. Department of Agriculture was, so to speak, an island of state strength in an ocean of weakness. Although it did not achieve cabinet status until 1889, the Department of Agriculture was founded during the Civil War, when the southern states were out of the union and when it was both possible and necessary for unprecedented federal initiatives to be taken. Influenced by the period of its birth, Agriculture enjoyed from its inception an unusual degree of administrative unity and flexibility: few component bureaus were legislatively created by Congress, and all but the top officials (and the head of the Weather Bureau) were subject to appointment and removal by the head of the department. Thus, new offices could be created and periodic reorganizations could occur, subject only to post-hoc approval by Congress when appropriations were made. Much more than other department heads, agriculture secretaries (or, before 1889, commissioners) were able to regard—and shape—their department as a functionally unified domain.[132]

In key steps taken before and after World War I, secretaries of agriculture (especially David Houston and Henry C. Wallace) reorganized the department to heighten its capacities for policy-oriented research and for centrally coordinated policy implementation. Increasing emphasis was placed on agricultural economics rather than on the natural sciences, culminating in the 1922 establishment of the all-important Bureau of Agricultural Economics, formed through the consolidation of the Office of Farm Management, the Bureau of Crop Estimates, and the Bureau of Markets. During the 1920s, the "new Bureau performed important general-staff services for the Secretary and the Department in a period of formative development both in the field of agricultural economics as a social study and in the evolution of governmental policy on agriculture."[133] By 1931, the BAE's chief could rightly say of his bureau: "There is scarcely an economic phase of agriculture that is not comprehended in its services and research."[134] In the seven decades following its birth, the USDA had developed from "essentially a collection of natural-scientific research workers with attachés for informational and publication services" into an agency of government with extraordinary capacity to formulate and implement domestic economic and social policies.[135]

Moreover, well before the dawn of the Republican New Era, the USDA had become one of the heftiest civilian parts of the federal government. In 1915, the department's annual expenditures were about 8 percent of total federal civil expenditures (exceeded only by such other categories of civil expenditures as public improvements and marine transportation), while the Commerce Department accounted for about 5 percent of civil expenditures.[136] Herbert Hoover's Department of Commerce was the glamorous center of new governmental growth in the 1920s, but *both* Agriculture and Commerce grew by about 400 percent between 1915 and 1930, leaving Agriculture almost twice as big as Commerce at the end of that period, just as it had been at the beginning. Moreover, while the Office of the Secretary of Commerce did *not* keep up with Commerce's overall growth, the Office of the Secretary of Agriculture—the center of coordination and staff services for the whole department—*did* keep pace in terms of personnel with the Agriculture Department as a whole.[137] Hoover tried to weaken the Department of Agriculture and make it a satellite of his own Department of Commerce, but the net effect of his efforts was to strengthen the sense of solidarity among agricultural experts.[138]

The USDA and Professional Expertise

Tracing the genealogy of the USDA as an administrative part of government provides useful background information. Yet for the purpose of understanding the origins of agricultural planning in the New Deal, it is even more important to see the USDA as part of a larger nexus of institutions that functioned—to a degree unique in pre-1930s U.S. national politics—to bring professional expertise to bear on public issues and on governmental policy making about them. At about the same time as the USDA was created, the Morrill Act was passed, authorizing federal land grants to support the establishment in each state of a college oriented to agricultural research and education. In practice, these "land-grant colleges" were slow to establish themselves, and their greatest impact on farm practices came after the establishment of federally subsidized, state-run Experiment Stations in 1887 and the federalization of the Extension Service in 1914. By the end of the nineteenth century, though, the USDA was already recruiting many of its civil servants from the land-grant colleges. Indeed, characteristic career lines were beginning to carry individuals from the colleges to Experiment Stations (or Extension Service posts), then into the Department of Agriculture, and perhaps finally back to administrative positions in the colleges or in state agricultural programs.[139]

One impact of the connection between the USDA and the land-grant colleges was, predictably, to solidify the department's distinctive collective identity. From the "homogeneity of origin, training, and type of career and professional interest of those who were rising to the higher posts in the permanent civil service of the USDA there emerged a corporate atmosphere in the Department."[140] Thus, the authors of a 1940 Social Science Research Council (SSRC) study of public administration in the USDA were able to conclude that "the personality factor"—that is, the influence of extraordinary entrepreneurial secretaries or bureau heads—"has probably not been so important as perhaps in the history of other departments. Here [the personality factor] has been dissolved because a corporate factor—the influence of land-grant college training and tradition—has been overwhelmingly strong."[141]

Another important development flowing from the USDA's ties to the colleges was the symbiotic linking of academic life with the expanding domains of government research and policy making. As farmers faced new problems and as government officials groped for new policies, teachers and researchers in the land-grant colleges redefined the scope of instruction and research. Indeed, the new disciplines of agricultural economics and rural sociology emerged and flourished at this intersection of agricultural policy and land-grant education.[142] In turn, of course, answers and dilemmas arrived at in the colleges were carried into the Bureau of Agricultural Economics, where, partly under academic stimulation and partly because of the availability of accumulated statistics and experience, efforts were increasingly made to look holistically at U.S. agriculture, in order to understand and cope with its changing place in the American economy and the world economic order.

During the 1920s, farm pressure groups used statistics collected by government agencies to highlight the disastrous decline in farm income, and political demands mounted for government corrective action. Agricultural experts—whether current, former, or prospective government employees—grappled with politically proposed solutions and in many cases formulated proposals of their own. Many divergent answers were offered during the debates of the 1920s and the early depression. The sheer proliferation of demands for government action reflected the previous contacts of farmers with the USDA (and with the state-level programs associated with the department). Similarly, the proliferation of technically and administratively sophisticated proposals reflected the ease with which, in the agricultural sector of the U.S. political economy, professionally trained people had for some time moved freely from scholarship to application, from academia to government policy making and implementation. Both farmers and agricultural experts were, so to speak, "state-broken" well before the New Deal launched its planning efforts.

More than that, and perhaps most decisive of all, many agricultural experts were willing to make policy *for*, rather than just *with*, the farmers and their organizations.[143] Accustomed to the challenges of public office, their training and career experiences had given them a concrete sense of what could (and could not) be done with available governmental means. Having gained a public-service perspective—or, to put it another way, having learned to take the point of view of the state—agricultural experts could devise policies with means and even goals beyond those directly advocated by farm pressure groups. Two key examples are M. L. Wilson's advocacy of government-administered production controls and Howard Tolley's proposals for land-use planning. Although both Wilson and Tolley formulated policy proposals well before the New Deal, neither could successfully "sell" them to farmers' organizations or to Congress.[144] Without Roosevelt's support and without the Democratic ascendancy in 1932, these agricultural economists could not have translated their ideas into government action. Yet once the Agricultural Adjustment Act was passed, Wilson, Tolley, and other professionals associated with them could seize the opportunity to implement new policies. Familiar with the resources of the AAA, they quickly moved into key operational posts in the AAA, so as to launch the agency on a programmatically coherent course.[145] Had the agricultural economists merely responded to the diverse pulls of farmers' demands and of immediate political pressures in 1933, they would have bogged down in the omnibus possibilities of the Agricultural Adjustment Act and in the organizational contradictions of the AAA under George Peek. Instead, their ideas about production control and other types of government planning *for* agriculture helped them to set the AAA on a course that turned out to be relatively coherent and successful.

Intervention and Political Learning

Looking back historically from the New Deal, we can see that agricultural experts, their ideas, and the administrative means they could use to implement the ideas all were products of a long process of institution building whose roots go back to the Civil War, when the U.S. Department of Agriculture was chartered and the Morrill Act was passed. Two points of broader analytic significance are worth underlining about the political effects of the complex of agricultural institutions that developed in U.S. history between the Civil War and the Great Depression.

First, these institutions laid the basis for an *administrative will to intervene* in the national market economy. This happened in ways analogous to those analyzed by John Armstrong for European administrative elites and by Alfred Stepan for contemporary interventionist military regimes in Latin America.[146] Both of these authors place great emphasis on prior historical development of institutions and on patterns of elite socialization that forge a unified administrative leadership imbued with an "interventionist role definition," a collective sense that it can diagnose—and use state intervention to act on—socioeconomic problems. In his study of European administrators and state activities to promote economic development, Armstrong writes that a "large measure of organizational unity and homogeneity in socialization among elite administrators has been crucial for development [of an] interventionist role definition," and he also points to the importance of administrative field experience, scientific education, and exposure to "systematic economics training."[147] Stepan asks how certain militaries in Latin America in the 1960s moved from a narrowly military definition of their roles to a collective belief that the military could and should take responsibility for national economic development. His answer focuses on the broadening of military education to include studies of society and the economy as a whole, as well as techniques of economic planning.[148] USDA administrators and agricultural economics experts went through experiences like those of Europe's interventionist administrators and Latin America's "new" military professionals: their education and career experiences tended to forge a corporate identity, the USDA itself was administratively unified to a high degree, and both government experience and social-scientific training encouraged the combination of technical expertise, orientation to practical action, and a holistic view of agriculture in the national economy.

Second, the U.S. agricultural complex historically nurtured not only an administrative will to intervene but also a process of "political learning" about what could be effectively done for farmers and society as a whole through public agricultural policy. In his study of the long-term development of social policies in modern Britain and Sweden, Hugh Heclo maintains that politics "finds its source not only in power but also in uncertainty—men [that is, people] collectively wondering what to do."[149] He argues that social policy developments have not usually come simply as a result of electoral competition, pressures from interest groups, or programmatic initiatives by political parties. The *occasion* for new policy departures may be created by such precipitants: "Changes in the relationship of power—wide political participation, election results, party government turnovers, new mobilizations of interest groups—have served as one variety of stimulus, or trigger, helping to spread a general conviction that 'something' must be done."[150] But *what to do* is another matter, argues Heclo. Here the answers—the actual contents of workable policies—tend to come from government administrators and other expert elites who have been closely in touch over time with attempts and failures in a given field of public-policy endeavor. "Even [successful] increases in administrative power," says Heclo in a passage that sounds ideally suited for a discussion of the New Deal's NRA versus the AAA, "have had as their basis less the ability to issue authoritative commands than the capacity to draw upon administrative resources of information, analysis, and expertise for new policy lessons and appropriate conclusions on increasingly complex issues."[151]

In the case of the relatively successful AAA, the New Deal was indeed able to draw on a well-established governmentally centered tradition of political learning about what needed to be done and could be done through government intervention in agriculture. The policy innovators and eventual policy implementers were not simply government officials, for they had moved into and out of government posts and carried experiences back and forth from government to educational institutions, maintaining contacts in the process with major farm interest groups.[152] Yet there was an important thread of continuity in the succession of programs implemented by the USDA. As the authors of the 1940 SSRC study of the USDA put it, in a formulation strikingly like Heclo's "political learning" argument:

> Since 1932 public attention has been centered upon the New Deal program as marking a sharp reversal in trends in governmental policy; nevertheless, the more we study the evolution of agricultural policies the more we are impressed with their continuity over

an extended period, notwithstanding changes in party control of government. Changes occur, but the new policy will be found to have roots in some undramatic research, fact-gathering, information-providing, or similar "noncoercive" activity. . . . Civil servants assigned to the task of analysis come upon situations in which a public interest is discovered because hitherto it had been no one's business to study them. In this evolutionary process the functions of government are changed.[153]

What is more, the SSRC authors might have said, in this way the basis is laid for a *successful* extension of government administrative intervention when a political conjuncture such as that of 1932–1933 creates the opportunity.

Like the Agricultural Adjustment Act, the National Industrial Recovery Act created an extraordinary opportunity to extend government intervention into the economy. But, at the beginning of the Depression, no properly *political* learning had been going on to lay the basis for the NRA. Such learning as was going on in the 1920s about how to plan for industry was happening within particular industries, with trade association leaders doing the learning.[154] When the federal government withdrew from even nominal control of industry after World War I, it left the field clear to the giant corporations and to the trade associations, whose efforts Hoover simply encouraged and attempted to coordinate, instead of building up independent governmental apparatuses. Thus, when the Depression struck and the New Deal found itself committed to the sponsorship of industrial planning, there was only the "analogue of war" to draw on—an invocation of the emergency mobilization practices used during World War I.[155]

Government's job in depression was much more difficult than in war: not just exhorting maximum production from industry but stimulating recovery and allocating burdens in a time of scarcity. For this, a tradition of political learning—from prior public administrative supervision of industry—would have been invaluable. But, in contrast to the situation in agriculture, the U.S. state lacked the "administrative resources of information, analysis, and expertise for new policy lessons and appropriate conclusions" on the "increasingly complex issues" presented by the challenge of industrial planning. Thus, the NRA failed in its mission of coordinating industrial production under the aegis of public supervision, and the apparent opportunity offered by the NIRA's extraordinary peacetime grant of economic authority to the U.S. government was lost. The reach of the New Deal's ambitious early venture into industrial planning simply exceeded the grasp that could be afforded by the public institutions and intelligence of the day.

Conclusion

As this overview of New Deal programs has illustrated, socioeconomic interests are not fixed and do not reductively determine public policies. State and party organizations are sites for political actors with goals and values of their own. In addition, state and party organizations may influence the capabilities and alliances of socioeconomic interests, and those interests may themselves be reoriented or reorganized in the process. Armed with this understanding, we are now in a position to offer precise and detailed explanations of the similarities and differences between the origins, implementation, and socioeconomic effects of the National Recovery Administration and those of the Agricultural Adjustment Administration. The next three chapters of this part are devoted to analyzing each phase of the development of these two New Deal programs in turn.

3

The Origins of the NRA and the AAA

The National Recovery Administration and the Agricultural Adjustment Administration were each responses to the national economic crisis. Neither program fixed prices, but both programs sought to raise prices indirectly. Recovery was to be achieved by adjusting supply to demand. Analysis of the origins of each program shows policy formation over time: the response to depression changed from the Republican administration of Herbert Hoover through the 1932 election, the preinaugural transition, and then the first "Hundred Days" of the Democratic administration of Franklin Roosevelt. Comparison of the origins of the two programs shows that industry and agriculture differed in their relation to state and party organizations, as well as in some intrinsic characteristics of production and consumption.

The central question about the origins of each program is: Which policies were selected when? Which policies were selected means choice among a range of alternatives supported by mobilized publics or considered by policy-making elites at some stage of the policy process. Policy origins are thus understood as more than who suggested the enacted policies first or how the relevant bills became laws, although the answers to both questions can be telling. When policies were selected means the timing of policy choices; when a choice was made is treated as evidence about the conditions under which it occurred.

Which policies were selected? In both industry and agriculture, a key Democratic constituency was able to elicit, as part of President Roosevelt's New Deal, federal intervention beyond what President Hoover had been willing to endorse. But these constituencies could not control the choice among competing interventionist proposals. Workers' representatives backed the Black Bill for a thirty-hour work week; farmers' representatives wanted the national government to boost prices without controlling production. Roosevelt, however, endorsed alternative policies that did not have popular support, drawing on the ideas of agricultural economists to create the AAA and on the ideas of business planners to create the NRA.

When were these choices made? The National Industrial Recovery Act and the Agricultural Adjustment Act both became law during Roosevelt's "Hundred Days." Yet there were important differences in the timing of the process by which they were selected over alternative proposals. Production control was selected as the basis for agricultural policy within the context of Roosevelt's 1932 campaign. The administration's farm program was further developed during the transition period between Roosevelt's election in November 1932 and his inauguration in March 1933. Codification, in contrast, became the basis for Roosevelt's industrial policy only in response to the emergence of the Black Bill as a policy threat: a proposal that policymakers define as unacceptable but, for electoral reasons, cannot simply reject without providing an alternative.

The selection and timing of the NRA and the AAA suggest that electoral shifts produce policy change, but within limits that reflect the structural imperatives of a capitalist economy, as understood by elected officials. Proposals within these limits compete for policymakers' attention; proposals outside these limits are rejected as unacceptable and met with counterproposals when they win popular and congressional support.

The selection and timing of the NRA and the AAA also point to the importance of assembled expertise as a prerequisite for policy innovation. Preexisting state capacities in agriculture produced policy proposals independent of agricultural capitalists' own demands. The absence of comparable governmental or quasi-governmental organizations for industry led to reliance on industrial capitalists for policy proposals. State capacity is thus important for policy formation as well as for policy implementation. The outcome of the interaction of interests and ideas in policy making depends on the characteristics of the institutions that organize the process.

From the Black Bill to Business Planning

The NRA's regulation of production under "codes of fair competition" was neither an automatic nor an immediate response to the collapse of American industry in the Great Depression. As we have already noted, presidents Hoover and (initially) Roosevelt both opposed such a policy. Codification became the basis for U.S. industrial policy in response to the possibility that Congress would enact Senator Hugo Black's bill for a thirty hour week. This policy threat forced the Roosevelt administration into a hurried search for a policy alternative. The alternative embodied in the National Industrial Recovery Act (NIRA) most closely resembled business proposals for recovery. The NIRA also contained concessions to organized workers; by their presence and by their dubious impact, these concessions reflected the secondary position of labor within Roosevelt's 1932 electoral coalition.

Business, Labor, and Proposals for Recovery

Most business recovery proposals focused on the limited goal of relaxing the antitrust laws. Even before 1929, capitalists in "profitless" industries, including cotton textiles, oil, and rubber, sought antitrust revisions that would permit sectoral cooperation. Capitalists from additional sectors endorsed revision as markets, prices, and profits declined in the Great Depression.[1] General Electric's Gerard Swope and the U.S. Chamber of Commerce, led by Henry Harriman, introduced ambitious programs for business planning that went beyond antitrust revision to encompass national economic councils; industry-by-industry self-regulation of wages, hours, and prices; and even industry provision of social insurance.[2] Proposals by "start-up planners" represented another variety of business recovery programs: these called for government loans to help firms expand employment and production.[3] Though legitimized by the example of the War Industries Board created for mobilization during World War I, support for either kind of business planning remained a minority view.[4]

All of these business proposals went against an antitrust tradition that remained popular in the nation's agrarian peripheries, the South and the West. For antitrusters such as Louis Brandeis, the cure for economic problems was what it had been under Woodrow Wilson: more competition, not less. Intellectuals' proposals for national planning, in which business was put under government direction or placed within a tripartite framework with representatives of labor and consumers, also challenged antitrust.[5]

Purchasing power proposals reflected underconsumptionist and technocratic theories that a mature capitalist economy had become stagnant. The solution was to "share the work": a shorter average work week would expand employment and increase mass purchasing power. Voluntary action to reduce working hours was endorsed by unions and employers. Secretary of Labor Frances Perkins had worked for legislation setting minimum wages and maximum hours in New York State and wanted similar national regulations. Senator Black's simpler bill set hours only.[6]

Though Hoover responded to the industrial collapse, he did not offer or endorse sectorally specific programs. He opposed proposals for either antitrust relaxation or business planning, rejecting the Swope Plan as "the most gigantic proposal of monopoly ever made in history."[7] A "Share the Work" campaign emerged from Hoover's Conference of Banking and Industrial Committees, held in August 1932, but unlike the Black Bill it relied on voluntary reemployment rather than federal compulsion.[8]

Roosevelt's initial program, as developed in the course of the 1932 campaign and then during the preinauguration "interregnum," also avoided sectorally specific industrial policy. Roosevelt instead set out to reverse industrial decline through banking reform, budget cuts, agricultural recovery, and unemployment relief.[9] Antitrust revision, except in the special circumstances of coal and oil, was rejected as too controversial to propose during the congressional session.[10] States were to be encouraged to pass wages and hours legislation; Secretary of Labor Perkins's March 31 conference with labor leaders endorsed federal standards as well.[11] Raymond Moley, a member of Roosevelt's Brains Trust, collected the various business planning proposals and asked James Warburg to synthesize them. But Moley was not convinced by Warburg's start-up proposal, and on April 4, 1933, he and Roosevelt agreed to do nothing.[12] As late as April 13, Roosevelt expressed strong skepticism about any comprehensive program for industrial regulation and recovery.[13] A month later, Roosevelt was willing to endorse the NIRA as an alternative to the Black Bill.

The bill that Hugo Black introduced during the lame-duck congressional session of December 1932 set a six-hour day and a five-day week by prohibiting the shipment in interstate commerce of goods produced by male workers with longer hours. The Black Bill would have mandated a dramatic reduction in the work week, which averaged 37.0 hours in April 1932 and had averaged 49.6 hours under the predepression conditions of 1929. Even protective laws for women workers, passed by many states during the Progressive Era, typically set a work week of at least forty-eight hours.[14] The Black Bill represented a simple statutory solution to a social problem, a type of policy response that Elizabeth Sanders has described as typical of social movements and their congressional allies.[15]

Senator Black, an Alabama Democrat, said he had come up with the thirty-hour-week idea himself.[16] However, William Green, the president of the American Federation of Labor, had endorsed the thirty-hour week in 1930. In keeping with the voluntarist policy established under Samuel Gompers, Green's initial proposal made no provision for government enforcement. In November 1932, one month before Black introduced his bill, the AFL took an important move away from labor voluntarism and endorsed legislation for the shorter work week.[17] Green appeared as the first witness in the subcommittee hearings on the Black Bill, concluding his testimony with a discussion with Black, in which he explained that voluntary action would not achieve the shorter week. The only alternative to the legislative force of the bill was economic force:

> Senator BLACK. By universal strike?
> Mr. GREEN. By universal strike.
> Senator BLACK. Which would be class war, practically.
> Mr. GREEN. Whatever it would be, it would be that.[18]

Despite the supposed prospect of class war, Congress took no action during the lame-duck session. In the new Congress, however, the Black Bill passed the Senate on April 6, 1933, by a 53-to-30 vote.[19] The House Committee on Labor had already approved a counterpart measure, sponsored by Massachusetts Representative William P. Connery, on April 4.[20] In Roosevelt's view, the Black Bill would probably be declared unconstitutional. Moreover, the bill was impractical, likely to paralyze industry and demoralize business, because of its inflexible standards applying across all industries. "There have to be hours adapted to the rhythm of the cow," the president said.[21] Amendments added to the Senate bill met this specific objection by exempting dairy workers, among others, but did not end administration opposition.[22] Employers mobilized against the bill.[23]

The administration's first counterproposal was the kind of discretionary administrative response that Sanders suggests is often favored by the executive branch.[24] In testimony to the House Committee on Labor, Secretary of Labor Perkins, building on her own and Roosevelt's long-standing concern to regulate conditions of employment, proposed an alternative bill raising the maximum hours standard and making it more flexible, instituting minimum wages, and assigning great authority to supervise the new regulations to the Secretary of Labor. Business opposition led Roosevelt to abandon Perkins's proposed substitute. The AFL also rejected the Perkins substitute because it contained a minimum wage; opposition to the minimum wage, which it believed would become a wage ceiling, was one Gompers legacy the AFL had not yet abandoned.[25]

The complicated drafting policy that produced the NIRA has been traced by several authors.[26] Roosevelt authorized several groups within the administration to prepare general industrial recovery plans. Each group contained seasoned advocates of business planning.[27] Given Roosevelt's resistance to any programs calling for large amounts of federal spending, the business regulators were able to get their low-cost ideas accepted as the cornerstone of the NIRA by presenting them as the best available route to industrial recovery. No doubt half-convinced themselves, the business planners made extravagant projections of an economic upturn and expanding employment—if only business could eliminate cutthroat competition and put its own industries in order.[28]

The National Recovery Act that emerged resembled the Swope Plan and other business planning schemes, without social insurance and with what appeared to be more interventionist governmental supervision. The antitrust laws were effectively suspended, causing insurgent western Republicans, led by Senator William Borah, to oppose the bill. Hugo Black voted against it for the same reason.[29] Industrial capitalists did have to accept Section 7(a), guaranteeing labor the right to organize and bargain collectively with employers. Business opposed this section, which had no counterpart in the Swope Plan and which threatened the open shops and company unions created during the anti-union offensives of the 1920s, but even with its inclusion business supported the recovery package.[30] Inclusion of Section 7(a) and of the requirement that NRA codes stipulate minimum wages, maximum hours, and employment conditions reflected the determination of congressional liberals that the bill address the concerns of industrial workers. Particularly important in this regard was Senator Robert Wagner, the New York Democrat who participated in drafting the NIRA and was also the administration's point man in the Senate.[31] Section 7(a), public works, and regulation of working conditions were all written into the draft of the Recovery Act by Senator Wagner's legislative assistant, Leon H. Keyserling.[32]

Institutional and Electoral Contexts

The formation of New Deal industrial policy was reactive. Roosevelt's policy preferences, apparent by the first month of his administration, were altered by the possibility that the Black Bill would win congressional approval. The alternative that resulted contained concessions to the Black Bill's labor supporters, but within a framework closest to business proposals for recovery. As Roosevelt said of the NIRA in one of his Fireside Chats, "It is a partnership . . . between government and . . . industry . . . , not partnership in profits, for the profits still go to the citizens, but rather a partnership in planning and a partnership to see that the plans are carried out."[33]

Congressional support for the Black Bill and presidential opposition to it both reflected the nature of the Democratic coalition at the beginning of the New Deal. Congress, in its attention to the Black Bill, as well as in its advocacy of public works spending, was more sensitive than Roosevelt to the distress of the industrial working class. The more localized electoral constituencies of congressional representatives made them inherently more likely than the president to respond to pressures from such sources as unemployed workers, bankrupt local governments, and construction firms seeking subsidies. Moreover, urban Democrats had achieved substantial influence in Congress well before they became important in presidential politics. From the mid-1920s on, increasing numbers of Democrats from urban backgrounds or constituencies were appearing in Congress. During Hoover's final years in office, key northern urban liberals (such as Robert Wagner) allied with Progressive Republicans (such as George Norris) and with southern mavericks (such as Hugo Black) to propose measures for unemployment relief and public works.[34] The 1932 elections strengthened congressional willingness to support such measures, for the many newly elected Democrats were especially anxious to consolidate their electoral majorities by enacting popular programs to alleviate unemployment.[35]

Urban workers were less important to President Roosevelt's electoral coalition than they were to congressional Democrats, and so electoral pressures, even when supplemented by the prospect of "universal strikes," could not overcome Roosevelt's constitutional and practical objections to the Black Bill. In 1932, labor was less important to the Roosevelt coalition than it would become later in the New Deal. As Raymond Moley observed, Roosevelt's 1932 strategy "might be called essentially agrarian, an appeal to rural elements—farmers and residents of small towns and cities." The same strategy had gained Roosevelt unusual upstate support in his gubernatorial races.[36] Roosevelt won the 1932 nomination without much support from urban Democrats, who remained loyal to Al Smith. Strategy for the general election focused on contesting midwestern states that normally voted Republican by attacking Hoover on agriculture. The inside groups of the post-1896 Democratic minority, southerners and urban workers, were taken for granted. With the religious issue of 1928 removed, southerners could be expected to return to their tradition of solid Democratic support. Democratic strategy assumed urban workers would vote for Roosevelt because of the strength of party machines, because of ethnic loyalties carried over from the 1928 campaign, or because workers blamed Hoover for the Depression.[37] The 1932 Democratic platform did not endorse shortened hours or collective bargaining guarantees; in fact, it did not mention unions at all. Roosevelt's campaign speeches also gave labor issues little attention.[38] In the 1932 election, voters were not yet divided along class lines, as they would be in 1936 and thereafter.[39]

The influence of urban workers within the Roosevelt coalition was further diminished by the weaknesses of labor as an organized interest group. Union membership had declined from 3.4 million in 1929 to less than 3 million in 1933.[40] Moreover, the AFL had been neutral in the 1932 campaign. AFL President William Green and Daniel Tobin of the Teamsters supported Roosevelt, but other AFL leaders supported Hoover despite the Depression.[41]

Without support from either industrial capitalists or industrial workers, recovery proposals centering on use of state authority, whether through the Department of Labor or through the new agencies envisioned by national planning advocates, had little impact on the NIRA. Even within the Brains Trust, Rexford Tugwell was isolated as a national planning advocate; Moley and Adolph Berle, Jr., both supported business planning instead.[42] Frances Perkins, who sought to vest authority for industrial policy in her department, was left "outside the whole circle of developments" after industrial capital and labor mobilized against her recovery proposal.[43]

A wide range of ideas came into play in the making of New Deal industrial policy, including underconsumptionist notions that prefigured Keynesianism. As the subsequent failure of the NRA proved, business recovery plans were inherently no more sound than share-the-work programs or national planning schemes. Interest group resources, as mediated through party coalitions, determined which ideas won out. Business, whose ultimate resource was perhaps Roosevelt's own sense of what was needed for a healthy capitalist economy, triumphed. Labor's preferred solution to the industrial crisis, the thirty-hour week, was rejected; instead, the unions received Section 7(a) as part of the program of business recovery. The value of this concession to labor would depend on how 7(a) was interpreted by employers, by NRA officials, and by the workers themselves.

From Agrarianism to Adjustment

Like the NRA, the AAA was a state response to sectoral crisis. As we explain below, farmers responded to the long agricultural depression by supporting several broad policy alternatives: agrarianism, progressivism, cooperativism, and McNary-Haugenism. Yet New Deal agricultural policy was founded on another policy alternative, production control, which before Roosevelt's election had been rejected by farmers and farm groups. In the words of Michel Petit,

> Farm organizations do not seem to have played a significant role in the process of adopting these major policy innovations. Clearly, many of the ideas they had been fighting for during the previous decade were implemented by the new administration, but observers agree that leadership was given by the administration economists. Thus the hypothesis that policies are the result of a process driven by the struggle among conflicting interests must be reexamined, or one must conclude that in this case the process started well before the 1932 presidential election. The Democrats harvested a ripe fruit.[44]

Previous Plans

Agrarianism blamed the farm crisis on an "imbalance" between the agricultural and industrial sectors, to be "readjusted" by legislation of specific benefit to farmers. This analysis was tied to an ideology of "agricultural fundamentalism," which held that farming was the ultimate source of all wealth, more basic, virtuous, and democratic than other occupations.[45] During the 67th Congress (1921–1923), agrarian legislation was advanced by a bipartisan Farm Bloc including twenty to twenty-five senators and nearly one hundred representatives. The Farm Bloc was first organized in the office of Gray Silver, Washington representative for the American Farm Bureau Federation (the Farm Bureau), and Silver continued to coordinate the Bloc. Among the Farm Bloc's accomplishments were passage of the Packers and Stockyards Act, aimed at raising livestock prices by prohibiting unfair practices, and the Federal Highway Act, designed to better link farms to markets.[46]

Progressivism blamed the farm crisis not on an imbalance between agriculture and industry but on "plutocracy" and the monopolies that stood between the farmer and the urban consumer. The Progressives' solution to the farm crisis was government ownership of such intermediary services as the railroads, waterways, and grain elevators. Unlike the agrarians, the Progressives did not appeal to farmers alone but sought to unite farmers and workers against the forces that exploited them both. The products of this union included farmer-labor parties in Minnesota and North Dakota that provided examples of successful state-level radicalism; the Conference for Progressive Political Action, which successfully targeted several congressional and gubernatorial candidates for defeat in 1922; and Robert La Follette's independent presidential candidacy in 1924.[47]

The cooperativist explanation for the farm crisis was that farmers, unlike the industrial trusts, lacked control over their markets. Cooperatives had been established much earlier, but it was during the mid-1920s that the movement had its greatest impact. Aaron Sapiro, a charismatic entrepreneur who helped form cooperatives for a fee, successfully organized producers of such diverse commodities as wheat, corn, cotton, tobacco, and California fruits. Less centralized cooperatives sprouted among producers of livestock, potatoes, and dairy products.[48] The total membership of the cooperatives themselves exceeded that of the three major peak associations, the Farm Bureau, the National Farmers' Union, and the National Grange. In 1923, Sapiro-formed cooperatives alone included 709,669 farmers.[49] The peak associations themselves became involved in the cooperative movement, with the Farm Bureau the most committed of the three: Oscar Bradfute, its president from 1922 to 1925, declared cooperative marketing the central focus of the organization and employed Sapiro as advisor.[50] The cooperativist approach to the farm crisis emphasized self-help and thus required less state intervention than either agrarianism or Progressivism. The cooperatives did mobilize in support of proposals that would facilitate their operations or establish programs that would be channeled through them and thereby increase their membership, finances, and opportunities for self-perpetuation.[51]

Agrarianism, Progressivism, and cooperativism each mobilized large numbers of farmers. But the movement that mobilized the most farmers and, for a time, united farmers of different organizations, sections, and ideologies was McNary-Haugenism. Like the Black Bill in industry, McNary-Haugenism shows the mass appeal of relatively simple solutions that could be captured in slogans. The McNary-Haugen movement had its origin in the pamphlet "Equality for Agriculture," published by George N. Peek and Hugh S. Johnson in January 1922. Agriculture, Peek and Johnson argued, needed the same protection industry received from the tariff, but agricultural tariffs alone were insufficient. Production, they pointed out, was set by six million individual farmers and subject to weather conditions. No matter how high agricultural tariffs were set, farmers would produce a surplus, which would have to be sold on the world market, and the world price would determine the domestic price. To "make the tariff effective for agriculture," Peek and Johnson proposed establishing a corporation to purchase the domestic surplus at the domestic price and dump it abroad at the world price. This market segregation, financed by an "equalization fee" on producers, would keep domestic prices high.[52]

As opponents of the export ban pointed out, by boosting prices without controlling production, the Peek-Johnson proposal would encourage farmers to increase their acreage. In the long run, production would increase, the export corporation would be forced to dump an ever-larger surplus, and the farmers' problems would be intensified.[53] Such effects have indeed been exhibited in recent times by the European Community's Common Agricultural Policy (CAP), which has been roughly similar to the Peek-Johnson plan in its maintenance of high domestic prices through import restrictions and export subsidies.[54] Yet the CAP also demonstrates that such policies, however unwise, can be sustained without extinguishing overall economic prosperity.

Despite opponents' claims that the export plan would make the farm problem worse, advocates of the proposal were eventually able to win the support of midwestern Republicans, southern Democrats, the major farm organizations, and the cooperatives. In the fall of 1923, Secretary of Agriculture Henry C. Wallace endorsed the proposal and commissioned his deputies to prepare a bill incorporating its principles. This bill was the first of five introduced in the Senate by Charles L. McNary and in the House by Gilbert N. Haugen. Subsequent versions of the McNary-Haugen bill expanded regional support by adding to the list of commodities covered and won the cooperatives over by providing that the new farm corporation contract with them to export surpluses rather than do the job itself. Following a change in leadership, the Farm Bureau made support for McNary-Haugen instead of cooperativism its main task. In February 1927, the fourth McNary-Haugen bill became the first to win congressional approval; support was bipartisan and based in South, Midwest, and West. The bill was vetoed by President Coolidge. Coolidge's veto message, written mostly by Secretary of Commerce Herbert Hoover and his protégé, Secretary of Agriculture William Jardine, argued that it helped only a few crops, constituted government price fixing and "the most vicious form of taxation," would stimulate production and breed bureaucracy, and was unconstitutional to boot. In April 1928, the McNary-Haugen coalition passed the fifth version of the bill, but once again it was vetoed by Coolidge.[55]

The Origins of Production Control

The first significant proposal for federal intervention to control farm production in the twenties was advanced by W. J. Spillman of the Bureau of Agricultural Economics in a February 1926 article and, more fully, in a January 1927 book. Like Peek and Johnson, Spillman sought to give farmers the equivalent of tariff protection, but his plan also would have encouraged restriction of production to the level of domestic consumption. Allotments equal to the estimated domestic consumption (the "domestic allotment") of every commodity would be distributed to individual farmers according to recent production levels. For production up to their allotment, farmers would receive the market price (equal to the world price) plus the value of the tariff. Farmers could produce beyond their allotment but would receive only the world price on this additional product. In 1929, John D. Black, a Harvard economist, published a plan developed by Beardsley Ruml of the Rockefeller-funded Laura Spelman Rockefeller Memorial. The Ruml-Black plan was similar to Spillman's except that it applied only to cotton and wheat and allowed farmers to transfer allotment rights. Mordecai Ezekiel, assistant chief economist with the Federal Farm Board, proposed that acreage controls be incorporated into the domestic allotment plan after a European trip convinced him that foreign markets would remain closed to American farmers. Henry I. Harriman of the United States Chamber of Commerce proposed a processing tax to finance the plan. M. L. Wilson, an agricultural economist at Montana State, added to the plan the important feature of local participation. Producers of each commodity would meet in their communities to decide whether their product should be included in the allotment program. Even if the decision was to join the program, individual farmers could choose not to participate in production control.[56]

Despite Wilson's provisions for local autonomy and individual freedom, farmers and farm leaders viewed the domestic-allotment plan with suspicion. Earl Smith of the Illinois affiliate of the Farm Bureau, for example, wrote George Peek that the allotment plan would "only operate to bring forth more confusion rather than the much needed crystallization of sincere thought" behind the McNary-Haugen Plan. Farm leaders also questioned the administrative feasibility of the plan; Ralph Snyder, the president of the Kansas Farm Bureau Federation, wrote that the "problem of putting such a plan into effect rather staggers my imagination." From 1930 to 1932, bills based on the domestic-allotment plan elicited little congressional response, even among legislators active in support of other proposals for farm relief. And, as Gilbert C. Fite has shown, both before and after adjustment became government policy, farmers preferred legislation that would guarantee them prices at least equal to the cost of production over programs for production control.[57]

Even among agricultural economists, support for production control was a minority position. Most of the discipline, including the chief of the Bureau of Agricultural Economics (BAE), Nils A. Olsen, favored a more limited approach combining voluntary planning by individual farmers with tariff liberalization and elimination of industrial oligopolies. Like the farm leaders, Olsen thought that production control would be impossible to administer; when the Roosevelt administration's Farm Bill was pending, he wrote in his journal that "the bill of course had colossal weaknesses and imposes a burden upon the Department that is just unthinkable."[58]

Republican Agricultural Policies

Republican agricultural policies reflected the concerns of farm groups and agricultural economists less than they reflected the concerns of eastern industrial and financial interests inside the party's coalition. The agrarianism of the Farm Bloc did not contest the inviolability of private property but did threaten the meat and grain trusts with regulation and sought to interfere with the financial system by requiring Federal Reserve Board representation for farmers and more generous agricultural lending policies. The Harding administration accepted some of the farm-bloc proposals but at the same time tried to break up the bloc by denouncing "class legislation," by appointing the leader of the bloc to the judiciary, and, apparently, by tapping the phones of the Farm Bureau's Washington office and having the head of that office trailed by detectives.[59] Progressive demands for government ownership were steadfastly resisted by the Republican majority. Cooperativist efforts mandated little state action and seemed to parallel and thus legitimate industrial trade associations. Hence, cooperativism received a generally favorable treatment from the Republican administrations.[60] The McNary-Haugen Plan would have provided cheap food for European workers, allowing their employers to pay lower wages and thus compete more successfully with American manufacturers. Secretary of the Treasury Andrew Mellon (who explicitly made this argument), the Chamber of Commerce, the National Association of Manufacturers, and the *Wall Street Journal* all strongly opposed the plan. The business interests supporting McNary-Haugenism were those dependent on farmers: rural bankers and agricultural implement producers. Peek and Johnson were themselves employed by Moline Plow at the time they developed the export proposal.[61]

The Republicans of the 1920s were able to win elections despite such pro-industry agricultural policies because the Democrats did not challenge them with policies appealing more closely to farmers' economic interests. Had the Democrats mounted such a challenge, the Republicans might have had to make concessions. Throughout the 1920s, however, Democratic party politics was waged along purely ethnocultural lines. An urban bloc identified with Alfred E. Smith appealed to Catholics, wets, and immigrants. Its mirror image was a rural bloc identified with William G. McAdoo and based on fundamentalism, prohibition, and the Ku Klux Klan. The struggles between the two factions were devoid of economic content, and so to a large extent were the interparty contests that followed. In 1924, the deadlock between McAdoo and Smith led to the nomination of John W. Davis, a conservative Wall Street lawyer, who spent more of his campaign attacking La Follette than going after Coolidge. In 1928, Smith did try to win farm support by a vague endorsement of McNary-Haugen "in principle." George Peek, with the unofficial assistance of the Farm Bureau, organized farmers in support of Smith, but the farm issue was overshadowed by the great cultural conflicts of that campaign.[62] Insurgents within the Republican party, such as Robert La Follette and George Norris, posed a more consistent challenge to the probusiness policies of the dominant Republican faction, but this group had virtually no impact on the Republican party's presidential nominations or platforms and achieved only very limited success in Congress.[63]

During the Hoover presidency, Republican agricultural policy moved beyond opposition to McNary-Haugen to a positive program consistent with Hoover's preference for associationalist cooperation over economic competition.[64] The Agricultural Marketing Act of June 15, 1929, set up the Federal Farm Board, empowered to establish stabilization corporations that would hold surpluses for future domestic sale and to provide low-interest loans to cooperatives, which would be merged into centralized "national associations." The Farm Board made genuine efforts to improve farm conditions but in ways that safeguarded the interests of industrial capitalists: processors occupied key positions, agricultural production for export was discouraged, and the centralized organization of farmers legitimized Hoover's support for industrial trade associations.

The general economic collapse soon rendered the Farm Board both economically and politically ineffective. David E. Hamilton suggests that the Farm Board would not have fared much better under more favorable conditions:

> What began as a bold departure in farm policy aimed at restructuring the farm economy quickly turned into another failed attempt at organizing farmers and commodity cooperatives. Instead of building self-governing cooperatives, the board was organizing remote agencies and led by self-serving managers and directors. By mid-1931 its policies were under attack from the established cooperatives, whose leaders had come to see the board as a threat to the survival of cooperative marketing. What emerges from a closer look at the national associations is a picture of a president and a Farm Board adhering to unrealistic expectations and willing to ignore the tremendous discrepancy between their goals and the reality of their creations.[65]

With the failure of the Farm Board, the farm organizations, which had been induced to support the board through participation in its stabilization corporations, returned to their earlier advocacy of McNary-Haugen or other panaceas.[66]

Openings for the Democrats

The general economic collapse also produced a change in business attitudes toward the farm crisis and proposals for farm relief. Leaders of the insurance industry, which had invested heavily in farm mortgages, and general business leaders, who believed a revived farm market was necessary for national recovery, endorsed programs of agricultural relief through state intervention. Henry Harriman of the Chamber of Commerce was a particularly active and early proponent of production control. Beardsley Ruml and the Laura Spelman Rockefeller Memorial sponsored John Black's 1929 study of alternative agricultural recovery proposals and suggested that Black review the domestic allotment plan.[67] However, business did not unite in support of any one plan for resolving the farm crisis. Production control did not subsidize European industry, but processors such as the cereal companies and cotton textile firms, which were otherwise greatly interested in farm relief, opposed a plan that would cut their profits by reducing the volume of their operations. These firms resisted even more strenuously proposals for financing production control by a processing tax.[68]

The shift among industrial capitalists did not in itself produce policy change. The Hoover administration sponsored no new farm proposals following the failure of the Farm Board. Nor did Hoover support the early bills for government-enforced production restrictions, which he believed would be fascism.[69] The enactment of the AAA was possible only because Hoover and the Republicans, whose conception of the role of the state remained narrow even when industrial capitalists were seeking its expansion, were replaced in power by Franklin Roosevelt and the Democrats. Because Roosevelt and his advisors sought to win the farm vote on economic rather than ethnocultural grounds, they developed an alternative conception of the state's role in agriculture.

During the 1920s, Smith and McAdoo mobilized support within the Democratic party by appeals to their ethnocultural bases rather than by policy stances that might have unified the Democratic party and appealed to voters outside the party as well. Roosevelt's initial strategy for obtaining the 1932 nomination was no more policy-oriented. Under the counsel of the "Albany advisors"—Louis Howe, James Farley, and Colonel Edward M. House—Roosevelt sought to coast to victory on personal attractiveness, while avoiding controversy of any sort. When Roosevelt did poorly in several early primaries and a Smith-McAdoo anti-Roosevelt coalition threatened to form, the Brains Trust—Raymond Moley, Adolph Berle, Jr., and Rexford Guy Tugwell—partially supplanted Howe, Farley, and House, and the Roosevelt campaign placed more emphasis on policy. The new strategy allowed Roosevelt to win southern and western votes by his position on farm issues. Support from these sections was crucial to Roosevelt's nomination, since Smith maintained the support of eastern party leaders. As mentioned above, the strategy of emphasizing agricultural policy proved equally successful in the general election, helping Roosevelt to win in normally Republican farm states.[70]

Roosevelt was able to win farm votes without committing himself to any of the specific proposals advanced by farm leaders. Though Tugwell and M. L. Wilson, whom Tugwell brought into the campaign, were both advocates of domestic allotment, specific references to this proposal were avoided as well. Instead, Roosevelt spoke in general terms of the goals a farm policy need accomplish, suggesting to each farm leader that the candidate endorsed that leader's preferred solution to the farm crisis. In his major farm policy address, delivered at Topeka, Kansas, on September 14, 1932, Roosevelt endorsed the McNary-Haugenite goal of making the tariff effective for agriculture and listed the necessary features of a farm relief plan. Among the requirements were that the plan not stimulate production, that it not lead to European retaliation, and that it be voluntary or at least based on the support of a majority of producers.[71] In retrospect, only the domestic allotment plan met all these conditions. Yet such farm leaders as George Peek, John Simpson of the Farmers' Union, and Edward O'Neal of the Farm Bureau were convinced Roosevelt would enact the policies they advocated, and each of them allied with the Democrats.[72]

After Roosevelt's election, the president-elect and his advisors were able to use the ties developed with the farm organizations during the campaign to persuade those organizations to accept production controls. The farm organization in turn won the consent of their members for the new direction in federal farm policy. Ironically, campaign support by the farm groups ultimately worked against their prior policy preferences. Having backed Roosevelt, the leaders of the farm groups needed to be able to claim to their members that he was adopting their ideas. In return for endorsing the Roosevelt administration's production control program, the peak association leaders were given official access, influence over appointments, and ambiguous statements within the Agricultural Adjustment Act, all of which allowed them to claim credit with their members.[73] Between the election and Roosevelt's inauguration in March, the Grange and the Farm Bureau each endorsed production control for the first time. Meetings were then held between Roosevelt's advisors and representatives from the peak associations and the major cooperatives. All the farm leaders except Simpson of the Farmers' Union agreed to endorse "adjustment payments" to farmers who reduced their 1933 acreage.[74] One consequence of the farm groups' new position was the relatively easy and rapid passage of the administration farm bill establishing the AAA. Congress did tack on an amendment authorizing the president to expand the money supply, but a more radical amendment embodying the Farmers' Union view that prices should be fixed at cost of production levels was defeated.[75]

Pre–New Deal Republican agricultural policy had been reactive, but New Deal agricultural policy was proactive. During the 1920s, the Republicans viewed farmers as a class whose demands were to be resisted. Roosevelt and the Brains Trust, in contrast, saw farmers as contested voters, to be won through policy appeals. The difference between the two parties can be explained by their electoral coalitions and strategies. Before 1932, the Republican party could pursue nakedly probusiness policies and still enjoy the votes of western and midwestern farm states under the sectional alignment of 1896. The Democratic party, split along ethnocultural lines, posed no policy challenge, and profarmer insurgents within the Republican ranks were too weak to have much impact. Roosevelt changed farm politics and farm policy because he found it advantageous to win farmers' votes through policy appeals that would convince them to vote as farmers rather than as members of a particular region or ethnocultural group.

The Democrats, then, came into power ready to formulate a new farm policy. The Agricultural Adjustment Act made concessions to the McNary-Haugen movement, including provisions for marketing agreements and the use of processing taxes to cover export losses. George N. Peek was named as the AAA's first administrator.[76] Roosevelt had actually endorsed McNary-Haugen in a telegram to *Collier's* and in a ghostwritten article for *Liberty*.[77] But McNary-Haugenism violated the conditions of Roosevelt's Topeka speech, which may be read as the constraints that even a collapsed industrial economy still imposed on agricultural policy. Peek would be out after seven months, and New Deal agricultural policy would not be based on McNary-Haugenism but on production control.

If New Deal agricultural policy was not made by the farm groups, by whom was it made? Certainly not by farm workers, who lacked either votes or organizations and were completely excluded from the policy process. Production control had important business support, but industrial capitalists were not united in its support, and those who did support it could not convince Hoover. Roosevelt's selection of production control as the basis for New Deal agricultural policy was most directly attributable to agricultural economists trained in the land-grant colleges and the Department of Agriculture. W. J. Spillman, a Bureau of Agricultural Economics professional who acted unofficially in creating his plan, was one of the leaders in the organization of agricultural economics within the Department of Agriculture. John D. Black was a Harvard economist who had been trained at the land-grant University of Wisconsin. Black had previously taught at land-grant Minnesota and worked at the BAE. Before moving to the Federal Farm Board, Mordecai Ezekiel had been an economist for the BAE, which had hired him even though he had no formal training in economics or statistics; Ernest K. Lindley described him as "the brilliant young economist and part author of the revolutionary farm bill, who can demonstrate by logarithms how to raise hogs." M. L. Wilson taught agricultural economics at Montana State, also a land-grant college, after service in the BAE and studies at Iowa State, Wisconsin, Chicago, and Cornell (all except Chicago were land-grant colleges.).[78] Wilson is particularly important because he became a near-fanatical advocate of the plan. Among his many converts were Henry A. Wallace, then publisher of *Wallace's Farmer*, and Rexford Tugwell, by then a campaign advisor to Franklin Roosevelt.[79]

Electoral incentives pushed Roosevelt to do something for agriculture; economic constraints prevented him from doing what the farmers wanted him to do—enact McNary-Haugen or cost-of-production legislation. Agricultural experts generated a policy alternative. The victory of the idea of production control over the interests of agricultural capitalists reflected the institutional context of the land-grant colleges and the Department of Agriculture.

Interests, Ideas, Institutions, and Policy Threats

At the beginning of the New Deal, business planning defeated work sharing for industry and production control defeated export marketing for agriculture. New Deal policies in both sectors were thus alternatives to proposals with more popular support. The two policies came from different sources: the NRA grew out of proposals by capitalists such as Gerard Swope, whereas the AAA was based on proposals by the agricultural economists, Spillman, Black, Ezekiel, and Wilson, as well as by the Rockefeller-connected Ruml. The NRA can thus be interpreted as the product of the politics of interests, the AAA as the product of the politics of ideas.

Rational choice, pluralist, elitist, and Marxist approaches to politics all emphasize self-interest, as each approach construes it. Several recent authors have argued that the cost of this emphasis is inadequate attention to the influence on public policy of ideas, which are either neglected entirely or treated as masks for the real interests involved.[80] The ideal way to test this argument for the power of ideas, Mark H. Moore suggests, would be

> to do a series of experiments in which public ideas that were more to less orthogonal to the play of interests were introduced into the domain of public deliberation and action, and measurements were taken of how often and to what degree the ideas shifted the nature of the discussion and the subsequent actions. But just to describe these conditions reveals the absurdity of a rigorous analytic approach to this question. There are many ill-defined terms in this analytic framework. And it is quite implausible that one could experiment with our own policy-making processes by systematically varying the character of the ideas available for discussion.[81]

Given the impossibility of such a pure experiment, the next best research strategy might be to treat historical cases as quasi-experiments in order to evaluate what Judith Goldstein calls the "supply of ideas" as a factor in policy change.[82] Goldstein finds that the liberalization of U.S. industrial trade policy and the simultaneous refusal to liberalize agricultural trade policy were "determined by more than the structural needs of the economy."[83] Martha Derthick and Paul J. Quirk show that ideational variables had more impact than interest group resources on the success of efforts to deregulate assorted sectors of the U.S. economy during the 1970s and 1980s.[84] Peter Hall sums up a collaborative project on the impact of Keynesianism as confirming

> that ideas have an existence and force of their own that cannot be reduced to complete dependence on some set of material circumstances. . . . Keynesian ideas did not simply reflect group interests or material conditions. They had the power to change the perceptions a group had of its own interests, and they made possible new courses of action that changed the material world itself. In these respects, Keynesian ideas had a good deal of independent force over circumstances.[85]

Hugh Heclo, in his study of the origins of British and Swedish social policies, says that

> finding feasible courses of action includes, but is more than, locating which way the vectors of political pressure are pushing. Governments not only "power" (or whatever the verb form of that approach might be); they also puzzle.[86]

Of course, most of the scholars who argue for the importance of ideas to policymaking are not so naive as to think ideas have influence solely according to their merit. Rather, these authors distinguish, in various ways, between the context and the content of policy ideas. The fit between an idea and its political environment, they suggest, matters more than substantive soundness in determining how much force the idea will have.[87]

"To some degree," Derthick and Quirk say, "whether analysis is likely to meet both substantive and political requirements for effectiveness depends on how it is conducted and on the organizational arrangements under which it is produced."[88] The effects of organizational arrangements on the politics of ideas—and thus on policy formation—are best demonstrated through comparison. Alexis de Tocqueville sketched a classic cross-national contrast:

> In England writers on the theory of government and those who actually governed co-operated with each other, the former setting forth their new theories, the latter amending or circumscribing these in the light of practical experience. In France, however, precept and practice were kept quite distinct and remained in the

hands of two quite independent groups. One of these carried on the actual administration while the other set forth the abstract principles on which good government should, they said, be based; one took the routine measures appropriate to the needs of the moment, the other propounded general laws without a thought for their practical application; one group shaped the course of public affairs, the other that of public opinion.[89]

Another form of comparison is analysis of a single polity over time. James Q. Wilson and Hugh Heclo both say that ideas are more important in American politics today than in the recent past. They trace this transformation to organizational changes: the decline of party in Congress and the replacement of "iron triangles" of interest groups, congressional committees, and bureaucratic agencies by more fluid, idea-based "issue networks."[90] In comparing patterns of policy formation across nations or over time, it is important not to lose sight of a third form of comparison: analysis of the variations across policy areas in a single nation at a single time.[91] Derthick and Quirk's study of deregulation is an example of a cross-sectional comparison in the politics of ideas.[92]

The selection and timing of the NRA and the AAA suggest that in the formation of American public policy, the power of organized interests and the power of ideas are both dependent variables, the importance of which is determined by configurations of state and party organizations. New Deal policies for industry reflected the power of organized interest groups. Business groups got what they wanted; labor unions, which supported the blocked Black Bill, received concessions whose value seemed to be questionable. New Deal policies for agriculture followed a different pattern. Agricultural capitalists were not able to control the policy process, and unorganized farmworkers were completely excluded.

The two U.S. economic sectors also provide contrasting evidence about the power of ideas in public-policy making. Goldstein argues that New Deal debates over state intervention in agriculture took place within a cohesive intellectual framework that was absent from debates over intervention in industry. " 'Ideas'," in turn, "reflect variations in the development trajectories of each sector."[93] The idea of production control, germinated in the Department of Agriculture and the land-grant college system and disseminated to the Roosevelt camp, shaped the AAA. Similar ideas about industrial planning, championed by some of the same people, had less impact on the NRA. Heclo cites the Department of Agriculture as an example of the recent rise of the policy intellectuals he labels "technopols."[94] The origins of the AAA and the NRA suggest that it might be more appropriate to say that other policy areas have lately come to resemble the agricultural issue network of the 1930s.

Policy threats, defined earlier in this chapter as proposals that policymakers define as unacceptable but for electoral reasons cannot simply reject without providing alternatives, represent one pattern of interaction between ideas, interests, and institutions in the process of policy formation. McNary-Haugenism and the Black Bill both demonstrate the importance of this pattern. Each proposal had support among interest groups and within the Democratic party; the combination drove Roosevelt to do more than Hoover had done to bring about industrial and agricultural recovery. But the McNary-Haugen and Black bills also violated Roosevelt's conception of what could or should be done within the context of a capitalist economy. Each proposal thus resulted in a search for policy alternatives. The search for an alternative to export marketing took place within the 1932 campaign because Roosevelt's strategy identified farmers as the crucial contested group. Industrial workers, in contrast, were taken for granted as safely inside the Democratic coalition. The search for an alternative to the thirty-hour week took place only after the Black Bill passed the Senate, following the AFL's post-election shift from its long-time voluntarist opposition to such policies.

The contrasting sources of alternatives to the policy threats in industry and agriculture reflect differences in state capacities for intervention in the two sectors, as well as the relationship of experts to governmental agencies. Experts trained in the land-grant colleges and the Department of Agriculture developed domestic allotment into a policy proposal and communicated the proposal to the Roosevelt campaign, whose electoral needs it met. The adoption of agricultural policies originally opposed by organized agricultural capitalists reflected the match between state capacity and party strategy. No such match occurred in the making of New Deal industrial policy. Rexford Tugwell was an advocate of national planning within the Roosevelt camp. Frances Perkins, who sought discretionary wages and hours regulation, was Roosevelt's Industrial Commissioner in New York and could draw on a network of officials who had administered state-level protective legislation. But Roosevelt did not make industrial policy a campaign priority and was inaugurated without any program for intervention in the industrial economy. Roosevelt did not use his election to convert industrial capitalists and workers to wages and hours regulation as he converted farm leaders to production control. The result was that Perkins's hastily drafted substitute for the Black Bill confronted immediate and fatal opposition from interest groups representing both sides of the industrial class conflict.

Drawing on organizational theory, John W. Kingdon has developed a model of policy formation that treats problems, politics, and policies as three separate streams. The problems stream and the political stream set the policy agenda; alternatives are generated in the policy stream.[95] The origins of the NRA and the AAA confirm several of Kingdon's insights into the policy process. Kingdon's three streams sometimes come together to provide policy windows when policies can change.[96] The combination of crisis and electoral turnover made Roosevelt's "Hundred Days" such a period of opportunity. The roles of Hugo Black, Gerard Swope, George N. Peek, and M. L. Wilson, among others, support Kingdon's emphasis on the role of policy entrepreneurs, who join the three streams by taking advantage of problems and politics to promote their policy solutions.[97] Kingdon suggests that policy communities, not individuals, develop policy proposals; infinite regress (ideas can always be traced back further in time) and multiple authorship make it impossible ever to say who invented a proposal.[98] The origins of the thirty-hour-week proposal (Hugo Black or William Green?), the AAA (W. J. Spillman, John D. Black, M. L. Wilson, Mordecai Ezekiel, or Beardsley Ruml?), and the NRA (Swope and Harriman or its architects within the Roosevelt administration?) demonstrate the problem.

The origins of the NRA and the AAA also demonstrate the limits of Kingdon's approach. Kingdon's policy stream is a "primeval soup" in which ideas are as important as interest group pressures and technical feasibility is one criterion for survival.[99] This conception assumes that experts exist and are available to public officials. Contemporary Washington consultants in health and transportation, the two policy areas Kingdon studied, meet these criteria. But they meet them in different ways than the agricultural experts of the land-grant college system do today or did in the 1930s. And in industrial policy, experts who meet these criteria were not available in the 1930s and do not exist today. Business groups consequently exercised influence over the NRA beyond the negative blocking that Kingdon describes as the main activity of organized interests.[100] During the 1930s, expertise was more available to the executive branch than to the legislature, which lacked the staff it has today. This differential access to expertise, along with differences between local and national constituencies, may explain why Congress was more willing than the president to endorse such technically infeasible ideas as exporting the farm surplus during a worldwide depression and mandating a thirty-hour work week.

Kingdon's vision of technical competition between policy ideas may be valid for ideas that policymakers consider acceptable, such as the different drafts for the NIRA. But policymakers such as Franklin Roosevelt judge some ideas as unacceptable threats. Only those ideas that survive this primary test can be considered on their merits. The failure of the Black Bill and the McNary-Haugen Plan in the early New Deal suggests that proposals become threats when they violate the constraints of a capitalist economy (as the policymaker interprets those constraints) but must still be met with some alternative lest a part of the party coalition be lost.

The importance of threats has been emphasized by scholars who look at pressures from below as the cause of new policy initiatives.[101] But this approach has not given sufficient emphasis to the ability of policymakers to respond to threats with alternatives. William Green's warning of massive strikes did not force either Hoover or Roosevelt to accept the thirty-hour week. Farm strikes during the fall of 1933 did not lead to replacement of the AAA with policies guaranteeing farmers that prices would at least equal production costs.[102] Direct actions such as strikes or protests may or may not push policymakers to do something. Whether policymakers do have to respond depends on the position of the insurgents in the governing party's electoral coalition. Party strategy, an interpretation of the opportunities for success within an existing alignment, may define a group as safe supporters, as contested voters, as opponents, or as excluded from the electorate. Contested groups, such as farmers for the Democrats in 1932, must be appealed to but can sometimes be won with cultural symbols rather than policy decisions. Safe supporters, such as industrial workers for the Democrats in 1932, can be taken for granted unless they exercise influence from within the party organization. Excluded groups (for example, agricultural workers in 1932) and, usually, opposition groups can be ignored.

"My notebook," Raymond Moley wrote, "contains Roosevelt's reaction to the Black bill under the category of 'Threats.'"[103] Like Moley's notebook, the study of policy formation should have a special category for threats, proposals that policymakers define as unacceptable but cannot simply reject. The requirements of a capitalist economy, as policymakers understand them, combine with electoral alignments and party strategies to define policy proposals as threats. What policymakers choose to do then depends on the alternatives available to them. These alternatives, in turn, are influenced by the capacities of state organizations and allied experts as sources of policy proposals.

4

The Implementation of Industrial and Agricultural Planning

Both the National Industrial Recovery Act and the Agricultural Adjustment Act declared very broad objectives and granted enormous authority—and leeway in legislative interpretation—to the executive branch. Essentially, the two acts mandated the establishment of authoritative new administrative organizations, the National Recovery Administration (NRA) and the Agricultural Adjustment Administration (AAA), through which economic functions formerly shaped by market competition would be planned and regulated in the public interest. The "voluntary" participation of trade associations and farmers' committees was envisaged as the primary means for putting NRA and AAA programs into effect, but it was clear that the government had been granted authority to induce cooperation and coerce recalcitrants. Moreover, government officials were allowed plenty of space to initiate plans and regulations to achieve the desired broad goals of recovery, stabilization, and relief. An advocate of public planning such as Rexford Tugwell could be forgiven for hoping in the spring of 1933 that the NRA and the AAA had together opened the door for unprecedented government coordination and direction of the entire U.S. productive economy.

What actually happened was quite different. Despite the parallel broad grants of executive authority in the two acts, the administrative organizations established under their provisions had sharply contrasting trajectories of development. The NRA became, over time, increasingly unwieldy, conflict-ridden, and uncertain about its basic goals and preferred means for achieving them. The AAA, to a much greater degree, sorted out its priorities, resolved a major internal contradiction of programs and personnel, streamlined its organizational structure, and launched ambitious new plans for the future. When the Supreme Court declared the original Agricultural Adjustment Act unconstitutional, it was quickly replaced, whereas Title I of the National Industrial Recovery Act (NIRA), the part establishing the NRA, was not reformulated after it was invalidated in the *Schechter* decision of May 1935. In short, the main agricultural program of the early New Deal ended up being successfully institutionalized, but the main industrial program did not. The ulterior political consequences of the NRA's failure and the AAA's success reverberated throughout the rest of the New Deal and can still be felt today.

It is important, therefore, to understand why the NRA and the AAA had such different results, both for our understanding of U.S. industrial and agricultural policies and, more generally, for our understanding of the conditions for effectual policy implementation. Our explanations of the implementation of the NRA and the AAA are based on the concept of state capacity, defined in chapter 2 as the means by which state goals can actually be carried out. This is not a tautology: capacity, as an independent variable, is something an organization possesses or does not possess, in degrees and dimensions, before it even starts to implement a particular policy. The dependent variable is the policy's outcome, which can be categorized roughly as success or failure or according to a more refined scheme appropriate to the particular policy domain. Different governmental challenges require different kinds of capacities: the same administration organization may be quite able to carry out one innovative program and utterly unable to carry out another.

Both the NRA and the AAA demanded expertise for sectoral planning, that is, for making decisions at levels of aggregation above that of the firm or farm. The pre–New Deal development of the agricultural state had created experts with both the will to intervene and ideas about how they might do so. Moreover, these experts were located in positions within or connected with the United States Department of Agriculture (USDA). The prior development of the industrial state did not create similar experts for comprehensive, sectoral-level industrial planning. What industrial planning was done was done for particular firms and was done outside the Department of Commerce. Differences in the implementation of New Deal policies for industry and for agriculture would follow from these differences in preexisting state capacities.

The NRA and the Weakness of the Industrial State

The implementation of New Deal industrial policy bore out Alexis de Tocqueville's observation that in America, "there are some enterprises concerning the whole state which cannot be carried out because there is no national administration to control them."[1] In one way of looking at it, the NRA had to start from scratch to implement government-supervised industrial coordination. But in another way of looking at it, the NRA simply reproduced still another variant of the governmental strategies used to "mobilize business" for the First World War under Bernard Baruch's War Industries Board and used to "cooperate with business" under Herbert Hoover's "associative state" (see chapter 2). For the implications of the American state's persistent administrative weakness were to prove as telling for the NRA as they had been for the previous major phases of government-business relations in twentieth-century America.

Hugh Johnson Launches the NRA

To a discerning eye, the prodromal signs were already apparent in the spring of 1933 as Roosevelt became extraordinarily reliant on one man, General Hugh Johnson, to put together the entire apparatus needed to implement Title I of the National Industrial Recovery Act. Johnson was a veteran of the WIB, a coauthor of the agricultural relief proposal that became the basis for the McNary-Haugen bills, and a leading partici-pant in the drafting process that produced the NIRA. He was also "Bernard Baruch's man" in the Roosevelt entourage; through his af-filiation with Baruch, Johnson enjoyed a broad range of connections to the heads of corporations and to trade association leaders. Roosevelt's selection of Johnson as NRA administrator was a sop to Baruch, who had hoped for but not received the position of secretary of state. Johnson had the qualities that seemed appropriate to lead the program of business recovery the drafting process had produced: enthusiasm, knowledge, and experience. Like Roosevelt (who had served as presi-dent of a trade association, the American Construction Council, during the 1920s), Johnson was committed to industrial self-government. Arthur Krock of the *New York Times* noted approvingly that Johnson was a practical man, not an educator or a theoretician. Others, includ-ing Baruch, were perturbed by Johnson's erratic personality and his heavy drinking.[2]

　　Roosevelt responded to these concerns by making two changes in the plan of organization drawn up for the NRA by Johnson and Alexander Sachs, who became chief of the Research and Planning Division. First, Johnson, as NRA administrator, would not report directly to the president but to the Industrial Recovery Board, composed mostly of cabinet officials. This board never became effective and was abolished in December 1933.[3] Second, Title II of the National Industrial Recovery Act, the $3.3-billion public-works program under the new Public Works Administration (PWA), was separated from Title I, the program of sectoral codification under Johnson's NRA. Johnson had expected to head both programs, but Interior Secretary Harold Ickes was put in charge of the PWA. The separation and Ickes's cautious administration undermined the economic logic of the recovery program, according to which the stimulatory effects of public works spending would expand purchasing power, allowing the public to afford the higher prices generated by the NRA codes. The loss of control over public works also deprived Johnson of the ability to sanction employers who did not comply with the codes by keeping them out of the potentially lucrative public works program.[4]

The early NRA has been aptly characterized as "the swirling chaos over which Hugh Johnson reigned."[5] The tasks at hand were exhilarating and overwhelming. An entire NRA staff had to be instantly assembled; as Johnson later wrote, "We started with nobody in the Washington organization and at one time had nearly 3,000 people there."[6] Johnson quickly launched the "Blue Eagle Campaign" to persuade employers to agree immediately to the blanket provisions of the "President's Re-employment Agreement" (PRA): maximum hours (thirty-five hours a week for manufacturing, forty for white-collar workers), minimum wages (set according to the size of the town of employment, with the highest rate in the largest cities), and a ban on child labor.[7] Ever the pragmatist, Johnson believed "the quickest method is to *bring the uniform cases to swift action by a blanket rule and then to deal with the exceptions.*"[8] Moreover, the process of drafting codes for individual sectors was going slowly, and Roosevelt wanted to get people back to work at once.

Unlike the forthcoming codes (violations of which would be liable to prosecution as unfair competition under the Federal Trade Commission Act), the PRA was not enforceable by law. Johnson therefore relied heavily on the mobilization of mass pressure. As one participant put it, Johnson "was a very picturesque fellow; he stimulated a large part of the population and terrorized another part."[9] In an effort to put NRA "enforcement . . . into the hands of the *whole* people,"[10] Johnson consciously modeled the Blue Eagle campaign on successful precedents from World War I: the WIB's Mobilization of Industry, the Liberty Loan bond drives, the Food Administration's restrictions on meat and wheat consumption, and the local administration of the military draft. Cooperating employers would be allowed to display the Blue Eagle, an insignia based on a Navaho thunderbird design and carrying the slogan "We Do Our Part." Noncompliers were to be boycotted by code-signing firms and denied government contracts. All of this was accompanied by great public hoopla: 250,000 people joined an NRA parade in New York, and 8,000 children formed a giant eagle in San Francisco. Meanwhile, Johnson used his formidable powers of personal persuasion to prompt industries to draw up their own individual codes of fair competition. Participation in the code-making process promised to give businesses the higher prices they needed to pay the higher wages imposed by the PRA.

For the major industrial executives, as Louis Galambos notes, "working with Johnson—or as they referred to him privately, Old Ironpants—was like trying to tame a whirlwind: if they succeeded, they would hold the reins on a source of tremendous power; if they failed, the whirlwind might well destroy them and all of their plans."[11] When the dust settled after the first hectic months of the NRA, it certainly seemed that the business executives had succeeded in taming the whirlwind. Between June and October 1933, the major industrial sectors were brought under approved codes of fair competition, and processes were well under way that would result in 557 approved codes covering about 96 percent of U.S. industry.[12] All codes necessarily embodied wage and hours provisions for labor, along with the pro-forma Section 7(a) provision declaring labor's right to organize collectively. Despite these features, business leaders—especially the trade associations that represented many oligopolistic industries—succeeded in formulating the codes so as to allow many loopholes in prolabor provisions as well as production cutbacks and noncompetitive, higher prices for most industries.

The Staffing of the NRA

The NRA could not be staffed with trained government officials experienced in regulating or planning for industry with "the public interest" and some conception of the whole economy in mind, for few were at hand. Instead, the key officials of the early NRA (besides Johnson himself), those directly responsible for drafting the codes, were drawn from business. Table 5 shows that reliance on business, although pronounced at all levels, was less extreme among the division administrators, who included political appointments and long-time friends of

Table 5. Prior careers of NRA code officials (percentage distribution)[a]

Rank	Business	Government	Academic	Law	N[b]
Division Administrator	70.0	50.0	0.0	20.0	10 (1)
Deputy Administrator	89.6	35.4	10.4	12.5	48 (0)
Assistant Deputy	90.5	21.6	9.5	2.7	74 (8)
Total	88.6	29.5	9.1	7.6	132 (9)

Sources: U.S. Congress, Senate, *Employees of the National Recovery Administration*, Senate *Document No. 164*, 73d Cong., 2d sess., March 20, 1934, was the source for names of officials responsible for each proposed code, and the main source for career data on these officials. Information that was omitted or ambiguous in *Employees of the NRA* was obtained from *Dictionary of American Biography*, *National Cyclopedia of American Biography*, *Who's Who*, and *New York Times* obituaries.
[a] Includes officials with direct responsibility for codes serving as of or prior to March 20, 1934. Percentages sum to more than 100 since some officials had experience in more than one category.
[b] Totals and percentages do not include officials for whom career data could not be obtained. The number of such officials is shown in parentheses.

Johnson, than at the lower ranks of deputy administrator and assistant deputy, whose selection Johnson delegated to other officials, particularly John Hancock, a Wall Street banker. Some NRA officials came from the very same industries with which they had to negotiate over code provisions: for example, H. Nelson Slater, a cotton textile manufacturer, became deputy administrator with authority over the cotton textile code. Many of the NRA officials who did have prior governmental experience were career military officers, such as retired major general Clarence C. Williams, chief of ordnance in World War I, who "knew the chemical industry inside out and, as an old army man, could think in terms of the government interest." Others had served in temporary government positions during the war. The twelve code officials with academic experience included three engineers, two college administrators, two chemists, two economists, a geologist, a political scientist, and a professor of marketing. Of the twelve, only the political scientist, Lindsay Rogers of Columbia University, did not also have prior experience in business.[13]

Two contemporary observers were hardly exaggerating, therefore, when they described the early NRA as a "bargain between business leaders on the one hand and business men in the guise of government officials on the other."[14] Long before 1933, Adam Smith noted the distance between the mindset of "merchants and manufacturers" and the public interest: "As their thoughts, however, are commonly exercised rather about the interest of their own particular branch of business, than about that of the society, their judgment, even when given with the greatest candour (which it has not been upon every occasion), is much more to be depended on with regard to the former of those two objects, than with regard to the latter."[15] Confirming Smith's insight, the NRA "businesscrats" lacked "any set of concepts wherewith to consider the relations of government to business enterprise other than the hackneyed thought that the less government supervision there is the better."[16] They were strongly sympathetic to the demands of the industrialists for government action that would guarantee a profitable environment and an end to "cutthroat competition" in the deflationary crisis.

Academic economists participated in the NRA, but they were marginalized.[17] The NRA's two leading figures both expressed contempt for economists. Hugh Johnson criticized "economic kibitzers" in print; Donald Richberg, the NRA's general counsel (and later its administrator), wrote of economists as "dodos." In some cases, economists had to be reclassified as mathematicians or statisticians before their appointments would be approved. The hostility was mutual, for most economists rejected the NRA's price and production controls as a violation of the classical doctrines of Smith, David Ricardo, and Alfred Marshall. As noted above, only two of the twelve code officials with academic experience included in table 5 (Eugene W. Burgess and Earl Dean Howard) were economists.

The organizational base for economists within the NRA was the Division of Research and Planning, outside the structure of direct authority over the codes. Despite its name, the division did little long-range planning. Johnson saw it as a statistical bureau only and relegated it to routine data collection for code administration. Even in this area, the economists were hampered by lack of information. The economists' most significant victory was the release in June 1934 of Memorandum 228, weakening open-price and fair-trade provisions. Johnson, however, announced that the memorandum would apply only to codes that had not yet been approved, thus excluding almost 90 percent of the industries eventually covered by the NRA. Research and Planning's main ally in the battle against cartelization, the Consumers' Advisory Board, exercised even less policy influence. Johnson said, "Who the hell cares what the Consumers' Board thinks?"[18]

Besides economists, the other alternatives to business executives within the NRA were lawyers. Though most of Johnson's experience had been in the military and in business, he was also a lawyer who had practiced with the Army, the Bureau of Insular Affairs, and the Illinois Attorney General.[19] As general counsel, Richberg, a leading labor lawyer, was second in power only to Johnson at the start of the NRA; he would eventually head the agency himself.[20] Table 5 indicates that few of the officials with direct responsibility for codes came from legal careers. NRA lawyers were instead located primarily within the Legal Division. The necessity of legal clearance gave the NRA lawyers what the NRA economists lacked: entrée into the codification process that was central to the recovery program. The Brookings Institution's generally critical study described the NRA lawyers as a "source of advice detached from any one of the special interests represented in the code bargaining process," whose rulings often came to substitute for nonexistent general NRA policies.[21] Yet the NRA lawyers had personal characteristics that made them sympathetic to business: compared with the more liberal lawyers of the AAA and the NLRB, the NRA lawyers were older, less frequently educated at Ivy League law schools, and more experienced in business and politics.[22]

To the extent that the NRA lawyers did challenge the prevailing norms of the program, they did not necessarily improve the agency's capacity for sectoral intervention. Hugh Heclo lists four requirements for effective industrial policy: purposiveness, self-monitoring, ability to calculate quid pro quos, and procedural predictability.[23] The participation of lawyers in the code-making process guaranteed the last of these at the expense of the other three. Tocqueville observed that American lawyers are oriented to precedent, which makes them a conservative force within a democratic political system.[24] In the context of the NRA, an emphasis on precedent played into the hands of a predominantly conservative, Republican-appointed judiciary, which could issue interpretations of past cases that were unfavorable to the program and ultimately laid the basis for the *Schechter* decision.[25] Lawyers also seek cases they can win, which leads them to disregard economic criteria for decision making.[26]

In addition to their ability to deal mainly with inherently sympathetic NRA personnel who were much like themselves, industrial executives had other advantages. One was that the only organizational means that could conveniently be used to implement NRA codes were the trade associations. Code jurisdictions followed the boundaries of previously existing trade associations, and most of the code authorities established were selected and staffed by trade association personnel or industrial executives. For about one-fourth of the codes, the trade association simply became the code authority. The Cement Institute's Trade Practice Committee, for example, was transformed into the NRA's code authority for cement.[27] Not surprisingly, the trade associations took advantage of their dominance over code administration to expand their own memberships. Code authorities were supposed to counter business influence by including representatives of government, labor, and consumers, but the "government representatives" serving on code authorities were usually nominated by the Industrial Advisory Board of the NRA, a body made up of elite U.S. capitalists, whereas labor representatives appeared on less than 10 percent of the initially established code authorities and representatives of consumers made it onto a mere 2 percent.[28]

The trade associations, along with individual firms, were also indispensable as sources for industrial statistics. "With the possible exception of Russia," George Galloway wrote,

> more statistical information is available in the United States than in any other nation. A multitude of fact-gathering agencies, public and private, has been gathering a vast array of data. But the information has been collected individualistically, accidentally, haphazardly, not by one central bureau as in Germany according to an integrated, coherent plan.[29]

The result was that NRA planners were forced to depend on business, as organized in the code authorities, for the data they needed to make decisions. What they received was inadequate, yet efforts by Research and Planning to improve statistical capabilities were resisted by Johnson, who shared business's hostility to governmental data collection. It was thus impossible for the NRA to evaluate code provisions or to challenge sectoral data designed for advocacy more than for analysis.[30] "We have seen," a former Research and Planning economist concluded, "how NRA officials possessed inadequate statistics. Therefore they had to negotiate settlements. Indeed, the facts are that such compromising was the foundation of both NRA codemaking and administration; statistics counted but little."[31]

Business Conflicts Politicized

General Johnson corralled the various participants and made them play the codification game very quickly, but business executives and their organizations held all the good cards. So, naturally, they came up winners, at least in the first round of play. Rapid codification accomplished in this way soon led, however, to increasingly bitter controversies within the NRA. Business executives found that legalized regulation and planning by industries' own efforts, rather than by state initiative, resulted in an incoherent pattern of jurisdictions and a proliferation of administrative red tape. Ellis Hawley points out that "many businessmen found themselves subject to conflicting orders, multiple assessments, and overlapping interpretations, an experience that was at best irritating and at worst downright disillusioning."[32] Besides, by joining the NRA effort, business executives inevitably brought conflicts within and between industries into a political arena. There were "conflicts between large units and small ones, integrated firms and non-integrated, chain stores and independents, manufacturers and distributors, new industries and declining ones, and so on ad infinitum."[33] Industrial sectors and subsectors tried to use the NRA codes to their own relative advantage. And the NRA apparatus, itself thoroughly permeated by conflicting business interests, was unable to resolve disputes in an authoritative fashion. At worst, internecine feuds among business groups intensified; at best, they settled into uneasy stalemates. Either way, many business executives were bound to become increasingly frustrated with the NRA.

The NRA also provided openings for the opponents of business recovery, who claimed to speak for consumers, small firms, and labor. The Consumers' Advisory Board lost most of its battles within the NRA; one reason was that, as Persia Campbell wrote, "it proved an extremely difficult task to find personnel with a sufficient knowledge of industrial practices to be intelligent on their job and at the same time able convincingly to present a consumer point of view."[34] Another handicap was the unavailability of price and cost data that could be used to document the harms done to consumers by the NRA codes. Nonetheless, the board still gave consumers more representation within the national government than they had had before 1933, while stimulating the development of extragovernmental groups to challenge business's price, standardization, and advertising practices.[35] Antimonopoly forces, led by Progressive Republican senators Gerald Nye (North Dakota) and William Borah (Idaho), worked to revive the antitrust laws that had been effectively suspended by the NIRA. In response, Roosevelt created the National Recovery Review Board, headed by Clarence Darrow, to investigate the NRA's impact on small business. Richberg, who suggested Darrow's appointment, and Johnson, who endorsed it, expected that participation by the seventy-six-year-old veteran of earlier radicalisms would serve to legitimize NRA policies. Instead, the Darrow Board submitted a scathing report that hurt the NRA despite the sloppiness and bias with which it was prepared.[36] And, as we explore in chapter 5, NIRA Section 7(a), guaranteeing labor's right to organize under NRA codes, proved to be more than just a symbolic concession: to the surprise and dismay of industrial capitalists, Section 7(a) helped to generate a reinvigorated and more militant trade union movement.

Business disillusionment with the NRA was rooted in the failure of even the most successful self-regulatory codes to ensure market stability and steady profitability. From business's perspective, an NRA that could not deliver on its promises of recovery was not worth paying the costs associated with its expansion of conflict. Louis Galambos tells a revealing story in this respect for the cotton textile industry—an industry whose trade association, the Cotton Textile Institute (CTI), led the way in the fight for government-enforced industrial guilds and then drew up the very first code to be approved under the NRA. The code authority in cotton textiles was directly established by the CTI, and during 1933–1934 it was remarkably successful in maintaining its authority within the industry and its autonomy from unwanted interference by government officials. Nevertheless, the code authority in cotton textiles was still having difficulty in 1934 with the hoary problem of how to fine-tune flows of production in the industry to prevent inventory backlogs from building up and undercutting steady profitable yields. The trouble was that the code authority, as a representative of firms in the industry,

> could react to manifest problems but could not anticipate difficulties before they impinged directly and decisively upon a large majority of the members. By opting for self-regulation instead of central planning, CTI had ensured that this handicap would be built into its NRA program. Under these conditions the Authority was unable to prevent inventories from periodically building up to the point where the market was demoralized.
>
> Sloan and Dorr recognized by the summer of 1934 that prices could not be stabilized so long as the manufacturer's product groups had to initiate the decisions to cut production. They needed to give that responsibility to a person or persons who could keep in touch with the statistical reports and check any overproduction before it became serious. But that idea carried the association leaders onto dangerous ground: the experts who made these decisions might end up being government experts, and to the manufacturers that was an outcome to be avoided at any cost.[37]

Perhaps if there had existed from the start a well-established state administration knowledgeable about and sympathetic to the needs and aims of the business regulators, the NRA, in its capacity as a government agency responsible for coordinating the formation of cartels of U.S. business enterprises, would have worked as the U.S. industrialists who initially pushed for it hoped it would. Some American capitalists (at least) would have consistently benefited from state-enforced plans and regulations, and they would not have perceived state administrators as threatening "meddlers." But by the time expert administrators with their own ideas on how government intervention could induce recovery did emerge within the NRA, they were seen as very threatening by capitalists, because they were speaking for consumer and labor interests and were advocating social reforms as a concomitant of increased state regulation of certain aspects of business performance. Under these circumstances, even industries that might have benefited from more state planning—or at least from more effective state backing for their own attempts at market regulation—simply shied further away than ever from the notion of "government interference in industry."[38]

The Exceptional Petroleum Code

The petroleum code was the exception that proved the rule. In a sector that was already divided between the vertically integrated majors and the independents, the code did a satisfactory job of raising and stabilizing the price of oil by regulating output. When the Supreme Court struck down Section 9(c) of the NIRA, which had given the president authority to prohibit interstate transportation of "hot oil" produced in violation of state quotas (*Panama Refining Co. v. Ryan*, January 1935), Congress responded by passing the Connally Act, an even more sweeping ban. After *Schechter*, the essential provisions of the NRA petroleum code were continued, with congressional and presidential approval, under the Interstate Oil Compact.[39]

Why was oil exceptional? The peculiar physical and legal characteristics of petroleum—oil's underground migration towards the low pressure areas created by drilling, and the "law of capture" that makes recovery the basis for ownership—created a particular need for NRA regulation.[40] But this need cannot explain the relative success of the petroleum code; the highly competitive cotton textile industry was also in need of government stabilization. The distinguishing factor was that the petroleum code, alone among all the codes, was not administered by the NRA itself. Instead, administration was delegated to the secretary of the interior, Harold L. Ickes, whose department had traditionally concerned itself with oil policies. Governmental responsibility over oil had been expanded in 1924, when President Calvin Coolidge, in the wake of the Teapot Dome scandal involving naval oil reserves, established the Federal Oil Conservation Board, including the secretaries of interior, commerce, war, and the navy. By 1933, the board was drawing on the Interior Department's Bureau of Mines to investigate production and marketing methods, measure output, estimate future supply and demand, and plan conservation practices. These functions and many of the experts who performed them were transferred to the Petroleum Administrative Board created under the NIRA.[41] Because this preexisting state capacity, located in the Interior Department, was available for administration of the petroleum code, "the collusive action of the industry under the code was at all times subject to a degree of surveillance quite unknown among any of the multitudinous trades and industries operating under the general supervision of the National Recovery Administration. . . . [Ickes] had behind him, moreover, a corps of qualified civil servants built up gradually through many years and familiar with the industrial domain in the administration of which they were now vouchsafed a measure of participation."[42]

Business Repudiates the NRA

Reflecting the unhappy experiences of most capitalists in most other sectors under the codes, the business leaders and organizations that had supported and helped to formulate the NIRA turned against it.[43] Gerard Swope's business recovery plan had been a major influence on the NIRA, but in November 1933 the General Electric executive proposed that the NRA be replaced by a National Chamber of Commerce and Industry that would be even less independent of business. Another corporate liberal, Henry I. Harriman of the U.S. Chamber of Commerce, said in the same month, "I know of no representative group of businessmen today in which some do not question the whole program."[44] The December 1933 convention of the National Association of Manufacturers gave the NRA an unenthusiastic endorsement. As the NRA moved toward expiration in 1935, a majority of firms favored extension, but only with modifications to make the program less prolabor; a large minority opposed extension in any form. A few weeks before *Schechter*, Harriman's inability to bridge the widening gap between his organization and the administration over NRA policies led to his removal as Chamber of Commerce president.

Despite—indeed, because of—the enormous influence they had in its operations, the NRA did not meet the original hopes of industrial capitalists for economic recovery through government-backed industrial coordination. And as the NRA became ever more conflict-ridden in 1934–1935, it actually generated dysfunctional side effects for its original business advocates. It helped to arouse and politicize labor-management struggles, and it set increasing numbers of disillusioned capitalists on a collision course with New Deal politicians. The virtually complete absence of state capacity to administer industrial planning in the U.S. polity of the early 1930s condemned the NRA to be, at first, a charismatic mobilization effort and then an arena of bitterly politicized and inconclusive conflicts. Midway through the life of the agency, John Franklin Carter, writing under the pen name "Unofficial Observer," said:

> The N.R.A. needs a complete overhauling in personnel. Some of the newer men may show up well in time and some of the lesser lights among the Deputy Administrators are able, but on the whole the staff is distinctly inferior in brains and in efficiency to the staff of J. P. Morgan & Co. and to any one of fifty major industrial and financial organizations. The best brains in the country are not yet available for public service, even in the vital problem of industrial recovery.
>
> It is easier to see the need than to find the men to fill it. What the Roosevelt Administration needs more than anything else is one hundred alert, progressive, young business men and industrialists—men who will think of themselves neither as capitalists nor as agents for Wall Street, but as industrial managers. It would also be desirable that these men should have a smattering of economics. We should not be compelled to wait for the schools and universities to remodel themselves so as to produce such a breed, though men of that type are hard to find in the present day and age. Yet there must be a hundred of them in the country.[45]

Whether the NRA implied state planning for industry or merely state coordination and backing for business planning, it asked too much of the public intelligence and the government machinery of the time. In the words of an NRA lawyer, "The administration of the NRA was inadequate. Everything had to be done in such a hurry and no one had any experience. The result was a real lack of control."[46] Consequently, as the New Deal continued, U.S. capitalists would learn that it was perhaps worse to have tried the NRA experiment and failed than not to have tried at all. Commercial farmers, meanwhile, were learning a different lesson about the effects of government intervention in the agricultural economy. As we will show, the public intelligence and governmental machinery of the day were sufficient to realize the aims of the Agricultural Adjustment Act, for the schools and universities of the land-grant system, together with the USDA, were already producing the breed of personnel necessary for the AAA.

The AAA and the Strength of the Agricultural State

When the AAA was launched in the spring of 1933, there was as much potential for bureaucratic confusion as in the NRA and even more likelihood of policy conflict and stalemate. For agriculture as for industry, the omnibus possibilities of the enabling legislation had to be embodied in actual programs, and the organization of the AAA, like that of the somewhat smaller NRA, had to be assembled anew in a very short time.[47] In a sense the nascent AAA was even more handicapped than the NRA, because contradictory programmatic emphases had been deliberately built into its initial leadership and organizational structure.[48]

Origins and Early Operations

By the spring of 1933, Roosevelt was personally convinced that a program of government-induced production controls for major staple crops was the best way to raise farm prices to parity. But advocates of marketing programs for price fixing and export-dumping of surpluses were still strong within farmers' organizations, in the world of business, and in Congress. Characteristically, Roosevelt simply melded together the divergent approaches, not only in the Agricultural Adjustment Act but also in construction of the AAA itself. George N. Peek, a determined advocate of marketing programs, was named administrator of the AAA, yet he was made responsible to Secretary of Agriculture Henry A. Wallace, who, along with his assistant secretary, Rexford Tugwell, was a confirmed believer in production controls. Understandably worried that his policy preferences might lose out to the production-control advocates who were being recruited to head several of the commodity sections where policies for each major crop would actually be formulated, Peek insisted on a dual structure for the major crops. Thus, in an ideal formula for administrative confusion and stalemate, a Division of Processing and Marketing run completely by Peek and his appointees was set up to parallel the Division of Production, and duplicate sections for wheat, for cotton, and for the linked commodities of corn and hogs were established within the two divisions. There was no way to coordinate programs for these key commodities except by recourse to Peek himself or, if his decisions were disputed, by appeal to Secretary Wallace or the president.

And yet, on the whole, the AAA functioned well.[49] Policy clashes and appeals to higher authorities indeed abounded during the early months of the AAA. Nevertheless, the AAA's overall trajectory of development did not parallel the NRA's path toward greater divisiveness and ultimate stalemate. During 1933, a production-control program for wheat was formulated and implemented with some success, and (as plans were made for controls in 1934) emergency crop-destruction programs were carried through for cotton and hogs.[50] After Peek's removal in December 1933, the AAA's programs—except for the special cases of dairy products and fruits and vegetables—became consistently oriented toward raising farm prices by making payments to farmers to curtail their production. Overall plans were made by AAA experts in Washington and then implemented by committees of local farmers. And even as the NRA was coming under increasingly vociferous political attacks, the AAA benefited from a favorable review by Congress and gained support from farmers and their organizations.

Moreover, while its emergency programs did their job, the AAA began to think ahead: the Program Planning Division was set up in 1934, and by 1935 it was proposing ways to coordinate new and existing agricultural programs and formulating plans for land use and soil conservation.[51] Planning Division ideas were to prove timely in 1936, when the first Agricultural Adjustment Act was declared unconstitutional in the Hoosac Mills case (*United States v. Butler*) and a new approach to agricultural planning had to be quickly proposed to Congress. In fact, the invalidation of the first AAA gave planners a welcome opportunity to try some new approaches to overcome negative side effects of the original production-control programs, such as wasteful patterns of land use. New, substitute legislation (the Soil Conservation Act of 1936, followed by the second Agricultural Adjustment Act of 1938) was proposed and passed.[52] Appropriate plans were available, and there was widespread political support for continuing the relatively successful efforts at government intervention in agriculture. All of this was in contrast to the situation in industry, where the NRA was not revived after it was declared unconstitutional in the 1935 *Schechter* decision.

The Role of Public Experts

Why were the results of the AAA so much more favorable to the continuation of state intervention than the results of the NRA? The crucial difference was that the AAA, unlike the NRA, could draw on experts who were already prepared to carry out the tasks of sectoral planning. As Lewis L. Lorwin and A. F. Hinrichs observed, "Planning for agriculture has a longer history and a richer background in the United States than planning in any other area of economic life."[53] Agricultural planners were typically educated in the state land-grant colleges established under the Morrill Act of 1862 and employed either in the land-grant colleges or in the USDA, also founded in 1862 and elevated to cabinet status in 1889. "In the early days of [AAA] organization," Edwin G. Nourse, Joseph S. Davis, and John D. Black wrote,

> heavy drafts were made on the personnel of the Bureau of Agricultural Economics and also of the various state agricultural colleges and experiment stations. This brought to the important posts men who had a large amount of experience and professional training along the lines involved in the operation of this program. A lesser number of recruits were drawn from business connections, and while some of them have found important posts of permanent usefulness, their qualifications have in general been found less suitable than those of professionally trained men.[54]

Carter, the "Unofficial Observer" who was so critical of NRA personnel, explained why the qualifications of the agricultural experts proved more "suitable" than those of the business executives:

> Through the agricultural colleges of the States and the Federal Government, we have been developing men who think about agriculture in national terms. To-day, where industry has few men with a national social viewpoint, agriculture has hundreds of them and they are taking the social leadership of the nation away from the bankers whose mental range is limited by rediscount rates and from the industrialists who understand everything about their business except the actual process of economic exchange. There is no more pathetic spectacle in America to-day than that of our bewildered business executives contemplating the purposeful moves of these farm philosophers who do not believe that the mass production of Babbitts in Buicks is a sufficient answer to the demand for social justice.[55]

Even AAA officials with other backgrounds had to adapt to the primacy of expertise. Alger Hiss, a young, city-bred attorney in the AAA Legal Section, recalled that "we had to find out what the cotton experts wanted, and we had to learn something about cotton."[56]

Particularly prominent among the farm experts were agricultural economists, who exercised more authority over the commodity sections that were the AAA's operating units than economists of any sort exercised in relation to the NRA code authorities. Within the Division of Production, M. L. Wilson of Montana State, a leading proponent of the domestic allotment plan, became chief of the Wheat Section, and Albert G. Black, head of the department of agricultural economics at

Iowa State, became chief of the Corn and Hogs Section. (The Production Division was headed by Chester C. Davis, a farm journalist who had participated in the McNary-Haugen battles of the 1920s but had then been converted to production control.) The leadership of the commodity sections that functioned both for Production and for Processing and Marketing included John B. Hutson, a USDA agricultural economist who had also taught the subject at the University of Kentucky (tobacco), and Howard W. Tolley, from the University of California's Giannini Foundation of Agricultural Economics (special crops). Wilson, Hutson, and Tolley had all served in the USDA Bureau of Agricultural Economics (BAE). Tolley's New Deal career had no parallel in the NRA: he moved from special crops to become chief economist for the Division of Production, took charge of the new Program Planning Division, went back to the University of California in 1935, and returned to the AAA the following year to take its top position of administrator.[57]

The BAE, established in 1922 as the culmination of Henry C. Taylor's drive to make agricultural economics a distinctive discipline, was not only a source of personnel for the AAA but also a source of statistics on past, present, and expected future supply and demand at both the individual and the aggregate levels. The BAE Division of Crop and Livestock Estimates, for example, was given the task of setting county quotas for the complicated corn-hog program.[58] Thus, as Lorwin and Hinrichs said, the AAA

> is built on prolonged research. Data have been collected and analyzed with a comprehensiveness and a penetration that has not been applied to any but a restricted number of industries. There is a substantial knowledge as to the nature of the demand for most of the basic agricultural products. Despite the fact that millions of individuals are engaged in production, the conditions and technical possibilities of production are fairly well known.[59]

Other components of the agricultural policy infrastructure, which like the BAE had been established before the New Deal, contributed to the success of the AAA as well. Extension agents, employed by the USDA (through the land-grant colleges) under the Smith-Lever Act of 1914, helped to organize committees of local farmers for the AAA. The extension agents also improved the design of the production control program for wheat by discussing likely field problems with M. L. Wilson and his staff. The state agricultural experiment stations, created by the Hatch Act of 1887, worked with the AAA's Program Planning Division in formulating long-term adjustment recommendations. Scientists from the Bureau of Animal Industry, established in 1884, and the Bureau of Plant Industry, established in 1901, contributed their skills to such AAA activities as the planning of crop restrictions and the emergency slaughter of baby pigs.[60] The AAA's relationships with these other public agencies were frequently rough: BAE Chief Nils A. Olsen, a Republican holdover, resisted AAA demands until his resignation in 1935, when he was replaced by the AAA's Albert G. Black, and disputes between the USDA and the state agencies continued until the Mt. Weather agreement of 1938.[61] Yet these preexisting organizations gave the AAA resources that the NRA lacked.

Marketing Programs versus Production Controls

The initial obstacle to the agriculture economists' vision of the AAA as production control was its administrator, George N. Peek. Peek was in many ways a twin to the NRA's administrator, Hugh S. Johnson. Both men had served under Bernard Baruch at the WIB. Both subsequently went to work for Moline Plow, where they cooperated on the "Equality for Agriculture" proposal that gave rise to the McNary-Haugen bills. Both received their New Deal appointments via their connections to Baruch. The two men also had similar attitudes toward policy intellectuals. During the preinauguration conferences on the administration farm bill, Peek complained that "farm leaders were being led off by economists."[62] "The 'economists' and professors knew what they wanted," Peek wrote later, "and were determined to get it. I thought I had them checked, but events proved that I was mistaken."[63]

Production control, in Peek's view, was an attempt "to socialize farming" that violated Roosevelt's pledges—and Congress's intentions—"to achieve a balance in our economic system by taking measures to increase agriculture's share in the national income."[64] Peek saw the AAA as a collection of marketing programs that would raise agricultural prices, either by sending the farm surplus abroad, much as McNary-Haugen would have done, or by brokering agreements between farmers and processing firms. Processors, who would be hurt both by production control itself (since it reduced the volume of their operations) and by the processing tax to finance it, supported Peek's efforts; the processing companies also appreciated his determination to shield their records from AAA bureaucrats who were trying to keep down prices to consumers.[65] To administer his marketing programs, Peek relied heavily on agribusiness executives. Charles J. Brand, secretary-treasurer of the National Fertilizer Association, was brought in as coadministrator. William I. Westervelt of Sears, Roebuck, which did extensive mail-order business with farm households, headed the Division of Processing and Marketing. The commodity section chiefs in Westervelt's division included G. C. Shepard of the Cudahy Packing Company (corn and hogs) and J. D. Dole of the Dole pineapple empire (food products).[66] In its reliance on business executives as administrators and in its emphasis on bargaining among affected interests, the marketing part of the AAA under Peek looked much like the NRA under Johnson.

Peek's marketing projects led him into conflicts with the AAA lawyers, first over tobacco and then over dairy. Roosevelt resolved the tobacco dispute by backing Peek and the tobacco companies in their refusal to open their books as widely as the lawyers wanted. The dairy issue, however, precipitated the end of Peek's tenure as administrator. Tugwell and then Wallace refused to approve Peek's use of $500,000 in processing tax funds to subsidize butter exports to Europe. When Peek appealed to the president, Roosevelt removed him from the AAA and made him Special Adviser on Foreign Trade. Peek, who took with him several of his business appointees, had lasted seven months.[67] Chester Davis replaced Peek as AAA administrator and reorganized the agency, eliminating the parallel divisions by merging the sections under Processing and Marketing into the Division of Production.[68]

With Peek's exit, marketing programs for most commodities were subordinated to production control. For fruits and vegetables and for dairy products, however, the marketing approach to agricultural recovery continued after Peek, and the marketing approach continues to dominate policy for these commodities today.[69] Of the fifty-one marketing agreements approved by the AAA between 1933 and 1935, twenty-two were for fruits and vegetables and seventeen were for dairy. Fruits and vegetables were considered "special crops," which were not covered by the main provisions of the Agricultural Adjustment Act. There was thus no authorization for processing taxes or benefit payments, and government intervention to raise prices for these crops could only proceed under the marketing section of the act, which applied to all commodities.

Dairy, in contrast, was listed as a "basic" commodity eligible for AAA processing taxes and benefit payments. Yet only marketing programs were implemented, making dairy an exception to the AAA's emphasis on production control for the other basic crops (initially, wheat, cotton, corn, hogs, rice, and tobacco). The local nature of the market for dairy products facilitated organization by producers and processors. Before the AAA, therefore, cooperatives had "been utilized more comprehensively and more thoroughly by the milk industry, as a means of attacking its economic problems, than by any other major agricultural group."[70] The relative success of pre–New Deal cooperation, in turn, made the economic problems of dairy producers less severe and diminished the urgency with which either agricultural economists or producers searched for policy alternatives. Moreover, Clyde L. King, the first head of the AAA dairy section, had a very different background than officials like Wilson or Tolley, who emphasized production control. King was an economist but not an *agricultural* economist; he had been educated and employed at the University of Pennsylvania rather than in the land-grant colleges, he had served in Herbert Hoover's wartime Food Administration rather than in the USDA, and his expertise was in marketing rather than in production. Unlike the agricultural economists, King was close to Peek, and he left the AAA when Peek resigned.[71] After the departure of Peek and King, Wallace announced a proposal for dairy production controls, but "no such aggressive attempt was made by the AAA to 'sell' it to the producers as had been made in the cotton, wheat, and corn-hog programs,"[72] and the proposal was dropped once opposition emerged at a series of regional conferences.

Farmers' Organizations React to the AAA

Although the NRA was based on ideas promoted by business, the failure of its implementation drove business organizations away from the Roosevelt administration and from state intervention in industry. The AAA was based on ideas of production control that were abhorrent to most farmers, yet the successful implementation of state intervention in agriculture helped to solidify the alliances between the farm groups and the administration that had been forged in the 1932 campaign. Among the three peak associations, the Farm Bureau enjoyed the most access to the administration and gave it the most support: the organization lobbied for the 1936 and 1938 farm bills, to the drafting of which it had contributed, and helped to win the midwestern farm vote for Roosevelt in the election of 1936. The Farm Bureau also benefited the most from the New Deal, expanding its membership, particularly in the South, through its connections to AAA producer committees and Extension Service agents.[73]

The other two peak associations were less consistently enthusiastic about the New Deal. The Grange endorsed the 1933 and 1936 farm bills but not the 1938 bill, which it believed went too far toward compulsory production control.[74] The Farmers' Union was split between a moderate, pro–New Deal faction, emphasizing cooperative marketing and sympathetic to the New Deal and a radical, anti–New Deal faction, demanding legislation to ensure that farmers would earn back at least their costs of production. The radicals gained control in 1930, when they capitalized on the unpopularity of Hoover's Federal Farm Board, in which the moderates had participated, to elect John A. Simpson as the organization's president. Simpson rejected the Agricultural Adjustment Act and fought for cost-of-production legislation until his death in March 1934. Simpson's successors continued his opposition to the New Deal, but the radicals were ousted in 1936, when they were discredited by their support for William Lemke's third-party presidential candidacy.[75] Cooperatives representing producers of various commodities were generally wary of production control but swung behind the AAA as they were guaranteed more significant roles in its marketing programs.[76]

Early support for the AAA from the cooperatives, the Farm Bureau, and the Grange helped to marginalize the most aggressive organizational opponent of the agricultural New Deal, the Farmers' Holiday Association. After the Association, an Iowa-based offshoot of the Farmers' Union, called a farm strike in October 1933, five midwestern governors endorsed its program, which included cost-of-production guarantees. Roosevelt, Wallace, and other national officials rejected most Association demands, but Roosevelt did authorize gold purchases that resulted in the price inflation the Association and other farmers had wanted. With the dissipation of the farm strike and the impact of inflation, the Farmers' Holiday Association declined, leaving its national organization open to infiltration by Communists, whose views were distant from the opinions of most farmers. Another group, closer to the positions of the organization's recently deceased leader, Milo Reno, joined the doomed Lemke campaign.[77]

If the success of the Democratic program for agricultural recovery—and thus the ability of the Democrats to incorporate farmers and farm groups into their electoral coalition—depended on the presence of specifically trained and educated experts, the influence of these experts depended on the willingness of Democratic politicians to keep them in key positions. That willingness, originating in the 1932 campaign, diminished after 1938, when Henry Wallace, like many officials of the Roosevelt administration, began his quest for the 1940 presidential nomination.[78] Roosevelt, of course, eventually dashed all such hopes by breaking the third-term tradition and seeking renomination himself, but Wallace, by winning the vice-presidential nomination, ended up closer to his goal than the other contenders. In the interim, Wallace used his position as secretary of agriculture to elevate practical farmers who might do more than academic experts to further his national ambitions. Wallace reorganized the USDA, replacing the AAA commodity sections with geographical divisions that were more politically salient.[79] Howard Tolley was shifted from head of the AAA to head of the BAE, a move that he considered a politically motivated demotion. His replacement, Rudolph M. "Spike" Evans, was "a man of action, not a philosopher," who had done advance work for Wallace's Midwest tour during the 1936 campaign.[80]

From 1933 to 1938, however, agricultural experts were unusually prominent in the AAA and the USDA, and even thereafter Wallace and his successors were able to draw on their talents. John Franklin Carter found "more brains and more real ability per pound of human flesh in the agricultural wing of the New Deal than anywhere else."[81] This concentration of talent was the product of agricultural policies enacted long before 1933, and it made implementation of the New Deal's agricultural policies possible. Russell Lord, himself a veteran of the AAA, recognized the extent to which its success depended on preexisting state capacities:

> When we lament, as we often do in this republic, the lack of a college-trained group of civil servants specifically trained in tasks of administration and statesmanship, we overlook the fact that in one important particular we are well supplied. The Land Grant Agricultural Colleges, established by the states in the time of Lincoln, have been turning out year by year not only thousands of trained technicians in the special branches of agriculture, but economists, sociologists, and administrators whose approach to events is trained and generally realistic. And the in-service training which many such men and women acquire after graduation in the Agricultural Extension Service, as county agents, state supervisors, and state or regional administrators, for instance, inclines to instill a considerable degree of skill and competence in public affairs. These men and women customarily work facing real people, out on the ground. One reason that Triple-A was able to forward its programs, it may well be argued, where NRA so largely failed, lies in the fact that Triple-A could be and was staffed from the very first with specifically trained and, on the whole, educated people.[82]

State Capacity and Policy Implementation

Between 1933 and 1935, the AAA was consolidated while the NRA fell apart. The AAA addressed longstanding problems of American agriculture; the NRA created new problems for American industry. The

AAA mobilized groups of farmers in its support; the NRA drove business groups away. The lasting consequence of the NRA, unintended by either its business proponents or its sponsors in the Roosevelt administration, was to revive American trade unionism. The AAA, quite intentionally, benefited commercial farmers rather than sharecroppers, tenants, or farm workers.

These two programs and their contrasting results provide instructive comparative case studies, for the NRA and the AAA were alike in many of the conditions that have been found to facilitate or impede policy implementation. Implementation of the NRA and the AAA was attempted in the same period, under the leadership of the same president. The initial administrators of the two programs, Hugh Johnson and George Peek, were remarkably similar. The NRA and the AAA operated under the same constraints of the depression economy and the U.S. Constitution, as interpreted by the Supreme Court.[83] With allowances for differences between industry and agriculture, the two programs also shared a basic policy design, focusing on raising prices through sectoral intervention that would be carried out by powerful new public agencies in cooperation with affected private interests.[84]

Some of the social science literature on policy implementation suggests that effectual state intervention is so unlikely that government officials should not attempt it or they should try it only through marketlike mechanisms.[85] The AAA argues against these pessimistic conclusions.[86] The theory of agricultural adjustment, that farm purchasing power could be improved by production control, may or may not have been valid, but that theory was translated into action.[87] Bureaucrats planned allotments. Farmers complied and received subsidy payments. Prices increased.

Other authors have developed multivariate models that link implementation to a range of organizational, environmental, and statutory variables.[88] State capacity is a higher-level concept that encompasses many of the variables correlated with successful implementation and places them within a historical institutional analytical framework. One such variable is organizational capability.[89] Organizational capability is a narrower concept than state capacity, since it refers to attributes of a particular agency rather than to a whole system in which the strengths of some units may compensate for the weaknesses of others. Yet the availability of experts with the will and ability to intervene, the basis for our definition of state capacity, surely contributes to the capabilities of the organizations in which they serve.

Another variable employed in implementation studies is professionalism. Professionalism has been linked to innovation, communication, and the dispositions of public officials, all of which can in turn affect policy implementation.[90] Before professionals can contribute to implementation in these ways, the relevant professions must be created, organized, and connected with public authority. Professional roles in agriculture, from county agent to agricultural economist, were developed by government, and the same was true for such other professions as medicine, law, and education.[91] Fatally for the NRA, this was not true for industrial experts.

When implementation is viewed as a dynamic process, the possibility of learning becomes crucial. Implementation occurs over time: organizations like the AAA that can receive and respond to the results of their actions can improve their performance.[92] Learning can also occur in reverse. An organization like the NRA grows less, not more, adequate to the challenges that confront it. State capacity creates an environment in which learning can take place, for officials will then have the data they need, the conceptual tools to interpret them, and the strong desire to solve the problems that inevitably arise. Without state capacity, administrators will lack necessary information, theory, or will, and adaptation will probably be either nonexistent or dysfunctional.

State capacity is not the only variable relevant to the results of policy implementation. When it is present, however, public agencies seem more likely to be self-correcting.[93] In the absence of state capacity, everything seems more likely to go wrong.

5
The Consequences for Class Relations in Industry and Agriculture

In chapters 3 and 4, we showed how a U.S. polity organized by state and party interacted with a society organized by class and sector to shape the origins and implementation of the NRA and the AAA. Spurred by economic crisis, capitalists, farmers, and workers made demands on the national state. Which demands were answered and the extent to which the responses took the form of efficacious public policy depended on the autonomy and capacities of state organizations, as well as on the alignment and strategies of the political parties.

The consequences that followed the implementation of early New Deal interventions in industry and agriculture reveal how public policies can restructure politics and social relations. In this chapter, we analyze how the NRA and the AAA ended up restructuring class relations in industry and agriculture. Policies that responded to societal demands as mediated through political institutions in turn transformed the interests and relationship that would confront public policymakers in the future. Thus, the state- and party-centered perspective that we outlined in chapter 2 is not only useful for explaining the choice among competing policy proposals at the start of the New Deal. This perspective also helps us to understand shifting social and political alignments during the New Deal and subsequent governmental responses to unfolding class tensions in industry and agriculture.

Before the 1930s, state policies toward unions of industrial workers had been based on *repression*; the New Deal established a policy based instead on *recognition* of labor unions. Repression has remained the basis of state policies toward agricultural workers and was revived for use against industrial workers in the 1980s. Thus, class conflict does not necessarily trigger concessions from capitalists or their state, and the most fundamental question about labor policies is how we can explain the choice between repression and recognition.

A third approach to industrial labor policy emerged during the 1920s and was a viable alternative to repression or recognition. Under *company unionism*, firms established, financed, and controlled their own labor organizations. These "employee representation plans" did not link workers with their counterparts in other firms, did not engage in collective bargaining, and did not strike. Company unionism was promoted by the corporatist policies of the Hoover administration and, more effectively, by the "voluntarism" of the National Recovery Administration. Company unionism was never widely practiced in agriculture, and it disappeared as an industrial labor relations alternative after the Wagner Act of 1935, which made it an unfair labor practice for employers to dominate, interfere with, or support any labor organization.

We seek to explain the choice among the labor policy alternatives of repression, recognition, and company unionism, as well as the timing of these policy decisions for industrial and for agricultural workers. Our explanation emphasizes the interactions of state capacities with party alignments. In chapter 2, we defined state capacity as the ability of governmental organizations to implement official goals, especially when confronting the actual or potential opposition of powerful social groups or facing recalcitrant socioeconomic conditions. By this definition, capacity can vary within different policy areas of a single national state, so comparison requires reference to capacities, in the plural. During the New Deal, the capacities available for state intervention in agriculture were far more extensive than those available for state intervention in industry. The result was that the AAA succeeded while the NRA failed. These different outcomes, in turn, had important consequences for U.S. labor policies.

The collapse of the NRA doomed the voluntarist approach to labor issues favored by its central administrators, Hugh Johnson and Donald Richberg, while enhancing the prospects for the more extensive labor recognition favored by Senator Robert Wagner and the NRA's labor boards. The collapse of the NRA simultaneously prodded President Roosevelt from the business alliance formed in his 1932 campaign toward the laborist politics that would triumph in 1936.

The success of the AAA, in contrast, strengthened its most antilabor administrators, helped to make the conservative American Farm

Bureau Federation dominant among the farm organizations, and maintained the paradox of a Democratic party allied with organized industrial workers yet dependent on electoral support from the nonunionized agricultural South.

We defined party alignments in chapter 2 as the relationships that link organizations seeking to win elections with supporters who supply votes, money, and effort. Party alignments determine which interests will be represented, by whom, and at what stages of the policy process. The NRA and the AAA reflected Franklin Roosevelt's initial electoral coalition and would not have been possible under the preceding Republican administration of Herbert Hoover. Both programs were thus products of the electoral shifts that created a Democratic majority by 1932. Between 1932 and 1936, industrial workers replaced industrial capitalists within the Roosevelt coalition. But the agricultural component of the Roosevelt coalition was less plastic. Disfranchisement and the seniority system in Congress made it impossible for agricultural workers to push agricultural capitalists out of the New Deal Democratic party.

Industrial Class Conflicts and the NRA

Depressions are normally not auspicious times in which to organize a labor movement. Unemployed workers cannot pay union dues and are outside the workplace, in which grievances can be shared and bonds of solidarity forged. When unemployment is high, employers can more easily coerce workers who remain employed, for the supply of substitute workers is larger and few other jobs will be available for workers who are replaced. For these reasons, models of labor activity in the twentieth-century United States suggest a lagged but significant negative relationship between unemployment levels and union membership.[1]

Figure 2 shows that the American labor movement declined during the early years of the Great Depression, as it had declined in previous economic downturns.[2] The Great Depression also caused unions to decline in other advanced industrial societies. In Great Britain, where the long slump continued for most of the interwar period, union density (the proportion of the labor force that was organized) fell from 45.2 percent in 1920 to 30.2 percent in 1923 and 22.6 percent in 1933. Union density did not return to the 1920 level until 1948.[3] Union density in Australia dropped from 47 percent in 1927 to 35 percent in 1933.[4] German union density in 1932 was the lowest since 1919.[5]

After 1933, however, industrial workers in the United States be-

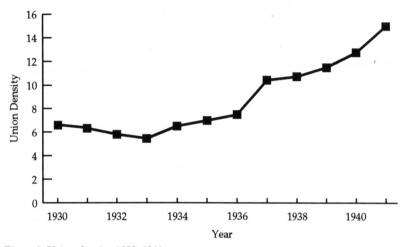

Figure 2. Union density, 1930–1941
(Union members as percentage of civilian labor force. Does not include company unions.)
Sources: Calculated from data on union membership in Leo Troy, *Trade Union Membership, 1897–1962* (New York: Columbia University Press for National Bureau of Economic Research, 1965), p. 1, and from data on civilian labor force in U.S. Department of Commerce, Bureau of the Census, *Historical Statistics of the United States, Colonial Times to 1970*, Bicentennial ed. (Washington, D.C.: U.S. Government Printing Office, 1975), 1:126.

came more organized. Though economic recovery came slowly and was actually reversed during the recession of 1937–1938, union density increased in every year from 1934 to 1947. Tactical and organizational innovations accompanied union growth. During its 1933 strike, the United Textile Workers made extensive use of the "flying squadron," which transported strikers from one plant to another to convince workers to join the strike or to picket.[6] The sit-down strike was revived, most famously in the United Auto Workers' victory over General Motors at Flint, Michigan, in 1936–1937.[7] As the Flint strike demonstrated, workers in mass production industries, most notably steel and automobiles, were mobilized into new unions organized by industry rather than craft. These industrial unions became the basis for the Congress of Industrial Organizations (CIO). With Labor's Non-Partisan League, sponsored by CIO unions for the 1936 elections, the labor movement provided organizational support and financing for Roosevelt and pro-labor Democrats.[8] Even before CIO secession and competition, unions of the older, craft-based American Federation of Labor (AFL) began to organize more broadly and more actively.[9]

The modern American labor movement thus emerged during the New Deal years. In the same period, three statutes created a new industrial order, redefining the relationships of capitalists and workers to each other and to the state. The National Labor Relations Act (Wagner Act) of 1935 gave official recognition to the revitalized unions. The Wagner Act required that employers bargain with unions endorsed by a majority of their workers. Employers were forbidden to establish company unions under their own control or to carry out other "unfair labor practices" that interfered with the process of labor representation. Managerial discretion was further limited by the Fair Labor Standards Act of 1938, which set minimum wages and maximum hours. The Social Security Act (1935) created programs of old-age and unemployment insurance, establishing a sphere outside of productive employment in which former workers, in categories defined as deserving, would receive minimal incomes from the state. Together, these three statutes created the modern American system of industrial relations.

The mobilization and recognition of industrial workers were in significant part consequences of the NRA, determined by the interactions of state capacities and party alignments. Section 7(a) created a system of labor relations, embedded within a more general framework in which business was regulated by industrial codes. This system, as it haphazardly emerged from decisions by President Roosevelt and NRA Administrator Hugh Johnson, encompassed company-dominated unions and established collective bargaining on the basis of proportional representation. Equivocal as it was for trade unions, Section 7(a) sparked labor mobilization, both into existing unions and in previously unorganized sectors. The labor relations system created under Section 7(a) might have continued had the NRA worked. Instead, the collapse of the NRA led to the replacement of Section 7(a) by the Wagner Act in 1935, creating a new set of class relations to be administered by the National Labor Relations Board (NLRB). Under the Wagner Act, company unions were prohibited and majority rule became the basis for collective bargaining.

After 1935, national policy toward unions of industrial workers was changed by the courts, labor's traditional enemy, and by a more conservative Congress. World War II and the Taft-Hartley Act of 1947 completed the transformation of national labor policies. These changes, not the Wagner Act itself, helped to undercut labor militancy and union expansion in the postwar years. Still, for all its limitations the postwar labor movement was more extensive and more powerful than it could have been under the NRA or under the repressive policies that preceded the New Deal. It was also more extensive and more powerful than the scattered and transitory groups of agricultural workers organized under the AAA and successor farm programs.

Labor Policy Before the New Deal

Before the New Deal, efforts to unionize industrial workers were repressed by employers and by the state. Employers responded to union membership gains during World War I and to the strike wave that followed the war with a successful offensive against labor unions. The "American Plan" pledged companies to maintain the open shop, by which was understood not just a workplace in which union membership was not required (the normal meaning of the term) but a workplace in which union membership was forbidden. A worker could be fired for joining a union or required to sign a "yellow-dog contract" stating he or she would neither join a union nor organize one. The effectiveness of anti-union propaganda was increased through use of spies, strikebreakers, and private industrial police forces.[10]

Federal repression of the postwar labor movement began with Woodrow Wilson's use of troops against the coal and steel strikes of 1919.[11] A U.S. Steel poster during the steel strike proved symbolic of state support for the anti-union drive in the decade to come: in seven languages, Uncle Sam ordered workers, "Go back to work!"[12] The open shop campaign had the full support of the Republican administrations of Warren G. Harding and Calvin Coolidge. President Harding's attorney general, Harry M. Daugherty, requested and received a wide-ranging injunction against the railway shop crafts strike of 1922. In 1924, the Republicans won with a national ticket that was unsurpassably antilabor: President Calvin Coolidge, who had first become prominent by breaking the Boston police strike as governor of Massachusetts, and Charles G. Dawes, who had founded the Minute Men of the Constitution, a quasi-military group active against Chicago-area unions. Throughout the twenties, federal troops, state militia, and local police intervened to end strikes by violence against strikers.[13]

Business's antilabor alliance with the national state reduced union membership from a peak of 4,881,200 in 1920 (11.8 percent of the civilian labor force) to 3,161,800 by 1930 (6.5 percent).[14] With the labor movement smashed, the gentler approach of welfare capitalism became viable, particularly for large firms. Companies practicing welfare capitalism offered more extensive benefits and improved working conditions. Scientific personnel management replaced the arbitrary power of the foreman—and diminished worker control over the labor process. Employee representation was provided by company unions, funded and controlled by employers. Though company unions discussed work conditions with management, they did not bargain over wages and hours. Membership in company unions was sometimes mandatory. In the railway shop crafts and in meat packing, company unions were installed after trade unions were defeated.[15]

The public-policy complement to welfare capitalism was Herbert Hoover's voluntarist corporatism. As vice-chair of the 1919 Second Industrial Conference and as secretary of commerce under Harding and Coolidge, Hoover opposed the open-shop campaign and the labor injunction. Hoover's preferred form of labor organization was the shop council; since the interests of labor and capital were, in his view, essentially harmonious, the councils would cooperate with management. In 1932, Hoover signed the Norris–La Guardia Act, which limited the use of anti-union injunctions and prohibited most yellow-dog contracts. Congress, not the administration, had originated the act and probably would have overridden a veto. Hoover's endorsement, moreover, was offset by a memorandum released by Attorney General William D. Mitchell suggesting a limited scope for the act and appealing to the courts, which had granted so many past injunctions, for definitive interpretation.[16]

The Republican administrations elected in the 1920s continued the attack on labor unions initiated by Democrat Woodrow Wilson. This repressive approach ended when another Democrat, Franklin Roosevelt, defeated Herbert Hoover and the National Recovery Administration became the basis for industrial policy.

The Origins of Section 7(a)

The National Industrial Recovery Act (NIRA), the Roosevelt administration's primary response to the industrial depression, was introduced to head off Senator Hugo Black's bill for a maximum thirty-hour work week, which seemed likely to win congressional approval.[17] The NIRA, signed into law in June 1933, enacted an industrial policy based on sectoral codes regulating minimum wages, maximum hours, and other conditions of production to indirectly regulate prices. These codes were to be formulated and implemented under the new National Recovery Administration. Section 7(a) stipulated that the codes include guarantees "that employees shall have the right to organize and bargain collectively through representatives" chosen by them, without employer interference, and "that no employee and no one seeking employment shall be required as a condition of employment to join any company union or to refrain from joining, organizing, or assisting a labor organization of his own choosing."[18]

Although Section 7(a) broke with the open-shop or corporatist policies of the pre–New Deal period, significant aspects of the recognition that would be granted with the Wagner Act were still either absent or ambiguous. In place of the open shop, Section 7(a) proclaimed workers' rights to organize and to bargain through representatives they chose for themselves. Management, however, was not obligated to recognize or to bargain with these representatives. Company unions and management support for them were permitted, but workers could not be required to join them or forbidden to join trade unions independent of management control. How workers' representatives would be chosen and what would happen when alternative groups of representatives (such as a company union and a trade union) each received the support of substantial numbers of workers were not explained in Section 7(a)'s paragraph of generalities. These questions would become central issues of conflict between 1933 and 1935.[19]

The legislative history of Section 7(a) suggests several important points. First, the Roosevelt administration would not have introduced comparable legislation except as part of the National Industrial Recovery Act. As David Plotke points out, the 1932 Democratic platform "made no reference to passing any such measure, or even to unions."[20] Secretary of Labor Frances Perkins, who had been Roosevelt's industrial commissioner in New York, sought regulation of wages and hours, not union recognition.[21] Section 7(a) was included in the NIRA for the same reason the NIRA itself became a sudden priority for the Roosevelt administration: to head off Black's bill setting a thirty-hour week. In order to woo union support from the Black Bill to the NIRA, Hugh Johnson assigned the drafting of labor provisions to Donald Richberg, a labor lawyer who had worked on the Norris–La Guardia Act and the Railway Labor Act of 1926. Richberg drew on these statutes and on bills that been submitted for regulation of the coal industry.[22]

Second, business opposed Section 7(a). Business ultimately acquiesced to the inclusion of 7(a), *not* because any organizations or sectors agreed with the right to organize or the restrictions on company unionism but because Section 7(a) was part of a larger measure that promised to bring industrial recovery and, better yet, to bring recovery through relaxation of the antitrust laws, for which many firms had long been lobbying.[23] The National Association of Manufacturers (NAM) opposed Section 7(a) from the time it was drafted. The Association tried to mobilize a mass meeting of its members against the labor clause, though it would not go so far as to call for the defeat of the entire measure if the offensive sections were unchanged. A NAM press statement claimed that Section 7(a) would force employers to deal with Communists and racketeers (as, in many cases, it did) and would destroy employee welfare plans.

The United States Chamber of Commerce, often contrasted with the NAM and identified with corporate liberalism, had an initial understanding with the AFL that it would accept the NIRA's labor provisions if the AFL accepted the industrial codes. After the NAM swung into action, however, the Chamber's Henry Harriman, whose proposals for "business planning" influenced the NIRA's code structure, gave Senate testimony opposing Section 7(a) and reaffirming the ideal of the open shop. No industrial capitalist testified in support of Section 7(a) during either the House or the Senate hearings.

Capitalist opposition to Section 7(a) engendered an amendment by Senator Bennett Champ Clark, a Missouri Democrat, to maintain the status quo created by the anti-union offensives of the 1920s. The Clark amendment would have protected company unions by adding to employee guarantees the right of "self-organization" and subjected the entire clause on the right to organize and bargain collectively to the condition "that nothing in this Title shall be construed to compel a change in existing satisfactory relationships between the employers and employees of any particular plant, firm, or corporation. . . ."[24] The Clark amendment was endorsed by Richberg (who suggested "satisfactory") and by Johnson. It was approved by unanimous vote of the Senate Finance Committee but defeated on the floor, 46 to 31.

The Clark amendment illustrates a third point about the origins of Section 7(a): Senator Robert Wagner, a New York Democrat, held very different positions on labor relations than Johnson and Richberg. Johnson and Richberg accepted the Clark amendment; Wagner, in contrast, fought against it.[25] These differences would crystallize within a National Recovery Administration that included Johnson as administrator, Richberg as general counsel (and eventually as Johnson's successor), and Wagner as head of the NRA's first labor board and the Senate's leading prolabor Democrat.

The Impact of 7(a)

By granting workers the right to choose their own representatives, Section 7(a) placed a new set of questions on the policy agenda.[26] The selection of bargaining agents through representation elections required the designation of bargaining units and the selection of an electoral system. The NIRA itself made no special provision for the administration of Section 7(a), but in August 1933, Roosevelt, at the proposal of the NRA's Industrial and Labor Advisory Boards, created the National Labor Board (NLB). The NLB was composed of three labor members, three industry members, and, as chairman, Senator Wagner, representing the public. Wagner voted with the labor members in support of the principle of majority rule: the union endorsed by the majority of workers bargains for all. The NLB was unable to enforce its decisions, however, even after Roosevelt issued executive orders authorizing it to mediate or arbitrate disputes that "tend to impede the purposes of the National Industrial Recovery Act" and empowering the board to conduct representation elections at the request of employees.[27] Supported by the NAM, several firms refused to appear at hearings or defied NLB rulings.

Since the NLB had no authority of its own, its interpretations would only have force if they were incorporated into the NRA codes. Johnson and Richberg, however, held a voluntarist conception of labor representation as a set of individual decisions.[28] As Richberg later wrote, "The right of men to associate together must embody also a right not to associate."[29] A theme of even-handed criticism of business and labor runs through the memoirs of both Johnson and Richberg.[30] Yet Johnson's belief that workers should not strike suggests that labor voluntarism was not truly a middle way between repression and recognition but a more presentable procapitalist alternative.[31]

Johnson and Richberg's procapitalist voluntarism led them to reject majority rule for the alternative principle of proportional representation: in state-sponsored elections, each worker could choose a different agent or none at all, even if the consequences would be reduced bargaining power for workers and innumerable administrative problems. Proportional representation of employees implied that trade unions, independent from employers and affiliated with the AFL, might have to share representation functions with company unions. Johnson wrote in his memoir that a truly independent company union was authorized by the NRA but that "I also must in frankness say that I have grave doubt that there are very many of such unions in existence" and that even an independent union organized by employees of a single company would work against the recovery program because it would not help to establish industry-wide wages, hours, or prices.[32] Richberg wrote, "If I were called upon to advise a particular group in a particular situation I should have an opinion definitely leaning toward a craft or industrial union (whichever would better tend to unity of purpose and action) with a strong belief in the value of an organization extending beyond the influence of a single employer."[33] Despite their skepticism about company unions, Johnson and Richberg were willing to endorse their participation in bargaining to the extent that they were voluntarily selected by employees.

Support for company unions and proportional representation was also expressed by the business members of the NLB, including Walter C. Teagle (from Standard Oil of New Jersey) and Pierre S. Du Pont.[34] These executives thus rejected the NAM's resistance to any accommodation with unions that were not company-controlled, but they were equally unwilling to accept the pro-union positions of Wagner and the NLB. The voluntarist policy supported by the NRA and the NLB business members won a crucial victory in March 1934, when Johnson, with Roosevelt's support, thoroughly undermined the NLB by establishing an Automobile Labor Board independent of its authority. This new board provided for proportional representation of minority unions and individuals in bargaining with the auto companies.

With their legality affirmed and their claim to proportional representation established, company unions flourished under the NRA. Seemingly compelled to accept some form of union, large firms established their own. Company unions grew more rapidly than trade unions, covering 1.25 million workers in 1932 (44.6 percent of trade union membership) and 2.5 million workers in 1935 (69.3 percent of trade union membership). Over 60 percent of the company unions in existence in late 1933 had been founded since the NRA began in midyear.[35] As had been true before the New Deal, most company unions did not engage in collective bargaining and did not challenge management authority over wages, hours, or personnel decisions.[36] One consequence of Section 7(a) was thus to revive welfare capitalism, which had declined when the Depression reduced company resources and dissolved labor-management cooperation.[37]

Figure 2 shows that trade unions also grew between 1933 and 1935, if less rapidly than company unions. These gains were made within an economy in which unemployment and GNP were still far from pre-Depression rates. Recent regression estimates, with other economic and political variables controlled, suggest that Section 7(a) had a significant, positive effect on unionization.[38]

Unions that had become moribund after the combined blows of the open-shop campaign, welfare capitalism, and the Depression were quickly revitalized. Using the appealing (though misleading) slogan "The President wants you to join the union," John L. Lewis's United Mine Workers (UMW) staged an enormously successful membership

drive (planned before the NIRA) and won agreement with the commercial mine owners by September 1933. The UMW met more resistance in its effort to organize the "captive mines" owned by the steel
companies, but the NLB ruled that the companies must negotiate with
the representatives chosen in NLB elections, though not necessarily
with the union as such.[39] In the movie industry, the Academy of Motion Picture Arts and Sciences had functioned as a company union
since the defeat of Actors' Equity in a 1929 strike; disputes over the
NRA movie code drafted by producers led actors and actresses into
the fledgling Screen Actors Guild, which replaced the Academy as
the main representative of Hollywood's on-screen performers.[40] The
International Ladies' Garment Workers Union (ILGWU), led by David
Dubinsky, joined with New York manufacturers to achieve standardization of the coat and suit industry through an NRA code and then
won a closed shop by striking the New York dress manufacturers days
before hearings on the dress code were to begin.[41] Rose Pesotta successfully organized for the ILGWU in Los Angeles, despite that city's
open-shop tradition and the anti-union bias of the local NRA office.
Pesotta recalled that Section 7(a) convinced garment workers throughout the country to contact the national office for organizing assistance
and that it also inspired organization by San Francisco longshoremen,
whose rebellion sparked the general strike of 1934.[42]

Even more important than the revival of older unions was the organization of workers in the mass-production industries. Before Section 7(a), these industries had remained open-shop through a combination of employer resistance, the reluctance of AFL unions to organize
unskilled workers, and the inadequacy of the AFL "federal union" as
an intermediate step to craft unionization.[43] Though all these barriers
to mass-production unionism remained during the early New Deal,
Section 7(a) encouraged organization in several industries. Despite the
complacency of its leadership, the Amalgamated Association of Iron,
Steel, and Tin Workers expanded with the formation of locals named
"New Deal," "NRA," or "Blue Eagle."[44] The Mechanics Educational
Society of America, a small organization of tool and die makers, became the first union in the auto industry to win company recognition.[45]

The newly organized workers were militant. Figure 3 shows that in
1933 and 1934, the number of strikes, the number of workers participating in them, and the aggregate strike volume (worker days lost per
one thousand employed in civilian labor force) increased above pre-
New Deal levels. Organizational strikes, though not strikes over wages
or working conditions, became significantly more frequent under Sec-

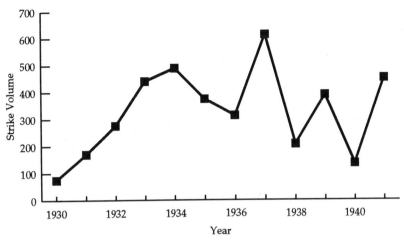

Figure 3. Strike volume, 1930–1941
(Worker days lost per one thousand employed in civilian labor force. This statistic is based on Douglas A. Hibbs, Jr., "Industrial Conflict in Advanced Industrial Societies," *American Political Science Review* 70(4): 1034–36 [December 1976]. Hibbs's denominator is the number of wage and salary workers; because this data is not available for the period of the table, the number of workers employed in the civilian labor force is used here.)
Source: Calculated from U.S. Department of Commerce, Bureau of the Census, *Historical Statistics of the United States, Colonial Times to 1970*, Bicentennial ed. (Washington, D.C.: U.S. Government Printing Office, 1975), 1:126, 1:179.

tion 7(a).[46] Conflicts between workers seeking to organize and employers determined to resist came to a head during the massive strike wave of 1934, when, as Irving Bernstein has concluded, "anybody struck." In Toledo, Minneapolis, and San Francisco, strikes broadened into all-out class warfare as other workers joined strikers to challenge employer associations backed by private and public military forces.[47]

These results bore out the initial hyperbole of AFL president William Green, who compared Section 7(a) to the Magna Carta, and of Lewis, who compared it to the Emancipation Proclamation.[48] Carl Leck participated in the 1934 Auto-Lite strike, which escalated into "the Battle of Toledo" between strikers and the National Guard. Asked by an oral history interviewer whether there had been much interest in organizing before 1933, Leck responded, "Nope. It was all on the q.t. then. Before that, you didn't hear much about it, until President Roosevelt come out and give us the right to organize."[49] Carey McWilliams, then a pro-union lawyer in open-shop Los Angeles, recalled that "the electrifying effect of the legislation was felt immediately; in plant after plant, industry after industry, workers wanted to know how to exercise the new rights they had been granted."[50] Ernest Weir of Weirton Steel, among the most virulently anti-union employers, blamed the strike against his company on "the deliberate misrepresentation of the meaning of this clause" by the trade unions; his own interpretation was that Section 7(a) reaffirmed the right of workers to participate in the company union![51] Hugh Johnson criticized both labor and management for misleading workers about the meaning of Section 7(a). While employers claimed presidential authorization for company unions, Johnson said,

> some labor organizers went out and unconscionably oversold the provisions of Section 7a. They told their men (who have not time to study the statutory facts and decide for themselves and who trusted their leaders) that the *President wanted them* to join this, that, or the other particular union, and some of them are still doing it. It was not true. It is not the function of government to organize labor.[52]

The great paradox of Section 7(a) is that the magnitude of the response was so much greater than the magnitude of the stimulus. A vague statutory promise, implemented so as to favor company-controlled representation plans, would not seem to have increased workers' incentives to join trade unions. Yet the trade unions did grow while Section 7(a) was in force, and those involved in the class struggle believed the provision was responsible for union growth. Why did Section 7(a) have such impact? The provision sent two simultaneous messages to industrial employees, both of which are expressed in Burr McCloskey's recollections about the origins of organization among Akron rubber workers:

> [Clark] Culver happened to know Stanley Denlinger, an Akron criminal lawyer who later went on John L. Lewis's staff. They got together and Culver said, "Stan, tell me what this Section 7(a) means." Denlinger studied it a day or two and then he said, "You can organize, the government *wants* you to organize."[53]

"The government wants you to organize" was one signal from the state. Clever organizers attached the imprimatur of a popular president to their unions. Despite that president's actual equivocation toward labor, workers responded.[54]

The second signal, no less important, was that "you can organize." The permissive tone of this statement suggests that violence, the defining characteristic of the state, would not be used against workers by the federal government. In 1919, the federal government responded to labor insurgency with repression, as it had done in earlier strike waves and would do again in 1946. In 1934, the federal response to labor insurgency was not repressive.[55] Even in Minneapolis, San Francisco, and Toledo, the three cities where strikes expanded into broader class conflicts and where state and local authorities did employ violence, the federal government did not send in troops but sought to mediate.

The next year, the federal response to labor unrest moved beyond nonrepression (that is, not killing workers) to recognition. The Wagner Act endorsed trade unions as legitimate representatives of organized workers while withdrawing such endorsement from their company-controlled rivals.

The Wagner Act

In 1935, the voluntarist labor policy of the NRA was reversed. Along with the rest of the NIRA, Section 7(a) was invalidated in the *Schechter* decision, issued on May 27. On July 5, President Roosevelt signed the National Labor Relations Act, sponsored by Senator Wagner and developed out of the experiences of the NRA labor boards. In 1937, the Supreme Court upheld the National Labor Relations Act (known as the "Wagner Act") as constitutional in the *Jones & Laughlin* case. Company unions, which had thrived under the formal neutrality of Section 7(a), could no longer benefit from employer support. Proportional representation under Section 7(a) threatened to weaken workers' bargaining power, even if company-controlled unions were excluded; its impact would have been especially devastating after the AFL-CIO split of 1936. The National Labor Relations Act reestablished majority rule as the basis for worker representation in collective bargaining. Section 7(a) had protected the right of workers to bargain but had not required that employers bargain with them. The National Labor Relations Act obliged employers to bargain in good faith with workers' elected representatives, though they still were not required to reach agreement. The policy of labor recognition was to be enforced by a new agency, the autonomous National Labor Relations Board, composed of three members independent of either industry or labor and endowed with quasi-judicial powers subject only to review by higher courts.

Wagner's effort to pass a similar bill in 1934 had failed. To provide for stronger administration of Section 7(a) and to clear up ambiguities such as the representation issue, Wagner introduced the Labor Disputes Bill, drafted by his office with the assistance of the NLB staff, in March 1934.[56] Employer participation in or support for company unions was banned; the choice between majority rule and proportional representation was left to a new, permanent labor board, established outside the NRA. The bill received support from the NLB and from the AFL. However, the Roosevelt administration was ambivalent, while most business groups were strongly opposed. A diluted version of the Labor Disputes Bill, drafted primarily by Charles Wyzanski, the Department of Labor counsel, was reported by Senator David Walsh's Labor Committee. In the Walsh bill, employers would be allowed to initiate company unions but not to support their administration.

The strike wave that came in the spring of 1934 did not revive Wagner's original bill but led to replacement of the Walsh bill by the even weaker Public Resolution No. 44. Leon Keyserling, Wagner's bill-drafting legislative assistant, said in retrospect, "I think the primary objective of '44' was to derail the 1934 Wagner Act."[57] Threatened by a steel strike, Roosevelt asked Wyzanski and Richberg to draft a new bill, which he then dictated to congressional leaders. Public Resolution No. 44 passed easily in June, after both Wagner and Walsh abandoned their earlier bills. The resolution did not provide substantive policies on representation, company unions, or other issues. Instead, it gave the president power to establish a board to investigate disputes. The board would supervise elections, and it was empowered to impose penalties for violations of the rules it established. Acting under the resolution, Roosevelt abolished the NLB and created the first National Labor Relations Board (NLRB), a body of three public members with semiautonomous status within the Department of Labor. The promise of representation elections led to cancellation of the steel strike.[58]

Business, which had opposed the Labor Disputes Bill, was divided over Public Resolution No. 44. Henry Harriman of the Chamber of Commerce thought the authority of the new board was dangerous.[59] A U.S. Steel vice president, however, wrote privately that "it is not going to bother us very much" and would contribute to the defeat of the more pernicious Labor Disputes Bill.[60] No business representative argued for Public Resolution No. 44 *because* it would be effective in expanding recognition for trade unions; the question was whether the dangers of the new NLRB outweighed the benefits of heading off the Labor Disputes Bill. For labor, the question was whether the potential benefits of the NLRB were worth the loss of the Labor Disputes Bill. William Green thought not, though his general counsel, Charlton Ogburn, expected the board to side with labor.[61]

The test of these conflicting views was the actual performance of the NLRB. The board made some contributions to labor policy, most notably by defining its mission as judicial action against violations of labor rights, rather than the mediation carried out under the NLB.[62] But this mission required enforcement, and the NLRB, lacking enforcement powers of its own, depended on Attorney General Homer Cummings, who proved reluctant to press cases the Justice Department did not believe could succeed in the courts. "Judgments," Irving Bernstein notes, "were not obtained in any of the thirty-three noncompliance cases referred to the [Justice Department] between July 1, 1934 and March 1, 1935."[63] Like the NLB before it, the NLRB came out for majority rule. In another parallel to its predecessor, the NLRB's authority was subordinated to that of the NRA by a presidential decision removing a particular sector from its jurisdiction.[64]

Though not a member of the NLRB, Wagner remained concerned about its problems. In the fall of 1934, he and his staff, together with the legal staff of the NLRB, drafted a new labor bill. The AFL was consulted about the bill, but—significantly—the Department of Labor, the NRA, and the White House were excluded from the drafting process.[65] The Senate committee reported Wagner's bill with only favorable amendments attached; the entire Senate then rejected unfavorable amendments and passed the bill 63 to 12. Roosevelt, previously indifferent, endorsed the bill on May 24, 1935. In June, the House passed it without a roll call vote. Roosevelt signed the "Wagner Act" into law on July 5.[66]

Explaining the Wagner Act

Why did the National Labor Relations Act become law in 1935, when the similar Labor Disputes Bill had failed in 1934? Neither the scheduled expiration of the National Industrial Recovery Act in June 1935 nor the *Schechter* decision invalidating the NIRA required that industrial labor policy be reshaped to establish majority rule and virtually abolish company unions.[67] The expiration or invalidation of the NIRA without new labor legislation to replace it would have simply meant reversion to the labor policy of early 1933; the Norris–La Guardia Act would still have protected unions against injunctions. Alternatively, Congress might have enacted legislation that continued the approach of Section 7(a) and Public Resolution No. 44, defusing class conflict through encouragement of company unions and proportional representation in collective bargaining. Henry Harriman of the Chamber of Commerce, for example, argued in the Senate hearings that the Wagner bill was unnecessary because Public Resolution No. 44 already provided for all the powers government might need.[68]

Did the Wagner Act pass because of support from industrial capitalists who were willing to trade labor recognition for industrial peace? Thomas Ferguson traces the Wagner Act to one particular group of industrial capitalists: executives of firms in capital-intensive sectors, which he argues could afford to accommodate labor in order to maintain production.[69] He emphasizes the role of the Twentieth Century Fund, founded by Edward Filene of the Filene's department store, in drafting the bill, as well as the critical support of Walter Teagle (Standard Oil of New Jersey) and Gerard Swope (General Electric).

There are several problems with Ferguson's brief account, the sources for which he only hints at. Contrary to Ferguson, the Twentieth Century Fund and Senator Wagner were not "working closely together" in drafting the bill. The Fund's report was prepared independently of what was occurring in Washington; though its recommendations about majority rule and company unions paralleled Wagner's, mediation received more attention, and a substantially different system for administration of labor policy by cease-and-desist orders was proposed.[70] Filene did not "control" the Twentieth Century Fund, as Ferguson suggests; Filene's biographer says that from the Fund's beginning he was often outvoted by the board and that Filene, who died in 1937, lost interest in the Fund toward the end of his life.[71] Filene himself was unlikely to oppose company unionism, for his department store had established the first company union in America, which continued to operate through the New Deal.[72] Filene's own economic program, a retailer's dream, called for higher wages but through government compulsion, as in the NRA, not through collective bargaining.[73] Filene, moreover, was a member of the Business Advisory Committee (BAC), which opposed the Wagner Act and which was more directly controlled by its corporate members than was the Twentieth Century Fund. That Swope and Teagle were also members of the BAC makes Ferguson's comment that "probably Swope, and perhaps Teagle" supported the Act puzzling.[74] Teagle's support for company unions while a member of the NLB was compatible with the BAC position, as was Swope's enthusiasm about company unionism at General Electric.[75]

Stanley Vittoz's comment that "business opposition to the Wagner Act was probably more unified than its response—positive or negative—to any other single piece of the New Deal legislation" is a more accurate assessment of corporate opinion.[76] Congressional hearings on the Wagner Act provide no evidence of extensive business support. The NLRB tried to find capitalists who would testify in favor of the bill, but its regional boards "reported 'almost unanimous' employer resistance."[77] The only employers who did testify for the bill were from two relatively small tobacco companies, which supported the bill because they were already unionized while their larger competitors were not and because higher wages might increase demand for their products, which had fallen sharply during the Depression.[78] Opposition to the Wagner bill, in contrast, was expressed in oral testimony and written statements from companies and trade associations in a wide range of sectors, including machinery, publishing, furniture, steel, rubber, meat packing, electric, food distribution, automobiles, mining, petroleum, textiles, chemicals, and construction.[79] Several opponents reaffirmed the statements they had presented against Wagner's Labor Disputes Bill the year before.[80] Capitalist opposition was spearheaded by Harriman and by James Emery of the National Association of Manufacturers; Emery gave fifty-five pages of testimony before the Senate.[81] Business opponents challenged the bill as unconstitutional and claimed it was one-sided because it proscribed unfair labor practices for employers but not for unions. Its premise, they argued, was the false theory that industrial relations were necessarily adversarial rather than cooperative. Cooperation was institutionalized in company unions, which employers defended as legitimate representatives of the workers, who allegedly preferred them to the AFL's outside agitators. "What is wrong with the company union or even a company-dominated union?" asked Guy L. Harrington of the National Publishers' Association.[82] Representatives of company unions gave similar testimony to rebut charges that their unions were "fake" because they did not engage in collective bargaining and did not sign written contracts.[83]

Capitalist opposition to the Wagner Act was no ruse disguising hidden support, for capitalists opposed the Wagner Act behind the scenes too. The Special Conference Committee, a secret organization of corporate leaders, worked with the NAM against the bill.[84] The Business Advisory Council (BAC), set up by the Commerce Department to support the New Deal, is sometimes seen as the embodiment of corporate liberalism during the 1930s.[85] The BAC opposed the Wagner Act and called for a two-year extension of the NIRA and its labor provisions.[86] G. William Domhoff concludes that even the BAC's capitalists "would not take the fateful next steps of supporting government sanction of majority rule and encasing collective bargaining within the rule of law."[87] Capitalists did divide over industrial labor policy. But these divisions were between advocates of company unionism and advocates of no unionism at all or between capitalists who acquiesced to labor recognition once it became national policy and those who continued to resist. And these divisions were intra- as well as intersectoral, reflecting differences in market position or managerial strategy.[88]

If capitalists did not bring about passage of the Wagner Act, did workers? Was the Wagner Act a response to labor insurgency? Michael Goldfield argues that strikes led New Deal Democrats and progressive Republicans to support government regulations "to constrain, limit, and control the increasingly militant labor movement."[89] Goldfield's evidence that the Wagner Act was designed to curb a militant labor movement includes the language of the bill and the arguments of its supporters.[90] He emphasizes the inclusion in Section 1 (the preamble and declaration of policy) of language describing the denial of the right to organize as the cause of strikes that burdened or obstructed the free flow of commerce. This statement of objectives cannot be taken as evidence of policymakers' intentions, for one of its purposes was to provide a constitutional basis for the act under the commerce clause.[91] Section 1, moreover, gave roughly equal weight to the objective of easing depressions that burden commerce by restoring workers' purchasing power, which was also included with a view to future constitutional tests.[92]

As figure 3 shows, strike activity actually peaked in 1934; the response that year was not Wagner's Labor Disputes Bill, which prefigured the NLRA, but Public Resolution No. 44, which reaffirmed the NRA's voluntarist interpretation of Section 7(a). From 1934 to 1935, when the Wagner Act was approved, the number of strikes increased, but the number of participants (the best indicator of the spread of insurgency) decreased, as did strike volume (the best indicator of capitalist losses).[93] Frances Perkins, who gave the act mild support while trying to get the NLRB placed within her Labor Department, said on May 20, 1935, that there was "no reality to the much-advertised strike epidemic," which she described as a normal accompaniment to economic recovery. Perkins pointed out that there had been more strikes in 1919 than there were in 1934.[94]

Goldfield cites Wagner, Connery, and Green to show that they did not perceive labor insurgency to be declining as they campaigned for the Wagner Act in 1935. The perception of labor unrest, however, was compatible with a wide range of alternative responses. Wagner and Connery argued that the strike wave demonstrated the need for the bill. Business opponents, however, suggested the opposite interpretation: that Section 7(a) had increased labor unrest and the current bill would only make things worse.[95] For James Emery of the NAM, the strike wave called for a president who would "protect the paramount public interest of the country" with repression, as Cleveland and Wilson had done.[96] Other opponents sought to continue company unionism under the NRA labor policy, as exemplified by the auto settlement.[97]

Despite Wagner's rhetoric, it would be incorrect to interpret his support for a policy of recognition as a reaction to labor unrest, for the National Labor Relations Bill embodied the principles he had advocated since 1933: majority rule and the restriction of company-controlled unions. If the Wagner Act was designed to restrain a militant labor movement, Wagner and Keyserling would not have inserted Section 13: "Nothing in this Act shall be construed so as to interfere with or impede or diminish in any way the right to strike." This language was chosen to forestall court interpretations that workers could only strike after collective bargaining. As this section was understood by Leon Keyserling, who drafted the act, even sit-down strikes and strikes during the life of a contract were permitted.[98] The Wagner Act was expected to foster labor peace by reducing what Keyserling described as "the most fractious and bloody types of industrial disputes": strikes stimulated by employers' refusal to recognize and bargain with unions. The act was to make such strikes less frequent by limiting the ability of employers to resist, not the ability of workers to strike.[99]

Strikes, if they can be maintained, can be very effective in winning union recognition, higher wages, and better working conditions from employers. What they do not necessarily do is win concessions from the state. A relatively high rate of strike activity was met with repression in 1894, 1919, and 1946, with NRA voluntarism in 1934, and with labor recognition in 1935. To understand why a policy of labor recognition emerged in 1935 but not in 1934, we must look away from labor insurgency and capitalist divisions to examine the intertwined processes of electoral change and policy failure. We can break down the question of why the Wagner Act was passed into three components: why Wagner sponsored the bill, why Congress approved it, and why Roosevelt went along.

Wagner's sympathy for the trade union movement was evident in his insistence on Section 7(a) and his alliance with the labor members of the National Labor Board. This sympathy reflected his position as "the first Senator at Washington who has represented industrial liberalism rather than agrarian liberalism."[100] What evolved after 1933 was not Wagner's policy of labor recognition but the method of its administration. The subordination of the National Labor Board and then of the first NLRB convinced Wagner that labor rights could only be enforced by an independent board with complete jurisdiction over collective bargaining and representation. The 1934 Labor Disputes Bill provided for an independent, tripartite board. The 1935 bill created an independent board composed only of public members, without representatives of labor or capital. Wagner's views also evolved from an

Table 6. Composition of congressional Democratic party, 1931–1936

Congress	Total	House Urban[a]	South[b]
73d	217	46	100
(1931–32)		(21.2)[c]	(46.1)
74th	313	73	100
(1933–34)		(23.3)	(31.9)
75th	322	86	100
(1935–36)		(26.7)	(31.1)

Congress	Total	Senate Urban	South
73d	47	5	22
(1931–32)		(10.6)	(46.8)
74th	59	7	22
(1933–34)		(11.9)	(37.3)
75th	69	10	22
(1935–36)		(14.5)	(31.9)

Sources: Kenneth C. Martis, *The Historical Atlas of United States Congressional Districts, 1789–1983* (New York: Free Press, 1982); idem, *The Historical Atlas of Political Parties in the United States Congress, 1789–1989* (New York: Macmillan, 1989); U.S. Congress, *Biographical Directory of the United States Congress, 1774–1989*, Bicentennial ed. (Washington, D.C.: Government Printing Office, 1989); U.S. Department of Commerce, Bureau of the Census, *Fifteenth Census of the United States, Population* (Washington, D.C.: Government Printing Office, 1931).
[a] Representatives from nonsouthern districts including all or part of cities over 250,000 population; representatives elected at large from nonsouthern states resident in cities over 250,000; senators from nonsouthern states resident in cities over 250,000.
[b] Representatives and senators from Alabama, Arkansas, Florida, Georgia, Louisiana, Mississippi, North Carolina, South Carolina, Tennessee, Texas, and Virginia.
[c] Figures in parentheses indicate percentage of total Democrats.

early emphasis on mediation to a focus on enforcement of collective bargaining rights.[101]

Electoral change helps explain why Congress endorsed Wagner's approach. Partisan realignment, a gradual process beginning in the 1920s, had transformed the Democrats into a party that mobilized increasing numbers of urban-ethnic voters into national politics.[102] Moreover, as table 6 shows, the congressional reapportionment of December 1930, the first since 1910, greatly increased urban representation in the House.[103] After the massive Democratic victory in 1932, Congress was more populated with urban Democrats such as Wagner than ever before. Their support was crucial to the inclusion of Section 7(a) in the NIRA and the defeat of the Clark Amendment. Still, had events in American politics followed their normal course, the 1934 elections would have brought setbacks for liberal Democrats, because the majority party usually loses seats in off-year elections. But instead of losing ground in 1934, the Democrats made significant gains. The Republican right was practically eliminated, and, as table 6 shows, urban Democrats moved closer to numerical equality with the southerners who had once dominated their party.[104] Congress thus became even more fertile ground for prolabor arguments than it had been in 1933 or 1934.

Congress was also influenced by the collapse of the NRA. The absence of state capacity for industrial policy made it impossible for the NRA to maintain business cooperation and further national economic recovery. Unable to draw on experts trained to plan for entire sectors, let alone for the economy as a whole, the NRA could only delegate public power to business executives, who used it to benefit their own firms. The failure of the NRA's "business commonwealth" approach to recovery gave added credence to Wagner's arguments that the Depression was caused by underconsumption, that increased consumption required higher wages, and that higher wages could be achieved only by government intervention. In the absence of another viable strategy for recovery, these arguments, prominent among those used by Wagner in congressional debates and incorporated into Section 1 of his bill, may have swayed members of Congress to ignore business opposition.[105]

In 1934, congressional sympathy for labor was stymied by Roosevelt's resistance to the Labor Disputes Bill. In 1935, the Wagner Act probably could not have passed in the face of presidential opposition; a presidential veto would certainly have been sustained.[106] The crucial shift was Roosevelt's. After substituting Public Resolution No. 44 for the Labor Disputes Bill in 1934, he remained neutral as Wagner introduced the 1935 bill and steered it through the Senate; then Roosevelt came out in support in time to influence the House.[107] His switch reflected the collapse of the NRA. The NRA's failure discredited Johnson, Richberg, and their voluntarist alternative to labor recognition. Had the NRA worked, Johnson and Richberg would have been as indispensable and influential in 1935 as they were in 1933. Instead, Johnson was removed from his position as administrator in September 1934. The immediate precipitant was an unauthorized speech against striking textile workers, but Roosevelt had earlier lost confidence in Johnson's administrative skills and was hoping to ease him out.[108] As Johnson's replacement in a reorganized NRA (after an interim period under S. Clay Williams, a tobacco executive), Richberg extended the controversial automobile labor code, but he was unable to convince Roosevelt to modify the Wagner bill to eliminate majority rule and permit company unions.[109]

The failure of the NRA also led, directly and indirectly, to a break between Roosevelt and the capitalists who opposed the Wagner bill with virtual unanimity. The inability of the NRA's sectoral planning to restore prosperity forced Roosevelt to develop alternative strategies for industrial recovery. As the Depression continued, Roosevelt purchased gold and increased expenditures for relief and public-works programs. The increased budget deficit and competition with private enterprise that these measures entailed, combined with the perception that the NRA itself was becoming overly responsive to labor, consumers, and government planners, increased business opposition to Roosevelt. Major corporate figures, including such breakaways from the Business Advisory Council as former NLB member Pierre Du Pont, launched the archconservative Liberty League in 1934. The National Association of Manufacturers, consistently anti-union since the progressive era, was transformed from an organization representing small- and medium-sized firms to a vehicle for big business opposition to the New Deal.[110] The most telling symbol of the business turnaround on the New Deal came at the April 1935 meeting of the U.S. Chamber of Commerce. The chamber, which had enthusiastically endorsed the NRA at its inception, rejected its extension along with social security, labor legislation, and other pending reforms. Faced with so much business opposition, Roosevelt moved closer to congressional progressives. His last-minute endorsement of the National Labor Relations bill was one manifestation of this shift.[111]

The inability of the NRA to stimulate industrial recovery and the temporary ascendancy of urban liberals within the Democratic majority combined in 1935 to foster passage of legislation granting full recognition to trade unions and delegitimating their company-controlled rivals. The Supreme Court upheld the constitutionality of the Wagner Act in the 1937 *Jones & Laughlin* case.[112] By the end of the New Deal, a part of the federal government, the National Labor Relations Board, had a vested interest in promoting unions, as well as the institutional capacities to carry out this aim.[113] Unions of industrial workers grew (see figure 2) and became more militant (see figure 3). In the decade after *Jones & Laughlin*, strikes stimulated membership, and membership stimulated strikes.[114]

The Aftermath

Why, then, is the contemporary U.S. industrial labor movement so small and so passive? The origins of the industrial labor movement's postwar accommodation and its more recent decline are to be found not between the lines of the Wagner Act but in its subsequent transformations, which created a labor policy system that limited union activities in ways the original legislation had not. Supreme Court interpretations of the act "deradicalized" it by placing constraints on unions while removing them from capitalists. Even the *Jones & Laughlin* decision affirmed that employers, though required to enter collective bargaining, were not required to reach agreements. The decisions that followed stated the right of employers to replace strikers, prohibited sit-down strikes, and limited the scope of protected collective bargaining to wage issues.[115] The failure of Roosevelt's 1938 purge attempts and the large Republican gains in the general election gave the conservative coalition an overwhelming majority in the House, which then created the Special Committee to Investigate the National Labor Relations Board. This committee, under anti-union conservative Howard Smith of Virginia, succeeded in moving the NLRB from pro-union activism to legalism: the NLRB's Division of Economic Research, whose findings had provided empirical support for many pro-labor decisions, was abolished, and radicals on the board and staff were replaced by advocates of cooperative "industrial relations."[116]

World War II and its aftermath contributed further to the development of more conciliatory class relations. Wartime labor policy spread the union shop under the National War Labor Board's maintenance-of-membership formula, which included the dues checkoff. This practice facilitated union financing and stabilized membership. But the checkoff also helped to bureaucratize the labor movement, because it reduced the need for union leaders to maintain contact with shop-floor workers.[117] The end of the wartime wage restraints and no-strike pledge produced a strike wave much greater than those of the New Deal.[118] This strike wave, unlike that of 1934–1935, did not produce expanded recognition. Instead, the postwar strike wave helped elect the first Republican Congress since the New Deal, which passed the Taft-Hartley Act of 1947 over President Truman's veto. That act gave capitalists amendments they had sought to add to the Wagner Act since 1935, including application of unfair labor practices to unions, protection of the open shop (in states that passed "right-to-work" laws), and expulsion of Communists from union leaderships.[119] Taft-Hartley established the framework for the long postwar settlement, in which unions bargained away control over the work process in return for wages and benefits tied to macroeconomic conditions, with the NLRB as "neutral" arbiter between labor and capital. The automobile industry, which had earlier set the pattern of class relations with the Auto Labor Board and the Flint Strike, did so again with the 1950 General Motors contract, also known as the "Treaty of Detroit."[120]

This system, in turn, came undone when international economic pressures produced intensified class conflict. The election of Ronald Reagan, supported by anti-union capitalists, produced an NLRB that rejected the board's postwar tradition of bipartisan moderation to work as aggressively against unions as the NLRB of the 1930s had worked for them.[121] In the 1980s, the national state again turned to a repressive labor policy. Reagan acted against the air traffic controllers as Cleveland had acted against the Pullman strike and Wilson against the strike in steel. Bankruptcy proceedings became as potent a weapon against unions as the labor injunction had been before Norris–La Guardia. Even at the end of the new Republican era, however, union density (about 12.9 percent in 1992) was higher than at any time during the New Deal.[122] Company unionism is still prohibited.[123] The Wagner Act has been transformed to the detriment of industrial workers, but it has not been eliminated.

Agricultural Class Conflicts and the AAA

All the gains described above, however, were for workers in industry and not for workers in agriculture. Unionization in agriculture remains so unusual that statistical sources often use nonagricultural employment as a measure of potential union membership.[124] In 1993, only 1.6 percent of agricultural wage and salary workers were union members.[125] Even during the New Deal, tenant farmers and sharecroppers in the South and agricultural wage laborers in California could not win class compromises with growers, who could still elicit repressive measures from political authorities. Workers in agriculture were not covered by minimum wages, maximum hours, unemployment insurance social security, or the Wagner Act.[126] The Farm Security Administration (FSA), in existence from 1937 to 1946, helped a small number of tenants, sharecroppers, and laborers to become farm owners but did not alter the status of those who remained without their own land. Despite its rather limited aims, the FSA was repeatedly restricted and ultimately abolished by the conservative coalition of southern Democrats and midwestern Republicans.

Given the preexisting structures of state and party organization, the NRA served to mobilize industrial workers and expand their claims to legally enforceable rights. The guarantees of Section 7(a), which stimulated trade union growth and militancy, were thus converted into the stronger and more permanent provisions of the Wagner Act. The AAA had no such impact on class conflicts in agriculture. Sharecroppers, tenant farmers, and wage laborers had grievances at least as great as those of their industrial counterparts, and committed radicals were active in organizing agricultural workers as well as workers in industry. Yet the consequences of the AAA did not include recognition of trade unionism or even establishment of company unions. Instead, workers in agriculture were repressed. Efforts to organize California farmworkers only stimulated capitalist counterorganization, which was backed up by the coercive authority of state and local governments. The tenants and sharecroppers of the cotton South were made worse off by AAA production controls, which facilitated their conversion into landless wage laborers and their displacement by mechanization. The comparison of agricultural and industrial class relations during the New Deal thus provides further support for the argument made above that sectoral intervention triggered working-class mobilization. The results of this mobilization were determined by two interactive variables: the incorporation of workers into (or their exclusion from) the New Deal Democratic coalition, and the efficacy of interventionist policies, which in turn was determined by the prior organization of state capacities.

Militancy and Repression

California's large-scale, "industrialized" agriculture depended on the wage labor of migratory farmworkers.[127] At the beginning of the New Deal, a majority of these workers were Mexicans; by the late 1930s, Mexican repatriation had combined with emigration from the Dust Bowl states of Oklahoma, Arkansas, and Texas to produce a predominantly white labor force.[128] While both farm owners and workers suffered from the Depression, only the owners benefited from the AAA. When demand dropped, employers cut wages, which represented their only variable cost. When farm prices improved, wages continued to drop under the demographic pressures of Dust Bowl emigration and urban unemployment.[129] Growers of fruits and vegetables, who accounted for more than a third of the state's agricultural production, were outside AAA production controls but participated in AAA marketing programs that contained no requirements that growers pass benefits on to workers in the form of higher wages.[130] Production of cotton did come under AAA acreage controls, which decreased demand for labor as they increased cotton prices.[131]

Even though they were not covered by Section 7(a) or other parts of the NIRA, agricultural workers organized and struck in response to Section 7(a)'s signals that unions would receive state support.[132] The militancy of California farmworkers was impressive considering the many barriers to their unionization, including workers' geographic mobility and ethnic heterogeneity, the widespread use of labor contractors, and growers' ability to keep organizers off farm property.[133] Another barrier was the indifference of conventional labor leaders, to whom farmworkers were even less promising trade unionists than unskilled industrial workers. As a California AFL official said, "Only fanatics are willing to live in shacks or tents and get their heads broken in the interest of migratory labor."[134] Because Communists were willing to endure such violence, two Communist-led unions, the Cannery and Agricultural Workers Industrial Union (CAWIU) and the United Cannery, Agricultural, Packing, and Allied Workers of America (UCAPAWA), assumed temporary leadership of the newly organized workers. CAWIU, formed in 1930 as a branch of the dual unionist Trade Union Unity League (TUUL), was dissolved after the Communist Party abandoned dual unionism and the TUUL in 1934.[135] UCAPAWA, founded as a CIO affiliate in 1937, ended its efforts to organize field workers in 1941.[136]

Growers and corporate landowners responded to union organization by forming the vigilante Associated Farmers and by joining antiunion state and local officials in acts of violence that included fatal shootings, kidnappings, and criminal syndicalism prosecutions.[137] Of course, industrial employers also met labor mobilization with repression. But industrial workers had recourse to Section 7(a) and later the Wagner Act, whereas agricultural workers did not. Dorothy Healey, a Communist active in both the CAWIU and the UCAPAWA, recognized the significance of this difference:

> One of the special problems we faced in UCAPAWA was that agricultural field workers were specifically excluded from the benefits of the Wagner Act. When we were organizing cannery workers or shed workers in the field, we could petition for representation elections, or file charges as we did in the case of the walnut growers. But that was not the case when we were organizing the workers who were actually out harvesting the fruit or cotton or vegetables.[138]

The exclusion of agricultural workers from Section 7(a) also ruled out state-sponsored class compromises like those of the NRA under Hugh Johnson and Donald Richberg. As the NRA's representative in California, George Creel claimed jurisdiction over the 1933 cotton strike even though agricultural workers were outside the NIRA and workers who were covered came under the NLB rather than the NRA itself. Creel used his self-proclaimed authority to promote a vision of class consensus much like that of Johnson and Richberg: no strikes, company unions, and dispute resolution through federal fact-finding. In the end, the cotton strikers won higher wages without union recognition. Lacking any real legal authority, however, Creel was unable to prevent growers from returning to repression as the solution to future strikes.[139] Pelham D. Glassford, a retired general sent to the Imperial Valley by Secretary of Labor Perkins, received employer cooperation when he acted against the CAWIU but not when he tried to curb anti-union violence or to reform labor relations in ways similar to those advocated by Creel.[140] Nor were growers interested in establishing company unionism on their own. The local Mexican consul set up a virtual company union for Mexican workers in the Imperial Valley, but it received employer support only as long as the CAWIU remained a threat.[141]

That the mobilization of California farmworkers resulted in repression rather than recognition or company unionism reflected their exclusion from the New Deal Democratic coalition. Mexican farmworkers, as noncitizens, could not vote and could be deported as political troublemakers.[142] Dust Bowl migrants were U.S. citizens, but the very fact of their migration reduced their electoral influence. Moreover, the highly individualistic Dust Bowl refugees were less likely to engage in collective action than were the Mexicans or other immigrant groups.[143] Farmworkers thus had only weak electoral claims on their own representatives, and California Democrats in Congress were divided over farm labor issues.[144] Liberal Democrats from other states, who championed industrial workers, gave farmworkers only lukewarm support. Robert Wagner agreed to George Creel's assumption of a role in the Imperial Valley that properly belonged to the NLB and dropped agricultural workers, who had been included in the 1934 Labor Disputes Bill, from the 1935 bill that became the Labor Relations Act.[145] Even Senator Robert M. La Follette, Jr., the Wisconsin Progressive whose committee exposed the violent anti-union activities of the Associated Farmers, was concerned that his staff's sympathy toward radical farmworker groups would hurt him in his agricultural home state.[146]

The limited results of mobilization in the California fields were also an indirect indication of the strength of the agricultural state. Farmworkers, despite George Creel's efforts, were outside the NRA and thus outside the dynamics by which the NRA's failure moved the industrial New Deal toward labor recognition. The AAA, better able to draw on preexisting state capacities, was more successful. This success reinforced, rather than eroded, the links between the administration and the commercial farmers who benefited from the AAA's production controls for cotton or its marketing programs for fruits and vegetables.

Planters versus Tenants in the South

Efforts to organize tenant farmers and sharecroppers in southern cotton fields had similar results. There too, the agricultural New Deal meant continued repression rather than recognition or company unionism. A contemporary writer said that "the Mexicans are to agricultural California what the Negro is to the medieval South, exploited and despised."[147] Although the institutions of southern cotton production had developed around black people's labor, during and after slavery, the combined effects of black out-migration to the North and white in-migration from the South's hill regions had made whites a majority of the Cotton Belt labor force by the 1930s.[148] Economic conditions, however, were no better for white workers than for black ones. Unlike the wage laborers of California, southern cotton workers were linked to land owners by paternalistic labor relations based on in-kind payment of rent in crops; in-kind provision by landlords of benefits such as food, housing, and medicine; limited labor mobility; and an exploitative crop-lien credit system. Tenant farmers provided their own tools and animals, paying landlords one-fourth of the cotton and one-third of the grain they produced in return for use of the land. Sharecroppers contributed only their labor and gave the landlord half their crop in return for the means of producing it, including tools and animals as well as use of the land.[149]

In the context of these class relations, it was predictable that AAA production limitations would serve the interests of cotton planters over the interests of the people who labored under their control. Acreage restrictions encouraged landlords to use less labor, while cash benefits allowed them to meet their remaining labor needs with wage workers rather than tenants or sharecroppers. AAA benefits were supposed to be shared with tenants and croppers, in proportion to their shares of the crop. In practice, though, most of the payments stayed with the planters through whom these funds were distributed.[150] The long-run effect of the AAA and successor programs was to further displace workers by giving cotton growers the capital needed to mechanize, in a region where capital had always been scarce.[151]

The visibility of displacement encouraged the mobilization of tenants and sharecroppers against planters and the AAA. The Southern

Tenant Farmers' Union (STFU) was founded in Tyronza, Arkansas, after Hiram Norcross evicted twenty-three sharecropper families from his Fairview Farms plantation. H. L. Mitchell and Clay East, two local merchants who belonged to the Socialist Party, helped to organize the biracial union. Mitchell and East had sponsored an earlier visit to Tyronza by the national Socialist leader, Norman Thomas, and Thomas publicized the STFU's grievances and activities in his speeches and articles. The STFU spread to neighboring states, elected East as Tyronza's constable, went to court on behalf of displaced croppers, won a wage increase by threatening a strike, and contacted the AAA with lists of landlords who had violated their cotton contracts. Like their California counterparts, southern growers responded to unionization with violence.[152]

Within the AAA, the STFU gained support from the Legal Section, headed by Jerome Frank. The section was a base for urban liberals, who looked to Undersecretary Rexford Guy Tugwell for leadership; among its young lawyers were members of a secret Communist cell.[153] The AAA Cotton Section, headed by Cully Cobb, was much less sympathetic to the STFU's complaints. Cobb and his subordinates had been trained in southern land-grant colleges that worked to maintain the plantation system.[154] Disputes between the Legal Section and the Cotton Section focused on the interpretation of Paragraph 7 in the standard cotton contract, which required that the participating planter

> endeavor in good faith to bring about the reduction of acreage contemplated in this contract in such manner as to cause the least possible amount of labor, economic, and social disturbance, and to this end, in so far as possible, he shall effect the acreage reduction as nearly ratably as practicable among tenants on this farm; shall, in so far as possible, maintain on this farm the normal number of tenants and other employees; shall permit all tenants to continue in the occupancy of their houses of this farm, rent free, for the years 1934 and 1935 (unless any such tenant shall conduct himself as to become a nuisance or a menace to the welfare of the producer). . . .[155]

As President Roosevelt later observed, "That can mean everything or nothing, can't it?"[156] To the Legal Section, Paragraph 7 provided tenants and croppers with firm guarantees. The Cotton Section, in contrast, viewed the ambiguous paragraph as no more than a moral proviso and advised planters that they could interpret it quite loosely.[157]

The final confrontation came over the meaning of the obligation that planters maintain "the normal number of tenants and other employees." In a case arising from another eviction by Hiram Norcross, this time directed at STFU members, Legal Section attorneys argued that planters were required to keep the same individual tenants, assuming reasonable behavior. The Cotton Section argued that Norcross and other planters could replace individuals as long as the total was not reduced. On February 5, 1935, AAA Administrator Chester Davis and Secretary of Agriculture Henry Wallace took the side of the Cotton Section and, in what became known as the "purge," fired Jerome Frank and staff attorneys Francis Shea, Lee Pressman, and Victor Rotnem from the Legal Section. Another pro-tenant urban liberal, Gardner Jackson, was dismissed as assistant consumers' counsel; his superior, Consumers' Counsel Frederic Howe, was demoted.[158]

As a center of prolabor sentiment within a procapitalist recovery program, the relation of the Legal Section to the AAA was not so different from the relationship of the NLB to the NRA, and the ambiguities of Paragraph 7 of the cotton contracts recalled those of the NIRA's Section 7(a). Why, then, didn't the conflicts within the AAA and the mobilization of workers by the STFU produce gains for the agricultural underclasses comparable to those made by industrial workers under the NRA? The electoral position of agricultural workers was much weaker than that of industrial workers, while the South's agricultural capitalists were in an even stronger position than the industrial capitalists of the North. Unlike the industrial workers, who could and did vote for Robert Wagner and other urban liberals, southern sharecroppers and tenants were largely disfranchised. White and black workers were barred by the poll tax; black workers were also subject to a variety of other Jim Crow devices.[159] White planters, in contrast, were well represented by (and often themselves served as) Democratic members of the U.S. Congress. The seniority system and the weakness of the Democratic party outside the South before the Great Depression gave crucial leadership positions to many of the southern Democrats, whose cooperation thus became necessary not only for the AAA but for the rest of the New Deal as well. Rexford Tugwell, of all people, pointed this out to Norman Thomas, asking, "What would you do if you had to deal with Joe Robinson, Cotton Ed Smith, and Pat Harrison?" "That's why I'm not a Democrat," Thomas replied.[160] Wallace also believed the purge was necessary if the AAA was to retain the officials who had made it work, including not only Cobb and the Cotton Section staff but also Davis, who in Wallace's view "more nearly has the necessary experience and grasp of all the details of the agricultural situation than anyone else who could be used at this time to run the

AAA," and A. G. Black, the agricultural economist who headed the Corn-Hog Section.[161]

At the time of the purge, Tugwell was in Florida and thus unable to protect his protégés.[162] When he returned to Washington and complained to Wallace and Roosevelt, offering his resignation, the president, characteristically, mollified him by giving him his own independent agency, the Resettlement Administration, to address the problem of rural poverty.[163] The Resettlement Administration was later incorporated within the USDA and, under the Bankhead-Jones Farm Tenant Act of 1937, transformed into the Farm Security Administration. Although the Resettlement Administration and the FSA did more for the rural poor than any other New Deal agencies, their programs, in contrast to the proposals of the STFU or the California farmworker unions, accepted the existing pattern of agricultural class relations. The FSA's best-funded programs, for tenant purchase and rural rehabilitation loans, each "skimmed the cream" of the South's agricultural underclasses, reaching only a small proportion of potential recipients and discriminating against black would-be borrowers. The FSA's program of camps for California migratory workers actually aided growers by socializing the costs of housing their labor force.

Mild as the programs of the Resettlement Administration and the FSA were, they did present the threat of class organization and thus aroused the antagonism of agricultural capitalists and their representatives. The American Farm Bureau Federation feared that the FSA and its clients would form a more powerful alliance than its own alliance with the Extension Service, and the California migratory camps proved good recruiting grounds for UCAPAWA. The FSA became a target for the conservative coalition of Republicans and southern Democrats, which gained an effective majority of Congress in the elections of 1938 and won control by an even larger margin in 1942. The "death appropriation" of 1943 cut the rural rehabilitation program by 43 percent and the tenant purchase program by 8 percent, placed stricter limits on lending, and eliminated FSA cooperative programs. In 1946, what remained of the FSA was absorbed into the even more mainstream Farmers Home Administration.

Recognition, Repression, and Company Unionism

Capitalism creates conflicting class interests. Whether in agriculture or in industry, capitalists and workers have competing claims to control over the production process and to consumption of what is produced or what it can be exchanged for. Capitalism does not, however, specify the extent or form of class organization. The coercive powers of the state can be employed to mobilize one class or the other and to mobilize them into particular organizations or alliances. The structure of state and party organization, not the level of capitalist development or the degree to which capitalism is in crisis, most directly determines how these powers will be used.

Between the beginning of the 1920s and the end of the 1930s, three alternative labor policies were in force in the United States. The repressive labor policies of the pre–New Deal era aimed to wipe out independent trade unions. Repression continued through the 1930s in agriculture, but in industry repression gave way to the voluntarism of Section 7(a), allowing competition between trade and company unions. Voluntarism in turn gave way to recognition as Section 7(a) was replaced by the Wagner Act, which provided state protections for unions participating in collective bargaining and excluded company unions from the representation process. The NLRB established by the Wagner Act could draw on prior state capacity in its regulation of labor relations; because that capacity depended on the expertise of lawyers, NLRB regulation became legalistic, particularly after the Smith Committee cut the NLRB off from economists as alternative sources of policy knowledge.

With unusual solidarity, American industrial capitalists opposed inclusion of Section 7(a) in the NIRA, supported the Clark Amendment to preserve the open shop, opposed the 1934 Labor Disputes Bill, and opposed the 1935 Wagner Act. Industrial capitalists opposed Section 7(a) and the Wagner Act because they threatened to stimulate union membership and strike activity. And the trade union growth and militancy of the New Deal era proved them right. Some capitalists could afford unions and strikes more easily than others, but none had reason to see them as desirable. Even such "corporate liberals" as Teagle and Swope would not go so far as to endorse the recognition of trade unionism contained in the Wagner Act. Instead, they embraced the labor voluntarism of the NRA under Johnson and Richberg, based on company unionism and proportional representation.

The concessions of Section 7(a), which grew into the broader and more permanent concessions of the Wagner Act, were the price industrial capitalists paid to get a program of business recovery instead of the Black Bill, mandating a thirty-hour week. Agricultural capitalists were offered a favorable recovery program without such concessions and thus had no reason to make them. Occupying a stronger position on their front of the class struggle than industrial capitalists did on theirs, agricultural capitalists also showed less interest in voluntarist compromises.

New Deal labor insurgency was a response to public policy, which was why trade union membership did not take off until 1933. Section 7(a) stimulated the strike wave of 1934–1935, including the radical revolts in Toledo and San Francisco. The drive to unionize the mass-production industries would have failed if organizers had not been able to promise that the president, far from using force against unionized workers, actually supported their unionization. Even farmworkers, to whom Section 7(a) did not legally apply, responded to its signals.

Senator Robert Wagner's participation was crucial to the inclusion of Section 7(a) in the NIRA and later to the passage of the National Labor Relations Act. Wagner's ideology of urban liberalism synthesized the substance of Progressive reform with the system of organizational politics practiced by machines such as Wagner's Tammany Hall.[164] Yet not all urban Democrats become laborist politicians: Al Smith, with the same roots in Tammany and Progressivism, ended up in the anti–New Deal Liberty League.[165] What was distinctive about Wagner was less his urban Democratic roots than the process of political learning by which his understanding of urban liberalism evolved into specific proposals for the empowerment of industrial workers. Wagner's political learning took place within the context of the NRA, through engagement with the difficulties faced by the National Labor Board. As the defeat of the 1934 Labor Disputes bill demonstrated, however, Wagner and his staff could not change labor law by themselves, even when militant labor unrest was at its height. They needed support from the rest of Congress and from President Roosevelt, which came only with the election of more urban liberals and the collapse of the NRA.

Agriculture shows the impact of elected officials such as Wagner and Roosevelt on the outcomes of class conflicts. Neither the blacks and poor whites of the southern cotton belt nor the Mexicans and "Okies" of the California fields could claim electoral representation as effectively as industrial workers. Neither group, therefore, received concessions in the Agricultural Adjustment Act comparable to those granted industrial workers in the NIRA, and over time the New Deal moved further away from their interests. Grievances under the AAA stimulated mobilization by the STFU, CAWIU, and UCAPAWA, but these unions' efforts ultimately failed to overcome the combined effects of repression and the inherent problems of agricultural unionism. The Resettlement Administration and then the FSA served as consolation prizes that helped some members of the agricultural underclasses while posing less severe challenges to the status quo. Even the FSA was taken away when the president who had sponsored it was weakened by domestic reverses and distracted by world events. In the end, all the tumult of the New Deal did not alter the traditionally repressive character of agricultural class relations.

With the Wagner Act, in contrast, the United States established an industrial labor policy based on recognition. Why not repression? Because the emerging party alignment gave Wagner, other urban Democrats, and progressive Republicans enough votes to insert Section 7(a) in the National Industrial Recovery Act. Why not company unionism? Because the absence of prior state capacity for intervention in industry made the NRA collapse. Roosevelt, whose support was crucial, then shifted from Johnson, Richberg, and business to Wagner and labor. Section 7(a) would not have become law outside the context of the National Recovery Administration. The Wagner Act would not have replaced Section 7(a) if the NRA had fulfilled its mission. The creation of the NRA made it more likely that workers in industry, unlike workers in agriculture, would have unions to join. The failure of the NRA made it less likely that those unions would be dominated by their capitalist employers.

Part 2

Dialogues with Alternative Theoretical Approaches

Introduction to Part 2

We, of course, are not the only scholars who have grappled with the challenges of explaining the New Deal's interventions into industry and agriculture, as well as comparable public policies in the United States and other capitalist democracies. In addition to our state- and party-centered institutional approach, other major theories of politics under advanced capitalism yield predictions about some aspects of New Deal industrial and agricultural policies. There have, in fact, been lively theoretical debates about state interventions in the New Deal. Proponents of several alternative perspectives have themselves commented on the NRA and the AAA or else have used their theories to interpret the New Deal more generally. In the few instances where competing theories of politics have not been applied to the New Deal programs in either of these ways, we can substitute our own speculations about how a theory might be applied. In this part of the book we engage in systematic dialogues with proponents of four other theoretical approaches: pluralism, elite theory, Marxism, and rational choice analysis.

Pluralist approaches emphasize access to top governmental decision makers by organized groups. Pluralists such as David Truman and Robert Dahl thus interpret policy outcomes as products of group resources. As we will show, however, pluralist approaches cannot explain why New Deal agricultural policy emphasized production control, which was opposed by organized farm groups, or why New Deal industrial policy, which followed the lines suggested by business leaders, worked against business interests.

Elitist approaches depict a political system based on concentrated power. Authors like Thomas Ferguson and G. William Domhoff argue that elite money can buy both elections and expertise. When elites disagree on policy issues, as they did about New Deal agricultural policy, this approach tells us that one of their alternatives will be chosen, but it cannot tell us which. When elites are relatively united, as they were in support of the National Industrial Recovery Act (NIRA), elite theory predicts that policies will conform to their preferences, perhaps with symbolic concessions to other groups, and that elites or their hirelings will be selected to implement these policies. What elite theory does not tell us is that such policies can work against elite interests. Instead of industrial recovery, the NRA produced the Wagner Act, in unsuccessful opposition to which elites were also united.

Marxist approaches, including those of Ralph Miliband, Nicos Poulantzas, and Fred Block, stress class conflict between capitalists and workers. Despite their differences, these writers all suggest that policies will serve capitalists' interests. Their theories are inadequate, therefore, to explain why the NRA worked against those interests or why the AAA broke with earlier responses of the capitalist state to the agricultural depression.

Rational choice approaches, finally, model the strategic decisions made by individual voters, politicians, or bureaucrats. Rational choice theorists such as Anthony Downs, William Riker, and Kenneth Shepsle assume that individuals are self-interested, that institutions aggregate individual preferences, and that these institutions evolve to more effectively provide the outputs desired by their members. These assumptions are particularly ill suited to the conditions of the early New Deal. They would lead us to expect an AAA based on export marketing rather than production control and an NRA that achieved its goals without unintended consequences.

Each of these major theoretical approaches is accurate for some aspects of the NRA and AAA but indeterminate (and thus irrelevant) or inaccurate for others. These evaluations, which we will substantiate in the chapters of part 2, may be summarized in the grid of figure 4. The implications of each theory for the origins, implementation, and consequences of state intervention in industry and agriculture can be evaluated as accurate (+), inaccurate (-), mixed (0), or indeterminate (?). Each theory is considered accurate for each phase of each program when it leads us to expectations that are reasonably close to what happened. Each theory is evaluated as inaccurate when it predicts the reverse of what happened: change in the opposite direction or a qualitatively different output or outcome. An evaluation of mixed indicates that the theory suggests both accurate and inaccurate predictions and that these are of roughly equal significance. A theory is evaluated as

	NRA	AAA
Origins	+	?
Implementation	-	0
Consequences	?	+

+   accurate
-    inaccurate
0   mixed
?   indeterminate

Figure 4. Sample evaluation grid

indeterminate when it yields no usable predictions or when its predictions are as compatible with what did not happen as with what did.

Systematic evaluation of the correspondence between existing theories and case studies can be used to build higher-level theories that explain when those theories will appear to succeed and when they will appear to fail. "We may have confidence in a theory," Harry Eckstein says,

> because it is derived logically from premises that have previously yielded valid theory in a field, or because it is derived from premises contrary to those that have led to major failures. We may also have confidence in a theory if it is able to account for both strengths and weaknesses in existing relevant hypotheses, or otherwise seems to organize considerable volumes and varieties of unexplained data.[1]

In this study, our state- and party-centered approach is employed to account for the strengths and weaknesses of pluralist, elitist, Marxist, and rational choice theories in explaining the NRA and AAA. These theories all rest on assumptions, often unrecognized, that state and party organizations can be understood in terms of the objective needs and subjective intentions of groups, elites, classes, or individuals, respectively. Our approach, by contrast, emphasizes the extent to which states and parties can be understood as institutions, organizations "in which powerful people are committed to some value or interest."[2] Individuals are influenced by their institutional positions and opportunities; they are not simply atomized beings with preformed preferences. Institutions are more stable than noninstitutions; their roles and practices usually persist despite personnel turnover.[3] Because their members are socialized into shared routines and because of stable patterns of resource allocation, institutions have a taken-for-granted quality. As institutions, state and party organizations operate, at least in part, according to their own internal logics and are not reducible to social forces or individual incentives.

As in part 1, we follow Max Weber in defining the state as a continuous organization with compulsory membership, territorial authority, and a monopoly of the legitimate use of force,[4] and we adopt E. E. Schattschneider's definition of party as "an organized attempt to get power."[5] Explicitly state- and party-based explanations not only yield more accurate predictions about the two programs than competing approaches do but also help us understand when other approaches will or will not appear correct. Pluralist, elitist, Marxist, and rational choice theories suggest various causal relations: if x, then y. We argue that these relations are only valid under particular conditions of state and party organization: if z and w, then x leads to y, but if not z or not w, then x may lead to a very different result, y'.

Pluralist theory, for example, suggests that whichever interest group is best organized will get what it wants from government. This notion assumes party alignments that place the group in a strategic position and state capacities that make it possible for such policies to be carried out with the intended effects. Between the onset of the agricultural depression in 1920 and the election of 1932, for example, farmers were mobilized but had little influence on policy: the first condition was not met because a party system based on ethnocultural loyalties meant their economic demands could be ignored. Business got what it wanted with enactment of the NRA, but the second condition was not met: the absence of state capacity meant that the program not only failed in its own terms but fostered the development of unions for industrial workers. Industrial capitalists' class enemies were thus mobilized into interest groups of their own.

Chapter 6 develops our critique of pluralist and elitist theories of politics in the advanced capitalist democracies. Chapter 7 does the same for Marxist theories, and chapter 8 focuses on rational choice models. Our argument throughout this part is that state- and party-centered theory can explain the origins, implementation, and consequences of the NRA and the AAA and that such a theory can also make sense of the explanatory accuracies, inaccuracies, and indeterminacies of competing approaches.

6

Pluralism and Elite Theories

Pluralist theories and elite theories have long been used by social scientists to analyze the roots and effects of New Deal programs such as the National Recovery Administration and the Agricultural Adjustment Administration. Although these approaches make contrasting assumptions about conflict and domination in the policy-making process, both nevertheless downplay the effects of governmental institutions and political-party organizations. We begin our discussion of alternative theoretical approaches with pluralism and elite theories, before turning to Marxist approaches and rational choice theories in chapters 7 and 8.

Pluralism and the Role of Interest Groups

Pluralist theories focus above all on the role of groups in democratic political processes. The classic statements of pluralist theory were presented by David Truman, Robert Dahl, Earl Latham, and Arnold Rose during the 1950s and 1960s. Though pluralism has been in theoretical disrepute since then, pluralist thought continues to shape many empirical studies in political science and provides an unacknowledged framework for much of American political journalism.[1] The key assumption of pluralism, that political outcomes are determined by the balance of group resources, is also shared by the Chicago School's "economic approach."[2] Even the best-known critic of pluralism, Theodore Lowi, accepts the pluralist claim that groups dominate American government as he challenges pluralist confidence that group politics can produce coherent or equitable public policies.[3]

Pluralist approaches explain political outcomes in terms of the resources of social groups, which compete and cut across one another so
as to achieve some, if not perfectly equal, substantive representation
for any affected interest.[4] Political institutions are understood as arenas
for the play of social groups; Latham, for example, suggests that "the
vectors which appear on Congress are merely local lines of force within
a larger field."[5] Occasionally, institutions are also treated as groups in
and of themselves. Thus, Latham also says,

> In these adjustments of group interest, the legislature does not play
> the inert part of cash register, ringing up the additions and with-
> drawals of strength, a mindless balance pointing and marking the
> weight and distribution of power among the contending groups.
> For legislatures are groups also and show a sense of identity and
> consciousness of kind that unofficial groups must regard if they
> are to represent their members effectively. In fact, the two houses
> of the Congress have a conscious identity of special "house" in-
> terest and a joint interest against the executive establishment.[6]

Pluralists reject alternative units of analysis as meaningless when
they do not correspond with group interests. Truman argues that "we
do not, in fact, find individuals otherwise than in groups," where their
attitudes and behaviors are collectively determined.[7] Pluralists are
equally critical of the concept of the state. Truman rejects the concept
because no nation, even in wartime, is ever completely unified.[8]
Latham concludes that private groups are "of the same genus, although a different species, as the state"; all are "structures of power."[9]
Pluralist theorists accept that classes may be important bases for group
mobilization but argue that classes are not necessarily more primary
than nonoccupational groups, organized and unorganized, to which
the members of any social class also belong.[10]

Pluralist theories place group politics within vague, evolutionist
schemes that posit institutional change as an inevitable progression of
ever-increasing democracy, governmental effectiveness, and the spe-
cialization of political arrangements, usually occurring in smooth, adap-
tive, incremental responses to the "modernization" of the economy
and society.[11] To the extent that pluralism is concerned with more
concrete historical transformations such as those of the New Deal, it
suggests that the best-organized interest groups in society—and those
with access to the greatest political skills and resources—would be the
ones to achieve their political goals. Some compromise might have to
be reached to satisfy other powerful and interested groups, but the final outcome should be in accord with the distribution of political re-

NRA   AAA

	NRA	AAA
Origins	+	-
Implementation	+	-
Consequences	-	0

+   accurate
-    inaccurate
0   mixed
?   indeterminate

Figure 5. Pluralism and the New Deal

sources brought to bear on "the governmental process."[12] Business interests constitute an important elite with significant resources, but business has often been defeated by the countermobilization of voters and volunteer activitists.[13]

Pluralist Theory on the NRA and the AAA

The implications of pluralist theory for the New Deal are evaluated in figure 5. The absence of preexisting capacity for state intervention in industry made the NRA pluralistic in its origins and its implementation: business interests won not only the effective repeal of antitrust but also the right to carry out the industrial policy that replaced it. The same absence of preexisting state capacity, however, led to the failure of the NRA, which pluralism would not predict, and empowered industrial workers as a countervailing interest group. The origins and implementation of the AAA did not follow the pluralist model. Because state capacity for intervention in agriculture did exist, an innovative policy was adopted against the expressed demands of well-organized farmers and then implemented as planned. As pluralism would predict, commercial farm owners, the group with the most resources, benefited most. The consequences of the AAA for the agricultural underclasses, however, belie pluralism's Panglossian faith that no affected group can ever be completely denied political power.

Origins

The struggle over New Deal industrial policy pitted organized business against organized labor. Business groups favored antitrust revision and wanted the government to sponsor coordination of prices, production levels, and conditions of employment within each industrial sector. The American Federation of Labor, in contrast, supported the Black Bill for a maximum thirty-hour work week, which business opposed.[14] That federal officials selected the policy alternative favored by business fits well with pluralist theory, for business was much better organized than labor. During the 1920s, industrial capitalists had formed many new trade associations, and existing associations had taken on new coordinating functions. Business associationalism had been actively encouraged by Herbert Hoover as secretary of commerce and as president.[15] Unions, in contrast, had been severely weakened, first by the open-shop and welfare capitalism campaigns that followed World War I and then by the Depression. Between 1920 and 1933, trade unions lost 42 percent of their membership.[16]

What pluralism cannot explain about the National Industrial Recovery Act is its timing. If the NIRA reflected the dominant resources of business, why could such a program not be enacted earlier, under Hoover? Why did Hoover term the Swope Plan, one of the progenitors of the NRA, " 'the most gigantic proposal of monopoly ever made in history' " and refuse "point blank to have anything to do with the proposals of the Chamber of Commerce and similar schemes for business rationalization"?[17] A pluralist explanation might be that industrial capitalists had greater access to Roosevelt than to Hoover. Yet Hoover's administration was unquestionably probusiness, whereas industrial workers and agricultural capitalists, two groups whose interests conflicted with those of industrial capitalists, had more influence with the Democrats than with the Republicans.

The origins of the AAA demonstrate pluralism in reverse. In pluralist theory, interest groups are political when, on the basis of shared attitudes, they make claims on government. Government will respond to those groups that have access.[18] Farm groups responded to the severe agricultural depression with policy demands and rallied behind Franklin Roosevelt's 1932 campaign in the expectation that these demands would be granted; Truman comments that farm groups "were assured access to the nominee."[19] The agricultural policy that was chosen, however, was very different from what the farm groups demanded, and their access to government made it possible for government to influence farmers more than farmers influenced government. By the late 1920s, the major farm groups had united in support of the McNary-Haugen export plan. After Roosevelt's election, the president-elect and his advisors were able to use the ties developed with the farm organizations during the campaign to "impose" their preference for a policy of production control on the organizations. The farm organizations, in turn, helped to get the Agricultural Adjustment Act through Congress and lessened the impact of protest by more militant farm groups.[20]

Lowi has described American agricultural policy as "How the Farmers Get What They Want."[21] Similarly, Latham describes "the whole program of farm subsidies which has evolved since the 1920's" as "an effort on the part of the farmer (organized) to make himself independent of the vicissitudes of the business economy, that is, to take the farmer out of the environment which he can control only imperfectly and to insulate him against economic adversity."[22] With the AAA, however, American farmers got what they and their organized groups had never wanted. Even after 1933, farmers disliked production control and strongly preferred legislation that would guarantee them the cost of production, as advocated by the Farmers' Union.[23]

Implementation

For Truman, the administrative process is a "web of relationships." Through lobbying and recruitment, interest groups have access to administrators. Yet "an administrative body is not necessarily a passive transmitter of interest group claims," for officials may identify with their administrative unit as a group and limit access or reject external demands in defense of organizational procedures and perspectives.[24] Any pattern of implementation can be accommodated within this framework. If external interests get what they want from government, they must have had access. If not, administrators must have identified more with the organization as a group. Lowi's conception of the bureaucracy includes access but not identification; as Donald Brand says, for Lowi there is no "genuinely autonomous institutional context."[25] Lowi's view is more purely externally oriented than Truman's and therefore more determinate. "Liberal governments," Lowi argues, "cannot plan."[26] They will exercise authority by delegating it to affected interests, and because they do so their policies will fail.

If pluralism predicts anything about policy implementation, then, it predicts that external interest groups will dominate. As Truman, Latham, and Lowi all recognize, the history of the NRA fits the pluralist model well. The NRA recruited its officials from the affected business groups and delegated regulatory authority to the trade associations.[27] Although the failure of the NRA supports the pluralist model, successful implementation of the AAA suggests that liberal governments *can* plan—when there is preexisting state capacity for doing so. Truman and Lowi both equate the AAA with the NRA as programs delegating authority to interest groups.[28] Implementation of the AAA followed the forms of producer representation, including recruitment from and delegation to farm groups. Yet the power to define policy alternatives, granted to industrial trade associations under the NRA, was not granted to farm groups. George N. Peek, coauthor of the McNary-Haugen Plan, was appointed as the AAA's first administrator but lost his battle to make export marketing and not production control the basis for New Deal farm policy. Peek left the AAA after seven frustrating months.[29]

Local farmer committees allocated AAA quotas to individual farmers and checked for compliance with adjustment contracts. This decentralization of field operations presented the appearance of "economic democracy" rather than centralized coercion.[30] The farmer committees, however, had no power to challenge the policy of production control; they could only carry it out. In the implementation of the AAA, interest groups did not use the state. Instead, the state used interest groups to administer a complex policy of production control that did not correspond with the original preferences of the farmers whose production was being controlled. Until the Supreme Court's Hoosac Mills decision of 1936 forced statutory changes, for example, tobacco

> policy was decided under the broad authority of the Agricultural Adjustment Act, with the result that the key decisions were taken within the AAA. The tobacco section did not simply respond to growers' pressure; rather it deliberately encouraged pressure from them. It could then respond to what it had itself created and by involving the growers facilitate the implementation of the production control program. When the growers made demands that the AAA believed were too narrowly sectional, the tobacco section rejected them.[31]

Consequences

Truman describes the New Deal as an "Unacknowledged Revolution," in which "certain groups secured a place at the political table from which they had previously been barred."[32] Industrial workers are clearly among these certain groups: Truman shows that Section 7(a) and the Wagner Act stimulated the expansion of trade unions, eliminated company unions as organizational rivals, spurred business countermobilization, and contributed to the AFL-CIO split.[33] Robert Dahl and Arnold Rose also portray the New Deal as a critical period in which business lost power, labor gained power by entering the Democratic party, and capitalism was reformed.[34] Yet if group resources were as all-determining as pluralist theory makes them seem, labor's increasing "need for positive recourse to political institutions" would not have been enough to defeat better-organized business groups.[35] By the pluralist model, company unionism or even the open shop of the 1920s should have remained the basis of American labor policy.

Within the pluralist model, groups with the most resources win, but no group ever completely loses: "Obstacles to the development of organized groups from potential ones may be presented by inertia or by the activities of opposed groups, but the possibility that severe disturbances will be created if these submerged, potential interests should organize necessitates some recognition of the existence of these interests and gives them at least a minimum of influence."[36] Even the disfranchised and disorganized black agricultural workers of the pre–civil rights Mississippi Delta, Truman claims, could exercise such indirect influence.[37] Latham says that just as farmers had organized against business, tenants and sharecroppers organized against farmers, so "organization begets counterorganization."[38] Possibilities for influence by relatively weak groups are enhanced by the fragmentation of American government, which offers groups multiple access points.[39] During the New Deal, however, limited access by agricultural workers to the federal government did not lead to enduring program changes addressing their concerns. What happened instead was that the governmental units that offered access to the agricultural underclasses—the AAA Legal Section and, later, the Farm Security Administration—were dismantled.[40]

Postpluralism and Beyond

In the pluralist world, competing groups are not necessarily equal in influence. But no group is so privileged as to be protected from the need to compete, and no group is so subordinated that it is excluded from competition. This model is almost completely wrong about the agricultural New Deal and only partially right about the industrial New Deal. In its classical forms, pluralism does not provide any way to understand its own explanatory limits. But the postpluralism of Charles Lindblom specifies some of the factors that determine how pluralistic politics will be.

Lindblom argues that "[b]usinessmen generally and corporate executives in particular take on a privileged role in government that is . . . unmatched by any leadership group other than the government officials themselves."[41] Though the achievement of foreign and domestic goals depends on business decisions about investment and allocation, government "cannot command business to perform."[42] Thus, business firms are given protections and benefits and enjoy tacit or explicit veto power over many policy areas.

In addition to stressing the importance in market societies of capitalist influences on the choices and actions of politicians, Lindblom pays attention to electorally mediated democratic influences on policy making and to those purely statist influences that are attributable to the ongoing struggles among politicians for authoritative control over governmental organs of administration, coercion, and legislation. Politics for Lindblom is "an untidy process" in which "people who want authority struggle to get it while others try to control those who hold it."[43] In struggling to achieve and maintain control, holders of top authority must rely on "supporting" political organizations, which themselves come to share authority and thus place constraints on top leaders. In liberal democracies with elements of "polyarchy" (rule by many), social groups will receive varying amounts and kinds of attention from elected politicians, depending not so much on their sheer weight in the voting process as on their strategic location (or lack of it) in the electoral process. Different forms of party organization, different party systems, and different historical conjunctures of competition for intraparty influence, for governmental office, and for influence within government will all affect which groups are attended to or ignored as politicians compete among themselves for authority.

Lindblom thus focuses simultaneously on two sets of controls operating on government officials in liberal-democratic capitalist orders: "those of polyarchy and those exercised by businessmen through their privileged position."[44] When these controls come into conflict, government officials have three options: they can choose between business and popular demands, formulate compromises, or somehow address each set of demands within separate political spheres. Franklin Roosevelt faced the conflict of business and polyarchal controls in 1933. In industry, popular demands for work sharing competed with business demands for antitrust relaxation. In agriculture, farmers supported recovery proposals that threatened the interests of industrial capitalists. The processes by which these conflicts produced the NRA and the AAA can only be understood if we pay attention to the patterns of party organization and electoral competition that Lindblom tells us are so important.

Lindblom's revisionist pluralism is more helpful in understanding the origins of New Deal industrial and agricultural policies than Truman's original version or Lowi's antipluralism. But what David Marsh argues about Western European states applies equally well to the U.S.:

Any empirical observation . . . shows that they are not undifferentiated wholes[;] there are more or less important divisions within the executive, between the executive and other branches of Government, and between the executive and the bureaucracy. In addition a brief analysis throws considerable doubts on the capacity of Government to control events sufficiently, given the number of constraints to which it is subject[,] to promote clearly and consistently the national interest, or its own interest, even if it should so wish. Once again, Lindblom's analysis is incomplete and the picture is much more complicated than his work implies.[45]

Lindblom's conception of a cohesive and capacious state is too undifferentiated to explain why the NRA could not bring about industrial recovery as planned, while the AAA at least contributed to recovery in agriculture. In addition to attending more to state structures to explain the consequences of the NRA's failure and the AAA's success for industrial and agricultural workers, it is necessary to pay more explicit attention to class relationships in society. Lindblom's society, like that of pluralist theory, is a collection of more or less organized social groups, differing in their declared interests and immediately available resources but not understood as systematically related to one another. In the sphere of the economy, however, systematic class relationships, fraught with actual and potential conflicts, tie workers to managers and owners. As both the NRA and the AAA show, state intervention in the economy may arouse new class-related issues and generate new political resources for classes to fight their battles with one another and with the government. Both state structures and class relationships need to be made analytically central.

Elite Theories and the New Deal

Elite theories of politics are defined by their emphasis on the dominance of "a relatively fixed group of privileged people."[46] Members of this elite exercise power through interest-group lobbies, through campaign contributions, through organizations of supposedly neutral experts, and through their own appointments to key government positions. Elitist arguments are often aimed directly at pluralism, which even in its milder versions portrays a more fluid set of power relations. In contrast to Marxist approaches, which view class as a relation rooted in production, elitist approaches can include the military, social notables, and even labor leaders among the "power elite."[47] Though G. William Domhoff, Thomas Ferguson, and Philip H. Burch, Jr., differ on some theoretical nuances and on some specific findings, each has been guided by elitist assumptions in research projects that include analysis of the New Deal.[48] Elitist assumptions also underlie "corporate liberal" interpretations of the New Deal by Barton Bernstein, Ronald Radosh, and Kim McQuaid.[49]

If political power is concentrated among an elite, that elite, or at least some portion of it, must be responsible for major policy changes such as those of the New Deal. In the elitist interpretation, the New Deal represents a particularly important period when vanguard capitalists who recognized the necessity of increased state intervention and expanded labor organization convinced politicians to enact their proposals, which then worked primarily to serve the interests of their corporate sponsors. The enlightened leadership group is identified with big business by Radosh; with capital-intensive, internationally competitive firms by Ferguson; with "an articulate minority of American capitalists" by McQuaid; and with upper-class rentiers such as Franklin Roosevelt by Domhoff, who argues that the diversified holdings of this class segment make them sensitive to capitalists' most general interests.[50]

Whatever its composition, the capitalist vanguard's clever strategies stabilized and revived a U.S. economy dominated by large corporations. Great stress is placed on the ultimate benefits gained by U.S. corporate capitalism, not only from government interventions to stabilize particular industries but also from such widely popular measures as unemployment insurance, social security, and the legalization of unions and collective bargaining. The appearance that such measures had been won by democratic pressure should not be accepted at face value but understood as an added advantage for capitalists. In this way, Radosh says, New Deal reforms "were of such a character that they would be able to create a long-lasting mythology about the existence of a pluralistic American democracy, in which big labor supposedly exerts its countering influence to the domination that otherwise would be undertaken by big industry."[51]

In ascribing New Deal policies to elite influence, these authors assume that electoral outcomes are not determined by votes but by money and other corporate contributions and that experts, whether inside or outside the state, cannot ever be autonomous. Ferguson's "investment theory of political parties" is the most formal—and the most extreme—statement of the elitist assumption that contributions determine electoral outcomes. Large corporate contributors control information and organization as well as money; the mass electorate, unless it sustains its own counterorganizations (such as Labor's Non-Partisan League, formed to support Roosevelt in 1936), can be excluded or manipulated. Ferguson asserts that major investors have effectively controlled American political parties and that significant political changes represent shifts in investment blocs. In Ferguson's interpretation, the New Deal represented the victory of the Rockefeller family and other financial interests allied with it in opposition to the House of Morgan.[52] Domhoff, more cautiously, says, "The fat cats who contribute $500 or more to individual candidates do not own the party lock, stock, and barrel. They do, though, have a dominant interest." Domhoff emphasizes the financial support that Roosevelt received from southerners, New Yorkers, and Jews among the economic elite.[53]

Elite research has demonstrated that it is worth paying attention to the power of money providers in party politics. Unfortunately, with that attention has come deliberate inattention to the power of voters, who are treated as completely manipulable. Voters do in fact respond to campaign spending, or to other organized contributions that are harder to measure.[54] But voters also respond to other factors, including ethnic and racial identities and retrospective judgments about incumbents' policies and performance.[55] And as Domhoff points out, wealthy people who donate to political campaigns often do so out of "such mundane factors as friendship with the fund-raiser, a personal liking of the candidate, long-standing party identification, or general social outlook" and not as an investment in preferred policies.[56] Unlike investors in a business enterprise, voters and campaign contributors both lack legally enforceable property rights. Thus, neither voters nor contributors have any way to prevent officials from reneging on campaign promises, except to punish such officials at the next election, when the alternative candidates might look even worse.

A second assumption typical of elite theory is that experts are never truly autonomous but always act to serve corporate interests. Domhoff considers any member of the power elite who is born into the social upper class, is educated in its universities, or participates in its institutions as effectively controlled by this upper class. In his view, such experts as M. L. Wilson and John R. Commons were connected to the corporate policy-planning network and so can be understood as acting in the interests of the corporate elites who financed and controlled that network.[57] Comparison between the NRA and the AAA suggests that experts are more usefully seen as *potentially* autonomous. Whether and to what extent that potential is realized depends on the exact institutional structures within which they operate.

	NRA	AAA
Origins	+	?
Implementation	0	-
Consequences	?	?

+   accurate
-    inaccurate
0   mixed
?   indeterminate

Figure 6. Elite theories and the New Deal

Origins

As the authors discussed here all note, elites played important roles in the origins of the NRA (see figure 6).[58] The NRA not only overrode the antitrust restrictions against business cooperation that had been targeted by business leaders throughout the 1920s but also used public authority to organize firms and implement their programs for what would previously have been illegal restraint of trade. The design of the recovery program resembled the Swope Plan of 1931, devised by Gerard Swope of General Electric. Swope, along with Henry Harriman of the Chamber of Commerce and other business leaders, contributed to the tripartite drafting process that produced the NIRA.[59]

Although the content of the NIRA and the process that produced it fit the elitist model well, the timing of the bill does not. We might expect that if business elites had purchased policy influence through participation in the Roosevelt campaign, the administration would have rushed to carry out already well-developed plans for business recovery. According to Ellis Hawley, however, "When Congress convened in March 1933 the new Administration had no plans for broad changes in the business structure."[60] Proposals for intervention in industry were considered seriously only after the Senate passed the Black Bill on April 6, 1933. In contrast, the new administration's proposal for broad changes in the agricultural structure was the product of a series of transition-period meetings involving Roosevelt, his advisors, and farm group representatives, and a farm bill was submitted to Congress within two weeks of Roosevelt's inauguration on March 4.[61]

Elite theories are less adequate guides to the origins of the AAA than to the origins of the NRA. Contacts between Roosevelt and corporate supporters of production control provide no evidence that elite support explains the policy shift, for there was also elite support for alternative agricultural policies. Even that portion of the corporate elite affiliated with Roosevelt was not united in support of any one policy approach. Henry Harriman endorsed production control, as did R. R. Rogers of Prudential Insurance, which like other insurance companies had invested heavily in farm mortgages.[62] Processors such as the cereal companies and the cotton textile firms, though interested in agricultural recovery, opposed production control plans that would reduce the volume of their operations.[63] Wall Street's Bernard Baruch supported the export plan developed by his protégés, Hugh Johnson and George Peek, and embodied in the McNary-Haugen bills.[64]

Compared with the NRA, the AAA owed less to elites and more to experts. The true progenitors of the AAA were not businessmen like Swope or Harriman but agricultural economists: W. S. Spillman of the USDA Bureau of Agricultural Economics, John D. Black of Harvard, M. L. Wilson of Montana State University, and Mordecai Ezekiel of the Federal Farm Board.[65] Rexford Guy Tugwell, the archetypical New Deal professor, introduced Roosevelt to Wilson's domestic allotment plan.[66] Analysis of the AAA as an example of elite influence thus requires an assumption that these experts acted to serve corporate interests. Domhoff and Ferguson both point to Beardsley Ruml as the link between industrial capitalists and agricultural economists. Ruml, as director of the Laura Spelman Rockefeller Memorial, funded Wilson's Montana experiments in mechanized wheat farming, asked Black to study the domestic allotment plan, and helped to bring Tugwell together with Wilson and Henry Wallace at the pro-allotment conference held in Chicago in June 1932. The Memorial also funded the Social Science Research Council and its agricultural programs, with which both Black and Wilson were involved.[67]

Do these expert-elite connections make the AAA a product of Rockefeller influence? Ferguson and Domhoff convey the ubiquity of corporate ties in a society where neither labor unions nor radical parties have been able to sustain counterhegemonic cultural institutions. But they also oversimplify the relationships among participants in the agricultural policy network. Though the AAA was more directly descended from Black's plan, an earlier domestic allotment proposal was published by W. J. Spillman, a scientific and economic expert who spent most of his career within the Department of Agriculture and served alongside Wilson in the Office of Farm Management.[68] Moreover, under Ruml's leadership the Laura Spelman Rockefeller Memorial operated with more independence from its benefactors than other Rockefeller family foundations or similar foundations organized by other wealthy philanthropists, and it distributed much of its money in the form of block grants that allowed extensive discretion to recipient institutions.[69] Black, Wilson, Spillman, Ezekiel, and other experts who contributed to the formulation of the Agricultural Adjustment Act may have been less independent than contemporary university professors, but that does not mean they were completely dominated by the Rockefellers or the Farm Bureau.

Implementation

The agricultural experts who formulated the AAA proved crucial to its implementation and were appointed to some of its key positions. M. L. Wilson headed the Wheat Section. Albert G. Black, the former chair of the Iowa State Agricultural Economics Department (and a former student of John D. Black at Minnesota), headed the Corn-Hog Section. The only USDA career official appointed to head a commodity section was John B. Hutson, an agricultural economist who had worked for the BAE and the Office of Foreign Agricultural Relations before he was put in charge of the Tobacco Section.[70]

Just as expert influence on the origins of the AAA carried over to its implementation, business influence over the NRA continued with the appointment of its officials, including the selection of Hugh Johnson, the Baruch associate who had written one of the two NIRA drafts, as administrator. Swope, Henry Harriman, and other corporate leaders joined Secretary of Commerce Daniel C. Roper to organize the Business Advisory Council (BAC), a secretive, semiofficial advisory group. The BAC, in turn, provided the basis for the NRA Industrial Advisory Board.[71]

If elite enthusiasm and participation were sufficient for administrative success, the NRA would have achieved its goals. Instead, the elite-based NRA followed a very different trajectory from the expert-based AAA. Can elite theory explain why the NRA collapsed? Ferguson attributes the failure of the NRA to elite divisions: the NRA "not surprisingly" self-destructed, he says, because internationalists swung against it once conditions began to improve, while protectionist firms, the program's more natural constituency, were divided by "the NRA's half-hearted and incoherently designed" efforts to allocate resources.[72]

Similar conflicts, however, did not completely undermine the AAA. As Ferguson notes, agriculture is objectively as divided as industry.[73] The stakes of international trade were different for cotton planters who produced for export than for sugar producers who needed protection against cheaper foreign sugar or for corn and wheat farmers who produced for the domestic market.[74] Policies benefiting corn growers hurt farmers who fed that corn to their hogs. Henry Wallace recorded that disagreements about production control by producers of different commodities almost broke up the March 1933 conference that he convened to work out a farm bill. The disagreements were resolved by giving the secretary of agriculture discretion to choose the programs best suited for each commodity.[75]

Domhoff argues that the inability of the NRA to foster recovery does not refute elite theory, which "only says that the power elite is dominant within the system, not that it is able to control the system as a whole and shape all the trends and problems that arise within it." The problems of the capitalist economic system were so severe that it was beyond the capacity of dedicated capitalist elites to cure or even to mitigate the industrial depression.[76] Again, the same could be said about agriculture. The agricultural depression had lasted longer, beginning in the early 1920s, and was at least as severe as the industrial collapse. Systemic problems, moreover, were arguably more important as causes of the agricultural depression, which was often blamed on overproduction, than as causes of the industrial depression, which had been exacerbated by counterproductive fiscal and monetary policies.

Comparison between industry and agriculture suggests that systemic problems are inherently neither solvable nor insolvable; whether they can be solved depends on the institutional capacities organized to solve them. The causes of the NRA's failure and of the AAA's success should be located at the level of the state, between the level of elites and the level of the "system." We can then ask why the NRA's administrative mechanisms were so poorly designed and so ill suited to the systemic problems they addressed—particularly in comparison with their agricultural counterparts. Elite theories that ignore this level of analysis, treating the state as a purchased tool of the ruling class and assuming that experts have no capacities other than those of the elites they serve, can make no consistent claims about what will happen once a program favored by the privileged few is actually implemented (see figure 6). Elite divisions might be mended or exacerbated; policies might achieve elite goals or backfire so as to make these goals less achievable in the future.

Consequences

The policy most directly contrary to elite goals—and thus the hardest case for elite theory—was the Wagner Act. In two years, the trade union movement was revived and the vague promises of Section 7(a) were transformed into the administrative guarantees of the National

Labor Relations Act. Some elitist interpretations treat the Wagner Act as an example of corporate power. In this view, there was a split within the corporate elite: while many industrial capitalists resisted unions, key corporate liberals or moderates supported the policy of union recognition, as a means to achieving labor peace or industrial recovery or as an alternative to craft fragmentation.[77] As we demonstrated in chapter 5, there is little evidence to support this interpretation. The real division among industrial capitalists was between employers who sought to keep out unions in any form and employers who developed company-controlled unions, which grew rapidly under Section 7(a). Virtually no capitalists supported either unions independent of company control or the Wagner Act's dangerous combination of majority rule, administrative enforcement, an outright ban on company unionism, and an affirmation of the right to strike. Even Gerard Swope and Walter Teagle, who served on the NRA's National Labor Board and are often presented as corporate liberal leaders, did not endorse the new labor policy, and the Business Advisory Council, to which they belonged, opposed it.[78] Henry Harriman, who is also frequently cited as a corporate liberal, testified against the Wagner bill.[79]

Other elitist interpretations recognize business opposition to the Wagner Act and interpret its passage as an exception to more general patterns. Domhoff, in an explicit shift from his earlier analysis of the act as a product of the corporate elite, argues that corporate moderates, normally a decisive swing group, were defeated as Roosevelt and other leaders of the power elite as a whole allied with industrial workers. Southern landowners were willing to accept this alliance, since their workers were specifically excluded from the act.[80] McQuaid shows that although the corporate liberals of the BAC were willing to recognize unions—and even grant majority rule—in the context of Section 7(a), the BAC strongly opposed Wagner's labor bill. Within the BAC, "business statesmen" Swope and Harriman lost or yielded to conservatives Pierre du Pont and Alfred Sloan, who shared smaller firms' hostility to organized labor.[81] Burch depicts the Wagner Act as a genuinely reformist measure, approved over the opposition of most business representatives.[82]

The analyses in this second group are descriptively accurate but theoretically incomplete. They fit the historical record within an elitist framework, but in so doing they suggest the limits of that framework. When is the position of corporate moderates decisive, and when is it not? Under what conditions do representatives of the entire class develop an independent position? Under what conditions do nonelites have bargaining power? A model of elite politics as shifting coalitions requires external factors to explain coalitional stability or change. In the case of the Wagner Act, the crucial shift was Roosevelt's switch from opposition to Wagner's labor bill in 1934 to support for its passage in 1935. This change is better explained by the collapse of the NIRA than by Roosevelt's personal background, which was no more or less elite in 1935 than in 1933 or 1934.

The resolution of agricultural class conflict during the New Deal would seem less problematic for elite theory. In agriculture, the elite, particularly southern planters, won. The AAA was implemented to favor farm owners over tenants and sharecroppers. Farm Security Administration (FSA) programs to benefit nonelites received low funding and were prematurely eliminated. Yet here too, elite theory explains too little. As the theory would predict, nonelites were excluded from power. The influence of specific elites, however, proved to be quite variable. Southern plantation owners were unable to determine what farm program would be enacted, but they were able to get that program implemented in ways that benefited them. Proposals for farm tenancy reforms were funded directly by the Rockefeller Foundation or by the University of North Carolina's Institute for Research in Social Science, which was then dependent on Rockefeller funding.[83] If, as elite theorists have argued, the Rockefeller bloc was central to the New Deal coalition, why weren't these proposals carried out more vigorously?

The AAA, like the NRA, did more than reflect patterns of elite power. It transformed those patterns in ways that made it more likely that landowners would triumph and less likely that either northern, industrial-based elites or the agricultural underclasses would determine the future of southern agriculture.

An Assessment of Elite Theory

Elite theory has stimulated programs of vigorous research into patterns of individual backgrounds and affiliations that other social scientists and historians have missed. But the significance of these patterns is not always what elite theory would suggest. As elite theory would predict, the NRA grew out of corporate proposals for industrial reconstruction, but these proposals became public policy only when a more radical alternative threatened. Both the AAA and the Wagner Act were enacted over alternatives preferred by the elites who were most directly concerned about them. The NRA's reliance on elite appointees ultimately worked against elite interests.

Elites participate within a context of state and party organizations, and it is in their assumptions about these institutions that elite approaches are too simple. Elite approaches assume that parties are controlled by their investors. Did elite investment in the 1932 Roosevelt campaign buy influence over industrial and agricultural policy? If anti-Morgan finance capitalists led by the Rockefeller family backed Roosevelt in 1932, as Ferguson argues, they were disappointed with the results. Louise Overacker's tabulations of large contributors show that in 1928 and 1932, bankers and brokers donated nearly as much to the Democrats as to the Republicans, suggesting that each party had substantial support within the financial community. In 1936, bankers and brokers showed their evaluation of the Roosevelt administration by giving the Republicans almost fourteen times as much money as they gave the Democrats.[84] Despite the influence of Rockefeller-connected experts on New Deal agriculture and labor policies, five members of the Rockefeller family donated at least five thousand dollars apiece to the Republican National Committee and allied organizations between 1933 and 1936.[85]

Elite theorists view experts as willing tools of the corporate elite and thus no basis for state autonomy. Yet the USDA-land-grant-college network was autonomous enough to give rise to and administer proposals for production control that were not tailored to the needs of capitalists from either agriculture or industry. These proposals were less threatening to the industrial elite than McNary-Haugenism, which is why some business interests responded positively to M. L. Wilson's zealous campaign for domestic allotment. The ultimate choice between competing farm proposals was made by Roosevelt; that choice reflected both his perceived electoral interests and the policy views that had been shaped by his advisors. Corporate alignments permitted him to choose a policy of production control but did not dictate this choice.

Elite theorists also assume that experts are available. This was true for the AAA and false for the NRA. The absence of autonomous expertise for industrial policy gave industrial capitalists what they wanted: state-sponsored cartelization and effective repeal of the antitrust laws. But without autonomous experts to make the new industrial policy work, they did not want it for long.

We are now ready to move on to a critical dialogue with Marxist theoretical approaches. Marxist analysts have written a great deal about New Deal programs in recent years. Like elite theorists, they are sharply critical of classical pluralist approaches to U.S. politics and emphasize the role of business interests. Yet Marxists, as we shall see, also privilege class relationships of domination and conflict.

7
Marxist Approaches to
Politics and the State

Karl Marx's scattered and somewhat inconsistent writings on the state do not add up to a unified theory.[1] Twentieth-century Marxists, seeking to understand why the advanced industrial societies have remained capitalist (and why underdeveloped Russia and China became Communist), have nonetheless drawn on Marx's concepts and historical examples to develop more systematic theories of the state. Marxist approaches share an emphasis on class, understood in terms of ownership of the means of production. The Marxist conception of class as analytically privileged over other social categories contrasts with the use of class in pluralist theory, where it is just one among many overlapping bases of collective action. Elitist theory also emphasizes class but treats it as a function of kinship or socialization, as well as ownership of the means of production. Marxist authors therefore pay more attention than elitist authors to patterns of working-class organization and pay less attention to patterns of elite organization, such as social clubs and debutante balls, that are not directly economic.

Varieties of Marxist Theory

Three approaches to politics and the state have often been distinguished within Marxist theory. The differences among these approaches can be summed up by their prevailing metaphors for the state: an "instrument" for class rule; a relatively autonomous "structure" for class domination; or an "arena" for class struggle.[2] Proponents of these competing approaches have often referred explicitly to the New Deal, perhaps because it was during the Great Depression that the United States came closest to fulfilling Marx's prophecy that under capitalism the "mass of misery, oppression, slavery, degradation, and exploitation" would grow and that with it would grow the revolt of the working class.[3]

The cases of the NRA and the AAA suggest that instrumentalist and structuralist conceptions of the state are most useful as ideal types within a broader analytical framework. That is, the state as instrument and the state as structure both represent possibilities. A third possibility is an autonomous state that does not necessarily meet the needs of capital or of capitalists. Whether a particular state, or a particular part of it, becomes a capitalist instrument, a capitalist structure, or an autonomous set of institutions depends in part on the social conflicts on which class-struggle Marxism focuses. More than the class-struggle Marxists, however, we emphasize the ways class struggle is translated, via party activities and alignments, into electoral behavior. We also maintain that whether a state or a portion of it is instrumental, structural, or autonomous depends on patterns of prior state development that cannot be reduced to past or present class struggles.

Instrumentalist Marxism

An instrument has no will of its own and thus is capable of action only as the extension of the will of some conscious actor. To understand the state as an instrument of the capitalist class is to say that state action originates in the conscious and purposive efforts of capitalists as a class. One expression of Marx's occasional view of the state as instrument is the *Communist Manifesto*'s claim that the "executive of the modern State is but a committee for managing the common affairs of the whole bourgeoisie."[4] Engels actually used the instrumentalist metaphor, describing "the modern representative state" as "an instrument for the exploitation of wage labor by capital."[5] An instrumentalist view of the state became official doctrine when orthodox Communist parties adopted the theory of state monopoly capitalism, which held that public authority had fused with private enterprise in the most advanced stage of capitalist development.[6]

An instrumentalist view of the American national state implies an interpretation of New Deal policy formation that is similar in substance, if not in terminology, to the elitist interpretation: the ostensibly liberal achievements of the New Deal originated with capitalist initiatives and became policy with capitalist support. This capitalist support was not unanimous: the New Deal, like other periods of American history, was marked by conflict among fractions of capital divided by size, sector, region, or other aspects of productive relations. But both an elitist and an instrumentalist approach imply that all measures enacted under the Roosevelt administration, even the Wagner Act, must have had *some* business support.

Some New Deal measures, including the NIRA, were supported by business. Business opinion was divided on others, including the AAA. The overall pattern, though, was that most of business was hostile to most of the New Deal.[7] Ralph Miliband, the author most often cited as exemplifying an instrumentalist approach, recognizes that capitalists saw the Roosevelt administration as acting against their interests:

> After all, it is quite probable that no leader of a government in this century has been more hated, and even feared, by business elites than was Roosevelt in the early (and even in the later) stages of the New Deal—much more so than any social-democratic prime minister in other capitalist countries. Yet no one believes that Roosevelt sought to (or did) weaken American capitalism. On the contrary it is now evident (and it was evident to many people at the time) that the New Deal sought to, and in fact did, restore and strengthen the capitalist system, at very little cost to the dominant classes.[8]

As Miliband points out, even though capitalists opposed Roosevelt, Roosevelt did not oppose capitalism. Joseph P. Kennedy wrote during the 1936 campaign that business hostility toward Roosevelt was

> the strangest hatred of history. . . . It certainly can be said without exaggeration that the Chief Executive has been at pains to protect the invested wealth of the nation. He has in every important speech, even when attacking the manifest abuses of irresponsible wealth, made clear that he advocates no policy of expropriation, no scheme of confiscation. At no time has he failed to assert or imply his belief in the essential capitalistic economy under which America and the American system have developed.[9]

This paradox suggests that a structuralist understanding of the New Deal is more plausible than an instrumentalist one.

Structuralist Marxism

Instrumentalist approaches posit a state that is not autonomous from the capitalist class. Structuralist approaches posit a state that can be autonomous and indeed must be if the system is to survive. Authority for a structuralist conception of the state can be found in the writings of

Marx and Engels, along with their more instrumentalist-sounding statements. Engels's comment that "the modern state, no matter what its form, is essentially a capitalist machine, the state of the capitalists, the ideal personification of the total national capital" can be interpreted in structuralist terms.[10] The most significant text for a structural reading of Marx is his own *Eighteenth Brumaire*. Marx depicts Louis Bonaparte as the head of a French state that was not controlled by the dominant class, the bourgeoisie:

> But under the absolute monarchy, during the first revolution, under Napoleon, bureaucracy was only the means of preparing the class rule of the bourgeoisie. Under the Restoration, under Louis Philippe, under the parliamentary republic, it was the instrument of the ruling class, however much it strove for power of its own.
>
> Only under the second Bonaparte does the state seem to have made itself completely independent.[11]

In Marx's analysis, the dictatorship of the executive branch under Louis Bonaparte was an alternative to direct class rule. Yet Marx still explained Bonapartism's origins and functions in class terms. Though the Bonapartist state robbed the bourgeoisie of both money and political power, it served the long-term interests of the bourgeoisie by preserving order—that is, by repressing the working class.[12] Marx later described Bonapartism as the consequence of a sort of equilibrium among contending class forces: "In reality, it was the only form of government possible at a time when the bourgeoisie had already lost, and the working class had not yet acquired, the faculty of ruling the nation."[13] In other writings, Marx and Engels found more examples of state autonomy from social forces, including the first Napoleon, Otto von Bismarck, Simon Bolívar, and absolutist monarchs such as Louis XIV. In these cases, too, state autonomy was the product of an equilibrium of class forces.[14] Antonio Gramsci formalized Marx's equilibrium analysis in his discussion of "Caesarism" as a political phenomenon in which the emergence of a "great personality" as a third force ends the deadlocked struggle of contending classes. For Gramsci, Mussolini, both Napoleons, and Bismarck were all cases of Caesarism.[15]

The early work of Nicos Poulantzas builds an elaborate structuralist theory of the state on a reinterpretation of the Marxist concept of Bonapartism. For Poulantzas, Bonapartism combines two distinct modes of state autonomy. As Gramsci had argued, Bonapartism is a concrete historical phenomenon, in which an equilibrium of forces produces executive dictatorship. But Bonapartism is also "a constitutive characteristic of the capitalist type of state."[16] All capitalist states, whether or not their forms are those of Bonapartist dictatorship, are relatively autonomous.

The "relative" that is always part of Poulantzas's concept of relative autonomy means that in the state's "relations to the class struggle," autonomy "allows the state to function . . . as the *unambiguous (univoque)* political power *of the dominant classes or fractions.*"[17] Since the bourgeoisie cannot organize itself as the dominant class, the capitalist state functions to do so. At the same time, the capitalist state functions to disorganize the working class into a collection of atomized individuals.[18] The relatively autonomous capitalist state is only as autonomous as is necessary for the hegemony of the dominant class or classes. In fact, only by being relatively autonomous from the ruling class can the state serve that class's interests: a state that was an instrument of the bourgeoisie would be no better able to organize bourgeois hegemony than the bourgeoisie itself.[19] Poulantzas's relatively autonomous state may be fragmented in form, but it is unified in its functions. It is thus impossible for the working class to gain power over a part of the capitalist state.[20] State and party strength are inversely related since states and parties are alternative mechanisms for performing the same functions of uniting the bourgeoisie and dividing its class enemies.[21]

Poulantzas's theory of the state sharply diverges from instrumentalism. State power "is not a machine or an instrument"; it is "an ensemble of structures."[22] The direct participation of capitalists in the state, imported into Marxism from elitist theory by Miliband, is irrelevant to the *"objective relation"* between the dominant bourgeoisie and the relatively autonomous state that makes the state a "factor of cohesion" and a "factor of reproduction."[23] One implication of Poulantzas's theory is that policies of government intervention to restructure the economy should originate within the state, since capitalists are incapable of acting in their own true class interests.[24] A second implication is that policies should be implemented autonomously; administrative organizations should not be "captured" by business interest groups.

The most fundamental implication of Poulantzian theory is that policies should be functional: they should have positive consequences for the capitalist system. Poulantzas's criticisms of functionalist tendencies in other approaches notwithstanding, his own arguments fit Arthur Stinchcombe's definition of functionalist explanations as those "in which a structure or an activity is caused (indirectly) by its consequences."[25] As Stinchcombe explains, the logic of functional explanation is that structures or processes maintain a condition despite tensions that threaten to alter it. The condition maintained in Poulantzas's theory is the capitalist mode of production; the tensions are the crises produced by the inherent contradictions of this system; the structures that preserve capitalism despite its crises are ideology and the state.[26]

Class-Struggle Marxism

Poulantzas's later work, culminating in *State, Power, Socialism*, abandons the metaphor of the state as structure for a description of the state as simultaneously a "material condensation of a relationship of [class] forces" and a "strategic field and process of intersecting power networks."[27] The state constitutes class struggle; that is, the division of labor within society requires the institutionalization of power in the state. But the state is itself an arena for class struggle, since the capitalist division of labor is reproduced within it.[28] Part of this reproduction is the separation between manual workers who produce commodities and intellectuals who produce science, statistics, and other forms of "state knowledge." These state intellectuals are distinct from the bourgeoisie yet "play a role in organizing its hegemony."[29] Class struggles have primacy over institutions: should some of the state organizations be captured by the Left, the bourgeoisie is somehow able to make other institutions dominant within the state.[30] Since the dominant class can in this way reshape the state to meet its needs, "change in the class relationship of forces always affects the state," though not always directly or immediately. Changes in the economic apparatus that carries out "crucial functions for capitalist relations of production and capitalist accumulation *as a whole* . . . cannot but *closely follow* the rhythm of change in the relations of production."[31]

The greater emphasis on class struggle in Poulantzas's later work reflects the lessened influence on him of the structuralism of Louis Althusser. Poulantzas was also concerned with debating Michel Foucault's poststructuralist conception of power, as well as what Poulantzas saw as an emerging technocratic strand within the Left.[32] But the resulting differences do not alter the assumptions of Poulantzas's theory of the state or their implications for the New Deal. Even in *Political Power and Social Classes*, Poulantzas invoked Marxist conceptions of class struggle, and *State, Power, Socialism* reiterates Poulantzas's earlier criticisms of instrumentalist Marxism.[33] In *State, Power, Socialism*, as in the earlier writings, the most fundamental characteristic of the capitalist state is still its functional unity. Can the state be absolutely or totally autonomous, independent from capitalists in a way that does not serve capitalists' larger interests? Both versions of Poulantzas answer that it cannot be.[34] Can workers achieve real gains within capitalist democracy? The early Poulantzas and the later Poulantzas agree that what might seem to be working-class gains (for example, the English factory legislation discussed by Marx in *Capital*) are really only short-term material concessions offered by the dominant classes in order to preserve their long-term domination.[35]

What is new in Poulantzas's later work is his argument that the state achieves its functions through apparent dysfunctions, that it demonstrates its unity through the appearance of chaos.[36] Thus, policies that are unsuccessful in their own terms, by virtue of their very failure, help to reproduce the capitalist mode of production. These changes make Poulantzas's theory even more flexible and even less determinate. They also make the internal logic of the theory even more confusing since, as Bob Jessop points out, Poulantzas never specified a causal mechanism by which micro-level processes that might work against capitalist interests are aggregated into necessarily functional macro-level outcomes.[37]

Marxist Theorists on New Deal Economic Interventions

Poulantzas's brief discussions of the New Deal demonstrate the continuity of his theory and its empirical implications. In both his early and his later work, the New Deal is an example of autonomous state intervention on behalf of monopoly capital, with concessions to medium-sized capital but not, apparently, to labor. Though both the New Deal and fascism strengthened the executive in the interest of capital, the New Deal and other variants of the bourgeois republic as the normal form of the capitalist state must be distinguished from fascism, understood as the exceptional form the capitalist state develops in crises.[38] Poulantzas also suggests that the comparatively weak party organization of the United States "has sometimes allowed a relative autonomy to the state, which came into play in Roosevelt's 'New Deal.'"[39]

Other authors taking approaches similar to Poulantzas's have discussed the New Deal at much greater length. Rhonda F. Levine's "class-centered" analysis of the industrial New Deal places particular emphasis on Poulantzas's later work, which she argues is not functionalist.[40] Jess Gilbert and Carolyn Howe analyze New Deal agricultural policy as the convergence of state structures with class capacities.[41] Steve McClellan also applies class-struggle Marxism to the agricultural New Deal. For McClellan, conflicts over the AAA reflect fundamental contradictions between present and future accumulation, with state managers acting to ensure future accumulation.[42]

Figure 7 sums up our evaluation of Marxism—as it is presented by

	NRA	AAA
Origins	0	+
Implementation	-	+
Consequences	-	+

+   accurate
-   inaccurate
0   mixed
?   indeterminate

Figure 7. Marxism and the New Deal

Poulantzas, Levine, Gilbert and Howe, and McClellan—as a framework for analysis of the NRA and the AAA. As figure 7 indicates, the AAA comes closer to Poulantzas's conception of the dynamics of state intervention than the NRA does. That is because the AAA was more successful at serving capitalist interests, and Poulantzas's theory of the state, even in its later version, predicts system-maintaining outcomes if it predicts anything at all.

Origins

To the extent that Poulantzas's theory does predict particular outcomes over their alternatives, it fits the purpose of the National Industrial Recovery Act and the process that produced it. The National Industrial Recovery Act explicitly authorized what Poulantzas depicts as the central function of the capitalist state, the organization of capitalists. Poulantzas also suggests that the state aggregates other interests to create a false national unity.[43] This aggregation can be seen in the drafting of the NIRA, with its many compromises and its deliberately ambiguous language. The drafting process melded together various proposals for government action to promote economic recovery: business schemes for government-backed industrial cartels were the primary basis for Title I, whereas Title II incorporated plans for stimulatory government spending. Section 7(a) made promises to labor, which capitalists opposed but were willing to accept as the price of the entire bill. There were also rhetorical concessions to consumers and to small business, which feared both the labor provisions and the antitrust revisions. Contradictions were, as Levine says, "glossed over" in the congressional debates.[44]

As Poulantzas might suggest, capitalists needed the state to regulate themselves. They did not, however, need the state to tell them they had this need. The NRA was based on proposals developed by capitalists, rather than by agents of an autonomous state. Business groups had long sought antitrust revision, and the Swope Plan suggested a positive program of state regulation for business recovery. Both kinds of state intervention in industry were opposed by the Hoover administration and thus required Roosevelt's election. Levine recognizes that monopoly capital's plans for industrial restructuring required Democratic victory in 1932, but her description of Hoover's policies as laissez-faire ignores revisionist arguments by Ellis Hawley and other scholars, who paint a more complex picture.[45] Levine also overstates the clarity of the choices offered in 1932 when she interprets the Democratic victory as a "mandate" for the "reformist wing of the capitalist class."[46] It has often been noted that there was little difference between the two parties' campaign positions.[47] If anything, Roosevelt and the Democrats, who emphasized a balanced budget, were more conservative than Hoover and the Republicans.

The origins of the NRA demonstrate that party organization is not always an alternative to state autonomy but may be a precondition for it. With Roosevelt's election, the partisan conditions for autonomous state action toward industry were met. Democratic victory, together with the policy threat of the Black Bill, was sufficient for enactment of the NIRA. But Democratic victory, the threat of more radical alternatives, and passage of the NIRA were not sufficient for successful implementation of the program or for consequences that would be functional for the capitalist system.

At the origin of the AAA, agricultural capitalists were too disorganized to act in their own collective interests. More than industrial capitalists, they needed a relatively autonomous state, in Poulantzas's sense of a state that could intervene on their behalf. The three peak associations (the Farm Bureau, the Grange, and the Farmers' Union) had failed to win adoption of the McNary-Haugen Plan and had been coopted into Hoover's unsuccessful Federal Farm Board. All three rapidly lost members after 1929. By 1933, only about one in ten farm families belonged to any of the three groups.[48] Agricultural policy innovation did not come from these groups, which had long opposed production control, but from within the state. The agricultural experts who developed and promoted the domestic-allotment proposal (W. J. Spillman, John D. Black, Mordecai Ezekiel, and M. L. Wilson) had been trained and socialized by the USDA and by the land-grant colleges, which were institutionally linked to the department.

Elitist or instrumentalist models of politics suggest that such policy innovations as production control originate outside the state. Gilbert and Howe, in contrast, locate the source of production control proposals in the USDA and the land-grant colleges but attribute a class basis (and a class bias) to these state structures.[49] Thus, though Gilbert and Howe offer a compelling plea to move beyond "state vs. society" debates and study the interaction of the two, their own way of connecting state and society is to trace state structures back to class forces. As they suggest, much of the agricultural state serves class interests. The Extension Service has worked primarily with the most affluent farmers, whom its agents view as "modern" producers most likely to adopt new methods.[50] The scientific research apparatus of the USDA and the land-grant colleges has had close ties to agribusiness, which has been the ultimate beneficiary of its achievements.[51] Most farmers are unable to retain any gains from improved technology because of the "technological treadmill." Individual farmers are compelled to adopt new technologies, because those who do not cannot compete effectively with those who do. But because demand for most commodities is inelastic, lower production costs are translated into lower prices for consumers, higher rents for landowners, or increased profits for intermediaries such as processors and supermarkets. Thus, the initial innovators are the only farmers who actually benefit.[52]

Class analysis of the agricultural state is least accurate for the part of it that was most involved in proposing and planning production control: the economic experts organized around the Bureau of Agricultural Economics (BAE). Internal dynamics of professionalization, rather than external class forces, led to the formation of agricultural economics as a discipline and to the creation of the BAE. Henry C. Taylor and his acolytes followed a model of academic organization developed at the University of Wisconsin. They first gained recognition for agricultural economics as a distinctive discipline in the land-grant colleges and then brought their discipline into the USDA. In 1922, with the help of a committee of outside economists, the agricultural economists attained policy supremacy within the USDA, defeating rivals in agronomy and marketing. The BAE was established, and Taylor, as its chief, was given direct access to the secretary of agriculture.[53]

The agricultural economists pursued professional goals even when these goals brought them into conflict with the big cotton producers. The BAE's correct prediction that cotton prices would drop in 1927 led southern members of Congress to insert language into subsequent appropriations acts that prohibited funding for cotton price forecasting.[54] During World War II, southerners in Congress mobilized against the BAE's plans for a postwar conversion program that would have allowed cotton prices to fall to world levels and shifted land and labor to other crops. They also criticized the BAE for supplying the Office of Price Administration with data that was used to support a 1946 price ceiling on cotton. Another target of southern conservatives was the BAE's 1944 study of Coahoma County, Mississippi, which drew on rural sociology and recognized the racial oppression of the plantation economy. A 1942 study of California's Central Valley prompted similar complaints from large fruit growers and from the district's congressional representative. These controversies ultimately led to congressional restrictions on BAE activities and to the departure of the BAE's controversial chief, Howard Tolley, "a man who had commitments growing out of his responsibilities as a scientist and whose work as an economist had led him away from [members of Congress's] agrarian philosophy."[55] One member frequently in conflict with the philosophies of the BAE and its successor, the Economic Research Service, was Mississippi Representative Jamie Whitten, whose seat on the House Appropriations Committee made him a powerful friend for planters to have.[56]

Another way Gilbert and Howe connect the AAA to class forces is by arguing that protests by family farmers made government intervention necessary. This is also the retrospective view of Harold F. Breimyer, an agricultural economist in the AAA's Program Planning Division.[57] Farm protests achieved quick results from state governments and private companies: local actions aimed at preventing foreclosures won suspension of foreclosures by nine midwestern states and by many insurance companies, and strikes against milk distributors also met with some success.[58] At the national level, though, protest at most contributed to a vague sense among policymakers that something should be done. Protesters' demands for legislation guaranteeing farm prices that would at least cover production costs did not move Hoover's farm policy away from the Federal Farm Board, nor did they move Roosevelt's farm policy away from the AAA. Cooptation of the mainstream farm groups—the peak associations and the cooperatives—into each program helped to insulate the national government from the effects of protest.

Gilbert and Howe emphasize the impact of the protests sponsored by the Farmers' Holiday Association, a radical, Iowa-based offshoot of the Farmers' Union. Yet the Holiday Association received only a scattered and sporadic mass response to its October 1933 call for a general farm strike to win passage of a program including federal refinancing of farm mortgages, nationalization of banking, and cost-of-production legislation. Several frightened governors responded favorably to the Holiday Association's demands, but Roosevelt, Wallace, and other federal officials, who did not have to maintain local order, denounced the strikers' proposals as regimental, illegal, and unsound. The strike did prompt Roosevelt to announce that the government would buy gold to lower the value of the dollar, indirectly raising farm prices. This was an important move, but given the collapse of the international economic system, Roosevelt might well have taken this first step away from the gold standard even without the impetus of the farm strike. Tellingly, when Milo Reno, the founder of the Holiday Association, was dying in 1936, he did not boast of what had been accomplished but expressed his disappointment at farmers who "would not cooperate to the extent that their problems might be solved."[59]

Implementation

The original version of Poulantzas's theory makes the very "French" assumption that there will always be a centralized, bureaucratic administrative apparatus capable of managing economic interventions on behalf of the capitalist class as a whole. Pre–New Deal episodes of state expansion did not create any such institutions for government intervention in industry. Theodore Roosevelt and other Progressive-era presidents attempted to expand administrative capacities beyond those of the nineteenth century "state of courts and parties," but their efforts were often frustrated by congressional resistance.[60] The industrial requirements of World War I were met by the ad hoc solutions of the War Industries Board, which relied on business executives for leadership and on trade associations for administration. With the end of the war, the WIB was dissolved. The WIB's most enduring organizational legacy was the myth of smooth business-government cooperation and coordination without conflicts of interest, all under the authority of Bernard Baruch. The myth of the WIB would be exploited by NRA Administrator Hugh Johnson, a WIB veteran, and by other New Dealers.[61]

The most logical source of expertise for industrial policy, the Department of Commerce, had been a decentralized combination of transplanted bureaus since its creation in 1903. As secretary of commerce from 1921 to 1928, Herbert Hoover was mostly unsuccessful in his attempts to reorganize the department. Hoover's Department of Commerce was an "adhocracy," as the WIB had been earlier and as the NRA would be later. Hoover's "associationalism" encouraged administrative development within industry, through the formation of trade associations, more than it enlarged the department's own capacities.[62]

In 1933, therefore, no part of the national government could provide the administrative apparatus the NRA would need to make and enforce hundreds of industrial codes regulating wages, working hours, prices, and production practices in every sector from steel and automobiles to textiles and consumer services. Because state capacities for industrial policy had never really developed in the United States, the NRA could not be autonomous in the Poulantzian sense. The NRA was not a centralized organization of experts acting in the interests of capitalists as a class; it was instead a conglomeration of capitalists using state authority to act in their own interests. An administrative apparatus was created from scratch through the emergency recruitment of business executives. The code authorities to which code enforcement was delegated typically replicated the distribution of power among firms within each sector. The NRA's administrator, General Hugh Johnson, tried to overcome his problems through a combination of patriotism, bluster, and misapplied wartime analogies. He lasted only till October 1934.[63] The absence of administrative capacities also made it difficult for the Roosevelt administration to build the public works funded under Title II fast enough to get the economy moving or to coordinate the public works program with the NRA regulatory codes.[64]

Though the necessary administrative capacity was not available for the NRA, the state organization developed in the land-grant colleges and the USDA since the Civil War provided such administrative capacity for the AAA. The land-grant system was the source of agricultural economics, which synthesized economic theory and practical knowledge in a way that had no industrial parallel. Unlike other economists, or the leaders of the earlier agricultural education movement, the agricultural economists were not doctrinaire adherents of laissez-faire. "To be sure," Breimyer recalled, "in those days most respectable economists quoted Marshall and Taussig, and anyone who dabbled in farm programs was déclassé. Nevertheless, then as now a few brave souls went against the tide."[65]

Agricultural economists exercised more policy influence than did economists studying other sectors.[66] Their research infrastructure had no counterpart within or even outside the federal government. "From 1933 through the 1960s," two economists noted, the USDA's

capacity to perform "in-house" analyses of complex economic programs on short notice has been almost unique among federal agencies. . . . The U.S. Bureau of Agricultural Economics . . . was a thoroughly professional research organization, with good equipment and ample clerical, stenographic, technical, and junior professional personnel to carry out the research plans of the senior agricultural economists.

Comparable facilities for quantitative and empirical research in other fields of economics were quite rare until the 1950s.[67]

The USDA as a whole was more centralized than other cabinet departments, and its secretary enjoyed exceptional reorganization authority. In both respects, the Agriculture Department was a contrast to Commerce.[68]

As Poulantzas might predict, the AAA was not captured by the farmers it regulated; it acted with autonomy. The AAA did not have to rely solely on farmers governing themselves because agricultural economists could help implement the policies they had previously advocated. Gilbert and Howe acknowledge that implementation of production control required the administrative capacities provided by the agricultural economists but see the agricultural economists as less important to the AAA than were representatives of agribusiness such as Chester Davis (who replaced George Peek as administrator) and Cully Cobb (head of the cotton section).[69] Though both Davis and Cobb were journalists, Peek himself had been president of Moline Plow. Executives from processors of agricultural inputs (for example, Moline Plow) and outputs (for example, the giant grain companies) represented capitalist agriculture even more than large commercial farmers did, for processing, which relies on wage labor, is more capitalist than farming per se, in which family production has survived into the 1990s.[70]

Nonetheless, the agricultural economists, who wanted to carry out production controls, defeated Peek and the processors, who favored export marketing, in the major internal battle of the AAA. Export marketing, as proposed in the McNary-Haugen bills, promised to expand demand for farm commodities and thus for the processors' products and services; production control, in contrast, reduced demand for processing and was financed by a processing tax. Even though farmers as well as processors preferred it to production control, export marketing was rejected as public policy. Peek was forced out of the AAA; Davis, his replacement as administrator, had been Peek's subordinate in the campaign for McNary-Haugen but had converted to production control in 1932.[71]

McClellan identifies Peek's marketing policy with present accumulation, and he associates production controls, which he suggests were more likely to yield stable world markets, with future accumulation. Peek's defeat is thus presented as the resolution of a latent contradiction of capitalist accumulation that had been incorporated within the state.[72] This "explanation" demonstrates the extent to which McClellan follows Poulantzas in assuming that state officials will be able to act in the long-term interests of capital. Again, the comparison with the NRA shows that this assumption is unwarranted. Moreover, it is not so clear that the triumph of production control did facilitate future accumulation. The impact of the AAA was to contract accumulation among processors, whose volume of operations was restricted, and among industrial capitalists, whose wage bill was raised by the higher price of food. And market-oriented critics of state intervention have argued that in the long run, New Deal programs hurt the farmers themselves: artificially high prices have caused them to lose world markets, and dependence on government has robbed them of their traditional self-reliance.[73]

Consequences

Had the NRA simply failed to achieve industrial recovery, it would have been no worse for American capitalism than any of the other New Deal programs whose macroeconomic impact was also disappointing. But the NRA was actually dysfunctional. The Poulantzian state is supposed to organize capitalists and disorganize workers; the NRA did the reverse. Industrial capitalists' conflicts over the content and administration of the NRA codes created divisions within and between sectors. Meanwhile, Section 7(a), accepted by industry as the price of codification, stimulated trade union organization and strikes. Disputes over Section 7(a) were resolved in labor's favor with passage of the Wagner Act in 1935. The new legislation defined company-controlled unions, which had grown even more rapidly than trade unions under Section 7(a), as an unfair labor practice.[74] If, as Poulantzas sometimes hints,[75] any outcome short of proletarian revolution is defined as functional for capitalists, then the consequences of the NRA were functional. By such other standards as trade union membership, strike volume, managerial autonomy, and labor's participation in the party system, industrial capitalists were worse off after the NRA and the Wagner Act than they had been in 1933.

Levine identifies several of the consequences of the NRA that are most relevant to Marxist theories of the state. She points to its unintended legacies of capitalist disunity and labor militancy.[76] Unlike instrumentalists or elitists who search for the monopoly-capitalist/corporate-liberal genealogy of the Wagner Act, Levine argues that capitalists resisted the shift in U.S. labor policy. Even after the Wagner Act was passed by Congress and approved by the Supreme Court, capitalists were unwilling to recognize trade unions.[77]

To fit these important points within a Poulantzian frame, Levine uses several strategies. Her most instrumentalist explanation is that the NRA was dysfunctional because capitalists were disorganized at its origins.[78] The problem with this argument is that in 1933 industrial capitalists were better organized than industrial workers, who nonetheless were able to benefit from New Deal programs—most of all, by using these programs to overcome the collective action problems that had kept them disorganized. Moreover, Poulantzas's theory *assumes* that capitalists are disorganized; that is why the state must act as their factor of cohesion.

At other times, Levine agrees with our argument that what doomed the NRA was a lack of state capacity for industrial policy, but she asserts that this absence can be explained in class terms. If the state lacked the preexisting capacity to effectively regulate industry in the interest of monopoly capital, then it must have been the case that before the New Deal, monopoly capital, "while dominant within the economic sphere, had yet to secure political dominance."[79] This is an odd conclusion about the pre–New Deal period, when monopoly capitalists were personally well represented in government and claimed virtually uncontested ideological hegemony. Both aspects of capitalist influence were symbolized by Andrew Mellon, who dominated fiscal policy as the twelve-year secretary of the treasury and developed the trickle-down theory to legitimize reduction of progressive wartime taxes.[80]

Levine's most frequent—and most Poulantzian—explanation for the outcome of the NRA is that its very failures were functional for capitalism, resolving the organic crisis that had produced the Depression with a new structure of accumulation: "The concatenation of executive reorganization and monopoly capital's adjustment to industrial unionization provided the conditions for the unchallenged political hegemony of monopoly capital, and thus the foundation for a new political and economic order in the post–World War II years."[81] Industrial workers mobilized, but their militancy was diffused once labor unions were incorporated into an "unequal structure of representation."[82] The administrative shortcomings of the NRA stimulated Roosevelt's efforts for executive reorganization, as did the intracapitalist conflicts that grew out of the NRA and were voiced in the Temporary National Economic Committee (TNEC) antimonopoly hearings. Reorganization made the state more functional for monopoly capital, even if monopoly capitalists joined other fractions of capital to oppose the Roosevelt reorganization program.[83] The apparent disarray of New

Deal industrial policy thus had a coherent logic after all: the logic of capital accumulation.[84]

This analysis imposes the coherence of functional outcomes on the industrial New Deal by misattributing labor's postwar quiescence to the Wagner Act. By the 1950s, unions of industrial workers did reach an implicit accord with their capitalist employers, trading workers' residual controls over the work process for fringe benefits and for pay increases tied to inflation. But this outcome reflected developments after the Wagner Act, including conservative victories in the 1938 congressional elections (which led to formation of the anti-CIO Smith Committee), implementation of a special wartime labor policy, the strike wave of 1946, the Taft-Hartley Act of 1947, and a series of Supreme Court decisions that reinterpreted national labor laws in ways that favored employers.[85] The immediate impact of the Wagner Act was to make industrial workers more militant. The expansion of workers' right to organize and the competition to organize them that erupted between the AFL and the breakaway CIO increased union membership. Unions struck more frequently and employed effective new tactics such as the sit-down. Communists, who were particularly active in developing and using the new weapons, achieved their peak influence between the passage of the Wagner Act in 1935 and the Nazi-Soviet Pact of 1939.[86]

Levine also overstates the success of Roosevelt's reorganization efforts. The 1937 Brownlow Committee report, the source of Roosevelt's reorganization plan, proposed to enlarge the president's powers as chief executive by establishing positions for six executive assistants, revising the merit system, reforming government accounting and auditing, making the National Resources Planning Board a permanent agency for central planning, and moving all independent agencies into functionally appropriate cabinet departments, including new departments of public works and welfare. The Reorganization Act of 1939, passed after the defeat of a stronger bill in 1938, gave the president only the six administrative assistants and the power to submit administrative reorganization proposals, subject to legislative veto. Roosevelt quickly used his new reorganization powers, but the results fell short of the Brownlow Committee vision of a consolidated national government.[87]

The most important consequence of the 1939 legislation was the eventual creation of what became the presidential "counterbureaucracy," but even this was as much a product of later developments as a creation of the New Deal. The administrative assistants grew into the modern White House staff, and Roosevelt used his reorganization authority to create the Executive Office of the President, including the staff as well as several executive agencies. Under Roosevelt, however, the size and power of the White House staff remained limited, as in the original conception of the Brownlow Committee. The real takeoff period came during the Truman administration, when the staff became larger and more powerful, the National Security Council and the Council of Economic Advisers were established within the Executive Office, and the recommendations of the first Hoover Commission supported stronger presidential management. The size and influence of the White House staff and the Executive Office were also expanded as part of President Nixon's strategy to bypass and control the regular bureaucracy, which Nixon considered hostile.[88]

Levine's application shows how the late-Poulantzian concepts of class struggle within the state and unity through conflict can be rendered compatible with the most dysfunctional outcomes short of socialist revolution. The trick is to connect dysfunctional policy outcomes with later developments that were more functional for capitalist accumulation. Because the AAA came closer to relative autonomy than the NRA did, Gilbert and Howe, and McClellan, can fit New Deal agricultural policy into class-struggle Marxism without such efforts (see figure 7).

Poulantzian theory suggests that public policies will have procapitalist consequences. If the NRA shows this is not always true, the AAA shows this is not always false. New Deal agricultural policy helped agricultural capitalists and hurt the agricultural underclasses. State intervention under the AAA and successor programs worked to overcome the economic crisis of capitalist agriculture, leaving commercial farmers better off than they had been in 1933. Overproduction was reduced, first by emergency measures such as the slaughter of baby hogs and the plow-up of surplus crops, then by acreage restrictions.[89] Prices for key commodities improved, as did the parity ratio, a measure of agricultural prosperity relative to industrial economy (see table 3).

Agricultural sharecroppers, tenants, and workers, unlike their landlords and employers, were devastated by the AAA. AAA benefits gave large cotton growers capital to mechanize, displacing labor. Along with World War II and the mechanical cotton picker, the AAA thus contributed to what has been described as the South's "own enclosure movement."[90] Landlords increased their AAA benefits by withholding the payments to which sharecroppers and tenants were legally entitled. The abuses of cotton producers stimulated organization of the Southern Tenant Farmers' Union, which demanded better treatment by landlords and by AAA officials. AAA liberals in the AAA

Legal Division and the Consumers' Counsel Division, who were sympathetic to the tenants, were purged in February 1935 after a dispute over the interpretation of tenancy provisions in the cotton contracts. Secretary of Agriculture Henry Wallace feared that if he took the tenants' side, he would lose cotton growers, southern Democrats in Congress, and key AAA officials.[91] The Resettlement Administration, later renamed and reorganized as the FSA, attempted to integrate tenants into the new agricultural order but on terms that did not organize agricultural workers as a class or challenge property rights, as the STFU had done. Its major program provided loans to the most productive workers so they could buy land and become small-scale agricultural capitalists themselves.[92]

The conflicts over the USDA purges and the fate of the FSA fit Poulantzas's concept of class struggles within the state, with the agricultural underclasses relying on lawyers, social scientists, and other professionals to advocate on their behalf. McClellan suggests that the AAA purge, like the ouster of George Peek, marked the resolution of a contradiction of capital accumulation that had been reproduced within the state. The AAA favored landlords over tenants, he argues, because doing so released surplus labor, promoting future accumulation. Even the FSA, in McClellan's view, "was a necessary component of the effective articulation of accumulation oriented farm policy," which transformed some tenants into farm owners while rechanneling discontent.[93]

Yet the concepts of contradictions and class struggles within the state fit equally well with the battles over the interpretation of Section 7(a), which ended in capitalist defeat. The National Association of Manufacturers was as conservative a force within industry as the Farm Bureau was within agriculture, and by the late 1930s the NAM had added many large firms to its original small-business membership.[94] It nonetheless failed in its campaigns against the Section 7(a) National Labor Board and the Wagner Act NLRB, whereas the Farm Bureau was able to eliminate the organizational and ideological threat of the FSA. Why did agricultural capitalists come out ahead?

Gilbert and Howe explain the regressive consequences of New Deal agricultural policy in terms of the class capacities of agricultural capitalists, represented through the Farm Bureau.[95] Before the New Deal, agricultural capitalists were in a stronger position relative to their workers than industrial capitalists were relative to theirs.[96] Agricultural workers were isolated and replaceable. Living and working on land owned by others, they lacked access to any space that was not controlled by landlords. Southern tenants, sharecroppers, and wage workers, who were at the center of political conflicts over agricultural class during the 1930s, were disfranchised, enmeshed in paternalism, and divided and oppressed by racial segregation. But what is most striking about class relations during the New Deal is that the relative position of agricultural capitalists improved, while the relative position of industrial capitalists deteriorated.

The Farm Bureau was able to shape New Deal agricultural policy in the interests of large commercial farmers because the AAA enhanced their capacity for collective action. The economic benefits of production control meant more farmers could afford to pay peak association dues.[97] By using AAA state and local committees as the nuclei for its own membership drive, the Farm Bureau was able to expand and achieve a dominant position among the farmers. This tactic was especially successful in the South, where the Farm Bureau had previously been weak.[98] The Farm Bureau's expanded southern membership linked the organization with southern Democrats, who enjoyed disproportionate power in Congress. Even during the liberal "Second" New Deal (1935–1938), southern cotton planters were able to get their workers excluded from the Wagner Act, the Social Security Act, and the Wages and Hours Act. After the bipartisan conservative coalition won effective control of Congress in the 1938 elections, the Farm Bureau and its allies could go further, crippling the FSA and restricting the purview of the BAE.[99]

Poulantzas posits that the state functions as a factor of cohesion for capitalists. The case of the AAA suggests that when the state does perform this function, its very success may have negative consequences for the state autonomy that Poulantzas also posits. By cooperating with the Farm Bureau's organizational drives, the AAA served as a factor for cohesion among agricultural capitalists. But this state-assisted cohesion enabled the Farm Bureau to more effectively challenge the autonomous agricultural state when the FSA tried to mobilize poorer farmers.[100] The Farm Bureau eventually was able to capture and use for its own organizational ends the agricultural state it had challenged. During and after World War II, geopolitical concerns led Roosevelt and Truman to reduce the importance of agricultural economists and other civilian-oriented planners in federal policy making. In the absence of presidential support for USDA autonomy, the Farm Bureau, acting in the interests of agricultural capitalists, was able to penetrate the department.[101]

An Assessment of Marxist Arguments

An instrumentalist Marxist understanding of the New Deal is plagued by the same problems as an elitist interpretation, particularly the problem of explaining how the Wagner Act could be a capitalist product when capitalists opposed it. Poulantzian theory resolves this problem by taking the autonomous state to be the source of policy change, thus shifting the focus of class analysis from who supported policy change to who benefited from it. Structuralist Marxism asserts the functional unity of the capitalist state; class-struggle Marxism differs from structuralism only in identifying working-class resistance, instead of the state, as the ultimate source of policy change in the functional interests of capital. But if the AAA was functional for agricultural capitalists, the NRA was dysfunctional for industrial capitalists. Moreover, the ability of industrial workers' unions to influence, if not control, the part of the state most directly involved in regulation of labor relations, the NRA labor boards and the Wagner Act NLRB, contradicts Poulantzas's view that it is not possible for the working class to gain power over a part of the state. Instrumentalist Marxism might attribute dysfunctional outcomes to capitalists' disorganization or their lack of class consciousness. In Poulantzas's theory, however, these weaknesses are both given and beside the point; the state is to compensate for the inability of capitalists to act in their own systemic interests.

Instrumentalism and structuralism are more useful when they are not taken to be full-blown theories of the state in themselves but are employed as the sources of ideal types for relations between capitalism and the state. Poulantzas warns against any use of ideal types to analyze the capitalist state.[102] But Paul Cammack implies such usage when he says that instrumentalist Marxism explains New Deal industrial policy and structuralist Marxism explains New Deal agricultural policy:

> As we shall see, in the case of the NIRA the legislation was requested, framed and instituted by the industrial capitalists themselves, and ditched only when an emerging autonomous state project appeared to threaten their class interests. The AAA, in contrast, organized the commercial farmers for their own collective good, and was eventually taken over by them. The cases thus demonstrate the usefulness of structural and instrumental perspectives.[103]

Cammack's empirical assessments are close to ours, as summarized in figure 7. But we arrive at our assessments from quite different theoretical premises. Any explanation of the NRA and the AAA that leaves out the Democratic party is incomplete. It is also misleading to say, as Cammack does, that the NIRA was "ditched" when it threatened capitalists; after all, the NIRA's labor provisions were replaced by those of the Wagner Act, which threatened capitalists even more! Even if we accept Cammack's characterization of each program and agree with his judgment that each case fits the story implied by an alternative Marxist approach, some more general framework is necessary to explain which version of Marxism will be appropriate when. Whether instrumentalism and structuralism represent the only ideal-typical patterns for relations between capital and the state should also be theoretically addressed. Can the state be absolutely autonomous, that is, independent from capitalists in a way that does not serve capitalist interests at some higher level? Can the state be an instrument for workers, one used by them to achieve real gains within capitalist democracy? In the absence of a framework that adequately deals with these issues, Cammack's maneuvers merely confirm the criticism of Axel van den Berg that " 'the' Marxist theory of the state now consists of a convenient grab bag of theories from which one can pick and choose as the occasion requires."[104] Such a "grab bag" is, of course, not really a theory at all; it is merely a set of interpretive labels.

The Post-Marxism of Fred Block

The independence of the state and its ability to intervene on behalf of the working class are both real possibilities in Fred Block's "Post-Marxist" model of three-way class struggle among capitalists, workers, and state managers.[105] Like the structuralists, Block views capitalists as incapable of acting in their own long-term interests by accepting, let alone sponsoring, major reforms or extensions of state power. Such changes are instituted instead by state managers, who do so in opposition to capitalist preferences and when prodded by workers. Class struggle thus pushes forward the political development of capitalism, pressuring state managers to introduce economic regulations and social reforms.

Unlike the structuralists, Block identifies specific mechanisms that usually prevent the reform process from expanding state power to an extent that threatens the capitalist system. The most important of these mechanisms is business confidence: to raise revenues and maintain their own public support, state managers need a healthy economy, which under capitalism requires continual reinvestment by the private owners of the means of production. Policies that make reinvestment unprofitable will trigger an effective capital strike against the state. Thus, even when they act only in their individual, short-term interest, capitalists can normally exercise a veto on public policy.

Under certain conditions, however, business confidence becomes a less effective mechanism of capitalist control. According to Block, the biggest spurts forward in state activity come during major crises such as wars and depressions. During depressions, the usual constraints on state policy are weakened:

> Low levels of economic activity mean that the threat of declining business confidence loses its power, at the same time that popular demands for economic revival are strong. In such periods, the state managers can pay less attention to business opinion and can concentrate on responding to the popular pressure, while acting to expand their own power.[106]

State managers may thus find it both expedient and possible to grant concessions to the working class. Yet they will do so only in forms that simultaneously increase the power of the state itself. What is more, over the longer run, especially as economic recovery resumes, the state managers will do the best they can to shape the concessions won by the working class to make them function smoothly in support of capital accumulation and existing class relations. Reforms and extensions of state power originally won through "pressure from below" can in this way become functional for capitalism and accepted by many of the very capitalists who at first strongly resisted the changes.

Using Block's model, there is no need to attribute reformist policies to the farsighted planning of the capitalist class or to the automatic intervention of a capitalist state smoothly functioning to preserve order and promote economic recovery. Instead, according to Block, these measures were made possible by a conjunction of working-class pressures with the willingness of state managers to increase their own institutional power at a time when capitalists' veto power was unusually weak. The reforms provided benefits to many members of the working class, strengthened the state in relation to the working class, and increased the state's capacity to intervene in the capitalist economy. The eventual result was that working-class struggle ended up contributing to the further development of American capitalism.

As a general sketch of the causes and eventual consequences of the Wagner Act and the Social Security Act, this is impeccable. If we stretch Block's model slightly to include commercial farmers along with workers, on the grounds that farmers were also a subordinate class within American capitalism, this sketch can also encompass the AAA. Still, it must be emphasized that at the very points where Block's class-struggle model of capitalist rationalization becomes most analytically relevant, it also becomes quite vague. What forms does working-class pressure take? What is the relationship between working-class pressure and the activities of state managers? Do the state managers only respond to pressures from below, or are they likely, under certain kinds of circumstances, to stimulate pressure from noncapitalists as well?

Another key New Deal statute, the NIRA, shows that Block's model is not just vague but, in some circumstances, perverse. Block suggests that the low level of investment in periods of economic depression reduces the importance of business confidence as a check on state initiatives. Yet in 1933, when the Roosevelt administration sought to restore prosperity, it did so by giving state authority to business. Block also hypothesizes that capitalists' veto power will be restored as the economy revives, because state managers rely on capitalist investment to sustain recovery.[107] By 1935, U.S. economic conditions were improving, though they remained far below pre-Depression levels (see table 1). Capitalists were nevertheless unable to block the Wagner Act, which almost all of them strenuously opposed. Moreover, Block's approach does not suggest any answer to the most fundamental question about the NRA: why it did not succeed. The NRA might be interpreted as an attempt at rationalization, but in practice the experiment deepened economic and social conflicts and produced unforeseen political effects.

Many of these problems result from Block's conception of state managers. In his model, state managers are actors in their own right; they respond to their own particular incentives and are subject to their own particular constraints. This approach allows Block to offer plausible and stimulating hypotheses about variations in the politics of capitalist democracies over time or between nations.[108] But Block's state managers are so abstractly rendered as to limit his model's applicability to any actual set of capitalists, workers, and public officials.

Block's abstract conception of state managers also permits a functionalist interpretation of his model that makes it little different from that of the later Poulantzas. The original formulation of Block's model is ambiguous as to whether reforms *always* become functional for capitalists in the end. He says that the pattern of capitalist reform "is not a smoothly working functional process, always producing the same result," and that "state managers have no special knowledge of what is necessary to make capitalism more rational; they grope toward effective action as best they can within existing political constraints and with available economic theories."[109] Yet Block also describes state managers as "capable of intervening in the economy on the basis of a more general rationality" than individual capitalists, and he suggests that "the more power the state possesses to intervene in the capitalist economy, the greater the likelihood that effective actions can be taken to facilitate investment."[110] Block has since disclaimed any functionalist intent and described the free market policies of the 1980s as "dysfunctional."[111]

The state managers of Block's model seek simply to maintain capitalist prosperity. In the government of the United States or in any other collection of bureaucratic agencies, roles and tasks are more sharply differentiated. No one manages the state per se; instead, officials of specific agencies carry out organizationally defined tasks in pursuit of organizationally defined missions.[112] Presidents or prime ministers may come closer than anyone else to Block's ideal. As he points out, they have electoral incentives to maintain economic prosperity: voters evaluate incumbents retrospectively, and officials whose economic performance is judged inadequate will not be continued in office.

Just as the roles of bureaucrats are products of the state organizations in which they serve, however, the roles of electoral politicians are products of the party alignments that put them in office. Partisan affiliations shape both voters' evaluations of elected officials and those elected officials' choices among alternative economic policies: Democratic voters and Democratic politicians place more emphasis on unemployment relative to inflation than do their Republican counterparts.[113] In any party system, voters who are inside the majority coalition or for whom competing parties contend are also likely to have more influence than voters for the minority party or potential voters who have been excluded from the electorate. Commercial farmers received the AAA and industrial workers received the Wagner Act because the New Deal Democratic party linked them with Roosevelt and the congressional majority. Agricultural workers, who lacked these electoral connections, were denied comparable or enduring gains despite their protests and the widely recognized justice of their cause.

Block's managers represent a more human version of the state than the instrumentalists' passive tool or the structuralists' ideal collective capitalist. The cases of the NRA and the AAA suggest that these managers act within a state that is more variegated and institutionally structured than Block's schema allows. What is more, the electoral pressures that influence certain state actors are patterned by electoral strategies and party alignments that Block omits altogether. Nonetheless, Block's conception of state managers as active participants in class struggle closes some of the gap between Marxist theories of the state and the realities of twentieth-century capitalism. If this gap can be closed further, it will more likely be through concrete, historical specification of states and parties as political organizations than through more elaborate theorization or more scrupulous exegesis of what Marx really meant.

8
Rational Choice
Actors and Institutions

Chapters 6 and 7 discussed pluralist, elite, and Marxist approaches and their implications for explaining the NRA and the AAA during the New Deal. This chapter continues our review of competing analytical frameworks with discussions of rational choice approaches. We conclude by showing how the strengths and weaknesses of all four of the approaches we have considered in part 2 follow from their conceptualizations—often incomplete and implicit—of state and party organizations. By making the institutional contexts of party and state central rather than peripheral to explanation, we not only have done a more consistent and complete job of accounting for the origins, implementation, and consequences of the NRA and the AAA; we also are able to situate the strengths and weaknesses of the alternative accounts offered by pluralists, elite and Marxist theorists, and—as we show in this chapter—rational choice analysts.

Premises of Rational Choice Approaches

Rational choice approaches begin with the individual as the unit of analysis.[1] The conception of the individual that underlies all rational choice approaches is taken from neoclassical economics. "In contemporary economic theory," Morris Fiorina explains,

> the assumption of "rational" behavior means no more than the notion that individuals engage in "maximizing" behavior. In any

200

situation the alternatives open to an individual lead to various benefits (typically in some probabilistic fashion). These alternatives entail various costs. The individual chooses so as to maximize the difference between expected benefits and costs, where there are wide varieties of theories about how to calculate those expectations.[2]

As Fiorina suggests, rational choice theorists disagree about how expected benefits and costs are calculated. They also disagree about who the politically relevant individuals are and just what it is that they maximize. Anthony Downs and William Niskanen have derived extensive equilibrium models of political action from a few postulates about the behavior of rational individuals. Scholars who are more skeptical about political equilibria, including Fiorina, William Riker, and Kenneth Shepsle, have given greater emphasis to the role of institutions, which they analyze as sets of choices made by individuals in response to their preferences and constraints. This more recent rational choice approach has been identified as collective choice, the positive theory of institutions, or the new institutionalism; it will be referred to here as rational choice institutionalism.[3] Fiorina, Riker, and Shepsle have each applied rational choice institutionalism to analyze specific historical cases.[4] Both versions of rational choice, however, fail to explain important aspects of the NRA and the AAA. They fail because they assume that institutions will be designed to fit the preferences of the individuals who create them. This assumption is compounded by a further assumption that Congress is the source of all institutional innovation within American government.[5]

Downs's economic theory of democracy is based on interaction between voters who seek to maximize their utility income and politicians who seek to maximize their votes. Individuals in both groups are rational, which for Downs means that whatever ends they choose, they efficiently select the means of pursuing them. The rational voter decides whether and for whom to vote by evaluating his or her party differential, that is, by comparing the benefits and costs implied by each party's policies. Parties, as teams of rational politicians, formulate these policies "in order to win elections, rather than win elections in order to formulate policies."[6] Downs's most famous contribution, the spatial model of party competition, follows from these postulates and the additional assumption that voters' preferences can be aggregated to form a single ideological continuum. The spatial model predicts that in a society where there are no strong class divisions and where most of the voters are located toward the middle of the ideological range, the parties will compete by taking virtually indistinguishable centrist positions. The United States, presumably, is an example of such a society.[7]

This focus on the relationship between voters and parties makes the state unproblematic. For Downs, the ruling party is the state; he fuses the two with the European term, "government." Since the party in power has selected positions that maximize its vote, once in office it simply carries these out. There is thus no possibility that the state may lack the capacity to implement party policies, as in the case of the NRA. There is also no possibility in Downs's model that the state may pursue goals contrary to those of the governing party, as may have happened when Republicans inherited a bureaucracy shaped by the New Deal and the Great Society.[8]

William Niskanen's theory of representative government focuses on the bureaucratic agencies that Downs takes for granted. The maximizing behavior that drives Niskanen's model is that of bureaucrats seeking to expand their budgets.[9] Of course, in a representative democracy, bureaucrats cannot claim public money by themselves: funds must be appropriated by a legislature, and services are expected in return. But the legislature's budgetary review process is typically inadequate, because the bureau is a monopoly provider of its service and legislators lack "the incentive or opportunity to obtain information on the minimum budget necessary to provide this service."[10] Bureaucrats can thus effectively determine their own budgets, subject to the constraint of supplying the expected output. The result is that spending is higher than optimal and inequitably allocated. Parties, the linchpin of Downs's analysis, do not play an important role in Niskanen's model. In making budgeting decisions, legislators respond to the preferences of their constituents, among whom the salient division is by demand for government services. The minority of voters with a high demand for services, Niskanen suggests, is able to dominate both political parties as well as the media.[11]

The shared weakness of the models proposed by Downs and Niskanen is that they assume—and thus do not specify—particular institutional environments. These institutional environments orient the actions of their politicians and bureaucrats. Downs's image of two parties meeting at the center of the ideological continuum is a reasonable approximation to the party system that emerged after the New Deal. By the 1950s, the Democrats and Republicans were contending for control of Congress and the presidency and had reached a near-consensus on such key issues as the Cold War, the Social Security system, and NLRB supervision of labor-management cooperation in industry.[12] This pattern of party politics, however, was very different from that of the 1920s, under which ethnocultural issues were paramount and the Democrats seemed to have become a permanent minority party.[13] Relatively close competition within a system based on issues of state intervention in the economy, which Downs takes as a given in a society like the U.S., is thus only one possible pattern of electoral politics. Downs's model would cause us to overlook the fundamental question of how politics gets organized along these particular lines of conflict.

Similarly, Niskanen may be right that officials generally seek more funds for their agencies.[14] Niskanen's abstract economic framework assumes agencies with no distinctive ethos, organizational history, or capacities. This theory leaves unexplained which agencies are assigned to provide which outputs. Niskanen's model would thus cause us to miss the importance of various patterns of administrative and economic organization.[15]

The organizational contexts that Downs and Niskanen take as given have become the explicit concern of rational choice institutionalism, which seeks to derive institutions from the action of rational individuals. Kenneth Arrow's general possibility theorem states that under any fair method of aggregating individual preferences into collective majorities, outcomes will depend on the order in which choices are made.[16] William Riker draws from Arrow's theorem the conclusion that democratic politics is characterized by disequilibria: any result is unstable because a different decision-making process would produce a different result. Political outcomes therefore do not depend on majority preferences but on what Riker calls "heresthetics," the artful use of speech by individuals who structure the decision-making process to generate the result they want. In several of the cases discussed by Riker, however, such a strategy was only effective in the context of a specific institutional setting, such as the U.S. Congress, or a specific party alignment, such as the system of the 1850s.[17]

The centrality of institutions to democratic politics is emphasized by Kenneth Shepsle, who also sees direct majority rule as producing disequilibria but suggests that equilibrium solutions are possible when decisions are delegated to institutions; political equilibria are thus "structure-induced" rather than "preference-driven." Relatively stable institutional rules determine the order in which choices are made and thus which outcomes will be produced. "If institutions matter," Shepsle says, "then which institutions are employed becomes a paramount concern."[18] The creation or reform of particular institutions is explained by the behavior of individual political actors seeking to attain their individual goals. Thus, Shepsle and Barry Weingast treat the congressional committee system as a rational adaptation to the problem of cooperation among autonomous, reelection-seeking individual members with different constituencies and policy concerns.[19]

Critiques of rational choice have typically focused on the implications of its conception of rationality.[20] Applying rational choice notions to the NRA and the AAA as historical cases points toward other problems. Rational choice approaches cannot explain much about the origins, implementation, or consequences of the NRA and the AAA because they fail at aggregation, that is, at connecting the rational individuals they assume to the collective institutions within which those individuals act. Since Downs and Niskanen take particular institutional contexts as given, their approaches cannot say anything meaningful about how particular configurations of state and party organizations come into place. Rational choice institutionalism posits a functional process that matches institutional forms to individual ambitions. This process requires an evolutionary mechanism to ensure that anyone who does not act in rational pursuit of self-interest is punished. Stanley Kelley summarizes this premise best: "Yet, just as firms that do not engage in the rational pursuit of profit are apt to cease to be firms, so politicians who do not pursue votes in a rational manner are apt to cease to be politicians."[21] Similarly, Riker says, "The political world selects for people who want to win politically; that is, those who do not want to win are more likely than others to lose and thus be excluded form political decisions."[22] Shepsle suggests the biological analogy of "the mechanism of environmental suitability or natural selection that permits genotypes to prosper or decline and phenotypes to increase or decrease their presence in the gene pool."[23]

Rational choice institutionalism is thus premised on the assumption of historical efficiency that March and Olsen describe as characteristic of microeconomic models and their application to politics: "An efficient historical process, in these terms, is one that moves rapidly to a unique solution, conditional on current environmental conditions, and is thus independent of the historical path."[24] But is politics so ruthlessly efficient? As Herbert Hoover learned in 1932, election outcomes are often determined by macroeconomic conditions outside a candidate's control.[25] More important, politicians who depart from vote-maximizing behavior are not always defeated by challengers who conform more closely to the rational ideal. Effective political organizations or representational styles may provide officials with enough slack to win reelection even as they pursue policy goals or institutional ambitions that do not correspond to constituent demands.[26]

It follows that political innovation is not necessarily efficient: politicians will introduce new policies and institutions that do not improve their chances of meeting electoral goals, and they will not always be punished for doing so. Moreover, as March and Olsen point out, if adaptation is not instantaneous, some apparent survivors will always be on their way out.[27] At any given time, the political environment will thus include politicians who have not adapted to new conditions, for example the anti–New Deal Democrats of the 1930s. One of them, Senator Carter Glass of Virginia, told "an irate constituent from Lynchburg who wondered if Glass were aware of strong support for the NRA in that city . . . 'I have not troubled myself to find out what the people of Lynchburg think of the N.R.A. I know perfectly well what I think of it.' "[28] Senator Glass's attitude—that his own views were more important than his constituents' preferences—may not have maximized his vote. But neither did it keep him from getting reelected.

An even more dubious assumption that Congress dominates American politics may not be intrinsic to the rational choice approach. Yet many of the leading rational choice analyses of American political institutions do exaggerate congressional power. The assumption of congressional dominance is particularly marked in rational choice studies of regulation. Congressional committees, this literature argues, delegate exactly as much authority to regulatory agencies as serves individual members' electoral interests, while maintaining complete control through various oversight mechanisms. Committees are thus understood as principals, bureaucratic agencies as agents.[29] Both the National Industrial Recovery Act and the Agricultural Adjustment Act delegated authority to the executive branch; indeed, the *Schechter* decision invalidating the NIRA remains the key precedent for judicial action against legislative delegation.[30] Both acts, however, originated with Roosevelt and his advisors, not with Congress.

Rational Choice and the New Deal Interventions

Within the framework of rational choice institutionalism, whatever happens in American politics happens because Congress wants it, and whatever Congress wants must in some way promise to improve members' prospects for reelection. The unwarranted assumptions of congressional dominance and political efficiency limit the utility of rational choice institutionalism in explaining the NRA and the AAA. Figure 8 summarizes our evaluations, which can now be spelled out for the analysis of the origins, implementation, and consequences of the NRA and the AAA.

	NRA	AAA
Origins	+	-
Implementation	?	?
Consequences	?	+

+   accurate
-    inaccurate
0   mixed
?   indeterminate

Figure 8. Rational choice institutionalism
and the New Deal

Origins

The most extensive application of rational choice institutionalism to
the New Deal is John Mark Hansen's work on farm group access to
Congress.[31] Hansen's central political actors are reelection-seeking legislators, for whom parties and interest groups are alternative sources of
information about constituent attitudes. In Hansen's model, legislators
will grant access to interest groups when two conditions are met. First,
legislators must come to believe that interest groups offer competitive
advantages over parties or other information sources. This occurs
when electoral results suggest the salience of interest groups' issues.
Second, legislators must be convinced that these issues are recurring
and thus will affect the results of future elections.

During the pre–New Deal period, Hansen argues, interest groups
displaced parties as the primary influences on congressional decisions
about agricultural policy making; farm groups testified at congressional hearings more frequently and were received more sympatheti-
cally. This shift occurred because the continuing agricultural depression convinced legislators their contacts with farm groups would be
enduring, while partisanship seemed to provide little electoral security. In Hansen's terms, midwestern Republicans "granted access" to
farm groups after the elections of 1926. Because the farm groups were
weakly organized in their region and because the price of cotton remained high through most of the 1920s, southern Democrats remained
more oriented to their party than to the farm groups until the early
1930s, when the severity of the Depression and the resulting political
agitation made them more willing to grant access.

Hansen describes his goal as "an analytic history of interest group
access in agriculture" rather than "a comprehensive history of agricultural price support policy."[32] Yet interest group access is only worth

studying to the extent that it tells us something about policy outcomes, and Hansen assumes that to explain patterns of access is also to explain patterns of policy making. Thus, he presents the Agricultural Adjustment Act as a congressional response to the preferences of the farm organizations, "the capstone of the farm lobby's ten-year battle for farm relief."[33] But even if we accept Hansen's theory of access and his assessments of how much access different members of Congress granted to different interest groups at different times, there remains an explanatory gap between access and policy.

The McNary-Haugen bill and the "three-headed monster" of 1932 each demonstrate how large this gap can be. The McNary-Haugen bill, based on proposals by George N. Peek and Hugh S. Johnson, would have established a corporation to buy farm surpluses (thus maintaining high domestic prices) and dump them abroad at low world prices. By 1927, the major farm organizations (the American Farm Bureau Federation, the National Farmers' Union, and the National Grange) had united in support of the bill. Since farm groups had gained access to midwestern Republicans but not to southern Democrats, by that time, the theory of access would lead us to expect that congressional Republicans were more likely to support McNary-Haugen. Such was the case for the first three versions of the bill, but the 1927 and 1928 bills, the fourth and fifth, passed Congress with support from both the agricultural blocs. The southerners shifted after the export program was revised to include cotton on favorable terms.[34]

After President Coolidge vetoed the McNary-Haugen bill in 1927 and again in 1928, the farm groups gave grudging support to Hoover's 1929 Federal Farm Board. When the general economic collapse caused the failure of the Farm Board, the peak associations returned to McNary-Haugen or other export schemes.[35] The views of the farm groups were perfectly mirrored in Senator McNary's "three-way bill" of 1932, also known as the "three-headed monster." This bill gave simultaneous authorization to the McNary-Haugen equalization fee, still favored by the Farm Bureau; to the export debenture plan, a variant of the McNary-Haugen Plan favored by the Grange; and to guarantees that farm prices would at least equal the cost of production, favored by the Farmers' Union. All three of the national farm organizations agreed to disagree over which form of farm relief was best and supported the bill. Although the farm groups had gained access to both Democratic and Republican members of the House Agriculture Committee by this time, the three-headed monster was blocked by Agriculture Committee Chair Marvin Jones in the House and killed with a recommittal vote in the Senate.[36]

The three-way bill did not include any provisions for production control, and bills that would have enacted production controls received little support from Congress or the farm groups before the election of 1932. Production control became a viable alternative when Roosevelt brought Rexford Guy Tugwell and M. L. Wilson into his 1932 campaign as farm policy advisors. Wilson, an agricultural economist, had been a zealous advocate of the Domestic Allotment Plan of production control for several years; Tugwell had been converted at a University of Chicago conference sponsored by Wilson and other agricultural economists. Tugwell and Wilson subsequently helped to draft Roosevelt's proposals. Farm interest groups followed the president-elect, not the other way around; these organizations did not endorse production control until after Roosevelt's victory. Farm Bureau President Edward O'Neal then chaired a secret meeting of representatives from the peak associations and the major cooperatives with Tugwell and other Roosevelt advisors. All the farm leaders except John Simpson of the Farmers' Union agreed to endorse "adjustment payments" to farmers who reduced their 1933 acreage.[37] Further meetings in January and March 1933 helped consolidate support and work out the details of the AAA. After Roosevelt gave these recommendations his approval, the Farm Bill that became the Agricultural Adjustment Act was drafted by Department of Agriculture officials.[38]

Thus, the Agricultural Adjustment Act passed in 1933 did correspond to the preferences of the Farm Bureau and the Grange, but only as those preferences had been altered by the new administration. As Hansen points out, interest groups played a similar, secondary role in the AAA amendments of 1935 and the replacement legislation of 1936 and 1938: to ease congressional approval, the farm organizations were mobilized in support of measures whose substance had already been determined by the Department of Agriculture.[39]

The Farmers' Union did not accept production control in 1933. Throughout the legislative process that led to the AAA a sizable bloc within the Senate pushed for the Farmers' Union solution to the agricultural depression: cost of production legislation. Hansen assesses interest group access by how group representatives are treated at congressional hearings; John Simpson, the Farmers' Union president, "consumed more time than any non-governmental witness" during the Senate Agriculture Committee hearings on the Farm Bill.[40] By a 47-to-41 vote, the Senate went against the administration and attached a cost-of-production amendment to the bill. After the House rejected such provisions, the Senate voted 48 to 33 to remove the language from its version, but some farm-state senators wanted to continue the fight.

Senator Burton Wheeler, a Montana Democrat, said, "We ought to have the courage to stand up and express our own views and not take the dictation of some professor down there in the Department of Agriculture."[41]

If the AAA did not mark the culmination of interest group access, neither did it mark the end of party influence over agricultural policy. Jones, the House Agriculture Committee chair, was so unenthusiastic about production control that he refused to sponsor the administration farm bill that became the Agricultural Adjustment Act. When Jones did endorse a revised version of the bill, he cited party unity and deference to the president.[42] The very fact that farm policy remained open for congressional decision making in 1933 reflected partisan considerations: Democrats, including then-Speaker John Nance Garner, had opposed the three-way bill in 1932 because they did not want to pass any legislation that might allow the Hoover administration to claim credit for improving farm conditions.[43] Partisan affiliation was also related to support for the AAA among the general public: a December 1935 Gallup poll found that 70 percent of Democrats but only 8 percent of Republicans favored the program.[44]

House and Senate floor votes on the act show the interaction of party with region (see table 7). Southern Democrats gave overwhelming support to the bill; the region's only two Republicans, both representatives from eastern Tennessee, also voted for it. Though members from the Midwest, according to Hansen, had been open to farm group influence longer, they did not give the bill as much support as their more recently accessible southern colleagues. Midwesterners from both parties supported the bill in similar proportions. Western representatives split along mildly partisan lines, but western senators from both parties gave the bill nearly unanimous backing. The most partisan region was the northeast, which was also the least agricultural section and hence the least likely to grant access to the farm groups. Northeastern Democrats were the president's most loyal supporters in the Senate, where they voted against amendments that would have weakened the AAA and against amendments such as cost of production that would have made the program more radical than Roosevelt wanted it to be.[45]

Hansen's theory of interest group access, together with his assumption (typical of rational choice approaches) that Congress dominates policy, suggests that export marketing should have become the basis for New Deal agricultural policy. But that is not what happened. The source of the New Deal transformation of American farm policy was the president, not Congress, and the change was contrary

Table 7. Party and sectional voting on the Agricultural Adjustment Act

Senate

	Democrat		Republican		
Region[a]	Yes	No	Yes	No	Index of Likeness[b]
Northeast	6	0	1	11	8.3
South	20	2	0	0	—
Midwest	6	2	9	4	94.2
West	15	0	5	1	83.3
Total	47	4	15	16	56.2

House

	Democrat		Republican		
Region[a]	Yes	No	Yes	No	Index of Likeness[b]
Northeast	57	7	9	55	25.0
South	106	4	2	0	96.4
Midwest	79	12	23	12	78.9
West	30	1	5	6	48.7
Total	272	24	39	73	42.9

[a] Northeast: Connecticut, Delaware, Maine, Maryland, Massachusetts, New Hampshire, New Jersey, New York, Pennsylvania, Rhode Island, Vermont, West Virginia; South: Alabama, Arkansas, Florida, Georgia, Kentucky, Louisiana, Mississippi, North Carolina, Oklahoma, South Carolina, Tennessee, Texas, Virginia; Midwest: Illinois, Indiana, Iowa, Kansas, Michigan, Minnesota, Missouri, Nebraska, North Dakota, Ohio, South Dakota, Wisconsin; West: Arizona, California, Colorado, Idaho, Montana, Nevada, New Mexico, Oregon, Utah, Washington, Wyoming.

[b] The index of likeness is equal to the difference between the percentage in each party voting for the measure, subtracted from 100. An index of 100 would indicate no difference in voting proportions between the parties. An index of 0 would indicate complete dissimilarity, that is, each party voting with perfect unity on opposite sides. See Lee F. Anderson, Meredith W. Watts, Jr., and Allen R. Wilcox, *Legislative Roll-Call Analysis* (Evanston, Ill.: Northwestern University Press, 1966), pp. 44–45.

to the previously expressed preferences of the farm organizations. The congressional-interest-group policy network switched to production control only after this policy innovation was adopted by the Roosevelt campaign and after Roosevelt won the general election. Party ties, which linked congressional Democrats with the president-elect, did not conflict with interest group connections; as president-elect, Roosevelt eliminated any such conflict by moving farm interest groups into his party (and policy) coalition.[46]

Hansen's conception of policy making as acquiescence to interest groups actually fits the NRA better than the AAA, because in the industrial case state intervention did accord with interest group demands. With the National Industrial Recovery Act, trade associations such as the Cotton Textile Institute and peak organizations such as the

National Association of Manufacturers achieved their goal of legalizing cartel arrangements by revision of the antitrust laws.[47] As with the AAA, though, a focus on congressional incentives is misplaced. The process of drafting the NIRA was dominated not by Congress but by the executive branch.[48] A group led by Assistant Secretary of State Raymond Moley and Hugh Johnson submitted a draft bill for industrial recovery to Roosevelt; another group headed by Senator Robert Wagner and Undersecretary of Commerce John Dickinson presented a different proposal. At Roosevelt's direction, the competing drafts were merged. Senator Wagner, who sponsored the administration's recovery bill, played an important role in the development of the NIRA, but he did so by stepping outside the normal legislative process to become Roosevelt's "chief planner" in Congress.

Another reason why the presidency, not the Congress, should be seen as the source of the NIRA is that the substance of the legislation did not match congressional preferences. As we showed in chapter 3, the administration's frantic drafting of a recovery bill was a response to the Senate's approval of a measure Roosevelt (and business groups) considered unacceptable: Senator Hugo Black's bill prohibiting shipment in interstate commerce of goods produced by workers employed for more than a thirty-hour week. The final bill accepted milder versions of the wage and hour limitations favored by Congress but incorporated them within a code structure that gave business groups the relaxation of the antitrust laws that they could not previously obtain from Congress. Because the policymakers who drafted the NIRA believed their own misleading analogy between the Depression and World War I, the form of administration created for the new powers of industrial regulation owed more to the precedent of the War Industries Board than to the electoral interests of either Roosevelt or congressional Democrats.[49]

Implementation

Rational choice institutionalism finds the genesis of public policies in the desire of individual politicians to maximize their utility functions. This usually means that policy origins are traced to the efforts of members of Congress to improve their chances for reelection. If institutions always worked as intended, the consequences for policy implementation would be clear: institutions would serve the individual interests of the officials who set them up. Fiorina, however, rejects as naive "the principle of intentionality: whatever exists was deliberately planned by some pivotal actor." Similarly, Gerald Gamm and Kenneth Shepsle suggest that rational foresight is not necessarily perfect and consequences may be unforeseen.[50] Under these more realistic assumptions, policy implementation becomes indeterminate. Rational choice institutionalism thus suggests no meaningful predictions about the implementation of the AAA or the NRA (see figure 8) and cannot explain why the AAA succeeded while the NRA failed.

Implementation of both programs depended on state capacities that had developed before 1933, along paths that would not necessarily correspond to the needs of New Deal policymakers. The match between program demands and administrative capacities proved closer in agriculture than in industry. Previously developed administrative capacities allowed the AAA to conquer the inherent problems of central planning. Agricultural experts from the land-grant colleges or the United States Department of Agriculture (USDA) carried out the tasks of production control by formulating, disseminating, and supervising programs for specific commodities.[51] Their ability to do so was noted by Edwin G. Nourse, Joseph S. Davis, and John D. Black, who wrote in 1937:

> While agricultural adjustment bills were under consideration and during the early life of the Adjustment Administration, it was freely predicted that, whatever the economic merits of the adjustment plan, the whole undertaking would break down because of purely administrative difficulties. Actual events have not borne out these dire predictions. In fact, the AAA stands out as one of the best administered of New Deal agencies.[52]

Implementation of AAA production controls required not only that plans be made but also that farmers comply with those plans. The AAA met both requirements. Margaret Levi defines "quasi-voluntary compliance" with tax policy as self-enforcement, whereby most taxpayers consent to pay because they expect to share benefits provided by the state. This self-enforcement by most subjects allows rulers to focus their coercive efforts on the relatively small number of violators.[53] The AAA likewise mixed coercion and consent to achieve widespread, quasi-voluntary compliance. Local implementation of production control posed the classic problem of collective action: every farmer stood to gain by nonparticipation, enjoying the benefits of higher prices while continuing to grow as much as was expected to be profitable. The AAA's solution built on producer groups to create what was called "economic democracy." The allocation of quotas to individual farmers and the checking of compliance with adjustment contracts, as well as the mobilization of social pressures to cooperate, were left largely to the farmers themselves, organized into local producer committees. For cotton and tobacco farmers, supplemental legislation made production control compulsory by imposing taxes on production above quota levels. Participation in other commodity programs was voluntary, but when participating farmers exceeded their quotas, their benefits were reduced or their excess produce was destroyed.[54]

Combining administrative capacities with quasi-voluntary compliance, the AAA worked. Participation rates were high, production decreased, and farm prices went up.[55] The National Recovery Administration made an even more ambitious effort to induce compliance, but the program was doomed by the absence of necessary administrative capacities.

The essential task of the NRA was to write codes that would govern wages, hours, and working conditions in the different industrial sectors. Primary responsibility for this work rested with the very firms to whom they applied, organized into code authorities that often built on previously established trade associations. The public interest was represented within the code authorities by administration-appointed members, and the codes were reviewed by NRA deputy administrators. Both groups of officials demonstrated that a

> problem in public personnel administration more difficult than that of securing industrial specialists for code drafting and code enforcement can scarcely be imagined. To secure at once persons well versed in the intricacies of the industry and yet free from bias and questionable interests was a difficulty of the first magnitude.[56]

The AAA could resolve this dilemma by drawing on a preexisting set of experts, autonomous from and trained to plan for entire sectors of agriculture. Unable to draw on any similar group of industrial planners, the NRA's only alternative to blatant conflicts of interest was to appoint a business executive from one industrial sector to regulate a different sector. Such appointees knew little about the industry to which they were assigned.[57]

Early delays in a codification process that depended on the initiative of the industries themselves led to enactment of the President's Reemployment Agreement and the Blue Eagle campaign. The Reemployment Agreement of July 1933 was a blanket code eliminating child labor and setting wage and hour standards, to apply until an industry had drafted its own code. To achieve widespread compliance, NRA Administrator Hugh Johnson fell back on his experiences with the War Industries Board during World War I. Consumers were urged to patronize only those businesses displaying the insignia of the Blue Eagle, indicating that they met NRA standards.[58] The tremendous publicity campaign sped up the code-making process, but haste only exacerbated the NRA's administrative incapacities. Walter Lippmann complained that "a kind of breathless anxiety that certain definite results had to be achieved on a particular day," such as Johnson's promise that the blanket code would create six million jobs by Labor Day, 1933,

> inspired the N.R.A. administrators to attempt much more than they could effectively handle. Instead of taking up the problem of making codes for industries in the order of their importance, achieving a series of definite reforms where they were most urgently needed, the N.R.A. jumped for the blanket code and got itself entangled in a maze of inconsequential matters pertaining to little industries and little shops, to industries which are relatively in good condition, and left itself all too little energy and time for considered action on the industries that most needed attention.[59]

The NRA, then, was created without the administrative capabilities that would have been necessary to make it work, and the Blue Eagle campaign to mobilize quasi-voluntary compliance, backed by the sanction of government-sponsored boycott, was more a symptom than a cure. Coverage was high, with 557 codes reaching most of American industry, but noncompliance was widespread and enforcement was haphazard.[60] Conflicts escalated within sectors, between sectors, and among representatives of business, labor, consumers, and government. Both the Roosevelt administration and its original business sponsors abandoned an agency unable to carry out its basic tasks and therefore unable to meet its political and economic goals. By 1935, the NRA was an example of institutional collapse, which rational choice approaches cannot easily explain. As Stephen D. Krasner says, "From an actor-oriented utilitarian or functional perspective, unambiguously dysfunctional behavior presents an anomaly."[61]

Consequences

Rational choice institutionalism accurately predicts the consequences of the AAA for agricultural class relations but does not seem to yield determinate predictions about the consequences of the NRA for industrial class relations (see figure 8). Rational choice institutionalism would lead us to expect that industrial and agricultural policies have winners and losers and that these consequences be related to electoral support. Through political institutions, rational choice approaches suggest, the powerful carry out policies that work to maintain their power.

It follows that the consequences of public policy are to enhance the position of the economic interests that can do the most for state officials. In political systems where state power is maintained through competitive elections, the groups that will benefit are the groups that can help officials secure votes. Payoffs to supporting groups can take the form of governmental subsidies, paid for by others. Supporting groups can also receive payoffs through state action to organize them and to create disorganization among opposing interests.[62]

The NRA and the AAA each produced changes in prices and wages that benefited some interests at the expense of others. Each program simultaneously transformed patterns of class organization. By 1936, the class actors who had gained the most, industrial workers and agricultural capitalists, had become the twin foci of the New Deal Democratic coalition. What rational choice institutionalism cannot explain about the New Deal's winners and losers is who was which. Franklin Roosevelt's desire for reelection did not dictate any particular class alliances; no one best strategy for electoral success was apparent at the time or can be inferred in retrospect. Though Roosevelt's position was usually decisive, measures regulating class relations were often initiated by members of Congress who more directly represented specific class interests. Thus, Senator Robert Wagner's urban liberalism reflected his New York working-class constituency,[63] whereas Representative Marvin Jones's agrarian ideology and his sponsorship of farm tenant legislation reflected the small-holding agriculture of his Texas Panhandle district.[64] Even members of Congress, however, have some freedom to decide which constituents they will represent and how.[65] New York's other senator, Royal Copeland, was a Tammany Democrat like Wagner, but from 1934 till his 1938 death in office Copeland consistently opposed the New Deal that Wagner championed.[66] Democratic Senator Carter Glass of Virginia was more responsive to low-wage industrial producers opposed to the NRA than to economic interests who supported the program, perhaps because he himself came under the codes as a newspaper publisher.[67]

Rational choice institutionalism seems compatible with many different patterns of class conflict in industrial sectors and so cannot distinguish the actual results of the program from other possible outcomes. From 1932 to 1936, Roosevelt offered several different responses to class conflict in industry, each of which proved compatible with electoral success. Which position, then, was determined by the goal of electoral success that Roosevelt undoubtedly held? During the 1932 campaign, Roosevelt's appeals to industrial workers promised jobs, unemployment insurance, and regulation of wages and hours.

Though Roosevelt had supported collective bargaining and curbs on antilabor injunctions as governor of New York, issues surrounding union organization received little attention in the national campaign.[68] The 1932 Democratic platform did not even contain any reference to unions.[69] Roosevelt's nomination and election received stronger support from the agricultural South and West than from his own industrial Northeast.[70] In 1934, after Roosevelt had equivocated on two key issues of labor organization under Section 7(a), the Democrats gained nine seats in the House and another nine in the Senate. These gains gave northern Democrats temporary numerical superiority over the southerners who normally dominated and thus created an unusually prolabor Congress.[71] After Roosevelt belatedly endorsed the Wagner bill that became the National Labor Relations Act of 1935, industrial workers became a major component of his electoral majority. Roosevelt received organizational support from Labor's Non-Partisan League, formed by the new Committee for Industrial Organization, and the class-based voting that would characterize the New Deal party system emerged.[72]

The electoral incentives emphasized by rational choice approaches do lead us to expect that the AAA would enhance rather than challenge the dominance of commercial farmers within agriculture. What Rexford Guy Tugwell said about Secretary of Agriculture Henry A. Wallace could apply just as well to Roosevelt: "His base was in agriculture and tenants did not vote."[73] Disfranchised and impoverished, tenants, sharecroppers, and farmworkers could offer little to the Democratic party and received little in return. AAA cotton administrators allowed plantation owners to withhold subsidy payments from tenants and to meet quotas through evictions. Efforts by the AAA's Legal Division to enforce tenant rights led to its "purge" in February 1935.[74] The Farm Security Administration of the later New Deal, though activist enough to arouse the ultimately fatal opposition of midwestern Republicans and southern Democrats, effectively defined the agricultural underclasses as poor people or as potential farm owners, not as workers. FSA field personnel did not support the organizational efforts of the Southern Tenant Farmers' Union.[75]

Yet even in this case, an explanation based on electoral self-interest is incomplete. The Roosevelt administration *might have* pursued a strategy of empowerment for tenants, sharecroppers, and farmworkers, particularly after the 1934 elections, when southern power within the Democratic party was at an ebb. After all, industrial workers were also disorganized and outside the electoral system before the New Deal, and in 1965 a later Democratic president would mobilize his own exceptional congressional majority for an attack on the southern political and economic order. That the Roosevelt administration did not attempt to lead such an attack reflected not only electoral incentives but also administrative and legislative concerns. The AAA cotton program was formulated with governmental resources, but it probably could not have been implemented without officials who had been plantation managers or had been trained in the conservative land-grant colleges of the South. More obviously, even so liberal a New Dealer as Rexford Tugwell recognized the need to cooperate with the conservative southerners who chaired key congressional committees.[76]

An Assessment of Rational Choice as Applied to the New Deal

The contributions and limitations of rational choice institutionalism are summed up in Fiorina's statement that in his model of regulation, "the focus is on the legislators, whom I treat as maximizing actors rather than passive registers of outside demands."[77] Unlike the socially determinist approaches of pluralism, elitism, and Marxism, which emphasize groups, elites, or classes, respectively, rational choice institutionalism has emphasized the extent to which policy outcomes can reflect incentives internal to institutions as well as external demands. This approach can help us understand why some political institutions seem to produce inefficient and inequitable policies.[78] But because rational choice approaches reduce institutions to machines for individual utility maximization and because the utility that is maximized is too narrowly interpreted as the reelection prospects of members of Congress, the explanatory power of these approaches is also less than their proponents would claim. Rational choice institutionalism fits the origins of the NRA better than it fits the origins of the AAA and fits the consequences of the AAA better than it fits the consequences of the NRA. Some rational choice institutionalists have recognized that it is untenable to assume that policies always work, but rational choice institutionalism without this assumption predicts little about the implementation of either the NRA or the AAA.

Rational choice theory presents itself as so universal that it applies to contexts as different from the contemporary United States as ancient Rome.[79] This theory therefore cannot itself explain why it should fit some cases better than others.[80] A more historically oriented institutionalism would suggest that rational choice explanations do not always work because state structures and party coalitions have properties as collectivities that shape—but do not derive from—individual rational action and that these properties should be studied, not deduced.[81] Even those versions of rational choice that claim to take institutions seriously, then, do not take institutions seriously enough.

The New Deal as Institutional History

The NRA and the AAA are consistent with the most general premises of pluralist, elitist, Marxist, and rational choice theories of politics. Organized groups of capitalists, farmers, and workers did play important roles in the formulation and implementation of public policies. Elites did enjoy personal and financial connections to top officials and their key advisors. Class struggle did break out, from the halls of Congress to the docks of San Francisco, as well as in Michigan auto factories and Mississippi cotton fields. And Franklin Roosevelt and other politicians usually did act in their own electoral self-interest.

Each of these theories, however, is inconsistent with specific aspects of the origins, implementation, and consequences of the NRA and the AAA (see figures 5 through 8). Structuralist Marxism fits the AAA well but fits the NRA much less well; of the four approaches, it is the only one that is not accurate about the origins of New Deal industrial policy. Pluralism provides the best guide to the NRA and the worst guide to the AAA. So many policy alternatives would in some way help politicians get reelected that rational choice approaches are indeterminate with regard to much of the New Deal. Similarly, so many policy patterns are influenced by the proposals or needs of *some* elite that any number of alternative policy scenarios are compatible with elitist approaches.

The strengths and the weaknesses of these approaches derive from their conceptions of state structures and party alignments. These conceptions are summarized in figure 9. Rational choice approaches treat state structures as functional and party alignments as flexible. Marxist approaches also treat state structures as functional but treat party alignments as fixed. In pluralist approaches, state structures are permeable and party systems are flexible. The elitist state is permeable; the elitist party system is fixed.

Both rational choice and Marxist approaches portray the state as functional, that is, as an organization whose structure is determined by its purposes. In rational choice theory, the purpose of the state is to serve the interests of reelection-seeking politicians, most especially members of Congress. In Poulantzian Marxism, the purpose of the state is to serve the interests of the dominant capitalist class. State form follows state function in either approach.

State Structure

		Functional	Permeable
Party Alignment	Flexible	Rational Choice	Pluralism
	Fixed	Marxism	Elitism

Figure 9. State structures and party alignments
in theories of capitalist democracy

Functionalist explanations are not necessarily false.[82] But functional explanations are incomplete without some "reverse causal links from consequences back to structures."[83] Rational choice models are driven by the notion that politicians seek reelection. Issues, events, and economic conditions will threaten, with varying severity, to prevent attainment of this goal. The forward causal link is that government policies and organizations will help politicians get reelected despite these difficulties. The reverse causal link is that those politicians will then select or reinforce the policies and organizations that contribute to their reelection, as against those that do not.[84] The reverse causal pattern of structuralist or class-struggle Marxism works in a similar way; ideology and the state, originally products of the capitalist system, continually reproduce it.

Functionalist explanations of politics also require state autonomy. For the state to act in ways that reelect reelection-seeking politicians or maintain capitalism, that state must enjoy some degree of independence from interest groups and elites, whose demands may be selfish or shortsighted. The agricultural state, built on the expertise of agricultural economists, was to a significant extent autonomous from affected interests—with regard to price and production levels if not class relations. Thus, rational choice and Marxism are both consistent with the consequences of the AAA.

Pluralist and elitist approaches, in contrast, assume that the state is not autonomous. Pluralists view the state as permeated by interest groups. Elitists view the state as permeated by elites. In their theories, state structure changes with changes in group or elite demands, not functional needs. Capitalists in pluralist theory act as members of organized groups such as the Chamber of Commerce and the trade associations. Capitalists in elitist theory act as corporate liberals. Either label—and either approach—is compatible with the business origins of the NRA. The National Industrial Recovery Act thus suggests that there are at least some cases where public authority is thoroughly penetrated by private interest.

State organizations can be functional or permeable but are not necessarily either. The precise nature of specific institutions is determined by patterns of development that are never instantaneous and are rarely historically efficient. These patterns of development are path-dependent—that is, they are processes in which "initial choices, often small and random, may determine future historical trajectories."[85] In turn, prior institutional routines, not just optimization processes, determine responses to new situations.[86] Thus, the origins, implementation, and consequences of public policies are limited by institutional development. The challenges of the New Deal expansion of state intervention in agriculture and industry were met by reliance on preexisting routines. The AAA could act on the routines of the USDA–land-grant network. The NRA could only act through the routines of private firms and existing trade associations.

Just as we can distinguish theories of politics by their conceptions of state structures as functional or permeable, we can distinguish theories by their conceptions of party alignments as flexible or fixed. Rational choice and pluralist approaches depict electoral politics as flexible: parties continuously adjust their positions to the preferences of discrete individuals (rational choice) or groups (pluralism). In Anthony Downs's spatial model of party competition, an example of rational choice theory, this adjustment is an equilibrium process. For David Truman, a leading pluralist, parties are "protean" alliances of interest groups.[87]

Elitist and Marxist approaches treat party alignments as fixed. Fixed in this context does not mean static but rather unchanging relative to a given set of social cleavages. For elitists and Marxists, what rational choice or pluralist theorists depict as real alternatives are only choices between different fractions of the ruling class or between different conceptions of ruling-class interests.[88] If there are no real choices, there is no real competition for votes. In the absence of competition, there is no need for parties to continuously adjust to the preferences of the electorate. Party alignments can change but only in response to underlying social change.

Rational choice, pluralism, elitism, and Marxism are all "sociological" approaches to politics, "in which the parties found in a political system reflect directly the social base in which they operate." "Institutional" approaches, in contrast, see organizational intermediation as the source of incongruity between party systems and social structures.[89] To understand what was fixed and what was flexible about American politics during the 1930s, we need to take the latter view and examine the roles of politicians and party organizations seeking to construct favorable party alignments.

Amidst all the tumult of the Great Depression and the New Deal, some aspects of American politics were unchanged. White Protestants in New England, for example, remained Republicans; "As Maine goes, so goes Vermont," Jim Farley remarked after the election of 1936.[90] Southern whites remained Democrats. Southern blacks remained disfranchised. Had the partisan affiliation and participation rates of all social groups remained the same as in the 1920s, though, there would have been no national Democratic majority. The dynamic aspects of New Deal politics demonstrate the interaction of social change and electoral strategy. If midwestern farmers went from voting Republican as drys to voting Democratic as victims of the agricultural depression, it was because Roosevelt worked to accomplish the shift. If immigrants from eastern and southern Europe became Democrats, it was because the Democratic party and the trade unions succeeded in mobilizing them. If northern blacks switched from heavily Republican in 1932 to majority Democratic in 1936, it was not only because they were hit hard by the Depression and welcomed New Deal relief but also because the Democratic party convinced them to say "farewell to the party of Lincoln," despite the administration's weak civil rights stand.[91]

Pluralist, elitist, Marxist, and rational choice theories of politics all derive their analyses of historical processes from general explanatory frameworks that are big, abstract, and complex. "Institutional theories of politics," in contrast, explicitly consider "how historical processes are affected by specific characteristics of political institutions."[92] As we spelled out in part 1 of this book, we have taken an institutional approach, focusing on the impact of America's historically evolved state and political parties on policy making for the economy during the New Deal. Our approach stands in clear contrast to the functionalism, ahistoricism, and social reductionism of the other major theoretical approaches to U.S. politics that we have explored in this part. We have discussed theoretical and empirical disagreements in detail so readers can judge for themselves which approach seems most convincing.

9

Conclusion

The New Deal and the Next Deal

American industrial and agricultural policies demonstrate the impact of policy on policy or, more specifically, the influence of the policy past on possibilities for policies in the present.[1] Past and present policies are connected in at least three different ways. First, past policies give rise to *analogies* that affect how public officials think about contemporary policy issues. Second, past policies suggest *lessons* that help us to understand the processes by which contemporary policies are formulated and implemented and by which the consequences of contemporary policies will be determined. Third, past policies impose *limitations* that reduce the range of policy choices available as responses to contemporary problems.

The relationships of contemporary U.S. policies for industry and agriculture to the industrial and agricultural policies of the early New Deal, the NRA (National Recovery Administration) and the AAA (Agricultural Adjustment Administration), illustrate each of these kinds of connections. Analogical conclusions about the NRA made policymakers more dubious about state intervention in industry, while similar conclusions about the AAA convinced some policymakers that state intervention in agriculture worked. Arguments about contemporary U.S. industrial and agricultural policies are thus also arguments about the NRA and the AAA, and vice versa. In more analytical terms, each policy provides lessons that emphasize the importance of state and party organizations in the policy process. The historical characteristics of these institutions explain why the policies that became the NRA and the AAA were selected over competing policy proposals and why they had such contrasting results. The failure of the NRA imposed limitations on future policymakers by encouraging the disaggregation of business organization and the mobilization of a larger and more militant labor movement. Finally, the success of the AAA imposed different limitations on future policymakers for agriculture: the dominance of a conservative peak association, the American Farm Bureau Federation, and the rigidification of policy decisions made during the New Deal, in response to the conditions of the Great Depression.

The next part of this chapter elaborates on the concepts of analogies, lessons, and limitations as distinctive kinds of connections between past and present policies. The two sections that follow identify some analogies, lessons, and limitations of the NRA and the AAA for contemporary industrial and agricultural policy. The conclusion offers some more general observations, based on the comparison between the two cases of administrative intervention in the national economy.

Analogies, Lessons, and Limitations

Public officials are aware of the relevance of policy history. Unfortunately, they generally invoke the past so simplistically that it might be better if they focused their attention solely upon current events. History is misused not only in defending policy choices, which might be expected, but in the actual choosing. Reasoning by analogy to recent or familiar cases, policymakers give little consideration to specific historical contexts and how they might compare with present circumstances. Cause and effect are linked by unexamined, often fallacious presumptions, such as *post hoc ergo propter hoc* (after this, therefore because of it). The results of such thinking include some of the most notable blunders in domestic and international affairs.[2]

The beliefs of policymakers about the clear-cut "lessons" of history may be influential even when those beliefs are inaccurate or irrelevant. One way past policies exercise influence is thus by generating policy analogies, transmitted beliefs about the "lessons" of earlier episodes. Such analogical lessons may be positive or negative: "policy," Hugh Heclo says, "invariably builds on policy, either in moving forward with what has been inherited, or amending it, or repudiating it."[3] The NRA, for example, was influenced and justified by the apparent success of the War Industries Board in coordinating American industry during World War I.[4] The NRA that built on the WIB provides contemporary policymakers with the sole peacetime example of coordinated industrial policy in American history.[5] Its failure has thus been used to argue against current proposals for state intervention to revive industrial competitiveness.

Although history is often misused in the policy process, valid lessons can be drawn. Drawing true lessons from the past requires more careful attention to similarities and differences between past and present cases.[6] Lessons should also be drawn from more carefully specified causal explanations, which means that they require theory.[7] The argument of this book is that a historical-institutionalist approach based on state and party organization explains the origins, implementation, and consequences of the NRA and the AAA better than competing approaches. If this argument is correct, such an approach should also enable us to derive insights from the New Deal for contemporary policy. The lessons presented here involve state capacities, party alignments, and unintended consequences, all of which are more important to the fate of a policy proposal than that proposal's avowed intentions or intrinsic merits from some normative standpoint.

A recurring lesson of policy history is path dependence: what paths are available now depends on what paths were chosen before. Economists have outlined formal conditions of technological competition under which "insignificant circumstances become magnified by positive feedbacks to 'tip' the system into the actual outcome 'selected.' The small events of history become important."[8] The policy process exhibits similar properties. "Small," contingent events can have big impacts on policy choice. At any future time, opportunities for policy change are limited by the effects of these earlier choices. The success of the AAA, for example, reflected a fortuitous combination of administrative developments dating back to the Civil War with electoral conditions peculiar to the Democratic party of the 1930s. By its success, the AAA set in place the most fundamental components of modern American agricultural policy: price supports, acreage controls, and support for large-scale, capital-intensive production. Proposals for policy change that go beyond tinkering with the existing system necessarily attack that system at its historical basis.

The NRA and Contemporary Industrial Policy

The industrial policy debate that began in the early 1980s offers several parallels to the policy debate preceding the New Deal. In both periods, analysts who claim the industrial economy is fundamentally sick offer remedies that are rejected by others who declare American industry fundamentally healthy.[9] One proponent of industrial policy is a prominent capitalist (Gerard Swope in the 1930s, Felix Rohatyn in the 1980s and 1990s), whose participation makes it clear that some version of industrial policy has some business support.[10] The revision of antitrust laws enjoys broader business support. The laissez-faire rhetoric of Republican administrations does not prevent them from engaging in extensive state intervention. But efforts to construct a more cohesive industrial policy (for which antitrust revision is only a starting point) and the institutions that would accompany it are attached to the fortunes of the Democrats.

Participants in today's debate can be grouped into three broad camps: "hards," "softs," and "antis."[11] Felix Rohatyn, Lester Thurow, Robert Reich, and *Business Week* were among the first advocates of a hard industrial policy in response to what they feared was deindustrialization and decline.[12] These writers favored sectoral interventions to support sectors targeted as prospective winners in international economic competition. Labor and capital would be removed from sectors with bleaker prospects, but the effects on workers and communities would be less harsh than if the market were allowed to carry out the same process. Sectoral interventions would be carried out by governmental organizations with New Deal–like forms; Otis Graham has used the generic terms *Forum, Council,* and *Bank* to describe the ones most commonly proposed.[13] The Forum, like the National Industrial Recovery Board of the NRA's last year, would be a tripartite body in which representatives of business, labor, and government meet to recommend policy directions.[14] The administrative Council would be modeled after, or at least inspired by, Japan's fabled Ministry of International Trade and Industry (MITI), but it would also resemble the National Recovery Administration. The Bank would explicitly be an attempt to revive the New Deal era's Reconstruction Finance Corporation, which had been organizationally separate from the NRA and established earlier, under Hoover.

Opponents of industrial policy included supply-side conservatives, whose rival program of lower marginal tax rates provided another echo of the pre–New Deal years.[15] Critics on the Left denounced industrial policy as corporatist and called for more democratic means of economic renewal.[16] But the most politically damaging opposition came from the normally liberal (that is, Keynesian) Brookings Institution, most notably from Charles L. Schultze, who had been budget director for Lyndon Johnson and chaired the Council of Economic Advisers for Jimmy Carter.[17] Backed by other Brookings experts, Schultze argued that the U.S. was not deindustrializing or uncompetitive; that current problems could be corrected with better macroeconomic policies, in particular by devaluing the dollar; and that MITI had played a negligible role in Japan's economic achievement. Schultze also made political claims: that the state was incapable of choosing sectoral winners and losers and that any attempt at industrial policy would inevitably turn into one more source of pork-barrel benefits to privileged special interests.

In between the hards and the antis and less vulnerable to the antiindustrial policy arguments were proponents of a soft industrial policy. Amitai Etzioni rejected a MITI-type central agency for many of the same reasons cited by Schultze but supported nonsectoral forms of state intervention, including support for research and development, infrastructure improvements, and incentives for capital investment.[18] Much of the soft agenda is also endorsed by proponents of harder approaches, whose views have generally softened as their hopes were frustrated. Even antis can accept some soft proposals, as long as they are called something besides industrial policy.

What can an analysis of U.S. industrial planning in the past tell us about today's debates? Investigation of the NRA cannot help us choose among contradictory assessments of current economic trends or among different views of the importance of MITI and its European equivalents to their nations' economic growth. But such analysis can help us to evaluate claims such as Schultze's about the fit between industrial policy and U.S. government, as well as claims about the NRA itself. Analysis of the NRA can also help us to understand the relationship between industrial policy debate and electoral politics.

Reference to the NRA in the industrial policy debate has been made almost exclusively by the softs and the antis, who cite its failure as an indication of the likely results of future sectoral intervention.[19] Analogical thinking about the NRA has thus given rise to skepticism about the possibility that national microeconomic policy could ever contribute to economic growth. Is the skepticism justified? Is this policy analogy a legitimate policy lesson?

One valid lesson to be drawn from the NRA experience highlights the importance of state capacities. Under the National Industrial Recovery Act, governmental authority was effectively delegated from Congress, via the president and the NRA administrator, to code authorities established to govern the various industrial sectors. The business representatives who served on the code authorities proved themselves quite capable of determining sectoral policies—in their own interests. The officials who were charged with representation of the public interest and with coordination of the 557 different codes were less adequate to their tasks. The results varied somewhat from code to code, depending on the configuration of firms and the previous level of trade association development for that sector. But the codes did not add up to either a cohesive industrial policy or a positive contribution to economic recovery.

The economic problems of today are not the same as those of the Great Depression, nor are they as severe. And none of the industrial policies suggested today follows the exact model of the NRA, with code authorities based on trade associations empowered to regulate wages, hours, and working conditions to expand domestic demand. Contemporary proposals are typically more focused on promoting technological innovation and production for export. They do, however, follow the NRA in relying on private firms, individually or in association, to make fundamental decisions about sectoral policies.[20] As much as or more than the NRA, contemporary industrial policy proposals would require governmental oversight to achieve coordination and protect the public interest. Any industrial policy would thus demand, in Heclo's words, an administrative apparatus characterized by "purposiveness, self-monitoring, bargaining acumen, and procedural predictability."[21]

Does the national government have the necessary capacities? No. The U.S. still lacks the state capacities necessary for industrial policy. Today as in the 1930s, the likely location of state capacity for sectoral intervention would be the Department of Commerce. Under presidents Ronald Reagan and George Bush, the Commerce Department proved more ready than other federal agencies to abridge the principles of free trade and free markets in the interests of American industry. Commerce has not, however, been able to assert its supremacy over the Office of the U.S. Trade Representative or other organizational rivals.[22] In 1983, the Reagan administration proposed a merger of the Commerce Department and the Trade Representative's Office into a Department of International Trade and Industry. As with many reorganization proposals in U.S. political history, nothing happened.

Commerce has also lacked the statistical resources that would be needed to carry out an industrial policy. The Carter administration proposed but did not act on the establishment of a Bureau of Industrial Economics, and the Reagan administration actually cut the collection and dissemination of economic statistics.[23] A former official recalled, "with respect to the Lockheed case, the Penn Central case, and the steel decisions[,] that in virtually every case we had great difficulty in getting unbiased, objective information at the level of the Executive Office of the President."[24]

To the extent that the United States has had a de facto industrial policy, an important component of it has been military security policy, which means that the Defense Advanced Research Projects Agency (DARPA) has been the closest equivalent to an American MITI, sponsoring the development of leading computer technologies and the organization of the Sematech semiconductor consortium.[25] Yet the disadvantage of a defense-based de facto industrial policy is that it is driven by noneconomic needs. High performance in military situations, regardless of cost, is the goal; commercially marketable spin-offs are only bonuses.

The public organizations that have most actively sought economic growth through industrial policies have not been at the national level but in state and local governments.[26] Subnational industrial policies originated as "smokestack chasing," that is, efforts to lure factories (and offices) from other jurisdictions. Southern states were particularly active in offering low taxes, low wages, and, with help from Section 14(b) of the Taft-Hartley Act, a nonunion workforce. One of Governor Bill Clinton's aides described the recruitment staff that Clinton inherited as "entertainment directors for visiting industrialists. . . . They had these nice cars and jobs and expense accounts, and they liked taking the boys out to the bars and tellin' 'em why they ought to come to Arkansas."[27] Under the leadership of governors like Clinton and Massachusetts's Michael Dukakis, this competition, which places governments against each other in a zero- or negative-sum game, began to give way to attempts to create jobs through programs encouraging capital formation and technological innovation.

Agencies associated with this new approach to state job creation are potential sources of capacity for national-level industrial policy. The new industrial policymakers have the will to intervene. What they do not yet have is any systematic knowledge of how to do so.[28] A discipline of "industrial economics" would, at a minimum, keep policymakers from continually reinventing each other's wheels. But from where would such a discipline come? Mainstream economists, whether Keynesians or monetarists, are mostly hostile to industrial policy, as their predecessors in the 1930s were hostile to the NRA. Business schools have been accused of contributing to America's problems by teaching their students to focus on short-term profitability rather than long-term industrial development.[29] Industrial policy practitioners have scattered academic allies, including maverick economists as well as some scholars teaching in political science departments and public policy schools. They lack more regular networks and institutional homes, such as the Department of Agriculture and the land-grant colleges provided for the agricultural economists of the 1920s and 1930s.

A true understanding of what happened to the NRA, then, suggests that industrial policy requires state capacities, and the continued
absence of these capacities from the U.S. national government suggests
that a comprehensive and activist industrial policy, based on sectoral
intervention, would probably fail. In this respect, opponents of industrial policy are right. Without more appropriate personnel, the industrial policy apparatus would have to rely on conventionally trained
M.B.A.'s, who would not know how to make long-term decisions in
the public interest, or on lawyers, whose orientation to precedent, ill-
suited to industrial policy in the 1930s, would be even less appropriate
to the continual technological innovation of the contemporary world
economy. Without the relevant statistics, public policymakers would
be dependent on the data gathered by firms and trade associations and
thus would be captives of private perspectives.[30] Opponents of industrial policies are wrong, however, in asserting that governments are inherently incapable of sectoral intervention[31] or that such intervention
is inherently incompatible with U.S. political culture[32] or the U.S. political system.[33] Beginning with the AAA, sectoral intervention has
been carried out in agriculture, where the cultural and political barriers
would be even greater than for industry. This suggests that state capacity might also be built for sectoral intervention in industry.

A second lesson of the NRA, as of many other governmental initiatives, is that policies have unintended consequences. Among the
limitations that the NRA has placed on subsequent industrial policy
are its provisions for minimum wages, maximum hours, and prohibition of child labor, required features of NRA codes that were invalidated by the *Schechter* decision, reinstated by the Wages and Hours Act
of 1938, and strengthened by subsequent congressional amendments.[34]

The limitations imposed by the NRA's reshaping of interest group
politics are probably even more significant. Contemporary patterns of
interest group politics, cited by opponents as additional obstacles to effective industrial policy, are in large part products of the NRA and its
failure. William Hudson, for example, finds that

a crucial flaw in the corporatist framework of representation is the
absence in the United States of genuine "peak associations" or na-
tionwide federations representing entire economic sectors such as
labor, business, and farmers, which are characteristic of countries
like Sweden, where corporatist policy making prevails. Without
such organizations, no concrete group can realistically claim to
represent a broad sector of society.[35]

A more viable NRA might have strengthened the peak associations by involving them in tripartite executive bodies with significant policy-making authority. Instead, attempts at coordination were replaced by sector-by-sector "partial planning."[36] These programs encouraged capitalists to seek frequent legislative recourse and to mobilize at no higher level than the trade association. Thus, observers of American business organization in the 1950s and the 1960s noted the isolation and infirmity of the peak associations, the Chamber of Commerce and the National Association of Manufacturers. A more vigorous peak association, the Business Roundtable, emerged in the 1970s. Though the Business Roundtable showed some interest in tripartite bargaining as a way to fight inflation, it was mainly concerned with overturning the new "social" regulation and with opposing pro-union labor law reforms.[37]

The other major consequence of the NRA for interest group organization was the mobilization of what was for much of the postwar era a broader and more effective trade union movement. Before the New Deal, organized labor had suffered from the combined effects of government repression, open-shop campaigns, welfare capitalism, and the Depression. To the surprise of capitalists and policymakers, the ambiguous guarantees of Section 7(a) of the National Industrial Recovery Act stimulated a genuine revival of the trade union movement. This contributed to the growing breach between Roosevelt and business, which led the president to reverse his earlier stance and support Robert Wagner's 1935 labor relations bill. The National Labor Relations Act of 1935 was more permanent than Section 7(a), and it decided the two persistent questions of NRA labor policy—majority rule versus proportional representation, and the status of company unions—in favor of the trade union position.

By the 1980s, organized labor was in decline, suffering from the contraction of unionized basic industries such as automobiles and steel as well as from anti-union tactics by corporations and the White House. In this context, it is not surprising that the labor movement embraced industrial policy proposals targeting basic industry for renewal. Nor is it surprising that labor support for industrial policy had little influence on other political actors.[38] Support from a weakened labor movement was in fact a mixed blessing for industrial policy, since union influence would pose problems for any program of sectoral intervention. Even if workers were to receive adequate retraining assistance, as provided in most industrial policy proposals, the unions, to maintain their membership, might still seek to preserve the numbers of workers in autos, steel, textiles, or other "sunset industries." And if retraining was as inadequate as it has been in the past, the workers as well as their unions could be expected to oppose efforts to shift their labor, along with capital, to the sectors policy experts considered more efficient.

The consequences of the NRA for interest group organization do limit the possibilities for industrial policy today. Yet the consequences of the NRA also demonstrate that interest group politics is more malleable than we might sometimes believe. Any industrial policy substantial enough to address America's fundamental economic problems could also be expected to have a substantial impact on interest group organization. What that impact would be and whether it would make industrial policy more or less workable would depend on the details of the policy.

The details of industrial policy and whether it is ever enacted at all depend on party alignments and strategies. This is a third lesson of the NRA. Herbert Hoover, Roosevelt's predecessor and his opponent in 1932, opposed any program of sectoral intervention that went beyond his own vision of "voluntaryism." Industrial policy thus required Democratic victory. Even after Roosevelt's election, state intervention in industry was a low priority for the incoming administration. The NRA came to be only because of the emergence of a policy threat, the Black Bill for a mandatory thirty-hour work week. Roosevelt and his business supporters could not accept the Black Bill, but they also could not reject it without a substitute recovery program. Business proposals for recovery through codification became the basis for the administration program.

As the origins of the NRA would lead us to expect, conflicts over industrial policies in the 1980s and the 1990s have followed party lines. The Republicans, while opposing industrial policy per se, have pursued a de facto industrial policy, driven by national defense and amenable to rescue operations for electorally important constituencies.[39] Hard and soft versions of explicit industrial policies have issued from the Democrats. Industrial policy proposals actually began near the end of Jimmy Carter's presidency, as he faced the twin threats of a Republican opposition that had made big gains in the 1978 congressional elections and a labor-based challenge by Edward Kennedy within his own party. The high point of Carter's industrial policy was his August 28, 1980, declaration of an "Economic Revitalization Program," including a board, a bank, and tripartite committees. Carter lost the election, and the board was appointed but never met.[40]

Industrial policy then became a favorite hope for Democratic policy intellectuals seeking an alternative to Reagan's supply-side economics as the 1984 election approached.[41] The severe recession of 1982–83 made the promise of reindustrialization especially attractive. The 1984 results, however, were as devastating for industrial policy as they were for the Democratic party. Gary Hart, who championed an industrial policy oriented toward high tech, lost the presidential nomination to Walter Mondale, who gave industrial policy lukewarm and wavering support, deciding ultimately to devote more campaign attention to his promise to raise taxes. While Mondale's loss to Reagan could be attributed to matters besides industrial policy, the defeat that same year of Rhode Island's Greenhouse Compact could not be. This proposal, developed by Robert Reich's coauthor, Ira Magaziner, represented the first comprehensive industrial policy that any state had submitted for popular approval. Its rejection by an overwhelming four-to-one margin, despite support from business, organized labor, and the media, thus represented a major defeat for proponents of industrial policy.[42]

After 1984, proponents of hard industrial policies softened their views. Even the term "industrial policy" was generally dropped in favor of the less controversial "competitiveness."[43] It is in this form that industrial policy became a minor theme in the presidential campaigns of Michael Dukakis (1988) and Bill Clinton (1992). Dukakis and Clinton had both been among the "new breed" of economic development governors, and both counted Reich among their policy advisors. Clinton's economic program emphasized infrastructure improvements and investment tax credits rather than new institutions for industrial policy, though it did suggest creating a civilian version of DARPA.[44] As president, Clinton named Reich as secretary of labor and Laura D'Andrea Tyson, another advocate of industrial policy, as chair of the Council of Economic Advisers. In February 1993, Clinton proposed several measures to promote high-technology sectors, including conversion of the Commerce Department's National Institute of Standards and Technology into a civilian technology agency, manufacturing extension centers modeled on the agricultural extension program, a permanent tax credit for research and development, and government financing for a national high-speed computer network or "information superhighway." The Clinton administration also pushed DARPA toward commercial technologies and established a partnership with the auto industry to develop more energy-efficient vehicles.

Clinton did not, however, describe these measures as industrial policy.[45] With Republican help, the concept of industrial policy has become identified with much that Democrats like Dukakis and Clinton have sought to avoid: liberalism, protectionism, big government, and, in general, economic losers rather than winners. The 1992 candidate willing to endorse the most extensive industrial policy was Ross Perot, who did not face the same strategic problems as the Democrats. His economic program, unlike Clinton's, called for an American MITI to target growth industries.[46]

An analogical conclusion often glibly drawn from the history of the NRA is that government intervention in industry must fail. The valid lessons of the NRA are that the origins and outcome of sectoral intervention will reflect preexisting patterns of state and party organization and that sectoral intervention will have consequences, possibly unintended, for patterns of interest group organization. Present circumstances are not conducive to successful industrial policy, but, as the case of the AAA suggests, those circumstances might be modified.

The AAA and Contemporary Agricultural Policy

The different language used to discuss state intervention in industry and in agriculture demonstrates the contrasting analogical policy learning to which the NRA and AAA experiences have given rise. The very term *industrial policy* has been a source of controversy in America and in recent years has been dropped by its proponents. In contrast, no one would deny that the U.S. has an agricultural policy, and no one seems to object very much to calling it such. This does not meant that there is consensus over what that policy should be. It does mean that since 1933, debate has taken the form of conflicts over policies modeled on or reacting to the provisions of the AAA. Even more important, possibilities for policy change have been limited by the consequences of the AAA's success.

Supporters of industrial policy cite U.S. agricultural policy as a model for sectoral intervention. "What Americans tend to forget," Thurow says,

> is that American agriculture was not always a success story. . . . In the 1930s, agricultural productivity was far below that of the rest of the economy. American agriculture was an industrial loser—a sunset industry.
>
> After 1940, agricultural productivity grew at more than 6 percent per year and the gap between agriculture and industry quickly narrowed. The shift from failure to success depended not upon good soil or good climate or hard-working farmers—all three were there during the period of failure—but upon an elaborate industrial strategy that heavily depended upon government funds and cooperative arrangements.[47]

For members of the agricultural policy network who share this view, the AAA experience is a source of confidence that government can successfully intervene to overcome agriculture's characteristic price and income instability. Sectoral intervention, in combination with the achievements of federally sponsored agricultural research, has made American farmers the most productive in the world, since government programs to assure income security allow them to take the risks associated with technological innovation.[48] Even the more radical adherents of this view do not wish to overturn the agricultural New Deal but to extend it to smaller farmers and to farm workers. They would do so by reorienting the land-grant system and by enforcing stricter production controls with benefits targeted to family-sized farms.[49]

For opponents of state intervention, the AAA has negative overtones. From the New Deal to the present, they argue, state intervention in agriculture has wasted taxpayers' money, discouraged farm exports, and restricted property rights without doing farmers all that much good. Like the opponents of industrial policy, they argue that sectoral problems have macro-, not micro-, level causes. "It would have been better," Don Paarlberg has written,

> had our monetary and credit system been so managed that the Great Depression would have been averted. Granting the fact of the Great Depression, it would have been better to put a government check in each farmer's mailbox and avoid tampering with the market. Accepting the existence of the depression and the fact of government price-fixing and production control, it would have been better to terminate the programs with the outbreak of World War II, when the depression disappeared. We missed all of these better options and continued the programs for more than fifty years.[50]

In this view, any inherent tendencies toward instability or uncertainty in agriculture are better addressed by market solutions such as futures trading or crop insurance than by more government intervention.[51]

Analytically speaking, the history of the AAA, like the history of the NRA, shows that policy formation reflects party alignments and strategies, that policies of state intervention require state capacities, and that these policies are likely to have unintended consequences. Production control became U.S. policy because Franklin Roosevelt became president, as the nominee of a Democratic party that needed to mobilize farmers on the basis of their economic grievances rather than their ethnocultural identities. The preceding Republican administrations had resisted both production control and the McNary-Haugen plan to export the farm surplus. Herbert Hoover, who was the driving force of Republican farm policy even before he became president, condemned the USDA's Bureau of Agricultural Economics, saying in 1924, "Being naturally Socialistic in my mind they turn to Socialism as a solution."[52] Hoover's was an ideological stance, but it was also one that fit the needs of the eastern financial and industrial capitalists who dominated the Republican party. Roosevelt too rejected McNary-Haugenism, but he accepted a program of production controls that originated with agricultural economists located in or connected to the BAE. Moreover, Roosevelt was able to enlist some of the leading farm organizations in support of production control, which these organizations had previously opposed and which ordinary farmers never much liked.

Contemporary conflicts over agricultural policy also follow party lines. Each party, in power, has maintained continuity with the personnel and ideas of its earlier administrations. Thus, the USDA of the Reagan years, led by Richard Lyng, echoed the USDA of Nixon and Earl Butz, and the Nixon-Butz USDA echoed the department of Ezra Taft Benson during the Eisenhower administration. Efforts to get government out of agriculture are supported by the Republicans (including Reagan and Bush), the Farm Bureau, and a network of agricultural economists led by Don Paarlberg, Benson's chief economic advisor and a professor at land-grant Purdue University.

Support for continued state intervention in agriculture comes from the Democrats and allied interest groups and policy advisors. Three factions can be distinguished within the Democratic camp. Incremental changes in the existing system are advocated by the National Farmers Union and a network of agricultural economists whose leading figure was for many years Willard Cochrane, chief economic advisor to Agriculture Secretary Orville Freeman during the Kennedy and Johnson administrations and a professor at the land-grant University of Minnesota. This was also the perspective adopted by the 1992 Clinton campaign, which expressed confidence that "our current farm programs, properly managed, can achieve reasonable prices for producers and guarantee a safe and stable food and fiber supply for consumers."[53] Despite pressures for budgetary savings, Clinton as president acted on this view by proposing to cut only the notorious commodity programs for honey, wool, and mohair.[54] Stricter versions of supply management are backed by such "neopopulist" Democrats as Senator Tom Harkin of Iowa and Jim Hightower, the former Texas agriculture commissioner. In contrast, a network of agricultural economists around Earl O. Heady, a professor at land-grant Iowa State, would modify government controls to make them more market-oriented. In his recent work, Cochrane has moved into this group, although he remains sharply critical of Republican laissez-faire.[55]

These alliances, as well as the terms of today's policy debate, reflect the original, successful implementation of the AAA, which in turn reflected the formation of state capacity for agriculture *before* the early 1930s. Agricultural economists from the BAE and the land-grant colleges provided the capacity to plan production and prices for entire regions and crops. At the local level, extension agents worked with farmer committees to translate the plans into individual allotments. The Agricultural Adjustment Act thus built on earlier legislation: the Morrill Act of 1862, creating the land-grant colleges; the Hatch Act of 1887, providing federal support for state agricultural research stations (the source of the soil conservation measures attached to New Deal production controls); and the Smith-Lever Act of 1914, allocating federal matching funds for county extension agents. All three measures had been enacted in response to the politics and problems of their times, with no effort made to construct a foundation for future policies of sectoral intervention. Yet that is what they did. Contemporary policymakers still draw on the sources of state capacity available for agriculture in the 1930s. As in the 1930s, this capacity makes it possible for public officials to carry out a more extensive policy of sectoral intervention than could be implemented for industry.

At the same time, unintended consequences of the AAA's success include the reshaping of American farm politics and the limitation of possibilities for future policy change. The policy of production control selected by the Roosevelt administration was not the preferred approach of the farm groups, who favored McNary-Haugen or cost-of-production schemes. But Roosevelt was able to use the farm organizations, at the national level, to legitimize the administration's farm program and, at the local level, to join extension agents and other federal officials in calculating allotments and applying social pressures to noncooperators. The Farm Bureau was able to use the AAA to build its own membership base, particularly in the South. The Farm Bureau emerged from the New Deal as the most powerful of the farm organizations, linking midwestern corn and southern cotton in a conservative alliance against farm workers and, after 1940, against the Democratic party and its proposals for agricultural reform. Farm Bureau hegemony has given way in recent years to a new pattern of fragmentation as the Farm Bureau and the other general farm organizations are partially displaced by such commodity groups as the American Soybean Association and the National Pork Producers Council. The new commodity-based farm politics reflects the commodity-based organization of the USDA and the House and Senate agriculture committees, as well as the commodity distinctions written into the various farm bills, especially since 1948. The new system of farm representation (which is also more open to participation by agribusiness, environmentalists, and other outsiders) does not have the specific biases of the Farm Bureau, but neither does it promise greater coherence and coordination.[56]

The success of the AAA also limits contemporary farm policy by building into it choices of instruments and goals that were of dubious merit in the 1930s and are even more questionable today. George Peek and Hugh Johnson's 1922 proposal, "Equality for Agriculture," and the McNary-Haugen bills to which the Peek-Johnson plan gave rise would have raised farm prices to "fair" levels that gave farmers purchasing power equivalent to what they enjoyed in the base period of 1906–1915. Though Roosevelt rejected McNary-Haugenism, his administration's farm bill, which became the Agricultural Adjustment Act, set a similar objective. The goal of the 1933 act was parity, defined as farm purchasing power equivalent to that in the high-price "golden age" of 1910–1914. The term *parity* itself gained legal significance as part of the Agricultural Adjustment Act of 1938, which authorized the AAA to support wheat, cotton, and corn prices at 52 to 75 percent of parity levels. Formally, the 1938 act remains in effect; should "temporary" programs such as those of the 1985 or 1990 farm bills lapse, price supports revert to the lower levels of the 1938 legislation. Later legislation revised the parity standard, replacing the original 1910–1914 base with moving averages and allowing for changes in relative prices between commodities. The 1985 and 1990 farm bills omitted the term, although parity remained the basis for wool, tobacco, and peanut prices. The USDA still calculates parity levels for 142 commodities, and some farm groups still use the old parity language to express their demands.[57]

If the base-period standard of parity has eroded, its definition of the goal of agricultural policy as maintenance of prices has not. Actually, a better policy goal would be maintenance of farm *income*, either through expansion of the current deficiency payments (based on the difference between market and target prices) or through some system of direct transfers. An income-based farm policy would not distort the domestic market as much as price adjustment does, nor would it assist foreign competitors by setting U.S. prices at levels that cannot be sustained on the world market. There is widespread agreement, moreover, that most of the benefits of existing programs go to large, land-owning farmers. It would be hard to achieve price goals without doing so, since large producers account for a disproportionate share of crop production.[58] An income-based farm policy, in contrast, could be targeted at smaller producers, without regard for ownership status. But continuities from past price-support programs make it hard to switch to an income-oriented approach today.[59]

In rejecting McNary-Haugen, Roosevelt, like his Republican predecessors, also rejected efforts to reduce the farm surplus through export expansion. Secretary of Agriculture Henry Wallace told AAA Administrator George Peek, "My views are well known to you. It is my feeling that aside from cotton, we ought not to depend on a foreign market for any considerable outlet of agricultural commodities for some time in the future and that, with this in view, we ought to act for the moment as if we were a self-contained agricultural economy."[60] Wallace embraced the Democrats' traditional low-tariff position and supported the efforts of Secretary of State Cordell Hull to liberalize international trade, which achieved legislative success with the Reciprocal Trade Agreements Act of 1934. But as Wallace recognized, the opportunities for export solutions to the problems of American agriculture were limited throughout the 1930s by European policies that emphasized self-sufficiency, both as a response to the Depression and as a means of preparing for war.[61] Thus, in the Roosevelt administration's view, any solution to the farm program would have to adjust domestic production. As Andrew Mellon had argued in the 1920s, exporting the farm surplus would have also given an effective subsidy to European industrialists, who would be able to pay lower wages because their workers could buy cheaper food.

Instead, U.S. policy, from the New Deal on, has given an effective subsidy to foreign agriculture. In recent years, the United States has run a consistent trade surplus in agriculture, where it is comparatively advantaged, both for classic Ricardian reasons of factor endowments (the fertile soil of the Midwest) and because of national economic strategy (high agricultural productivity due to state-supported research and dissemination). Artificially high domestic prices, together with the production controls used to achieve them, prevent American farmers from exporting even more and bringing in resources that could be used to restructure industrial sectors in which the U.S. does not enjoy comparative advantage.[62] Peek, among others, warned of this at the beginning, writing in 1933 that it was "not in the interest of industry, banking, or transportation and certainly not in the interest of the farmer; that we should be drying up acreage in the United States while other exporting countries—Canada, Australia, Argentina, etc.,—were increasing theirs to fill the vacuum created by our withdrawal."[63]

Along with the goal of price parity and the restriction that this goal is to be achieved within the domestic market, the success of the AAA determined that the primary instrument of American farm policy would be production control. For most commodities, the AAA and successor programs did not control production output per se but reduced production indirectly, by reducing the input of land.[64] Robert Paarlberg has described acreage controls as the most distinctive characteristic of American agricultural policy. Other advanced industrial nations also subsidize their farmers, but only the U.S. does so by land set-asides. U.S. reliance on acreage controls reflects the administrative capacities available in 1933. Monitoring actual production was considered impractical except for perishable fruits and vegetables, which could not be held in long-term storage and thus could be regulated by marketing programs enforceable at the point of sale. For storable basic commodities such as wheat and cotton, monitoring land was practical, given that the AAA was able to draw on local land records and extension agents. The AAA combined these local forms of state capacity with the ability of farmers to keep track of what each other was doing.[65] Acreage, however, is at best a short-term proxy for total production. In the long run, farmers can continue to qualify for subsidy payments by withdrawing acreage, while expanding yield on acreage that remains in production. This behavior, although individually rational, eventually wipes out the collective reduction of output and thus any price increase achieved through production control. Moreover, since the typical methods of increasing yields have included intensive use of pesticides and chemical fertilizers, this behavior has been environmentally destructive.[66]

The AAA and successor programs have also encouraged farmers, particularly southern cotton producers, to displace labor through mechanization. New Deal subsidies and loans gave southern planters the capital with which to mechanize.[67] AAA payments were supposed to be shared with tenants, but this provision was laxly enforced, and the AAA officials (based in the Legal Section) who sided with the tenants in a related dispute were purged in February 1935. Sharecroppers and tenants, a large minority of them African-Americans, were converted into wage laborers. During and after World War II, many left the South to take factory jobs. Large numbers of people thus moved from the rural South, where they were disfranchised, to northern cities, where they were able to vote. To attract their support, the Democratic party took a more active position in support of civil rights.[68] By 1968, the agricultural economy of the South was capital-intensive and diversified, the Civil Rights Act and the Voting Rights Act had become law, and the Democrats were no longer the New Deal party of northern workers and white southern farmers.

Hybrid Vigor and the Logic of Appropriateness

The United States does not now have an explicit industrial policy to compete with Japan and the nations of the European Community, who do. Even if the United States were to adopt an industrial policy tomorrow, that policy would probably fail for lack of appropriate personnel and statistical capacities. Meanwhile, U.S. agricultural policy has raised and stabilized farm incomes, but it has also dampened exports, damaged the environment, and displaced the rural poor.

Differences in the situations facing U.S. industry and agriculture today can be traced back to the different results of state intervention during the New Deal. The AAA drew on agricultural economists from the land-grant colleges and the USDA to carry out an extensive program of production control. The NRA drew on business executives from private firms to carry out an equally extensive program of industrial codification. The AAA succeeded and survived to become the direct ancestor of contemporary farm policy, while the NRA failed and came to be seen as a negative precedent in later debates about industrial policy.

The proximate cause of the different outcomes of state intervention for agriculture and for industry was the availability of agriculture economists in the one case and the absence of comparable experts in the other. But more was involved than the presence or absence of talented individuals. In December 1935, Secretary of Agriculture Henry A. Wallace told the annual meeting of the American Farm Economic Association:

> It is an unusual pleasure to meet with men of a group which has contributed so substantially to the welfare of the United States during the past fifteen years. Many of us in this group can recall the time in 1919 when the new Farm Economics Association emerged out of its Farm Management background. There were many who wished to make it clear on the one hand that farm economics had in it much more than farm management and on the other hand that it was different in certain respects from general economics. The new organization seemed to have a hybrid vigor derived from its dual source.[69]

"Hybrid vigor" was high praise coming from Wallace, who had developed the first commercial hybrid corn and for whom experimental breeding was a lifelong hobby.[70]

The hybrid vigor of agricultural economics and its contribution to the origins and implementation of the AAA are no evidence for (or against) the intellectual validity of the new discipline. Instead, we should understand this vigor in more institutional terms. The role of agricultural economics in the AAA is evidence for the fit between the norms and career lines of the previously developed discipline and the challenges of national policymaking for agriculture. James March and Johan Olsen distinguish between a logic of consequentiality, within which action is instrumental, and a logic of appropriateness, within which action is oriented toward norms and roles that are defined and transmitted by social institutions. Both logics are "rational," in that they apply reason to the choice among available courses of action. They do so, however, by fundamentally different processes. People operating according to the logic of consequentiality consider goals and alternatives by which they can best be achieved. People operating according to the logic of appropriateness implicitly consider roles and the alternatives they prescribe or prohibit.[71] Like other professions, agricultural economics established a logic of appropriateness. The particular set of norms and roles that constituted the "practice" of agricultural economics shaped the behavior of people like M. L. Wilson and Mordecai Ezekiel, who acted as agricultural economists in developing and implementing the domestic allotment plan for production control.[72]

As Franklin Roosevelt and the Democrats confronted the agricultural depression, agricultural economists oriented to norms of appropriate action were available to perform the tasks necessary for state intervention. They were available because of a series of small events, or rather, because of the long-run consequences of the smaller aspects of a series of large events. The founding of the USDA and the Morrill Act establishing the land-grant system (both in 1862) were minor aspects of the Civil War. The creation of the state experiment stations (1887) and extension agents (1914) and the elevation of the USDA to cabinet status (1889) were minor aspects of the federal response to the populist revolt against industrialism. The organization of agricultural economics as a distinct discipline was a minor aspect of the Progressive Era movement toward professionalization. The same large events—the Civil War, populism, and professionalization—had important impacts on the industrial sectors. But those impacts did not strengthen federal administration capacities or contribute to the cumulative construction of a professional discipline of industrial economists, oriented to a logic of appropriateness that fit the needs of the NRA.

The policies of the 1860s influenced the policies of the 1930s, and the policies of the 1930s influence our possible choices today. Capitalists, farmers, workers, and politicians often attempt to draw simple analogies to past policies—analogies that lead them to make big claims about what governments and markets can or cannot accomplish. Theoretically grounded lessons about the impact of past policies on present possibilities, about the importance of small changes at past junctures, or about the logic of appropriateness are thus unlikely to seem of great practical assistance to actors caught up in current ideological debates. But as our arguments about the NRA and the AAA have shown, these are the lessons that best help us to understand the roots and fate of public policies toward the economy that have been shaped and reshaped within the institutional context of the U.S. state and political parties.

History comprehended with due attention to institutions—and the often unintended processes they structure—is a much better guide to present realities than is history invoked in the form of simple analogies. Only with this kind of historical understanding can we grasp the true choices and the actual possibilities that face American makers of public policies for the future.

Notes

Index

Notes

Chapter 1. Introduction: New Deal Interventions in Industry and Agriculture

1. Samuel I. Rosenman, comp., *The Public Papers and Addresses of Franklin D. Roosevelt*, 13 vols. (New York: Random House, 1938), 2:246.

2. Quoted from the text of the act, reproduced in Leverett S. Lyon et al., *The National Recovery Administration: An Analysis and Appraisal* (Washington, D.C.: Brookings Institution, 1935), p. 895. Title II appropriated 3.3 billion dollars for public works, and Title III contained "Amendments to Emergency Relief and Construction Act and Miscellaneous Provisions."

3. Enforcement of these laws effectively, if inadvertently, promoted industrial integration and rationalization. See Thomas K. McCraw, "Mercantilism and the Market: Antecedents of American Industrial Policy," in Claude E. Barfield and William A. Schambra, eds., *The Politics of Industrial Policy* (Washington, D.C.: American Enterprise Institute, 1986), pp. 41–52.

4. Joseph A. Schumpeter, *Business Cycles: A Theoretical, Historical, and Statistical Analysis of the Capitalist Process*, 2 vols. (New York: McGraw-Hill, 1939), 2:992.

5. Elizabeth Brandeis, "Organized Labor and Protective Labor Legislation," in Milton Derber and Edwin Young, eds., *Labor and the New Deal* (Madison: University of Wisconsin Press, 1957), pp. 196–98.

6. Stanley Buder, *Pullman: An Experiment in Industrial Order and Community Planning, 1880–1930* (New York: Oxford University Press, 1967), pp. 183–85; Mark Perlman, "Labor in Eclipse," in John Braeman, Robert H. Bremner, and David Brody, eds., *Change and Continuity in Twentieth-Century America: The 1920s* (Columbus: Ohio State University Press, 1968), p. 124; Irving Bernstein, *The Lean Years: A History of the American Worker, 1920–1933* (Boston: Houghton Mifflin, 1960), pp. 211–12.

7. Lester V. Chandler, *America's Greatest Depression, 1929–1941* (New York: Harper & Row, 1970), provides an accessible overview.

8. Milton Friedman and Anna Jacobson Schwartz, *A Monetary History of the United States, 1867–1960* (Princeton: Princeton University Press, 1963), pp. 308–62.

9. Chandler, *America's Greatest Depression*, pp. 67–90, 145–60.

10. Ibid., p. 23.

11. Michael A. Bernstein, *The Great Depression: Delayed Recovery and Economic Change in America, 1929–1939* (Cambridge: Cambridge University Press, 1987), pp. 144–69.

12. These data combine coal and petroleum, for which separate codes were enacted. The other large sectors were garments, wholesale trade, retail trade, and construction. NRA Administrator Hugh S. Johnson decided that these were "too complex for immediate action," but all were eventually placed under NRA authority. See John Kennedy Ohl, *Hugh S. Johnson and the New Deal* (DeKalb: Northern Illinois University Press, 1985), p. 115.

13. The economic debates are reviewed in Bernstein, *Great Depression*, pp. 1–20, and in Peter Fearon, *War, Prosperity, and Depression: The U.S. Economy, 1917–45* (Lawrence: University Press of Kansas, 1987), pp. 149–59. The next paragraph draws on their surveys of the literature.

14. Alvin H. Hansen was Keynes's great Americanizer. Chapter 4 of his *Fiscal Policy and Business Cycles* (1941; reprint, Westport, Conn.: Greenwood Press, 1977) sets out the standard Keynesian interpretation of the New Deal: federal spending did increase but was offset by decreased state and local spending. A premature effort to balance the budget by cutting spending led to the second depression of 1937–1938. Only the military buildup after 1939 raised spending enough for an enduring recovery. See also Fearon, *War, Prosperity, and Depression*, pp. 150–51.

15. Paul A. Baran and Paul M. Sweezy, *Monopoly Capital: An Essay on the American Economic and Social Order* (New York: Monthly Review Press, 1966), p. 225. See also Paul M. Sweezy, *The Theory of Capitalist Development: Principles of Marxist Political Economy* (1942; reprint, New York: Monthly Review Press, 1970), pp. 133–236.

16. Friedman and Schwartz, *Monetary History*, pp. 299–419. Schwartz and her critics argue in Karl Brunner, ed., *The Great Depression Revisited* (Boston: Martinus Nijhoff, 1981), which also clarifies the monetarist perspective on the crisis.

17. Charles P. Kindleberger, *The World in Depression, 1929–1939* (Berkeley and Los Angeles: University of California Press, 1973).

18. Bernstein, *Great Depression*.

19. Ellis W. Hawley's introduction as editor of *Herbert Hoover as Secretary of Commerce: Studies in New Era Thought and Practice* (Iowa City: University of Iowa Press, 1981), pp. 1–16, is a helpful guide to the debates.

20. Albert U. Romasco, *The Poverty of Abundance: Hoover, the Nation, the Depression* (New York: Oxford University Press, 1965); Jordan A. Schwarz, *The Interregnum of Despair: Hoover, Congress, and the Depression* (Urbana: University of Illinois Press, 1970).

21. Robert F. Himmelberg, *The Origins of the National Recovery Administration: Business, Government, and the Trade Association Issue, 1921–1933* (New York: Fordham University Press, 1976); Ellis W. Hawley, *The New Deal and the Problem of Monopoly: A Study in Economic Ambivalence* (Princeton: Princeton University Press, 1966), p. 42.

22. William E. Leuchtenburg, *Franklin D. Roosevelt and the New Deal, 1932–1940* (New York: Harper Colophon, 1963), is a lucid introduction.

23. The gold-exchange standard of the interwar period and Roosevelt's decision to abandon it are explained in Fred L. Block, *The Origins of International Economic Disorder: A Study of United States International Monetary Policy from World War II to the Present* (Berkeley and Los Angeles: University of California Press, 1977), pp. 12–27, and in Kindleberger, *World in Depression*, pp. 63–64, 202–4.

24. The rest of this paragraph and the next draw on Himmelberg, *Origins*, pp. 181–212; Hawley, *New Deal*, pp. 35–52; Arthur M. Schlesinger, Jr., *The Coming of the New Deal* (Boston: Houghton Mifflin, 1959), pp. 87–102; Lyon et al., *National Recovery Administration*, pp. 3–7, 751–75.

25. Himmelberg, *Origins*, p. 181.

26. Hawley, *New Deal*, pp. 21–26.

27. Lyon et al., *National Recovery Administration*, pp. 751–877.

28. Charles Frederick Roos, *NRA Economic Planning* (Bloomington, Ind.: Principia Press, 1937), pp. 472–73 (quote p. 472), p. 436.

29. John Maynard Keynes, *The Collected Writings of John Maynard Keynes*, vol. 21 (Cambridge: Cambridge University Press, 1982), p. 291; similarly, pp. 299, 322–23.

30. Schumpeter, *Business Cycles* 2:992–96, 1010.

31. Michael M. Weinstein, *Recovery and Redistribution under the NIRA* (Amsterdam: North-Holland, 1980), pp. 109–48. Weinstein also suggests that by raising wages, the NRA increased unemployment 2 percent. This estimate, however, is based on the assumptions that NRA codes were equally effective in all industries and that the AAA set similar wage and hour regulations for agricultural workers. Both assumptions are dubious. NRA code provisions and enforcement varied among industries, since some were better organized to use the code authorities for business planning than others, and state actors lacked the capacity to impose uniformity. See Lyon et al., *National Recovery Administration*, pp. 394–97. The AAA did not regulate employment conditions for agricultural laborers, and their wages did not keep up with the increase in farm income. See Edwin G. Nourse, Joseph S. Davis, and John D. Black, *Three Years of the Agricultural Adjustment Administration* (Washington, D.C.: Brookings Institution, 1937), pp. 349–53. If significant sectors of the economy were outside the NRA or similar provisions, "then the net impact on the economy-wide average wage and unemployment would be ambiguous. Individuals released from the employment in the NIRA sectors might have been absorbed—at a lower wage—in the exempt industries" (Weinstein, *Recovery and Redistribution*, p. 136).

32. Milton Katz, quoted in Katie Louchheim, ed., *The Making of the New Deal: The Insiders Speak* (Cambridge: Harvard University Press, 1983), p. 123. See also Hawley, *New Deal*, pp. 111–31; Peter H. Irons, *The New Deal Lawyers* (Princeton: Princeton University Press, 1982), pp. 86–107.

33. Hawley, *New Deal*, pp. 205–69.

34. See *Papers and Addresses of Franklin D. Roosevelt* 2:74 for Roosevelt's re-

marks in submission of the Agricultural Adjustment Act to Congress, March 16, 1933.

35. M. L. Wilson, "Validity of the Fundamental Assumptions Underlying Agricultural Adjustment," *Journal of Farm Economics* 18(1): 20 (February 1936).

36. Gilbert C. Fite, *George N. Peek and the Fight for Farm Parity* (Norman: University of Oklahoma Press, 1954), pp. 3–13; Theodore Saloutos, *Farmer Movements in the South, 1865–1933* (Berkeley and Los Angeles: University of California Press, 1960), pp. 160–62, 173–79, 182–83, 203–5, 277–80; James H. Shideler, *Farm Crisis, 1919–1923* (Berkeley and Los Angeles: University of California Press, 1957), pp. 84–90; Elizabeth Hoffman and Gary D. Libecap, "Institutional Choice and the Development of U.S. Agricultural Policies in the 1920s," *Journal of Economic History* 51(2) (June 1992), pp. 399, 407.

37. Richard S. Kirkendall, *Social Scientists and Farm Politics in the Age of Roosevelt* (Columbia: University of Missouri Press, 1966), pp. 11–29, 175–78; William D. Rowley, *M. L. Wilson and the Campaign for the Domestic Allotment* (Lincoln: University of Nebraska Press, 1970), pp. 3, 150–52; Edward L. Schapsmeier and Frederick H. Schapsmeier, *Henry A. Wallace of Iowa: The Agrarian Years, 1910–1940* (Ames: Iowa State University Press, 1968), pp. 127–29, 149–51.

38. Gilbert C. Fite, "Farmer Opinion and the Agricultural Adjustment Act," *Mississippi Valley Historical Review* 48(4) (March 1962), pp. 656–73.

39. Because of wartime regulation of key commodities and the effects of climate and crop interdependence, Table 3 indicates a more varied pattern of expanded production than would have been the case in the absence of government controls or unforeseen events. The 1918 corn crop, for example, yielded 9 percent less than that of the previous year due to a shortage of seed. Still, the pattern of increased production is evident in the table. For accounts of the impact of the war upon the farmer and farm policy, see Murray R. Benedict, *Farm Policies of the United States, 1790–1950* (New York: Twentieth Century Fund, 1953), pp. 158–68; Shideler, *Farm Crisis*, pp. 10–19; Theodore Saloutos and John D. Hicks, *Agricultural Discontent in the Middle West, 1900–1939* (Madison: University of Wisconsin Press, 1951), pp. 87–98; Saloutos, *Farmer Movements in the South*, pp. 236–53. On Federal Reserve Bank policy, see Friedman and Schwartz, *Monetary History*, pp. 229–39.

40. Shideler, *Farm Crisis*, pp. 46–62; Saloutos and Hicks, *Agricultural Discontent*, pp. 98–110; Fite, *George N. Peek*, pp. 3–13; Benedict, *Farm Policies of the United States*, pp. 168–72; Saloutos, *Farmer Movements in the South*, pp. 253–57.

41. Fite, *George N. Peek*, pp. 119–22. H. Thomas Johnson, *Agricultural Depression in the 1920s: Economic Fact or Statistical Artifact?* (New York: Garland Publishing, 1985), argues that there was no agricultural depression between 1921 and 1929. As Johnson shows, the parity ratio, constructed during the postwar slump to demonstrate crisis conditions, is misleading because it does not show increases in input productivity, which allowed farmers to decrease costs by substituting capital for labor. His call for disaggregation of agricultural statistics, to capture differences by region, crop, and farm size, is equally compelling. However, Johnson's preferred indicator, net farm income, also points to a continuing depression. Net income rose with prices during the 1920s, but

never enough to make up for the terrible drop of 1919–1921. Johnson makes a convincing argument that inability to adjust inputs and outputs to new patterns of technology and factor prices—not overproduction—was the cause of farm distress. But it is not clear why this makes the period any less of a depression or why farmers should be blamed for decisions that reduced their individual risk.

Most important, Johnson's study shows that Department of Agriculture officials, politicians, and farm organizations all interpreted the period as a crisis. Economic conditions are *always* ambiguous. Crises are thus defined by political action, not objective indicators. The 1920s, then, were an agricultural depression because relevant state, party, and interest group actors called them one and behaved accordingly.

42. Benedict, *Farm Policies of the United States*, pp. 241, 243–44; John D. Hicks, *Republican Ascendancy, 1921–1933* (New York: Harper & Row, 1960), p. 264; John L. Shover, *Cornbelt Rebellion: The Farmers' Holiday Association* (Urbana: University of Illinois Press, 1965), pp. 13–17.

43. The most comprehensive discussion of the Federal Farm Board is in David E. Hamilton, *From New Day to New Deal: American Farm Policy from Hoover to Roosevelt, 1928–1933* (Chapel Hill: University of North Carolina Press, 1991). See also Joseph G. Knapp, *The Advance of American Cooperative Enterprise, 1920–1945* (Danville, Ill.: Interstate, 1973), pp. 122–42; Benedict, *Farm Policies of the United States*, pp. 257–67; Orville Merton Kile, *The Farm Bureau through Three Decades* (Baltimore: Waverly, 1948), pp. 163–69; Saloutos, *Farmer Movements in the South*, pp. 273–75; Bernard M. Klass, "The Federal Farm Board and the Antecedents of the Agricultural Adjustment Act, 1929–1933," in Carl E. Krog and William R. Tanner, eds., *Herbert Hoover and the Republican Era: A Reconsideration* (Lanham, Md.: University Press of America, 1984), pp. 191–219; Martin L. Fausold, "President Hoover's Farm Policies, 1929–1933," *Agricultural History* 51 (2): 362–78 (April 1977). This paragraph and the next draw on these sources.

44. Rowley, M. L. Wilson, chaps. 8–9; Kirkendall, *Social Scientists and Farm Politics*, pp. 30–49; Elliot A. Rosen, *Hoover, Roosevelt, and the Brains Trust* (New York: Columbia University Press, 1977), pp. 162, 175–78, 335–40; Bernard Sternsher, *Rexford Tugwell and the New Deal* (New Brunswick: Rutgers University Press, 1964), pp. 42–43; Gertrude Almy Slichter, "Franklin D. Roosevelt and the Farm Problem, 1929–1932," *Mississippi Valley Historical Review* 43(2): 248–58 (September 1956); Christiana McFadyen Campbell, *The Farm Bureau and the New Deal* (Urbana: University of Illinois Press, 1962), p. 51; Gilbert C. Fite, "John A. Simpson: The Southwest's Militant Farm Leader," *Mississippi Valley Historical Review* 35(4): 575–77 (March 1949); Fite, *George N. Peek*, pp. 237–41.

45. William R. Johnson, "National Farm Organizations and the Reshaping of Agricultural Policy in 1932," *Agricultural History* 37(1): 41–42 (January 1963); Kile, *Farm Bureau*, pp. 191–92; Campbell, *Farm Bureau and the New Deal*, pp. 52–54; Fite, "John A. Simpson," pp. 577–78; Schapsmeier and Schapsmeier, *Henry A. Wallace*, pp. 168–69; Henry A. Wallace, *New Frontiers* (New York: Reynal and Hitchcock, 1934), pp. 162–63.

46. Schlesinger, *Coming of the New Deal*, pp. 45–49; Van L. Perkins, *Crisis in*

Agriculture: The Agricultural Adjustment Administration and the New Deal (Berkeley and Los Angeles: University of California Press, 1969), chap. 4; Rowley, M. L. Wilson, pp. 195–97.

47. Perkins, *Crisis in Agriculture*, pp. 179–86; Fite, *George N. Peek*, pp. 243–66.

48. Nourse, Davis, and Black, *Three Years*, chaps. 2, 3, 4, 9.

49. Ibid., chaps. 5, 10, 14.

50. Keynes, *Collected Writings*, 21:323.

51. Schumpeter, *Business Cycles*, 2:992.

52. Benedict, *Farm Policies of the United States*, pp. 349–52, 375–84; Kirkendall, *Social Scientists and Farm Politics*, pp. 143–49; Irons, *New Deal Lawyers*, pp. 181–99.

53. Nourse, Davis, and Black, *Three Years*, pp. 266, 341–49; Campbell, *Farm Bureau and the New Deal*, pp. 88–89, 95, 100, 102; David Eugene Conrad, *The Forgotten Farmers: The Story of Sharecroppers in the New Deal* (Urbana: University of Illinois Press, 1965); Donald H. Grubbs, *Cry from the Cotton: The Southern Tenant Farmers' Union and the New Deal* (Chapel Hill: University of North Carolina Press, 1971).

54. Sidney Baldwin, *Poverty and Politics: The Rise and Decline of the Farm Security Administration* (Chapel Hill: University of North Carolina Press, 1968).

55. Kirkendall, *Social Scientists and Farm Politics*, pp. 195–254; Edward C. Banfield, "Organization for Policy Planning in the U.S. Department of Agriculture," *Journal of Farm Economics* 34:1 (February 1952), pp. 19–24.

56. The terms "commercial farmers" and "agricultural underclasses" refer to different groups of producers in each of the three basic regions of American agriculture. For the neoplantation system of the cotton South, the distinction is between the plantation owners and managers, on the one hand, and their sharecroppers and tenant farmers, on the other. Class relations on the "factory farms" of California and other western states more closely resembled those of industrial capitalism, and so the relevant distinction in this region is between the owners and managers of large-scale farms and the proletarianized wage laborers they employed. The "family farms" of the Midwest and Northeast were least reliant on outside labor; these varied by farm size, ownership status, and degree of indebtedness. See Jess Gilbert and Carolyn Howe, "Beyond 'State vs. Society': Theories of the State and New Deal Agricultural Policies," *American Sociological Review* 56(2): 209–10 (April 1991); Max J. Pfeffer, "Social Origins of Three Systems of Farm Production in the United States," *Rural Sociology* 48(4): 540–62 (Winter 1983); Susan Archer Mann, *Agrarian Capitalism in Theory and Practice* (Chapel Hill: University of North Carolina Press, 1990), pp. 6–8; Patrick H. Mooney, "Toward a Class Analysis of Midwestern Agriculture," *Rural Sociology* 48(4): 567–72 (Winter 1983); idem, "Class Relations and Class Structure in the Midwest," in A. Eugene Havens, Gregory Hooks, Patrick H. Mooney, and Max J. Pfeffer, eds., *Studies in the Transformation of U.S. Agriculture* (Boulder: Westview Press, 1986), pp. 214–23, 240–41.

57. Otis L. Graham, Jr., *Toward a Planned Society* (New York: Oxford Uni-

versity Press, 1976), p. 65. Graham takes the label "Broker State" from John Chamberlain, *The American Stakes* (New York: Carrick & Evans, 1940).

58. By-now-classic discussions of these patterns are J. Leiper Freeman, *The Political Process: Executive Bureau–Legislative Committee Relations*, rev. ed. (New York: Random House, 1965); Grant McConnell, *Private Power and American Democracy* (New York: Knopf, 1966); Theodore J. Lowi, *The End of Liberalism: The Second Republic of the United States*, 2d ed. (New York: Norton, 1979); and Morton Grodzins, "American Political Parties and the American System," *Western Political Quarterly* 13(4): 974–98 (December 1960).

59. Martin Shefter and Benjamin Ginsberg, "Institutionalizing the Reagan Regime," in Ginsberg and Alan Stone, eds., *Do Elections Matter?* (Armonk, N.Y.: M. E. Sharpe, 1986), pp. 191–203; Ginsberg and Shefter, "The Presidency and the Organization of Interests," in Michael Nelson, ed., *The Presidency and the Political System*, 2d ed. (Washington, D.C.: CQ Press, 1988), pp. 311–12; Benjamin Ginsberg and Martin Shefter, *Politics by Other Means: The Declining Importance of Elections in America* (New York: Basic Books, 1990), pp. 37–40. See also Barbara Sinclair, *Congressional Realignment, 1925–1978* (Austin: University of Texas Press, 1982), pp. 34–36.

60. J. David Greenstone, *Labor in American Politics*, Phoenix ed. (Chicago: University of Chicago Press, 1977), pp. 39–80.

61. Thomas Ferguson, "From Normalcy to New Deal: Industrial Structure, Party Competition, and American Public Policy in the Great Depression," *International Organization* 38(1): 41–94 (Winter 1984); Kathleen Kemp, "Industrial Structure, Party Competition, and the Sources of Regulation," in Ferguson and Joel Rogers, eds., *The Political Economy: Readings in the Politics and Economics of American Public Policy* (Armonk, N.Y.: M. E. Sharpe, 1984), pp. 104–111; Ginsberg and Shefter, "Presidency and Organization of Interests," pp. 312, 329 n. 2.

62. Richard Franklin Bensel, *Sectionalism and American Political Development, 1880–1980* (Madison: University of Wisconsin Press, 1984), pp. 191–222; James L. Sundquist, *Dynamics of the Party System: Alignment and Realignment of Political Parties in the United States*, rev. ed. (Washington, D.C.: Brookings Institution, 1983), pp. 241–52; David Rapp, *How the U.S. Got into Agriculture: And Why It Can't Get Out* (Washington, D.C.: Congressional Quarterly, 1988), pp. 27–32.

63. Jerome M. Clubb, William H. Flanigan, and Nancy H. Zingale, *Partisan Realignment: Voters, Parties, and Government in American History* (Beverly Hills, Calif.: Sage, 1980), pp. 122, 287.

64. Walter Dean Burnham, *Critical Elections and the Mainsprings of American Politics* (New York: Norton, 1970), pp. 132–33.

65. "Southern sectionalism and the special character of southern political institutions have to be attributed in the main to the Negro. The one-party system, suffrage restrictions departing from democratic norms, low levels of voting and of political interest, and all the consequences of these political arrangements and practices must be traced ultimately to this one factor. All of which

amounts to saying that the predominant consideration in the architecture of southern political institutions has been to assure locally a subordination of the Negro population and, externally, to block threatened interferences from the outside with these local arrangements." V. O. Key, Jr., *Southern Politics in State and Nation* (New York: Alfred A. Knopf, 1949), p. 665.

66. Sundquist, *Dynamics of the Party System*, pp. 352–75; Earl Black and Merle Black, *Politics and Society in the South* (Cambridge: Harvard University Press, 1987), pp. 259–75.

67. Mack C. Shelley II, *The Permanent Majority: The Conservative Coalition in the United States Congress* (University: University of Alabama Press, 1983); James T. Patterson, *Congressional Conservatism and the New Deal* (Lexington: University of Kentucky Press, 1967); David L. Porter, *Congress and the Waning of the New Deal* (Port Washington, N.Y.: Kennikat Press, 1980); James MacGregor Burns, *The Deadlock of Democracy: Four-Party Politics in America* (Englewood Cliffs, N.J.: Prentice-Hall, 1963).

Chapter 2. State, Party, and Policy: A Historical and Institutional Approach

1. The complexity of agricultural decision making is nicely illustrated by the input-output diagram in Nevin S. Scrimshaw and Lance Taylor, "Food," *Scientific American* 243 (September 1980): 86–87.

2. Theodore W. Schultz, *The Economic Organization of Agriculture* (New York: McGraw-Hill, 1953), pp. 186–91; Willard W. Cochrane, *Farm Prices: Myth and Reality* (Minneapolis: University of Minnesota Press, 1958), pp. 33–42; Daniel B. Suits, "Agriculture," in Walter Adams, ed., *The Structure of American Industry*, 8th ed. (New York: Macmillan, 1990), pp. 3–13; Richard Stone, *The Measurement of Consumers' Expenditure and Behaviour in the United Kingdom, 1920–1938*, 2 vols. (Cambridge: Cambridge University Press, 1954), 1:339–40.

3. Elasticity estimates for the United States and other advanced industrial economies, disaggregated by commodity groups, are presented in H. S. Houthakker and Lester D. Taylor, *Consumer Demand in the United States: Analyses and Projections*, 2d ed. (Cambridge: Harvard University Press, 1970), pp. 204–27, and in Stanley R. Johnson, Zuhair A. Hassan, and Richard D. Green, *Demand Systems Estimation: Methods and Applications* (Ames: Iowa State University Press, 1984), pp. 118–19, 126–34.

4. "The individual farmer is subjected to a greater range of intervening variables which affect his calling than is the businessman or the professional. Factors which cannot be anticipated with precision, such as weather, climactic changes, and natural disasters, can destroy at one blow a flourishing agrarian enterprise." Charles E. Jacob, *Policy and Bureaucracy* (Princeton: D. Van Nostrand, 1966), pp. 121–22.

5. James E. Boyle, *Agricultural Economics* (Philadelphia: J.B. Lippincott Company, 1921), pp. 17–20, 214–23; Edward L. Schapsmeier and Frederick H. Schapsmeier, *Henry A. Wallace of Iowa: The Agrarian Years, 1910–1940* (Ames: Iowa State University Press, 1968), pp. 27–28; Lawrence Busch, Alessandro Bo-

nanno, and William B. Lacy, "Science, Technology, and the Restructuring of Agriculture," *Sociologia Ruralis* 29(2): 121–27 (1989); Martin Kenney, Linda M. Lobao, James Curry, and W. Richard Goe, "Midwestern Agriculture in US Fordism: From the New Deal to Economic Restructuring," *Sociologia Ruralis* 29 (2): 138–39 (1989); Suits, "Agriculture," pp. 27–28.

6. Schultz, *Economic Organization of Agriculture*, pp. 192–94; Cochrane, *Farm Prices*, pp. 42–45; Suits, "Agriculture," pp. 13–25.

7. Clarence Alton Wiley, *Agriculture and the Business Cycle Since 1920: A Study in the Post-War Disparity of Prices* (Madison: University of Wisconsin, 1930), pp. 14–26, 60–65, 132–57; John K. Galbraith and John D. Black, "The Maintenance of Agricultural Production during Depression: The Explanations Reviewed," *Journal of Political Economy* 46(3): 305–23 (June 1938); J. R. Bellerby, *Agriculture and Industry: Relative Income* (London: Macmillan, 1956), pp. 281–83, 304–6; Glenn L. Johnson, "Supply Function—Some Facts and Notions," in Earl O. Heady, Howard G. Diesslin, Harold R. Jensen, and Glenn L. Johnson, eds., *Agricultural Adjustment Problems in a Growing Economy* (Ames: Iowa State College Press, 1958), p. 92.

8. Boyle, *Agricultural Economics*, p. 15.

9. D. Gale Johnson, *Forward Prices in Agriculture* (Chicago: University of Chicago Press, 1947), pp. 9–10; Suits, "Agriculture," pp. 2–3; Boyle, *Agricultural Economics*, pp. 117–25; A. Eugene Havens, "Capitalist Development in the United States: State, Accumulation, and Agricultural Production Systems," in A. Eugene Havens, Gregory Hooks, Patrick H. Mooney, and Max J. Pfeffer, eds., *Studies in the Transformation of U.S. Agriculture* (Boulder: Westview Press, 1986), pp. 43–45.

10. Galbraith and Black, "Maintenance of Agricultural Production," pp. 309–10, 321–22.

11. Schultz, *Economic Organization of Agriculture*, p. 176.

12. Susan Archer Mann, *Agrarian Capitalism in Theory and Practice* (Chapel Hill: University of North Carolina Press, 1990).

13. Mancur Olson, Jr., *The Logic of Collective Action: Public Goods and the Theory of Groups* (New York: Schocken Books, 1965), p. 148. See also Graham K. Wilson, *Special Interests and Policymaking: Agricultural Policies and Politics in Britain and the United States of America, 1956–70* (London: John Wiley & Sons, 1977), pp. 75–76, 99–100.

14. Angus Campbell et al., *The American Voter* (New York: John Wiley & Sons, 1960), pp. 414–16, 425–30. This study was based on 1952 and 1956 voter surveys. Michael S. Lewis-Beck, "Agrarian Political Behavior in the United States," *American Journal of Political Science* 21(3): 559 (August 1977), reports that farmers were still not joiners in 1972.

15. Adam Smith, *The Wealth of Nations* (New York: Modern Library, 1937), p. 429; Karl Marx, *The Eighteenth Brumaire of Louis Bonaparte*, in Karl Marx and Frederick Engels, *Collected Works* (London: Lawrence & Wishart, 1979), 11:187.

16. Karl Marx, *Capital: A Critique of Political Economy* (New York: Vintage, 1977), p. 638.

17. Max J. Pfeffer, "Social Origins of Three Systems of Farm Production in

the United States," *Rural Sociology* 48(4): 540–62 (Winter 1983); J. Craig Jenkins, *The Politics of Insurgency: The Farm Worker Movement in the 1960s* (New York: Columbia University Press, 1985), pp. 28–65.

18. Jenkins, *Politics of Insurgency,* pp. 66–85; Merle Weiner, "Cheap Food, Cheap Labor: California Agriculture in the 1930's," *Insurgent Sociologist* 8(2–3): 181–90 (Fall 1978); Linda C. Majka and Theo J. Majka, *Farm Workers, Agribusiness, and the State* (Philadelphia: Temple University Press, 1982).

19. Lee J. Alston and Joseph P. Ferrie, "Resisting the Welfare State: Southern Opposition to the Farm Security Administration," in Robert Higgs, ed., *Emergence of the Modern Political Economy* (Greenwich, Conn.: JAI Press, 1985), pp. 83–120; idem, "Labor Costs, Paternalism, and Loyalty in Southern Agriculture: A Constraint on the Growth of the Welfare State," *Journal of Economic History* 45(1): 95–117 (March 1985); Mann, *Agrarian Capitalism,* pp. 76–87, 168 (nn. 11, 13).

20. Mann, *Agrarian Capitalism,* pp. 7–8, 23–24.

21. Campbell et al., *American Voter,* pp. 416–25. Graham Wilson and Samuel Lubell also depict the farm vote of Eisenhower years as highly volatile. See Wilson, *Special Interests and Policymaking,* pp. 117–22; Samuel Lubell, *Revolt of the Moderates* (New York: Harper & Brothers, 1956), pp. 154–75.

22. Lewis-Beck, "Agrarian Political Behavior," pp. 556–61; David Knoke and David E. Long, "The Economic Sensitivity of the American Farm Vote," *Rural Sociology* 40(1): 10–17 (Winter 1975); Lee Sigelman, "Politics, Economics, and the American Farmer: The Case of 1980," *Rural Sociology* 48(3): 374–84 (Fall 1983).

23. Robert A. McGuire, "Economic Causes of Late-Nineteenth Century Agrarian Unrest: New Evidence," *Journal of Economic History* 41(4): 835–49 (December 1981).

24. David Burner, *The Politics of Provincialism: The Democratic Party in Transition, 1918–1932* (Cambridge: Harvard University Press, 1986), pp. 34–39.

25. Allen J. Matusow, *Farm Policies and Politics in the Truman Years* (New York: Atheneum, 1970), pp. 175–77, 185–88. Charles M. Hardin, "Farm Price Policy and the Farm Vote," *Journal of Farm Economics* 37(4): 610–15 (November 1955), while disputing the conclusion that the farm vote elected Truman, notes how much this belief influenced subsequent congressional behavior on farm issues.

26. Wilson, *Special Interests and Policymaking,* pp. 19–24; Peter Self and Herbert J. Storing, *The State and the Farmer: British Agricultural Policies and Politics* (Berkeley and Los Angeles: University of California Press, 1963), pp. 201–4; Sidney Tarrow, "The Urban-Rural Cleavage in Political Involvement: The Case of France," *American Political Science Review* 55(2): 349–50, 353, 356 (June 1971).

27. Wiley, *Agriculture and the Business Cycle,* p. 14. Emphasis in original.

28. O. V. Wells, "Agriculture Today: An Appraisal of the Agricultural Problem," in United States Department of Agriculture, *Farmers in a Changing World: The Yearbook of Agriculture 1940* (Washington, D.C.: U.S. Government Printing Office, 1940), pp. 386–87; Edwin G. Nourse, Joseph S. Davis, and John D. Black, *Three Years of the Agricultural Adjustment Administration* (Washington,

D.C.: Brookings Institution, 1937), pp. 20–22; Bellerby, *Agriculture and Industry*, pp. 187–89.

29. Raymond Moley, leader of Roosevelt's Brains Trust, later said that "every important venture from 1933 to the summer of 1935," including the AAA, "had been outlined" during the 1932 campaign, with "three exceptions": "(1) the abandonment of gold, (2) the 'borrow and spend' policies, and (3) the use of the N.R.A. as a quick recovery measure." Moley did think that the long-term planning aspects of the NRA were foreshadowed in a Roosevelt campaign speech. Raymond Moley, *After Seven Years* (New York: Harper & Brothers, 1939), pp. 62–63.

30. Robert L. Tontz, "Membership of General Farmers' Organizations, United States, 1874–1960," *Agricultural History* 38(3): 145–47, 150 (July 1964); Louis Galambos, *Competition and Cooperation: The Emergence of a National Trade Association* (Baltimore: Johns Hopkins Press, 1966), pp. 67–68.

31. Though highly competitive, textile manufacturers were well organized in the Cotton Textile Institute, formed with Hoover's encouragement in 1926. See Galambos, *Competition and Cooperation*, pp. 18–20, 89–112, 134–38.

32. Ibid., p. 271; Van L. Perkins, *Crisis in Agriculture: The Agricultural Adjustment Administration and the New Deal* (Berkeley and Los Angeles: University of California Press, 1969), pp. 54–56, 103; Anthony J. Badger, *Prosperity Road: The New Deal, Tobacco, and North Carolina* (Chapel Hill: University of North Carolina Press, 1980), pp. 118–21; Theodore Saloutos, *The American Farmer and the New Deal* (Ames: Iowa State University Press, 1982), pp. 126–32; Peter Irons, *The New Deal Lawyers* (Princeton: Princeton University Press, 1982), pp. 181–83. Hoosac Mills, the bankrupt cotton mill that brought the case, did so at the behest of the meat processor Armour & Company, to which it was financially connected; Armour sought to prevent AAA access to its books.

33. Perkins, *Crisis in Agriculture*, pp. 55–56, 182–85; Gilbert C. Fite, *George N. Peek and the Fight for Farm Parity* (Norman: University of Oklahoma Press, 1954), pp. 243–66; idem, "Farmer Opinion and the Agricultural Adjustment Act," *Mississippi Valley Historical Review* 48(4): 661–63, 671–73 (March 1962).

34. Irving Bernstein, *The New Deal Collective Bargaining Policy* (Berkeley and Los Angeles: University of California Press, 1950), pp. 58–62; Donald R. Brand, *Corporatism and the Rule of Law: A Study of the National Recovery Administration* (Ithaca, N.Y.: Cornell University Press, 1988), pp. 229–60.

35. Lawrence J. Nelson, "The Art of the Possible: Another Look at the 'Purge' of the AAA Liberals in 1935," *Agricultural History* 57(4): 416–35 (October 1983).

36. Bernstein, *New Deal Collective Bargaining Policy*, p. 27; J. Joseph Huthmacher, *Senator Robert F. Wagner and the Rise of Urban Liberalism* (New York: Atheneum, 1968), pp. 102–6; Sylvia Snowiss, "Presidential Leadership of Congress: An Analysis of Roosevelt's First Hundred Days," *Polity* 1(1): 67–77 (1971).

37. J. David Greenstone, *Labor in American Politics*, Phoenix ed. (Chicago: University of Chicago Press, 1977), pp. 40–49; Louise Overacker, "Labor's Political Contributions," *Political Science Quarterly* 54(1): 56–61 (March 1939).

38. E. E. Schattschneider, *Party Government* (New York: Rinehart & Co., 1942), p. 35.

39. Max Weber, *Economy and Society*, 2 vols., eds. Guenther Roth and Claus Wittich (New York: Bedminister Press, 1968), 1:285.

40. Joseph A. Schumpeter, *Capitalism, Socialism, and Democracy*, 3d ed. (New York: Harper and Brothers, 1950), pp. 269, 285, 287.

41. Anthony Downs, *An Economic Theory of Democracy* (New York: Harper & Row, 1957), pp. 115–23, 139–40.

42. C. B. Macpherson, *The Life and Times of Liberal Democracy* (Oxford: Oxford University Press, 1977), pp. 89–90; Alan Ware, *The Logic of Party Democracy* (London: Macmillan, 1979), pp. 32–43; idem, *Citizens, Parties and the State: A Reappraisal* (Cambridge: Polity Press, 1987), pp. 76–77; Janine Brodie and Jane Jenson, *Crisis, Challenge, and Change: Party and Class in Canada Revisited* (Ottawa: Carleton University Press, 1988), pp. 4–5.

43. See the data on these countries presented in Giovanni Sartori, *Parties and Party Systems: A Framework for Analysis* (Cambridge: Cambridge University Press, 1976), pp. 146–47, 305.

44. See Martin Shubik, *Strategy and Market Structure: Competition, Oligopoly, and the Theory of Games* (New York: John Wiley & Sons, 1959), and James W. Friedman, *Oligopoly Theory* (Cambridge: Cambridge University Press, 1983).

45. E. E. Schattschneider, *The Semisovereign People: A Realist's View of Democracy in America* (Hinsdale, Ill.: Dryden Press, 1975), p. 60. Emphasis in original.

46. Ware, *Logic of Party Democracy*, pp. 43–55; Macpherson, *Life and Times of Liberal Democracy*, p. 89; Brodie and Jenson, *Crisis, Challenge, and Change*, p. 5. The acme of oligopolistic behavior was reached in Austria from 1945 to 1965, when the country was governed by an interparty cartel. See Leon D. Epstein, *Political Parties in Western Democracies* (New York: Praeger, 1967), pp. 68–69.

47. Weber, *Economy and Society* 1:285.

48. Ibid., 1:286.

49. G. William Domhoff, *The Power Elite and the State: How Policy Is Made in America* (New York: Aldine de Gruyter, 1990), p. 225; Thomas Ferguson, "Party Realignment and American Industrial Structure: The Investment Theory of Political Parties in Historical Perspective," *Research in Political Economy* 6 (1983): 6–7, 11–12, 61.

50. Weber, *Economy and Society* 1:288.

51. Claus Offe, *Disorganized Capitalism* (Cambridge: MIT Press, 1985), p. 185.

52. Richard L. McCormick, *From Realignment to Reform: Political Change in New York State, 1893–1910* (Ithaca, N.Y.: Cornell University Press, 1981), p. 37.

53. Benjamin Ginsberg and Martin Shefter, *Politics by Other Means: The Declining Importance of Elections in America* (New York: Basic Books, 1990), pp. 1–9, 16–36; McCormick, *From Realignment to Reform*, pp. 37–38; William H. Riker, *The Art of Political Manipulation* (New Haven: Yale University Press, 1986), pp. ix–xi, 1–7.

54. McCormick, *From Realignment to Reform*, p. 37; Brodie and Jenson, *Crisis, Challenge, and Change*, p. 5.

55. McCormick, *From Realignment to Reform*, p. 37; G. Bingham Powell, Jr., "Party Systems and Political System Performance: Voting Participation, Government Stability, and Mass Violence in Contemporary Democracies," *American Political Science Review* 75(4): 865–67, 877 (December 1981); Peter Lange and Hudson Meadwell, "Typologies of Democratic Systems: From Political Inputs to Political Economy," in Howard J. Wiarda, ed., *New Directions in Comparative Politics* (Boulder: Westview Press, 1985), pp. 91–92; Epstein, *Political Parties*, pp. 147–48; T. J. Pempel, "Political Parties and Social Change: The Japanese Experience," in Louis Maisel and Joseph Cooper, eds., *Political Parties: Development and Decay* (Beverly Hills, Calif.: Sage, 1978), pp. 312, 327, 332.

56. On local party organizations, see David R. Mayhew, *Placing Parties in American Politics: Organization, Electoral Settings, and Government Activity in the Twentieth Century* (Princeton: Princeton University Press, 1986), pp. 19, 227. On party identification, see Paul Allen Beck and Frank J. Sorauf, *Party Politics in America*, 7th ed. (New York: Harper Collins, 1992), pp. 156–57, 179.

57. The perceptual definition of constituencies is emphasized in Richard F. Fenno, Jr., *Home Style: House Members in Their Districts* (Boston: Little, Brown, 1978), pp. 2–4, 27–29; John W. Kingdon, *Candidates for Office: Beliefs and Strategies* (New York: Random House, 1968), pp. 7, 10–11, 45–46.

58. Fenno, *Home Style*, p. 4.

59. This schematic representation incorporates nonvoting into the diagrams of Schattschneider, *Semisovereign People*, and James L. Sundquist, *Dynamics of the Party System: Alignment and Realignment of Political Parties in the United States*, rev. ed. (Washington, D.C.: Brookings Institution, 1983).

60. Fenno, *Home Style*, pp. 18–24.

61. Francis G. Castles, *The Social Democratic Image of Society: A Study of the Achievements and Origins of Scandinavian Social Democracy in Comparative Perspective* (London: Routledge & Kegan Paul, 1978), pp. 105–11; Pempel, "Political Parties and Social Change," p. 327.

62. Fenno, *Home Style*, pp. 8–18.

63. Morton Keller, *Affairs of State: Public Life in Late Nineteenth Century America* (Cambridge: Harvard University Press, 1977), pp. 532–533.

64. Aage R. Clausen, *How Congressmen Decide: A Policy Focus* (New York: St. Martin's Press, 1973), p. 128. Schumpeter made a similar point: "Evidently the will of the majority is the will of the majority and not the will of 'the people.' The latter is a mosaic that the former completely fails to 'represent.' To equate both by definition is not to solve the problem." Schumpeter, *Capitalism, Socialism, and Democracy*, p. 272.

65. Epstein, *Political Parties*, p. 245.

66. Even the most formal definitions of constituencies overlook the disfranchised. Clausen, for example, suggests as typical "a legal definition of constituency as the set of individuals who have the legal right to vote for a legislative representative upon reaching the age of competence, recently set at eighteen. The legal right to vote is established by the individual's place of legal residence within the boundaries of an areally defined legislative district." Clausen, *How Congressmen Decide*, p. 126.

67. Raymond E. Wolfinger and Steven J. Rosenstone, *Who Votes?* (New Haven: Yale University Press, 1980), pp. 79–83; Frances Fox Piven and Richard A. Cloward, *Why Americans Don't Vote* (New York: Pantheon, 1988), pp. 136–37, 178–80.

68. See Gerald M. Pomper, *Elections in America: Control and Influence in Democratic Politics* (New York: Dodd, Mead, 1970), pp. 149–203, on the United States, and Richard Rose, *Do Parties Make a Difference?*, 2d ed. (London: Macmillan, 1984), pp. 61–67, 144–45, on Great Britain.

69. David W. Brady, *Critical Elections and Congressional Policy Making* (Stanford: Stanford University Press, 1988), pp. 12–16, 115–35; Barbara Sinclair, *Congressional Realignment, 1925–1978* (Austin: University of Texas Press, 1982), pp. 4–9, 170–72, 182–86; Jerome M. Clubb, William H. Flanigan, and Nancy H. Zingale, *Partisan Realignment: Voters, Parties, and Government in American History* (Beverly Hills, Calif.: Sage, 1980), pp. 11–15, 36–41, 156–62, 252.

70. V. O. Key, Jr., *Politics, Parties, & Pressure Groups*, 5th ed. (New York: Thomas Y. Crowell, 1964), pp. 234–35, 671; David M. Potter, *The South and the Concurrent Majority* (Baton Rouge: Louisiana State University Press, 1972), pp. 44–51.

71. Alan Ware, *Citizens, Parties, and the State: A Reappraisal* (Cambridge: Polity Press, 1987), pp. 66–67.

72. Snowiss, "Presidential Leadership of Congress," pp. 67–77.

73. Miriam Golden, "Interest Representation, Party Systems, and the State: Italy in Comparative Perspective," *Comparative Politics* 18(3): 284 (April 1986).

74. Ware, *Citizens, Parties, and the State*, p. 65.

75. Michio Muramatsu and Ellis S. Krauss, "The Dominant Party and Social Coalitions in Japan," in T. J. Pempel, ed., *Uncommon Democracies: The One-Party Dominant Regimes* (Ithaca: Cornell University Press, 1990), pp. 286–98.

76. David J. Garrow, *Protest at Selma: Martin Luther King, Jr., and the Voting Rights Act of 1965* (New Haven: Yale University Press, 1978), pp. 212–36; Frances Fox Piven and Richard A. Cloward, *Poor People's Movements: Why They Succeed, How They Fail* (New York: Vintage, 1979), pp. 23–32; Robert Justin Goldstein, *Political Repression in Modern America: From 1870 to the Present* (Cambridge, Mass.: Schenkman, 1978), pp. 569–70.

77. Sundquist, *Dynamics of the Party System*, pp. 180–87; John D. Hicks, *Republican Ascendancy, 1921–1933* (New York: Harper & Brothers, 1960), pp. 24–27, 80–89; Ronald L. Feinman, *Twilight of Progressivism: The Western Republican Senators and the New Deal* (Baltimore: Johns Hopkins University Press, 1981), pp. 1–17; Richard M. Valelly, *Radicalism in the States: The Minnesota Farmer-Labor Party and the American Political Economy* (Chicago: University of Chicago Press, 1989), pp. 21–52.

78. David M. Potter, *The South and the Concurrent Majority* (Baton Rouge: Louisiana State University Press, 1972), pp. 31–32, 38, 59; Harvard Sitkoff, "The Impact of the New Deal on Black Southerners," in James C. Cobb and Michael V. Namorato, eds., *The New Deal and the South* (Jackson: University

Press of Mississippi, 1984), pp. 117–18; Brady, *Critical Elections and Congressional Policy Making*, p. 102.

79. Maurice Duverger, *Political Parties: Their Organization and Activity in the Modern State*, 2d English ed. (London: Methuen & Co., 1959), p. 308.

80. Ibid., pp. 386, 417–18.

81. Dewey W. Grantham, Jr., *The Democratic South* (New York: W. W. Norton, 1963), pp. 39–40; V. O. Key, Jr., *Southern Politics in State and Nation* (New York: Alfred A. Knopf, 1949), pp. 551–54. On domination and delegitimation in Israel and Italy, see Alan Arian and Samuel H. Barnes, "The Dominant Party System: A Neglected Model of Democratic Stability," *Journal of Politics* 36(3): 594–95 (August 1974); Ariel Levite and Sidney Tarrow, "The Legitimation of Excluded Parties in Dominant Party Systems: A Comparison of Israel and Italy," *Comparative Politics* 15(3): 297–303, 309–12, 319–20 (April 1983).

82. Burner, *Politics of Provincialism*, pp. 74–128, 130–37.

83. Ibid., pp. 179–243; Allan J. Lichtman, *Prejudice and the Old Politics: The Presidential Election of 1928* (Chapel Hill: University of North Carolina Press, 1979), pp. 40–76, 190–93, 231–46; Grantham, *Democratic South*, pp. 24–29, 42–44, 65–68; Key, *Southern Politics*, pp. 317–29; Alan Brinkley, "The New Deal and Southern Politics," in Cobb and Namorato, eds., *New Deal and the South*, p. 113. The only previous post-Reconstruction presidential election in which a Republican had won any of the eleven ex-Confederate states was 1920, when Harding carried Tennessee.

84. Frank Freidel, *Franklin D. Roosevelt: The Triumph* (Boston: Little, Brown, 1956), pp. 228–311; idem, "The South and the New Deal," in Cobb and Namorato, eds., *New Deal and the South*, p. 23; Roy V. Peel and Thomas C. Donnelly, *The 1932 Campaign: An Analysis* (New York: Farrar & Rinehart, 1935), pp. 27–32, 59–81, 91–105; James MacGregor Burns, *Roosevelt: The Lion and the Fox* (New York: Harcourt, Brace & World, 1956), pp. 123–38; Elliot A. Rosen, *Hoover, Roosevelt, and the Brains Trust: From Depression to New Deal* (New York: Columbia University Press, 1977), pp. 6–38, 95–275 passim; Earland I. Carlson, "Franklin D. Roosevelt's Post-Mortem of the 1928 Election," *Midwest Journal of Political Science* 8(3): 306–7 (August 1964).

85. Freidel, *Triumph*, pp. 312–71; Peel and Donnelly, *1932 Campaign*, pp. 213–21; Burns, *Lion and the Fox*, pp. 139–44; Louise Overacker, "Campaign Funds in a Depression Year," *American Political Science Review* 27(6): 770, 774–78, 783 (October 1933).

86. Sean J. Savage, *Roosevelt: The Party Leader, 1932–1945* (Lexington: University Press of Kentucky, 1991), pp. 113–28; Sundquist, *Dynamics of the Party System*, pp. 210–39; Burns, *Lion and the Fox*, pp. 197–203, 269–88; Kristi Andersen, *The Creation of a Democratic Majority, 1928–1936* (Chicago: University of Chicago Press, 1979); Greenstone, *Labor in American Politics*, pp. 39–49; David Plotke, "The Wagner Act, Again: Politics and Labor, 1935–37," *Studies in American Political Development* 3 (1989): 114; Nancy J. Weiss, *Farewell to the Party of Lincoln: Black Politics in the Age of FDR* (Princeton: Princeton University Press, 1983), pp. 180–208.

87. Philip Taft, *Organized Labor in American History* (New York: Harper & Row, 1964), pp. 607–8; Louise Overacker, "Campaign Funds in the Presidential Election of 1936," *American Political Science Review* 31(3): 476, 484–90, 497 (June 1937); idem, "Labor's Political Contributions," pp. 56–61; Burns, *Lion and the Fox*, pp. 286–87; Greenstone, *Labor in American Politics*, p. 49.

88. Brady, *Critical Elections and Congressional Policy Making*, p. 102.

89. Charles W. Eagles, *Democracy Delayed: Congressional Reapportionment and Urban-Rural Conflict in the 1920s* (Athens: University of Georgia Press, 1990); Laurence F. Schmeckebier, *Congressional Apportionment* (Washington, D.C.: Brookings Institution, 1941); Betty B. Rosenbaum, "The Urban-Rural Conflict as Evidenced in the Reapportionment Situation," *Social Forces* 12(3): 421–26 (March 1934). Congressional district boundaries are given in Kenneth C. Martis, *The Historical Atlas of United States Congressional Districts, 1789–1983* (New York: Free Press, 1982).

90. Savage, *Roosevelt: The Party Leader*, pp. 159–73; Sundquist, *Dynamics of the Party System*, pp. 226–28.

91. Savage, *Roosevelt: The Party Leader*, pp. 129–31, 153–58; James T. Patterson, "The Failure of Party Realignment in the South, 1937–39," *Journal of Politics* 27(3): 602–17 (August 1965); Brinkley, "New Deal and Southern Politics," pp. 102–9.

92. Walter Dean Burnham, "The United States: The Politics of Heterogeneity," in Richard Rose, ed., *Electoral Behavior: A Comparative Handbook* (New York: Free Press, 1974), p. 674. Southern Democratic control over congressional leadership positions underlies James MacGregor Burns's distinction between "the John Garner–Howard Smith–Harry Byrd–John McClellan congressional Democrats" and the presidential Democrats of Roosevelt, Truman, Stevenson, and Kennedy. Parallel distinctions between presidential and congressional Republicans lead Burns to describe the United States as having a four-party system. Burns, *Deadlock of Democracy*, p. 197. Giovanni Sartori, *Parties and Party Systems: A Framework for Analysis* (Cambridge: Cambridge University Press, 1976), pp. 189–90, 299, suggests sarcastically that the U.S. could also be considered a one-and-two-half party system or a two-and-one-half party system.

93. Robert R. Alford, *Party and Society: The Anglo-American Democracies* (Chicago: Rand McNally, 1963), pp. 232–41; Earl Black and Merle Black, *Politics and Society in the South* (Cambridge: Harvard University Press, 1987), pp. 50–72, 296–98.

94. On Canada, see Epstein, *Political Parties*, pp. 62–64; Ware, *Citizens, Parties, and the State*, p. 72; C. E. S. Franks, *The Parliament of Canada* (Toronto: University of Toronto Press, 1987), pp. 48–50; Hugh G. Thorburn, "Interpretations of the Canadian Party System," in Thorburn, ed., *Party Politics in Canada*, 5th ed. (Scarborough, Ont.: Prentice-Hall Canada, 1985), pp. 30–32. Mack C. Shelley II, *The Permanent Majority: The Conservative Coalition in the United States Congress* (University: University of Alabama Press, 1983), pp. 139–44, discusses the relative strength of each of the three congressional "parties" and lists the number of seats held in each year between 1933 and 1980.

95. Major works on these shifts include V. O. Key, Jr., "A Theory of Criti-

cal Elections," *Journal of Politics* 17(1): 3–15 (February 1955); Andersen, *Creation of a Democratic Majority*; Sundquist, *Dynamics of the Party System*, pp. 198–239.

96. On the importance of being FRBC, see Savage, *Roosevelt: The Party Leader*, pp. 23, 48–79, and Lyle W. Dorsett, *Franklin D. Roosevelt and the City Bosses* (Port Washington, N.Y.: Kennikat Press, 1977).

97. John M. Allswang, *The New Deal and American Politics: A Study in Political Change* (New York: John Wiley & Sons, 1978), pp. 48–52, 103–10, demonstrates how temporary Democratic gains among northern farmers proved to be.

98. Key, *Southern Politics*, pp. 531–663; Piven and Cloward, *Why Americans Don't Vote*, pp. 124–140; Andersen, *Creation of a Democratic Majority*, pp. 33–38, 107–10; Pete Daniel, "The New Deal, Southern Agriculture, and Economic Change," in Cobb and Namorato, eds., *New Deal and the South*, pp. 48–52, 55–61; Numan V. Bartley, "The Era of the New Deal as a Turning Point in Southern History," also in Cobb and Namorato, eds., *New Deal and the South*, pp. 138–41.

99. Weber, *Economy and Society* 1:54.

100. J. P. Nettl, "The State as a Conceptual Variable," *World Politics* 20(4): 564, 589–92 (July 1968); Charles Tilly, "Reflections on the History of European State-Making," in Tilly, ed., *The Formation of National States in Western Europe* (Princeton: Princeton University Press, 1975), pp. 34–35, 70–71; Stephen D. Krasner, *Defending the National Interest: Raw Materials Investments and U.S. Foreign Policy* (Princeton: Princeton University Press, 1978), pp. 55–70, 82–90; Bertrand Badie and Pierre Birnbaum, *The Sociology of the State* (Chicago: University of Chicago Press, 1983), pp. 23–24, 105–30; Ezra N. Suleiman, "State Structures and Clientelism: The French State versus the 'Notaires,' " *British Journal of Political Science* 17(3): 259–60 (July 1987); Michael M. Atkinson and William D. Coleman, "Strong States and Weak States: Sectoral Policy Networks in Advanced Capitalist Economies," *British Journal of Political Science* 19(1): 47–49 (January 1989).

101. S. N. Eisenstadt, *Social Differentiation and Stratification* (Glenview, Ill.: Scott, Foresman, 1971), p. 13. See also Badie and Birnbaum, *Sociology of the State*, p. 32. For alternative definitions, see Frederick Mundell Watkins, *The State as a Concept of Political Science* (New York: Harper & Brothers, 1934), pp. 71–76; Fred W. Riggs, "The Idea of Development Administration," in Edward W. Weidner, *Development Administration in Asia* (Durham, N.C.: Duke University Press, 1970), pp. 34–37.

102. Theda Skocpol, *States and Social Revolutions: A Comparative Analysis of France, Russia, and China* (Cambridge: Cambridge University Press, 1979), pp. 29–30; Gregory Hooks, "From an Autonomous to a Captured State Agency: The Decline of the New Deal in Agriculture," *American Sociological Review* 55(1): 32 (February 1990).

103. David Wilsford, "Tactical Advantages versus Administrative Heterogeneity: The Strengths and Limits of the French State," *Comparative Political Studies* 21(1): 157 (April 1988).

104. Eric A. Nordlinger, *On the Autonomy of the Democratic State* (Cam-

bridge: Harvard University Press, 1981), pp. 1, 9–20; William A. Niskanen, Jr., *Bureaucracy and Representative Government* (Chicago: Aldine-Atherton, 1971), pp. 36–42.

105. James Q. Wilson, *Bureaucracy: What Government Agencies Do and Why They Do It* (New York: Basic Books, 1989), pp. 179–95.

106. Skocpol, *States and Social Revolutions*, pp. 29–32.

107. Krasner, *Defending the National Interest*, pp. 10–13; Samuel P. Huntington, *Political Order in Changing Societies* (New Haven: Yale University Press, 1968), pp. 24–28.

108. Dietrich Rueschemeyer and Peter B. Evans, "The State and Economic Transformation: Toward an Analysis of the Conditions Underlying Effective Intervention," in Peter B. Evans, Dietrich Rueschemeyer, and Theda Skocpol, eds., *Bringing the State Back In* (Cambridge: Cambridge University Press, 1985), pp. 60–62; Fred Block, *Revising State Theory: Essays in Politics and Postindustrialism* (Philadelphia: Temple University Press, 1987), pp. 58–68.

109. Skocpol, *States and Social Revolutions*, p. 30; Suleiman, "State Structures and Clientelism," pp. 275–76.

110. Beth Walter Honadle, "A Capacity-Building Framework: A Search for Concept and Purpose," *Public Administration Review* 41(5): 577–78 (September/October 1981).

111. Nettl, "State as a Conceptual Variable," pp. 561, 567–70, 580; Krasner, *Defending the National Interest*, pp. 61–70; Badie and Birnbaum, *Sociology of the State*, pp. 125–30; Huntington, *Political Order*, pp. 100–106; Bert A. Rockman, "Minding the State—Or a State of Mind? Issues in the Comparative Conceptualization of the State," *Comparative Political Studies* 23(1): 35–37 (April 1990); Wilsford, "Tactical Advantages," pp. 132, 142.

112. Krasner, *Defending the National Interest*, pp. 11, 74–75, 85–88; Nettl, "State as a Conceptual Variable," p. 564.

113. Herbert Kaufman, *The Forest Ranger: A Study in Administrative Behavior* (Baltimore: Johns Hopkins Press, 1960), pp. x–xii, 161–200 (quote p. x); Rueschemeyer and Evans, "State and Economic Transformation," pp. 55–56; Wilson, *Bureaucracy*, pp. 50–71, 90–110.

114. Badie and Birnbaum, *Sociology of the State*, p. 73; Edward McChesney Sait, *Political Institutions: A Preface* (New York: Appleton-Century-Crofts, 1938), pp. 49–50; James G. March and Johan P. Olsen, *Rediscovering Institutions: The Organizational Basis of Politics* (New York: Free Press, 1989), pp. 54–56.

115. Suleiman, "State Structures and Clientelism," p. 276.

116. Joseph A. Schumpeter, *Business Cycles: A Theoretical, Historical, and Statistical Analysis of the Capitalist Process*, 2 vols., 2:1048 (New York: McGraw-Hill, 1939).

117. Stephen Skowronek, *Building a New American State: The Expansion of National Administrative Capacities, 1877–1920* (Cambridge: Cambridge University Press, 1982), pp. 19–35. This paragraph draws on Skowronek's analysis as a whole.

118. The phrase "businesscrat" comes from Galambos, *Competition and Cooperation*, p. 205. He attributes the word to Gerald D. Nash and comments

that it "accurately describes a twentieth-century breed of businessman who spends a significant part of his life working as a government bureaucrat" (p. 205 n. 3).

119. See Robert D. Cuff, *The War Industries Board: Business-Government Relations during World War I* (Baltimore: Johns Hopkins University Press, 1973).

120. Ellis W. Hawley, "Herbert Hoover, the Commerce Secretariat, and the Vision of an 'Associative State,' 1921–1928," *Journal of American History* 61 (1): 120 (June 1974).

121. Ibid., pp. 118–19.

122. See ibid. "Adhocracy" is Hawley's term for the links between the Commerce Department and private associations.

123. Ibid., p. 119.

124. On the situation before Hoover, see Lloyd Milton Short, *The Development of National Administrative Organization in the United States* (Baltimore: Johns Hopkins University Press, 1923), p. 408. Short points out that Commerce was put together from bureaus transferred from various other departments, and he comments: "While there is some evidence to indicate that Congress, in organizing this department, sought to give the Secretary a large measure of supervision and control over the organization and work of the several bureaus and offices, without regard to their status prior to their transfer to that department, this authority is not as complete as that possessed by the heads of some other departments, notably the Department of State and Department of Agriculture."

125. Hawley, " 'Associative State,' " pp. 138–39 n. 84; and Joan Hoff Wilson, *Herbert Hoover: Forgotten Progressive* (Boston: Little, Brown, 1975), p. 86.

126. Carroll H. Wooddy, *The Growth of the Federal Government, 1915–1932* (New York: McGraw-Hill, 1934), pp. 166–67.

127. Ibid., p. 176. Wooddy points out that the Bureau of Foreign and Domestic Commerce's work on export trade remained predominant in the 1920s. Work on domestic commerce grew, but less than one-fifth of the bureau's personnel specialized in this at the end of the decade (p. 177).

128. Paul M. Herzog, quoted in Katie Louchheim, ed., *The Making of the New Deal: The Insiders Speak* (Cambridge: Harvard University Press, 1983), p. 216. Both the NRA and, originally, the National Labor Board (where Herzog worked) were headquartered in the "four hundredth corridor" of the Commerce Building, although neither was ever part of the Commerce Department.

129. Van L. Perkins, *Crisis in Agriculture: The Agricultural Adjustment Administration and the New Deal* (Berkeley and Los Angeles: University of California Press, 1969), p. 97.

130. Nourse, Davis, and Black, *Three Years*, p. 59. Personnel also came from "the staff of the vanishing Federal Farm Board and from state agricultural college and experiment station staffs" (ibid.). On the BAE's contributions to the AAA, see also John M. Gaus and Leon O. Wolcott, *Public Administration and the United States Department of Agriculture* (Chicago: Public Administration Service, 1940), p. 54 n. 54.

131. Perkins, *Crisis in Agriculture*, pp. 97–99.

132. Short, *Development of National Administrative Organization*, pp. 393–94, and Wooddy, *Growth of the Federal Government*, pp. 277–78.

133. Gaus and Wolcott, *Public Administration*, pp. 277–78.

134. Quoted in Wooddy, *Growth of the Federal Government*, p. 209.

135. Gaus and Wolcott, *Public Administration*, p. 53.

136. Expenditure estimates are adapted from Wooddy, *Growth of the Federal Government*, using the total civil expenditure given in Table II (p. 543). Reflecting the government's own practice in his time, Wooddy presents figures on federal expenditures by functional categories rather than by department. Since breakdowns by bureaus are given in individual chapters, it proved possible to modify the functional totals for "agriculture" and "commerce" by reshuffling bureaus. Certain major bureaus were omitted: the Weather Bureau and the Bureau of Public Roads from Agriculture, and the Census Bureau from Commerce. Also (for minor deviations), the Food and Drug Administration was left in Commerce, and the (independent) Federal Farm Board was left in Agriculture (for 1930). The Agriculture Department expenditure figures are therefore not exact, but they are good rough approximations, consistent over time. Both departments' budgets are underestimated, Agriculture's probably more than that of Commerce. The figures are calculated in 1930 dollars.

137. Ibid., pp. 281, 166–67.

138. Gaus and Wolcott, *Public Administration*, pp. 53–54.

139. Ibid., p. 15.

140. Ibid., p. 16. Indeed, one sure indication of Agriculture's "corporate identity" over the decades is the presence in the library of many "in-house" histories of the department, as well as major social-scientific studies of its structure and operations. For an example of the former, see Gladys Baker et al., *Century of Service: The First 100 Years of the United States Department of Agriculture* (Washington, D.C.: Centennial Committee, USDA, 1963). No other federal cabinet department, except perhaps the State Department, has so much self-consciousness as Agriculture.

141. Gaus and Wolcott, *Public Administration*, p. 86.

142. Ibid., pp. 35–37.

143. Richard S. Kirkendall, *Social Scientists and Farm Politics in the Age of Roosevelt* (Columbia: University of Missouri Press, 1966), pp. 6, 257, argues that the agricultural experts were more than merely "servants of power," that is, paid experts working for farmers' organizations (or, for that matter, for business executives). He contrasts them to the experts working for industry discussed by Loren Baritz, *Servants of Power: A History of the Use of Social Science in American Industry* (Middletown, Conn.: Wesleyan University Press, 1960).

144. See Kirkendall, *Social Scientists and Farm Politics*, pp. 30–49, and William D. Rowley, *M. L. Wilson and the Campaign for the Domestic Allotment* (Lincoln: University of Nebraska Press, 1970), chaps. 7–9.

145. Wilson gave up the chance to be assistant secretary of Agriculture in order to head the more operationally crucial Wheat Section of the AAA.

146. John A. Armstrong, *The European Administrative Elite* (Princeton:

Princeton University Press, 1973), and Alfred Stepan, *The State and Society: Peru in Comparative Perspective* (Princeton: Princeton University Press, 1978), pp. 117–57.

147. Armstrong, *European Administrative Elite*, p. 305. See also Wilsford, "Tactical Advantages," pp. 140–41.

148. In addition to Stepan, *State and Society*, pp. 117–57, see Stepan, "The New Professionalism of Internal Warfare and Military Role Expansion," in Stepan, ed., *Authoritarian Brazil* (New Haven: Yale University Press, 1973), pp. 47–65.

149. Hugh Heclo, *Modern Social Politics in Britain and Sweden* (New Haven: Yale University Press, 1974), p. 305.

150. Ibid., p. 306.

151. Ibid., pp. 305–6.

152. Heclo argues that policy innovations usually come from "middlemen at the interfaces of various groups" (ibid., pp. 308–9). The interesting thing about the complex of agricultural institutions in the United States was that it encouraged (and allowed) people to *move about* from colleges to extension posts to the USDA and so forth, within the public world of American agriculture. Farmers' associations were active at many points in this world, so experts were never divorced from "politics" even as they maintained their own scientific and administrative roles.

153. Gaus and Wolcott, *Public Administration*, pp. 68–69. Part 1 of this study is, indeed, coherently constructed around a highly insightful "political learning" argument. The book bears reading not only for its "facts" but also for its sophisticated argument about the historical interplay of USDA development, farm politics, and agricultural policy making and implementation.

154. Galambos, *Competition and Cooperation*, focuses on the "organizational learning" of trade association leaders as one of its major themes.

155. See William E. Leuchtenburg, "The New Deal and the Analogue of War," in John Braeman, Robert Bremner, and E. Walters, eds., *Change and Continuity in Twentieth-Century America* (Columbus: Ohio State University Press, 1964), for an excellent discussion of the invocation of World War I symbolism and models, especially under the NRA.

Chapter 3. The Origins of the NRA and the AAA

1. Robert F. Himmelberg, *The Origins of the National Recovery Administration: Business, Government, and the Trade Association Issue, 1921–1933* (New York: Fordham University Press, 1976), chaps. 5, 7; Louis Galambos, *Competition and Cooperation: The Emergence of a National Trade Association* (Baltimore: Johns Hopkins Press, 1966), chaps. 7–8.

2. J. George Frederick, ed., *The Swope Plan* (New York: Business Bourse, 1931); Arthur M. Schlesinger, Jr., *The Crisis of the Old Order, 1919–1933* (Cambridge: Riverside Press, 1957), pp. 181–83; Ellis W. Hawley, *The New Deal and the Problem of Monopoly* (Princeton: Princeton University Press, 1966), pp. 36–43; Stanley Vittoz, *New Deal Labor Policy and the American Industrial Economy*

(Chapel Hill: University of North Carolina Press, 1987), pp. 79–82; Charles Frederick Roos, *NRA Economic Planning* (Bloomington, Ind.: Principia Press, 1937), pp. 18–20.

3. Himmelberg, *Origins*, pp. 192–95; Vittoz, *New Deal Labor Policy*, p. 81.

4. Roos, *NRA Economic Planning*, pp. 4–7, 12–13.

5. Elizabeth Sanders, "Industrial Concentration, Sectional Competition, and Antitrust Politics in America, 1880–1980," *Studies in American Political Development* 1 (1986): 184–86; Hawley, *New Deal*, pp. 43–51; Roos, *NRA Economic Planning*, pp. 11–12.

6. Vittoz, *New Deal Labor Policy*, pp. 81–82; Himmelberg, *Origins*, pp. 168–69; Roos, *NRA Economic Planning*, pp. 19, 28–30; Virginia Van der Veer Hamilton, *Hugo Black: The Alabama Years* (Baton Rouge: Louisiana State University Press, 1972), pp. 215–16; Irving Bernstein, *The Lean Years: A History of the American Worker, 1920–1933* (Cambridge, Mass.: Riverside Press, 1960), pp. 476–82.

7. Hawley, *New Deal*, p. 42 (Hoover quote); Himmelberg, *Origins*, pp. 151–80.

8. Himmelberg, *Origins*, pp. 170–71.

9. William E. Leuchtenburg, *Franklin D. Roosevelt and the New Deal, 1932–1940* (New York: Harper & Row, 1963), pp. 41–53.

10. Himmelberg, *Origins*, pp. 186–89.

11. Ibid., pp. 190–92; George Martin, *Madame Secretary: Frances Perkins* (Boston: Houghton Mifflin, 1976), pp. 251–56.

12. Raymond Moley, *After Seven Years* (New York: Harper & Row, 1939), pp. 184–86.

13. Frank Freidel, *Franklin D. Roosevelt: Launching the New Deal* (Boston: Little, Brown, 1973), p. 418.

14. National Industrial Conference Board, *Shorter Work Periods in Industry* (New York: National Industrial Conference Board, Inc., 1932), p. 44; Bernstein, *Lean Years*, pp. 223–24, 476.

15. Elizabeth Sanders, "The Institutional Conditions of an Instrumentalist Presidency: Contrasting Threads of Reform in American Political Development" (Paper presented to the American Political Science Association annual meeting, Atlanta, August 1989), p. 2.

16. Hamilton, *Hugo Black*, p. 215 n. 3.

17. Bernstein, *Lean Years*, pp. 481–82; Craig Phelan, *William Green: Biography of a Labor Leader* (Albany: State University of New York Press, 1989), pp. 59–60, 62.

18. Senate Committee on Judiciary, *Thirty-Hour Work Week: Hearings on S. 5267*, 72nd Cong., 2d. sess., 1933, pp. 21–22.

19. Jordan A. Schwarz, *The Interregnum of Despair: Hoover, Congress, and the Depression* (Urbana: University of Illinois Press, 1970), pp. 208–9; Hamilton, *Hugo Black*, pp. 217–18.

20. Vittoz, *New Deal Labor Policy*, pp. 84–85.

21. Frances Perkins, *The Roosevelt I Knew* (New York: Harper & Row, 1946), p. 194 (quote); Freidel, *Launching the New Deal*, p. 419; Moley, *After Seven*

Years, p. 186; idem, *The First New Deal* (New York: Harcourt, Brace & World, 1966), p. 287.

22. Hamilton, *Hugo Black,* p. 217.

23. Ibid., p. 218; Roos, *NRA Economic Planning,* p. 31.

24. Sanders, "Institutional Conditions," p. 2.

25. Moley, *After Seven Years,* p. 187; Hawley, *New Deal,* pp. 22–23; Phelan, *William Green,* pp. 61–62; Martin, *Madame Secretary,* pp. 261–63; Vittoz, *New Deal Labor Policy,* pp. 85–86; Roos, *NRA Economic Planning,* pp. 31–32.

26. Arthur M. Schlesinger, Jr., *The Coming of the New Deal* (Boston: Houghton Mifflin, 1959), pp. 96–98; Hawley, *New Deal,* pp. 23–26; Himmelberg, *Origins,* pp. 196–208; Vittoz, *New Deal Labor Policy,* pp. 87–93; Roos, *NRA Economic Planning,* pp. 36–40.

27. Galambos, *Competition and Cooperation,* pp. 195–96.

28. Himmelberg, *Origins,* p. 201, emphasizes that by mid-April 1933, business leaders had learned from their earlier failures to convert Roosevelt to antitrust relaxation "the lesson that their objective had to be cloaked more substantially in the rhetoric of recovery planning to attain success."

29. Ronald A. Mulder, *The Insurgent Republicans in the United States Senate and the New Deal, 1933–1939* (New York: Garland, 1979), pp. 56–60; Roos, *NRA Economic Planning,* pp. 45–46, 50–51; Hamilton, *Hugo Black,* p. 220. In the Senate, where the antitrust agricultural periphery was overrepresented, the NIRA passed by a 46–39 vote; the House, apportioned by population, voted 323–76.

30. Irving Bernstein, *The New Deal Collective Bargaining Policy* (Berkeley and Los Angeles: University of California Press, 1950), pp. 34–38.

31. On Wagner's role, see J. Joseph Huthmacher, *Senator Robert F. Wagner and the Rise of Urban Liberalism* (New York: Atheneum, 1971), pp. 147–48.

32. Leon H. Keyserling, quoted in Katie Louchheim, ed., *The Making of the New Deal: The Insiders Speak* (Cambridge: Harvard University Press, 1983), p. 197.

33. Samuel I. Rosenman, comp., *The Public Papers and Addresses of Franklin D. Roosevelt,* 13 vols. (New York: Random House, 1938), 2:164.

34. See Schwarz, *Interregnum of Despair.*

35. James T. Patterson, *Congressional Conservatism and the New Deal* (Lexington: University of Kentucky Press, 1967), pp. 4–6. Patterson notes that 131 of 311 House Democrats elected in 1932 were newcomers and that many of them were from normally Republican districts.

36. Moley, *First New Deal,* p. 524. See also Roy V. Peel and Thomas C. Donnelly, *The 1932 Campaign: An Analysis* (New York: Farrar & Rinehart, 1935), p. 31.

37. Moley, *First New Deal,* pp. 524–25; Peel and Donnelly, *1932 Campaign,* pp. 27–28, 216–17, 225; Frank Freidel, *Franklin D. Roosevelt: The Triumph* (Boston: Little, Brown, 1956), pp. 228–371.

38. Phelan, *William Green,* p. 63; David Plotke, "The Wagner Act, Again: Politics and Labor, 1935–37," *Studies in American Political Development* 3 (1989): 114; Freidel, *Triumph,* p. 358; Bernstein, *New Deal Collective Bargaining Policy,* p. 27.

39. James L. Sundquist, *Dynamics of the Party System: Alignment and Re-*

alignment of Political Parties in the United States, rev. ed. (Washington, D.C.: Brookings Institution, 1983), pp. 217–19.

40. Leo Troy, *Trade Union Membership, 1897–1962* (New York: Columbia University Press for National Bureau of Economic Research, 1965), p. 4.

41. Phelan, *William Green*, pp. 62–63; Martin, *Madame Secretary*, p. 253. Republican labor leaders who supported Hoover included John L. Lewis of the United Mine Workers, William Hutcheson of the Carpenters, and Matthew Woll of the Photo Engravers.

42. Himmelberg, *Origins*, pp. 182–83.

43. Charles E. Wyzanski, solicitor of the Labor Department, quoted in Martin, *Madame Secretary*, pp. 525–36 n. 6.

44. Michel Petit, *Determinants of Agricultural Policies in the United States and the European Community* (Washington, D.C.: International Food Policy Research Institute, 1985), p. 25.

45. Clifford B. Anderson, "The Metamorphosis of American Agrarian Idealism in the 1920's and 1930's," *Agricultural History* 35(4): 182–88 (October 1961); Joseph S. Davis, "Agricultural Fundamentalism," in Davis, ed., *On Agricultural Policy, 1926–1938* (Stanford University: Food Research Institute, 1939; [1st publ. 1935]). For a contemporary restatement of agricultural fundamentalism, see Wendell Berry, *The Unsettling of America: Culture and Agriculture* (San Francisco: Sierra Club, 1977).

46. Arthur Capper, *The Agricultural Bloc* (New York: Harcourt, Brace, 1922), pp. 117, 140–61, 177; James H. Shideler, *Farm Crisis, 1919–1923* (Berkeley and Los Angeles: University of California Press, 1963), pp. 155–65; Orville Merton Kile, *The Farm Bureau through Three Decades* (Baltimore: Waverly, 1948), pp. 92–103; Grant McConnell, *The Decline of Agrarian Democracy* (Berkeley and Los Angeles: University of California Press, 1953), pp. 57–59; Theodore Saloutos and John D. Hicks, *Agricultural Discontent in the Middle West, 1900–1939* (Madison: University of Wisconsin Press, 1951), pp. 321–41; Murray R. Benedict, *Farm Policies of the United States, 1790–1950* (New York: Twentieth Century Fund, 1953), pp. 181–84, 187–88; Theodore Saloutos, *Farmer Movements in the South* (Berkeley and Los Angeles: University of California Press, 1960), pp. 265–66; Donald L. Winters, *Henry Cantwell Wallace as Secretary of Agriculture, 1921–1924* (Urbana: University of Illinois Press, 1970), pp. 89–90.

47. Richard M. Valelly, *Radicalism in the States: The Minnesota Farmer-Labor Party and the American Political Economy* (Chicago: University of Chicago Press, 1989); Daniel P. Thelen, *Robert M. La Follette and the Insurgent Spirit* (Boston: Little, Brown, 1976), pp. 157–60, 163, 168–69, 170–72, 174–75, 182–92; Saloutos and Hicks, *Agricultural Discontent*, pp. 342–56, 361–71; Shideler, *Farm Crisis*, pp. 220–230, 235–39; Kenneth Campbell MacKay, *The Progressive Movement of 1924* (New York: Columbia University Press, 1947); John D. Hicks, *Republican Ascendancy, 1921–1933* (New York: Harper & Brothers, 1960), pp. 170–72; Russel B. Nye, *Midwestern Progressive Politics* (East Lansing: Michigan State University Press, 1959), pp. 300–302.

48. Shideler, *Farm Crisis*, pp. 95–104; Saloutos and Hicks, *Agricultural Discontent*, pp. 287–320; Saloutos, *Farmer Movements in the South*, pp. 260–64.

49. Shideler, *Farm Crisis*, p. 102. For peak association data, see Robert L. Tontz, "Memberships of General Farmers' Organizations, United States, 1874–1960," *Agricultural History* 38(3): 154–56 (July 1964).

50. On the Farm Bureau, see Kile, *Farm Bureau*, pp. 114–21, 134; Saloutos and Hicks, *Agricultural Discontent*, pp. 273–81; Joseph G. Knapp, *The Advance of American Cooperative Enterprise, 1920–1945* (Danville, Ill.: Interstate, 1973), pp. 35–53. On the Farmers' Union, see Shideler, *Farm Crisis*, pp. 106, 304–7, and William P. Tucker, "Populism Up-to-Date: The Story of the Farmers' Union," *Agricultural History* 21(4): 201–2 (October 1947). On the Grange, see Charles M. Gardner, *The Grange: Friend of the Farmer* (Washington, D.C.: National Grange, 1949), pp. 94–95.

51. Shideler, *Farm Crisis*, pp. 111–17; Saloutos, *Farmer Movements in the South*, p. 263.

52. George N. Peek and Hugh S. Johnson, "Equality for Agriculture," reprinted in Wayne D. Rasmussen, ed., *Agriculture in the United States: A Documentary History*, 4 vols. (New York: Random House, 1973), 3:2157–78.

53. Gilbert C. Fite, *George N. Peek and the Fight for Farm Parity* (Norman: University of Oklahoma Press, 1954), pp. 50–52, 78–84, 196–99.

54. See Simon Harris, Alan Swinback, and Guy Wilkinson, *The Food and Farm Policies of the European Community* (Chichester, Eng.: John Wiley & Sons, 1983), pp. 44–54, 323–39; Michael Tracy, *Government and Agriculture in Western Europe, 1880–1988*, 3d ed. (New York: New York University Press, 1989), pp. 331–36, 343–47.

55. Winters, *Henry Cantwell Wallace*, pp. 259–67; Fite, *George N. Peek*, pp. 44–72, 77–94, 106–208; Saloutos, *Farmer Movements in the South*, pp. 266–70; Christiana McFadyen Campbell, *The Farm Bureau and the New Deal* (Urbana: University of Illinois Press, 1962), pp. 35–40; Richard Franklin Bensel, *Sectionalism and American Political Development, 1880–1980* (Madison: University of Wisconsin Press, 1984), pp. 139–47. The cooperatives' attitude toward McNary-Haugen is discussed in Benedict, *Farm Policies of the United States*, pp. 223–24; Knapp, *Advance of American Cooperative Enterprise*, pp. 107–8. Coolidge's first veto message is reprinted in Rasmussen, ed., *Agriculture in the United States* 3:2190–2204.

56. W. J. Spillman, *Balancing the Farm Output* (New York: Orange, Judd, 1927), pp. 84–111; John D. Black, *Agricultural Reform in the United States* (New York: McGraw-Hill, 1929), pp. 271–301; William D. Rowley, *M. L. Wilson and the Campaign for the Domestic Allotment* (Lincoln: University of Nebraska Press, 1970), p. 123; Richard S. Kirkendall, *Social Scientists and Farm Politics in the Age of Roosevelt* (Columbia: University of Missouri Press, 1966), pp. 24–26; David E. Hamilton, *From New Day to New Deal: American Farm Policy from Hoover to Roosevelt, 1928–1933* (Chapel Hill: University of North Carolina Press, 1991), pp. 170–94.

57. Kirkendall, *Social Scientists and Farm Politics*, pp. 18–21, 30–32 (Smith

quote p. 32); Hamilton, *From New Day to New Deal*, pp. 189 (Snyder quote), 200–201; Gilbert C. Fite, "Farmer Opinion and the Agricultural Adjustment Act," *Mississippi Valley Historical Review* 48(4): 660–67, 672–73 (March 1962); idem, *George N. Peek*, p. 190.

58. Richard Lowitt, ed., *Journal of a Tamed Bureaucrat: Nils A. Olsen and the BAE, 1925–1935* (Ames: Iowa State University Press, 1980), pp. 141–42, 148–49, 152–54, 158-59, 161 (quote); Hamilton, *From New Day to New Deal*, pp. 171–80.

59. Kile, *Farm Bureau*, pp. 97–99, 101–2; Capper, *Agricultural Bloc*, pp. 118–19, 123; Saloutos and Hicks, *Agricultural Discontent*, pp. 331–32; Shideler, *Farm Crisis*, pp. 164–65.

60. Knapp, *Advance of American Cooperative Enterprise*, pp. 90–95, 100–106; Benedict, *Farm Policies of the United States*, pp. 221–23.

61. Fite, *George N. Peek*, pp. 68–69, 78–81, 148–49, 163–64, 182–83, 196–200; John P. Gleason, "The Attitude of the Business Community toward Agriculture during the McNary-Haugen Period," *Agricultural History* 32(1): 127–38 (January 1958). Wall Street's Bernard Baruch, a seemingly anomalous supporter of the McNary-Haugen Plan, had investments in cotton warehouses, farm implement companies, and land. Peek and Johnson were also his protégés from the three men's service together at the War Industries Board. See Jordan A. Schwarz, *The Speculator: Bernard M. Baruch in Washington, 1917–1965* (Chapel Hill: University of North Carolina Press, 1981), pp. 235–41.

62. David Burner, *The Politics of Provincialism: The Democratic Party in Transition, 1918–1932* (New York: Alfred A. Knopf, 1968), pp. 80–94, 117–28, 164–67, 190–243; Fite, *George N. Peek*, pp. 202–20; Kile, *Farm Bureau*, pp. 148–50.

63. Donald R. McCoy, "Election of 1920," in Arthur M. Schlesinger, Jr., and Fred L. Israel, eds., *History of American Presidential Elections, 1789–1968*, 4 vols. (New York: Chelsea House, 1971), 3:2351–53, 2355–59; David Burner, "Election of 1924," also in Schlesinger and Israel, *History of American Presidential Elections*, 3:2461–66; Hicks, *Republican Ascendancy*, pp. 62–64, 90–91, 123–24, 219–23; Roy V. Peel and Thomas Donnelly, *The 1928 Campaign: An Analysis* (New York: Richard R. Smith, 1931), pp. 8–9, 28–36; Thelen, *Robert M. La Follette*, pp. 169–75; Burner, *Politics of Provincialism*, pp. 161–68; Nye, *Midwestern Progressive Politics*, pp. 297–98.

64. The Federal Farm Board is discussed in Hamilton, *From New Day to New Deal*, pp. 26–147; Knapp, *Advance of American Cooperative Enterprise*, pp. 122–42; Benedict, *Farm Policies of the United States*, pp. 257–67; Kile, *Farm Bureau*, pp. 163–69; Saloutos, *Farmer Movements in the South*, pp. 273–75; Bernard M. Klass, "The Federal Farm Board and the Antecedents of the Agricultural Adjustment Act, 1929–1933," in Carl E. Krog and William R. Tanner, eds., *Herbert Hoover and the Republican Era: A Reconsideration* (Lanham, Md.: University Press of America, 1984), pp. 191–219; Martin L. Fausold, "President Hoover's Farm Policies, 1929–1933," *Agricultural History* 51(2): 362–78 (April 1977).

65. Hamilton, *From New Day to New Deal*, pp. 132–33.

66. Ibid., pp. 198–200.

67. Kirkendall, *Social Scientists and Farm Politics*, pp. 32–40; Rowley, *M. L. Wilson*, pp. 105–6, 114–16, 124–25, 128–29, 139–40, 154–55, 163–66; G. William

Domhoff, "Class, Power, and Parties in the New Deal: A Critique of Skocpol's State Autonomy Theory," *Berkeley Journal of Sociology* 36 (1991): 10–14.

68. Kirkendall, *Social Scientists and Farm Politics*, p. 52; Rowley, M. L. Wilson, pp. 154–55; Van L. Perkins, *Crisis in Agriculture: The Agricultural Adjustment Administration and the New Deal, 1933* (Berkeley and Los Angeles: University of California Press, 1969), pp. 54–55.

69. Kirkendall, *Social Scientists and Farm Politics*, pp. 40–41; Hamilton, *From New Day to New Deal*, pp. 208–9.

70. Elliot A. Rosen, *Hoover, Roosevelt, and the Brains Trust* (New York: Columbia University Press, 1977), pp. 6–38, 95–242 passim; Peel and Donnelly, *1932 Campaign*, pp. 59–81.

71. Rosen, *Hoover, Roosevelt, and the Brains Trust*, pp. 162, 175–78, 335–40; Rosenman, comp., *Public Papers and Addresses*, 1:702–5; Bernard Sternsher, *Rexford Tugwell and the New Deal* (New Brunswick: Rutgers University Press, 1964), pp. 42–43; Freidel, *Triumph*, pp. 342–50; Hamilton, *From New Day to New Deal*, pp. 210–12.

72. Gertrude Almy Slichter, "Franklin D. Roosevelt and the Farm Problem, 1929–1932," *Mississippi Valley Historical Review* 43(2): 248–58 (September 1956); Campbell, *Farm Bureau and the New Deal*, p. 51; Gilbert C. Fite, "John A. Simpson: The Southwest's Militant Farm Leader," *Mississippi Valley Historical Review* 35(4): 575–77 (March 1949); Fite, *George N. Peek*, pp. 237–41; Freidel, *Triumph*, p. 348.

73. "A basic principle of administrative planning . . . is that interested private groups should be sounded out and given an opportunity to work upon important Department policy proposals in advance of their public unveiling. The more drastic the changes being contemplated, the more imperative the necessity for such consultation.

"Given the chance to participate in a Department's planning program, private organizations can often make searching criticisms and contribute constructive suggestions. They can also, where this proves desirable, more easily shift their own policy positions and prepare their membership for those shifts." Reo M. Christenson, *The Brannan Plan: Farm Politics and Policy* (Ann Arbor: University of Michigan Press, 1959), pp. 173–74.

74. William R. Johnson, "National Farm Organizations and the Reshaping of Agricultural Policy in 1932," *Agricultural History* 37(1): 41–42 (January 1963); Kile, *Farm Bureau*, pp. 191–92; Campbell, *Farm Bureau and the New Deal*, pp. 52–54; Fite, "John A. Simpson," pp. 577–78; Edward L. Schapsmeier and Frederick H. Schapsmeier, *Henry A. Wallace of Iowa: The Agrarian Years, 1910–1940* (Ames: Iowa State University Press, 1968), pp. 127–29, 149–51; Henry A. Wallace, *New Frontiers* (New York: Reynal & Hitchcock, 1934), pp. 162–63.

75. Perkins, *Crisis in Agriculture*, pp. 36–78; John L. Shover, *Cornbelt Rebellion: The Farmers' Holiday Association* (Urbana: University of Illinois Press, 1965), pp. 103–12.

76. Fite, *George N. Peek*, p. 252.

77. Freidel, *Triumph*, pp. 274, 342.

78. Ernest K. Lindley, *The Roosevelt Revolution—First Phase* (New York: Vi-

king, 1933), p. 313; Gaus and Wolcott, *Public Administration,* pp. 35–36; Kirkendall, *Social Scientists and Farm Politics,* pp. 11–29; Rowley, M. L. Wilson, p. 3; Hamilton, *From New Day to New Deal,* pp. 180, 186–87.

79. Rowley, M. L. Wilson, pp. 150–52; Kirkendall, *Social Scientists and Farm Politics,* pp. 175–78; Schapsmeier and Schapsmeier, *Henry A. Wallace,* pp. 127–29, 149–51.

80. Robert B. Reich, "Introduction," in Reich, ed., *The Power of Public Ideas* (Cambridge: Ballinger, 1988), pp. 1–7; Gary R. Orren, "Beyond Self-Interest," also in Reich, ed., *Power of Public Ideas,* pp. 14–24; Mark H. Moore, "What Sort of Ideas Become Public Ideas?" also in Reich, ed., *Power of Public Ideas,* pp. 71, 77–78; Peter A. Hall, "Conclusion: The Politics of Keynesian Ideas," in Hall, ed., *The Political Power of Economic Ideas: Keynesianism across Nations* (Princeton: Princeton University Press, 1989),pp. 361–62; James Q. Wilson, "American Politics, Then and Now," *Commentary* 67(2): 46 (February 1979).

81. Moore, "What Sort of Ideas Become Public Ideas?" pp. 71–72.

82. Judith Goldstein, "The Impact of Ideas on Trade Policy: The Origins of U.S. Agricultural and Manufacturing Policies," *International Organization* 43(1): 32 (Winter 1989).

83. Ibid., p. 70.

84. Martha Derthick and Paul J. Quirk, *The Politics of Deregulation* (Washington, D.C.: Brookings Institution, 1985), pp. 238–39, 242, 245–52, 256–57; Paul J. Quirk, "In Defense of the Politics of Ideas," *Journal of Politics* 50(1): 31–41 (February 1988).

85. Hall, "Politics of Keynesian Ideas," p. 369.

86. Hugh Heclo, *Modern Social Politics in Britain and Sweden* (New Haven: Yale University Press, 1974), p. 305.

87. Hall, "Politics of Keynesian Ideas," pp. 362, 369–75, 389–90; idem, *Governing the Economy: The Politics of State Intervention in Britain and France* (New York: Oxford University Press, 1986), pp. 276–80; Moore, "What Sort of Ideas Become Public Ideas?" pp. 78–80; Derthick and Quirk, *Politics of Deregulation,* pp. 246–47; Goldstein, "Impact of Ideas," p. 71.

88. Derthick and Quirk, *Politics of Deregulation,* p. 247.

89. Alexis de Tocqueville, *The Old Régime and the French Revolution* (Garden City, N.Y.: Doubleday, 1955), pp. 145–46. See also Edmund Burke, *Reflections on the Revolution in France* (Indianapolis: Bobbs-Merrill, 1955), pp. 95–102.

Peter A. Hall suggests that for institutional reasons, France remains more open to policy innovation than Britain, with the United States in between. See Peter A. Hall, "Policy Innovation and the Structure of the State: The Politics-Administration Nexus in France and Britain," in Charles E. Gilbert, ed., *Implementing Governmental Change, Annals of the American Academy of Political and Social Science* no. 466 (March 1983): 46–47, 50–51, 58–59.

90. Wilson, "American Politics, Then and Now," pp. 44–45; Hugh Heclo, "Issue Networks and the Executive Establishment," in Anthony King, ed., *The New American Political System* (Washington, D.C.: American Enterprise Institute, 1978), pp. 88, 102.

91. Hall, "Policy Innovation," p. 59.

92. The logic of their case selection is explained in Derthick and Quirk, *Politics of Deregulation*, pp. 16–19, 27–28.

93. Goldstein, "Impact of Ideas," pp. 33–34 n. 3 (quote), 50, 56–57.

94. Heclo, "Issue Networks," pp. 113, 115.

95. John W. Kingdon, *Agendas, Alternatives, and Public Policies* (Boston: Little, Brown, 1984).

96. Ibid., pp. 173–79.

97. Ibid., pp. 129–30, 188–93. See also Nelson W. Polsby, *Political Innovation in America: The Politics of Policy Initiation* (New Haven: Yale University Press, 1984), pp. 55, 157–58, 174.

98. Kingdon, *Agendas, Alternatives, and Public Policies*, pp. 77, 81–82; see also Polsby, *Political Innovation*, pp. 155–57.

99. Kingdon, *Agendas, Alternatives, and Public Policies*, pp. 131, 138–39, 151.

100. Ibid., p. 52.

101. For example, Frances Fox Piven and Richard A. Cloward, *Poor People's Movements: Why They Succeed, How They Fail* (New York: Vintage, 1979); Michael Goldfield, "Worker Insurgency, Radical Organization, and New Deal Labor Legislation," *American Political Science Review* 83(4): 1268–78 (December 1989); idem, "Explaining New Deal Labor Policy," *American Political Science Review* 84(4): 1312 (December 1990).

102. See Shover, *Cornbelt Rebellion*, pp. 168–86.

103. Moley, *First New Deal*, p. 287.

Chapter 4. The Implementation of Industrial and Agricultural Planning

1. Alexis de Tocqueville, *Democracy in America* (Garden City, New York: Doubleday, 1969), p. 90.

2. John Kennedy Ohl, *Hugh S. Johnson and the New Deal* (DeKalb: Northern Illinois University Press, 1985), pp. 36–112; Arthur M. Schlesinger, Jr., *The Coming of the New Deal* (Boston: Houghton Mifflin, 1959), pp. 87–88, 103–7.

3. Charles Frederick Roos, *NRA Economic Planning* (Bloomington, Ind.: Principia Press, 1937), p. 58; Ellis W. Hawley, *The New Deal and the Problem of Monopoly: A Study in Economic Ambivalence* (Princeton: Princeton University Press, 1966), p. 73; Ohl, *Hugh S. Johnson*, pp. 107–8.

4. Ohl, *Hugh S. Johnson*, pp. 107, 111–12; Schlesinger, *Coming of the New Deal*, pp. 104–5, 109–10; Hugh S. Johnson, *The Blue Eagle from Egg to Earth* (Garden City, N.Y.: Doubleday, Doran, 1935), pp. 164, 200–201, 209–211; Roos, *NRA Economic Planning*, pp. 426–27; Bernard Bellush, *The Failure of the NRA* (New York: Norton, 1975), pp. 30–31; Charles E. Jacob, *Leadership in the New Deal: The Administrative Challenge* (Englewood Cliffs, N.J.: Prentice-Hall, 1967), pp. 6–8, 16, 25. Jacob points out that Roosevelt repeated the pattern of dividing authority between a vigorous leader such as Johnson and a careful administrator such as Ickes throughout the New Deal. See *Leadership in the New Deal*, pp. 25–26.

5. Louis Galambos, *Competition and Cooperation: The Emergence of a National Trade Association* (Baltimore: Johns Hopkins Press, 1966), p. 227.

6. Johnson, *Blue Eagle*, p. 286. Leverett S. Lyon et al., *The National Recovery Administration: An Analysis and Appraisal* (Washington, D.C.: Brookings Institution, 1935), p. 30, gives the NRA's peak size as 4,500. This was reached in February 1935, after Johnson had left the NRA.

7. The rest of this paragraph and the next draw on Lyon et al., *National Recovery Administration*, pp. 10, 30, 52–53; Ohl, *Hugh S. Johnson*, pp. 138–45; Hawley, *New Deal*, pp. 53–55; Roos, *NRA Economic Planning*, pp. 75–77, 92–93, 317; Johnson, *Blue Eagle*, pp. 250–70; Bellush, *Failure of the NRA*, pp. 48–52.

8. Johnson, *Blue Eagle*, p. 251. Emphasis in original.

9. Milton Katz, quoted in Katie Louchheim, ed., *The Making of the New Deal: The Insiders Speak* (Cambridge: Harvard University Press, 1983), p. 122.

10. Johnson, *Blue Eagle*, p. 261. Emphasis in original.

11. Galambos, *Competition and Cooperation*, p. 209.

12. Lyon et al., *National Recovery Administration*, pp. 29, 141; Johnson, *Blue Eagle*, p. 286. Different sources report varying figures for the number of approved codes; 557 codes were published as approved in the NRA's official *Codes of Fair Competition*.

13. John Franklin Carter [Unofficial Observer], *The New Dealers* (New York: Simon & Schuster, 1934), pp. 42–49 (quote on Williams p. 47); Hawley, *New Deal*, pp. 56–57; Johnson, *Blue Eagle*, pp. 191, 212–16; Ohl, *Hugh S. Johnson*, pp. 108–10; Galambos, *Competition and Cooperation*, p. 206. Slater's biography up to the New Deal can be found in *National Cyclopedia of American Biography* (New York: John T. White & Co., 1934), D:290.

14. Lewis L. Lorwin and A. F. Hinrichs, *National Economic and Social Planning: Theory and Practice with Special Reference to the United States* (Washington, D.C.: n.p., 1935), p. 85.

15. Adam Smith, *The Wealth of Nations* (New York: Modern Library, 1937), p. 250.

16. Lyon et al., *National Recovery Administration*, p. 280.

17. This paragraph and the next draw on ibid., pp. 130–31; Ohl, *Hugh S. Johnson*, pp. 182, 193; Hawley, *New Deal*, pp. 77–78, 100–103; Bellush, *Failure of the NRA*, p. 65; Galambos, *Competition and Cooperation*, pp. 236–39; George B. Galloway et al., *Industrial Planning under Codes* (New York: Harper & Brothers, 1935), pp. 52, 78, 417, 423; Roos, *NRA Economic Planning*, pp. 60, 62, 62 n. 9, 64, 71, 98, 461, 467; Lorwin and Hinrichs, *National Economic and Social Planning*, pp. 77, 93–94.

The analysis presented here is very different from that of Donald R. Brand, who argues that the growing influence of economists and consumer advocates made the NRA increasingly autonomous from business interests. Brand notes the number of professional economists within the NRA but not their marginal position, and he overstates the extent to which Memorandum 228 actually transformed NRA code administration. See Donald R. Brand, *Corporatism and the Rule of Law: A Study of the National Recovery Administration* (Ithaca, N.Y.: Cornell University Press, 1988), pp. 109, 115, 123–24.

18. Matthew Josephson, *Infidel in the Temple: A Memoir of the Nineteen-Thir-

ties (New York: Alfred A. Knopf, 1967), p. 267. On Johnson's relations with the Consumers' Advisory Board, see also Ohl, *Hugh S. Johnson*, pp. 179–83; Hawley, *New Deal*, pp. 75–78; Schlesinger, *Coming of the New Deal*, pp. 130–32; Persia Campbell, *Consumer Representation in the New Deal* (New York: Columbia University Press, 1940), pp. 31, 56, 67, 77–79.

19. Ohl, *Hugh S. Johnson*, pp. 17–20, 55, 68.

20. Thomas E. Vadney, *The Wayward Liberal: A Political Biography of Donald Richberg* (Lexington: University Press of Kentucky, 1970), pp. 119–21, 128–29; Peter Irons, *The New Deal Lawyers* (Princeton: Princeton University Press, 1982), pp. 28–30.

21. Lyon et al., *National Recovery Administration*, p. 64. See also ibid., pp. 63, 129–30.

22. Irons, *New Deal Lawyers*, pp. 30–31.

23. Hugh Heclo, "Industrial Policies and the Executive Capacities of Government," in Claude E. Barfield and William A. Schambra, eds., *The Politics of Industrial Policy* (Washington, D.C.: American Enterprise Institute, 1986), pp. 300–302.

24. Tocqueville, *Democracy in America*, pp. 267–69. See also Edward H. Levi, *An Introduction to Legal Reasoning* (Chicago: University of Chicago Press, 1949), pp. 1-2, 103; Robin Stryker, "Limits on Technocratization of the Law: The Elimination of the National Labor Relations Board's Division of Economic Research," *American Sociological Review* 54(3): 342 (June 1989); idem, "A Tale of Two Agencies: Class, Political-Institutional, and Organizational Factors Affecting State Reliance on Social Science," *Politics and Society* 18(1): 104–5 (March 1990).

25. Irons, *New Deal Lawyers*, p. 46.

26. James Q. Wilson, *Bureaucracy: What Government Agencies Do and Why They Do It* (New York: Basic Books, 1989), pp. 60–61; idem, "The Politics of Regulation," in Wilson, ed., *The Politics of Regulation* (New York: Basic Books, 1980), pp. 379–81. For perceptive observations about the differences between lawyers and economists within the same agency, see the 1939 statements by William Leiserson and Charles Fahy of the National Labor Relations Board, quoted in Stryker, "Tale of Two Agencies," pp. 119–20.

Again, our analysis contrasts with that of Donald Brand, who emphasizes the autonomy of the NRA lawyers and praises them for constructing regulations consistent with the rule of law. See Brand, *Corporatism and the Rule of Law*, pp. 123–24, 307–8.

27. Earl Latham, *The Group Basis of Politics: A Study in Basing-Point Legislation* (Ithaca, N.Y.: Cornell University Press, 1952), p. 71.

28. Lyon et al., *National Recovery Administration*, pp. 89–91, 166–69, 206–14; Galloway et al., *Industrial Planning under Codes*, pp. 416–17; Lorwin and Hinrichs, *National Economic and Social Planning*, p. 93; Hawley, *New Deal*, p. 61.

29. Galloway et al., *Industrial Planning under Codes*, p. 75.

30. Ibid., pp. 74–80; Roos, *NRA Economic Planning*, pp. 63–67, 466–67, 472; Lyon et al., *National Recovery Administration*, pp. 102, 111, 117–18, 130, 133, 205,

224–25; Bellush, *Failure of the NRA*, pp. 46, 143; Josephson, *Infidel in the Temple*, p. 270; Hawley, *New Deal*, p. 89; Lorwin and Hinrichs, *National Economic and Social Planning*, p. 77; Galambos, *Competition and Cooperation*, p. 205.

31. Roos, *NRA Economic Planning*, p. 67.

32. Hawley, *New Deal*, p. 69.

33. Ibid.

34. Campbell, *Consumer Representation*, p. 44.

35. Ibid., pp. 22–88; Lucy Black Creighton, *Pretenders to the Throne: The Consumer Movement in the United States* (Lexington, Mass.: D.C. Heath, 1976), pp. 22–29; Lyon et al., *National Recovery Administration*, pp. 123–29; Hawley, *New Deal*, pp. 75–79, 198–200; Schlesinger, *Coming of the New Deal*, pp. 128–30.

36. Hawley, *New Deal*, pp. 80–85, 95–97; Ronald L. Feinman, *Twilight of Progressivism: The Western Republican Senators and the New Deal* (Baltimore: Johns Hopkins University Press, 1981), pp. 68–73; Ohl, *Hugh S. Johnson*, pp. 187–90; Brand, *Corporatism and the Rule of Law*, pp. 157–62; Roos, *NRA Economic Planning*, pp. 409–11; Lyon et al., *National Recovery Administration*, pp. 710–11; Schlesinger, *Coming of the New Deal*, pp. 132–34, 167–68; Johnson, *Blue Eagle*, pp. 272–74; Kevin Tierney, *Darrow: A Biography* (New York: Thomas Y. Crowell, 1979), pp. 427–34.

37. Galambos, *Competition and Cooperation*, pp. 251–52. George A. Sloan and Goldthwaite H. Dorr were CTI officials.

38. Ibid., pp. 236–39.

39. Gerald D. Nash, *United States Oil Policy, 1890–1964* (Pittsburgh: University of Pittsburgh Press, 1968), pp. 128–56; Norman E. Nordhauser, *The Quest for Stability: Domestic Oil Regulation, 1917–1935* (New York: Garland, 1979), pp. 96–162; Ruth W. Ayres, "Petroleum Industry," in Galloway, ed., *Industrial Planning under Codes*, pp. 184–208; Harold F. Williamson et al., *The American Petroleum Industry: The Age of Energy, 1899–1959* (Evanston, Ill.: Northwestern University Press, 1963), pp. 548–51, 689–95; Myron W. Watkins, *Oil: Stabilization or Conservation? A Case Study in the Organization of Industrial Control* (New York: Harper & Brothers, 1937), p. 255; René de Visme Williamson, *The Politics of Planning in the Oil Industry under the Code* (New York: Harper & Brothers, 1936), pp. 49–51; Hawley, *New Deal*, pp. 212–20; Brand, *Corporatism and the Rule of Law*, pp. 175–206.

40. Ayres, "Petroleum Industry," pp. 186–88; Watkins, *Oil*, pp. 8–11, 38–39; Williamson, *Politics of Planning*, pp. 26–29, 70.

41. Watkins, *Oil*, pp. 72–88; Nordhauser, *Quest for Stability*, pp. 16-27, 33–35, 57–62, 97, 129, 133; Nash, *United States Oil Policy*, pp. 72–89; Williamson, *Politics of Planning*, pp. 22, 30–31, 60, 64–66; Williamson et al., *American Petroleum Industry*, pp. 308–13.

42. Watkins, *Oil*, p. 74.

43. This paragraph draws on Ohl, *Hugh S. Johnson*, p. 173; Hawley, *New Deal*, pp. 69–70, 92, 111, 121–22; Brand, *Corporatism and the Rule of Law*, pp. 113, 131, 143, 162–68; Albert U. Romasco, *The Politics of Recovery: Roosevelt's New Deal* (New York: Oxford University Press, 1983), pp. 195, 199–215.

44. Schlesinger, *Coming of the New Deal*, p. 121.

45. Carter, *New Dealers*, pp. 49–50.

46. Thomas I. Emerson, quoted in Louchheim, ed., *Making of the New Deal*, p. 208.

47. The AAA staff was normally about 5000 employees, with increases up to about 6500 in peak periods. See Edwin G. Nourse, Joseph S. Davis, and John D. Black, *Three Years of the Agricultural Adjustment Administration* (Washington, D.C.: Brookings, 1937), p. 60.

48. Schlesinger, *Coming of the New Deal*, pp. 45–49; Van L. Perkins, *Crisis in Agriculture: The Agricultural Adjustment Administration and the New Deal* (Berkeley and Los Angeles: University of California Press, 1969), chap. 4.

49. See the relatively favorable assessments of the Brookings Institution team, Nourse, Davis and Black, *Three Years*. Perkins, *Crisis in Agriculture*, chap. 9, also gives a favorable overall assessment of the AAA.

50. Perkins, *Crisis in Agriculture*, chaps. 6 and 7.

51. Richard S. Kirkendall, *Social Scientists and Farm Politics in the Age of Roosevelt* (Columbia: University of Missouri Press, 1966), chap. 5; Theodore Saloutos, *The American Farmer and the New Deal* (Ames: Iowa State University Press, 1982), p. 134.

52. The 1936 Act met the Supreme Court's objections to the original AAA by funding commodity programs from general revenues in place of the unconstitutional processing tax. The 1936 Act also shifted the mechanism of agricultural adjustment from production control to conservation; instead of simply removing acreage from production, participating farmers would plant soil-conserving crops such as grasses and legumes. The combination of bumper crops with the depressed demand of the 1937–1938 "recession" overwhelmed the new program and prompted a partial return to production control in the 1938 Act, which also incorporated Secretary Wallace's pet proposal for an "ever-normal granary" to carry over excess stocks. This second AAA nominally remains in effect, although it is usually superseded by more generous four- or five-year "temporary" programs passed by Congress. The conservation approach of 1936 was revived with the "sodbuster" and "swampbuster" provisions contained in the 1985 Food Security Act and continued under the Food, Agriculture, Conservation, and Trade Act of 1990. See Kirkendall, *Social Scientists and Farm Politics*, pp. 148–49; Saloutos, *American Farmer and the New Deal*, pp. 125–26, 135–36, 237–39, 242–43, 255–56; Murray R. Benedict, *Farm Policies of the United States, 1790–1950* (New York: Twentieth Century Fund, 1953), pp. 350–52, 375–78; Harold F. Breimyer, *Over-Fulfilled Expectations: A Life and an Era in Rural America* (Ames: Iowa State University Press, 1991), pp. 131–33; William P. Browne, *Private Interests, Public Policy, and American Agriculture* (Lawrence: University Press of Kansas, 1988), pp. 147, 232.

53. Lorwin and Hinrichs, *National Economic and Social Planning*, p. 99. See also Charles E. Jacob, *Policy and Bureaucracy* (Princeton: Van Nostrand, 1966), p. 120.

54. Nourse, Davis, and Black, *Three Years*, pp. 252–53.

55. Carter, *New Dealers*, pp. 102–3.

56. Quoted in Louchheim, ed., *Making of the New Deal*, p. 238.

57. George N. Peek with Samuel Crowther, *Why Quit Our Own* (New York: Van Nostrand, 1936), pp. 106–7; Perkins, *Crisis in Agriculture*, pp. 92–94; Kirkendall, *Social Scientists and Farm Politics*, pp. 63–66, 78; Pete Daniel, *Breaking the Land: The Transformation of Cotton, Tobacco, and Rice Cultures since 1880* (Urbana: University of Illinois Press, 1985), p. 112; Saloutos, *American Farmer and the New Deal*, pp. 57–58, 62, 236; Carter, *New Dealers*, pp. 99–102. On Hutson's career, see the obituary in the *Washington Post*, May 6, 1964.

58. Nourse, Davis, and Black, *Three Years*, pp. 52–54, 247–48; Saloutos, *American Farmer and the New Deal*, p. 74.

59. Lorwin and Hinrichs, *National Economic and Social Planning*, p. 129.

60. Nourse, Davis, and Black, *Three Years*, pp. 52–54, 263–65; Saloutos, *American Farmer and the New Deal*, pp. 70–71, 76, 134–35; Breimyer, *Over-Fulfilled Expectations*, pp. 90–91; Gladys Baker, *The County Agent* (Chicago: University of Chicago Press, 1939), pp. 39, 70–77; Joseph Stancliffe Davis, *Wheat and the AAA* (Washington, D.C.: Brookings Institution, 1935), pp. 70–74; John M. Gaus and Leon O. Wolcott, *Public Administration and the United States Department of Agriculture* (Chicago: Public Administration Service, 1940), pp. 10, 19.

61. Nourse, Davis, and Black, *Three Years*, pp. 247–48; Saloutos, *American Farmer and the New Deal*, pp. 87, 90–92, 243–44; Kirkendall, *Social Scientists and Farm Politics*, pp. 156–57; Richard Lowitt, ed., *Journal of a Tamed Bureaucrat: Nils A. Olsen and the BAE, 1925–1935* (Ames: Iowa State University Press, 1980), pp. 194–95, 197–98, 200–203, 205–6, 215–19.

62. Quoted in Gilbert C. Fite, *George N. Peek and the Fight for Farm Parity* (Norman: University of Oklahoma Press, 1954), p. 244.

63. Peek, *Why Quit Our Own*, p. 91.

64. Ibid., p. 342.

65. Ibid., pp. 144–46; Kirkendall, *Social Scientists and Farm Politics*, pp. 133–34; Saloutos, *American Farmer and the New Deal*, pp. 128–29; Fite, *George N. Peek*, pp. 253, 259; Carter, *New Dealers*, pp. 146–47.

66. Peek, *Why Quit Our Own*, pp. 105–7; Saloutos, *American Farmer and the New Deal*, pp. 55–58.

67. Peek, *Why Quit Our Own*, pp. 146–55; Fite, *George N. Peek*, pp. 258–66; Perkins, *Crisis in Agriculture*, pp. 179–86; Saloutos, *American Farmer and the New Deal*, pp. 88–90; Schlesinger, *Coming of the New Deal*, pp. 55–59. Peek's pursuit of bilateral agreements soon brought him into conflict with Secretary of State Cordell Hull, whose multilateralism was embodied in the Reciprocal Trade Agreements Act of 1934; by 1936, Peek was an ex–New Dealer campaigning for Roosevelt's Republican opponent, Alfred Landon. See Fite, *George N. Peek*, pp. 267–93.

68. Nourse, Davis, and Black, *Three Years*, p. 57.

69. New Deal marketing programs are discussed in Nourse, Davis, and Black, *Three Years*, pp. 217–45; Saloutos, *American Farmer and the New Deal*, pp. 78–84; Edwin G. Nourse, *Marketing Agreements under the AAA* (Washington, D.C.: Brookings Institution, 1935), pp. 32 n. 9, 46, 52, 119, 196, 221–23, 361; John D. Black, *The Dairy Industry and the AAA* (Washington, D.C.: Brookings Institution, 1935), pp. 23–24, 86–90, 373–96, 441–47; Brigitte Young, "The Dairy Industry: From Yeomanry to the Institutionalization of Multilateral Gover-

nance," in John L. Campbell, J. Rogers Hollingsworth, and Leon N. Lindberg, eds., *Governance of the American Economy* (Cambridge: Cambridge University Press, 1991), pp. 236, 243–54; E. C. Pasour, Jr., *Agriculture and the State: Market Processes and Bureaucracy* (New York: Holmes & Meier, 1990), pp. 124–36.

70. Nourse, *Marketing Agreements*, p. 353.

71. On King, see the obituary in the *New York Times*, June 22, 1937; Black, *Dairy Industry and the AAA*, pp. 90, 115; Nourse, *Marketing Agreements*, p. 207 n. 10; Saloutos, *American Farmer and the New Deal*, p. 78.

72. Nourse, *Marketing Agreements*, pp. 222–23.

73. Christiana McFadyen Campbell, *The Farm Bureau and the New Deal* (Urbana: University of Illinois Press, 1962), pp. 85–121.

74. Ibid., p. 113; Perkins, *Crisis in Agriculture*, pp. 37, 68; Charles M. Gardner, *The Grange: Friend of the Farmer* (Washington, D.C.: National Grange, 1949), pp. 83–84, 139, 145.

75. John A. Crampton, *The National Farmers Union: Ideology of a Pressure Group* (Lincoln: University of Nebraska Press, 1965), pp. 138–45; Gilbert C. Fite, "John A. Simpson: The Southwest's Militant Farm Leader," *Mississippi Valley Historical Review* 35(4): 577–83 (March 1949); William P. Tucker, "Populism Up-to-Date: The Story of the Farmers' Union," *Agricultural History* 21(4): 204–7 (October 1947).

76. Nourse, *Marketing Agreements*, pp. 255–58; Joseph G. Knapp, *The Advance of American Cooperative Enterprise: 1920–1945* (Danville, Ill.: Interstate, 1973), pp. 227–45.

77. John L. Shover, *Cornbelt Rebellion: The Farmers' Holiday Association* (Urbana: University of Illinois Press, 1965).

78. This is the argument of Saloutos, *American Farmer and the New Deal*, pp. 244–53, following views expressed by Howard Tolley and other agricultural economists.

79. A less cynical interpretation of the 1938 reorganization is suggested in Edward L. Schapsmeier and Frederick H. Schapsmeier, *Henry A. Wallace of Iowa: The Agrarian Years, 1910–1940* (Ames: Iowa State University Press, 1968), pp. 244–45.

80. The description is from Saloutos, *American Farmer and the New Deal*, p. 251. Evans's campaign role is mentioned in Schapsmeier and Schapsmeier, *Henry A. Wallace*, p. 230.

81. Carter, *New Dealers*, p. 75.

82. Russell Lord, *The Wallaces of Iowa* (Boston: Houghton Mifflin, 1947), pp. 380–81.

83. On the significance of administrative leadership and on the judicial aspects of implementation, see Paul Sabatier and Daniel Mazmanian, "The Conditions of Effective Implementation: A Guide to Accomplishing Policy Objectives," *Policy Analysis* 5(4): 494–95, 498–99 (Fall 1979). On the economic conditions of implementation, see Donald S. Van Meter and Carl E. Van Horn, "The Policy Implementation Process: A Conceptual Framework," *Administration and Society* 6(4): 470–72 (February 1975).

84. See Jeffrey L. Pressman and Aaron Wildavsky, *Implementation*, 3d ed.

(Berkeley and Los Angeles: University of California Press, 1984), pp. 143–46, on implementation and policy design.

85. Eugene Bardach, *The Implementation Game: What Happens After a Bill Becomes Law* (Cambridge: MIT Press, 1977), pp. 282–83; Pressman and Wildavsky, *Implementation*, pp. 147–62.

86. Sabatier and Mazmanian describe the early implementation literature as "generally quite pessimistic about the ability of important policy initiatives actually to effect the desired social changes." "Conditions of Effective Implementation," p. 482.

87. On policy as theory, see Pressman and Wildavsky, *Implementation*, pp. xxii–xxiii; Sabatier and Mazmanian, "Conditions of Effective Implementation," pp. 486–87; Van Meter and Van Horn, "Policy Implementation Process," pp. 448–49; Paul Berman, "The Study of Macro- and Micro-Implementation," *Public Policy* 26(2): 160–64 (Spring 1978).

88. For example, Sabatier and Mazmanian, "Conditions of Effective Implementation," pp. 484–500; Van Meter and Van Horn, "Policy Implementation Process," pp. 462–78, 484. Harry Hatry et al., *Program Analysis for State and Local Government*, 2d ed. (Washington, D.C.: Urban Institute, 1987), pp. 75–81, provides public officials with a guide to "implementation feasibility analysis" along these lines.

89. Hatry et al., *Program Analysis*, p. 77; Van Meter and Van Horn, "Policy Implementation Process," pp. 480–81; Herbert Kaufman, *Administrative Feedback* (Washington, D.C.: Brookings Institution, 1973), p. 3.

90. Erwin C. Hargrove, *The Missing Link: The Study of the Implementation of Social Policy* (Washington, D.C.: Urban Institute, 1975), pp. 48–49; Victor A. Thompson, *Bureaucracy and Innovation* (University: University of Alabama Press, 1969), pp. 69–72; Jack L. Walker, "The Diffusion of Innovations Among the American States," *American Political Science Review* 63(3): 894–95 (September 1969); Van Meter and Van Horn, pp. 472–73, 477–79.

91. Magali Sarfatti Larson, *The Rise of Professionalism: A Sociological Analysis* (Berkeley and Los Angeles: University of California Press, 1977), pp. 14–15, 18, 53, 70, 147–48, 156, 167, 179, 216; Robert H. Wiebe, *The Search for Order, 1877–1920* (New York: Hill and Wang, 1967), pp. 113–23.

92. Paul E. Peterson, Barry G. Rabe, and Kenneth K. Wong, *When Federalism Works* (Washington, D.C.: Brookings Institution, 1986), pp. 131–59; Berman, "Macro- and Micro-Implementation," pp. 172–79.

93. Martin Landau, "On the Concept of a Self-Correcting Organization," *Public Administration Review* 33(6): 533–42 (November/December 1973).

Chapter 5. The Consequences for Class Relations in Industry and Agriculture

1. Michael Wallace, Beth A. Rubin, and Brian T. Smith, "American Labor Law: Its Impact on Working-Class Militancy, 1901–1980," *Social Science History* 12(1): 14, 18–21 (Spring 1988); George Sayers Bain and Farouk Elsheikh, *Union*

Growth and the Business Cycle: An Econometric Analysis (Oxford: Basil Blackwell, 1976), pp. 65–67, 84–85, 90; Oscar Ashenfelter and John H. Pencavel, "American Trade Union Growth: 1900–1960," *Quarterly Journal of Economics* 83(3): 436–37, 444 (August 1969). See also Donald R. Brand, *Corporatism and the Rule of Law: A Study of the National Recovery Administration* (Ithaca, N.Y.: Cornell University Press, 1988), p. 258.

2. Leo Troy, *Trade Union Membership, 1897–1962* (New York: Columbia University Press for National Bureau of Economic Research, 1965), p. 4. The National Bureau of Economic Research (NBER) estimates of union membership, based on dues receipts, are more reliable for this period than the Bureau of Labor Statistics (BLS) estimates, published in U.S. Department of Labor, *Handbook of Labor Statistics*, Bureau of Labor Statistics Bulletin No. 2070 (1980). The BLS estimates are based on union self-reporting and thus are distorted by the inflated and unstable claims of the Congress of Industrial Organizations (CIO) in the first years after its secession from the American Federation of Labor (AFL). In fact, BLS estimates for CIO membership in 1939 and 1941 are based solely on the claims made in convention addresses by CIO presidents John L. Lewis and Philip Murray. These figures are not substantiated, are not disaggregated by individual unions, and are suspiciously well-rounded numbers: four million for 1939, five million for 1941. See U.S. Department of Labor, *Handbook of Labor Statistics*, Bureau of Labor Statistics Bulletin No. 1016 (1950); Congress of Industrial Organizations, *Daily Proceedings of the Second Constitutional Convention* (San Francisco, 1939); Congress of Industrial Organizations, *Daily Proceedings of the Fourth Constitutional Convention* (Detroit, 1941).

3. Arthur Ivor Marsh, *Trade Union Handbook: A Guide and Directory to the Structure, Membership, Policy, and Personnel of the British Trade Unions*, 4th ed. (Gower, Wales: Aldershot, Hants, England, 1988), pp. 6–8.

4. Norman F. Duffy, "Australia," in Albert A. Blum, ed., *International Handbook of Industrial Relations: Contemporary Development and Research* (Westport, Conn.: Greenwood Press, 1981), p. 3.

5. Jan Dhondt, "Government, Labour, and Trade Unions," in Herman Van Der Wee, *The Great Depression Revisited: Essays on the Economics of the Thirties* (The Hague: Martinus Nijhoff, 1972), p. 251.

6. Irving Bernstein, *Turbulent Years: A History of the American Worker, 1933–41* (Boston: Houghton Mifflin, 1970), p. 309.

7. Sidney Fine, *Sit-Down: The General Motors Strike of 1936–1937* (Ann Arbor: University of Michigan Press, 1969), pp. 121–33.

8. J. David Greenstone, *Labor in American Politics* (Chicago: University of Chicago Press, Phoenix Books, 1977), pp. 49–50; Louise Overacker, "Labor's Political Contributions," *Political Science Quarterly* 54(1): 58–60 (March 1939).

9. Milton Derber, "Growth and Expansion," in Milton Derber and Edwin Young, eds., *Labor and the New Deal* (Madison: University of Wisconsin Press, 1957), pp. 12–16; Christopher L. Tomlins, "AFL Unions in the 1930s: Their Performance in Historical Perspective," *Journal of American History* 75(4): 1021–42 (March 1979).

10. Irving Bernstein, *The Lean Years: A History of the American Worker, 1920–1933* (Cambridge, Mass.: Riverside Press, 1960), pp. 146–58; Larry J. Griffin, Michael E. Wallace, and Beth A. Rubin, "Capitalist Resistance to the Organization of Labor Before the New Deal: Why? How? Success?" *American Sociological Review* 51(2): 155–58, 160–61 (April 1986).

11. Robert Justin Goldstein, *Political Repression in Modern America: From 1870 to the Present* (Cambridge, Mass: Schenkman, 1978), pp. 151–54.

12. Bernstein, *Lean Years*, p. 51.

13. Ibid., pp. 211–12; Robert H. Zieger, *Republicans and Labor, 1919–1929* (Lexington: University of Kentucky Press, 1969), pp. 70–79; Goldstein, *Political Repression*, pp. 183–91.

14. Data sources are the same as in figure 2. Griffin, Wallace, and Rubin, "Capitalist Resistance," pp. 161–164, report time-series estimates in which membership and expenditures of the National Association of Manufacturers, the most virulently anti-union peak association of this period, significantly decrease union growth, density, and membership.

15. Bernstein, *Lean Years*, pp. 156–89; Griffin, Wallace, and Rubin, "Capitalist Resistance," pp. 158–60; David Brody, *Workers in Industrial America: Essays on the Twentieth Century Struggle* (New York: Oxford University Press, 1980), pp. 48–81; Daniel Nelson, "The Company Union Movement, 1900–1937: A Reexamination," *Business History Review* 56(3): 335, 341–47 (Autumn 1982).

16. Martin L. Fausold, *The Presidency of Herbert C. Hoover* (Lawrence: University Press of Kansas, 1985), pp. 119–23; Zieger, *Republicans and Labor*, pp. 64–66; Bernstein, *Lean Years*, pp. 413–14. The revisionist conception of Hoover as a corporatist, not an individualist, was introduced in an influential essay by Ellis Hawley: "Herbert Hoover and American Corporatism, 1929–1933," in Martin L. Fausold and George T. Mazuzan, eds., *The Hoover Presidency: A Reappraisal* (Albany: State University of New York Press, 1974), pp. 101–119.

17. Ellis W. Hawley, *The New Deal and the Problem of Monopoly: A Study in Economic Ambivalence* (Princeton: Princeton University Press, 1966), pp. 21–22.

18. Quoted from the text of the act, reproduced in Leverett S. Lyon et al., *The National Recovery Administration: An Analysis and Appraisal* (Washington, D.C.: Brookings Institution, 1935), pp. 895–96.

19. Irving Bernstein, *The New Deal Collective Bargaining Policy* (Berkeley and Los Angeles: University of California Press, 1950), pp. 35–36, 38–39.

20. David Plotke, "The Wagner Act, Again: Politics and Labor, 1935–37," *Studies in American Political Development* 3 (1989): 114.

21. Stanley Vittoz, *New Deal Labor Policy and the American Industrial Economy* (Chapel Hill: University of North Carolina Press, 1987), p. 82.

22. Bernstein, *New Deal Collective Bargaining Policy*, p. 37; Brand, *Corporatism and the Rule of Law*, pp. 85–86; Bernard Bellush, *The Failure of the NRA* (New York: Norton, 1975), p. 12. Since the coal bills had been drafted by the United Mine Workers, then in the AFL, Brand's comment that "the AFL had little to do with the drafting" of Section 7(a) (p. 85) is true but misleading. See John L. Lewis, "Labor and the National Recovery Administration," in Ernest Minor

Patterson, ed., *Towards National Recovery, Annals of the American Academy of Political and Social Science* no. 172 (March 1934): 58.

23. Business opposition to Section 7(a) is discussed in Robert F. Himmelberg, *The Origins of the National Recovery Administration: Business, Government, and the Trade Association Issue, 1921–1933* (New York: Fordham University Press, 1976), pp. 207, 209; Bernstein, *New Deal Collective Bargaining Policy*, pp. 34–37; Bellush, *Failure of the NRA*, pp. 16–17, 22; Brand, *Corporatism and the Rule of Law*, p. 90.

24. The full text is given in Bernstein, *New Deal Collective Bargaining Policy*, p. 36.

25. Ibid.

26. Ibid., pp. 58–62; Christopher L. Tomlins, *The State and the Unions: Labor Relations, Law, and the Organized Labor Movement in America, 1880–1960* (Cambridge: Cambridge University Press, 1985), pp. 109–13; J. Joseph Huthmacher, *Senator Robert F. Wagner and the Rise of Urban Liberalism* (New York: Atheneum, 1968), pp. 160–63.

27. Quoted in Bernstein, *New Deal Collective Bargaining Policy*, p. 59.

28. The significance and distinctiveness of voluntarism as a labor policy is forcefully presented in Brand, *Corporatism and the Rule of Law*, pp. 229–60.

29. Donald Richberg, *The Rainbow: After the Sunshine of Prosperity, the Deluge of Depression, the Rainbow of the NRA, What Have We Learned? Where Are We Going?* (Garden City, N.Y.: Doubleday, Doran, 1936), p. 56.

30. For a particularly revealing parable, see Hugh S. Johnson, *The Blue Eagle from Egg to Earth* (Garden City, N.Y.: Doubleday, Doran, 1935), pp. 345–46.

31. John Kennedy Ohl, *Hugh S. Johnson and the New Deal* (DeKalb: Northern Illinois University Press, 1985), pp. 196–97; Cletus E. Daniel, *Bitter Harvest: A History of California Farmworkers, 1870–1941* (Ithaca, N.Y.: Cornell University Press, 1981), pp. 171–72.

32. Johnson, *Blue Eagle*, p. 342.

33. Richberg, *Rainbow*, p. 55.

34. Tomlins, *State and the Unions*, p. 114.

35. Richard C. Wilcock, "Industrial Management's Policies Toward Unionism," in Derber and Young, eds., *Labor and the New Deal*, p. 288; Bernstein, *Turbulent Years*, pp. 38–40. Comparisons with trade union membership were calculated using trade union data in Troy, *Trade Union Membership*, p. 1.

36. Sanford M. Jacoby, "Reckoning with Company Unions: The Case of Thompson Products, 1934–1964," *Industrial and Labor Relations Review* 43(1): 24 (October 1989); Nelson, "Company Union Movement," p. 337.

37. Brody, *Workers in Industrial America*, pp. 66–78; Nelson, "Company Union Movement," p. 347.

38. Wallace, Rubin, and Smith, "American Labor Law," pp. 13, 21.

39. Bernstein, *Turbulent Years*, pp. 40–66, 90. "If pressed" on their slogan, Bernstein notes, organizers "admitted that they referred to the president of the United Mine Workers" (p. 41).

40. Ibid., pp. 137–42; Danae Clark, "Acting in Hollywood's Best Interest:

Representations of Actors' Labor during the National Recovery Administration," *Journal of Film and Video* 42(4): 4–6, 17 (Winter 1990).

41. Bernstein, *Turbulent Years*, pp. 77–89.

42. Rose Pesotta, *Bread upon the Waters*, ed. John Nicholas Beffel (1944; reprint, Ithaca, N.Y.: ILR Press, 1987), pp. 22–23, 31, 53, 81–82, 93–94, 97, 139.

43. Brody, *Workers in Industrial America*, pp. 82–119; Bernstein, *Turbulent Years*, pp. 92–125; Tomlins, "AFL Unions in the 1930s," pp. 1024–34.

44. Bernstein, *Turbulent Years*, p. 94.

45. Ibid., pp. 96–98.

46. Wallace, Rubin, and Smith, "American Labor Law," pp. 18–22.

47. Bernstein, *Turbulent Years*, pp. 217–317 (quote p. 316).

48. Ibid., p. 34.

49. Philip A. Korth and Margaret R. Beegle, *I Remember Like Today: The Auto-Lite Strike of 1934* (East Lansing: Michigan State University Press, 1988), p. 82. The Auto-Lite strike is described in Bernstein, *Turbulent Years*, pp. 218–29.

50. Carey McWilliams, *The Education of Carey McWilliams* (New York: Simon and Schuster, 1979), p. 81.

51. Ernest T. Weir, "New Responsibilities of Industry and Labor," in Patterson, ed., *Towards National Recovery*, p. 82.

52. Johnson, *Blue Eagle*, pp. 344–45 (emphasis in original).

53. Alice Lynd and Staughton Lynd, eds., *Rank and File: Personal Histories by Working-Class Organizers* (Boston: Beacon Press, 1973), p. 158 (emphasis in original). Dorothy Healey, a CIO activist and Communist Party member in this period, told David Plotke that union organizers used Roosevelt's supposed support for unionization as a central argument through the end of the 1930s. Plotke, "Wagner Act, Again," p. 140 n. 93.

54. This is the interpretation of Brody, *Workers in Industrial America*, pp. 145–46.

55. See Goldstein, *Political Repression*, pp. 14, 16, 51–57, on the nineteenth century; pp. 151–54 on 1919; and pp. 290–91 on 1946. Goldstein's discussion of the New Deal, pp. 209–36, emphasizes the generally nonrepressive character of the New Deal and the failure of conservative attempts to generate a new Red Scare that would discredit labor and Roosevelt.

56. Bernstein, *New Deal Collective Bargaining Policy*, pp. 57–75; Huthmacher, *Senator Robert F. Wagner*, pp. 163–69; Peter H. Irons, *The New Deal Lawyers* (Princeton: Princeton University Press, 1982), pp. 213–14; Kenneth M. Casebeer, "Holder of the Pen: An Interview with Leon Keyserling on Drafting the Wagner Act," *University of Miami Law Review* 42(2): 304 (November 1987).

57. Casebeer, "Holder of the Pen," p. 327.

58. Bernstein, *New Deal Collective Bargaining Policy*, pp. 76–83; Huthmacher, *Senator Robert F. Wagner*, pp. 169–71; Casebeer, "Holder of the Pen," pp. 304–5; Irons, *New Deal Lawyers*, p. 214. The National Labor Relations Board set up under Public Resolution No. 44 consulted Secretary Perkins "on major appointments, but retained control over decisions, hiring, firing, and funds" (Bernstein, *New Deal Collective Bargaining Policy*, p. 84).

59. Brand, *Corporatism and the Rule of Law*, p. 253.

60. Bernstein, *New Deal Collective Bargaining Policy*, p. 81.

61. Ibid.

62. James A. Gross, *The Making of the National Labor Relations Board: A Study in Economics, Politics, and the Law*, vol. 1 (Albany: State University of New York Press, 1974), pp. 76–88.

63. Bernstein, *New Deal Collective Bargaining Policy*, pp. 84–87 (quote p. 87); Irons, *New Deal Lawyers*, pp. 216–25. Keyserling suggested that the Justice Department's poor record did not reflect opposition to the policy itself: "I think that in the Justice Department, the question was purely lawyerlike: Could they defend themselves before the Supreme Court? In the Labor Department, however, it was mostly policy quarrels." Casebeer, "Holder of the Pen," p. 345.

64. Brand, *Corporatism and the Rule of Law*, pp. 254–55; Gross, *Making*, pp. 109–21. The NLRB came out for majority rule in the Houde Engineering case, involving an auto-parts firm; it was weakened when Roosevelt withdrew its jurisdiction over newspaper publishing.

65. Peter Irons points out that Wagner's bill, unlike the NIRA or the Agricultural Adjustment Act, was drafted by lawyers, who took care to write the statute in a way that would give the Supreme Court grounds for finding it constitutional. Irons, *New Deal Lawyers*, pp. 226–30.

66. The legislative history of the act is covered in Bernstein, *New Deal Collective Bargaining Policy*, pp. 88–128, and Huthmacher, *Senator Robert F. Wagner*, pp. 190–98.

67. Thomas Ferguson describes the coming expiration of the NIRA as an "Armageddon" that was "threatening to leave the country without any machinery for processing class conflict" in "From Normalcy to New Deal: Industrial Structure, Party Competition, and American Public Policy in the Great Depression," *International Organization* 38(1): 88 (Winter 1984); identically, "Industrial Conflict and the Coming of the New Deal," in Steve Fraser and Gary Gerstle, eds., *The Rise and Fall of the New Deal Order, 1930–1980* (Princeton: Princeton University Press, 1989), p. 19. Yet when Roosevelt, in February 1935, asked Congress for a two-year extension of the NRA, he praised the "pattern of a new order of industrial relations" developed under the program; his suggested modifications did not include stronger labor provisions along the lines of the Labor Disputes Bill. See Samuel I. Rosenman, comp., *The Public Papers and Addresses of Franklin D. Roosevelt* (New York: Random House, 1938), 4:81; Hawley, *New Deal*, p. 125.

Donald Brand, *Corporatism and the New Deal*, pp. 286–87, argues that by dissolving the NRA, the *Schechter* decision made direct public responsibility for workers impossible and so forced Roosevelt to use the state to develop the private power of labor unions. However, Roosevelt announced his support for the Wagner Act three days before the court decision; he responded to *Schechter* by making passage a higher priority. See Huthmacher, *Senator Robert F. Wagner*, p. 198.

68. Senate Committee on Education and Labor, *Hearings on S. 1958*, 74th Cong., 1st sess., 1935, pp. 463–64.

69. Ferguson, "From Normalcy to New Deal," pp. 49–53, 88. Another ar-

ticle by Ferguson recognizes that even the capital-intensive firms preferred company unionism to a genuinely independent labor movement. He attributes the success of industrial unions during the New Deal to their effective organization as investors, which he distinguishes from "simple rises in voter turnout." Since labor became organized for campaign support with the formation of Labor's Non-Partisan League in 1936, Ferguson's investment theory of politics sheds little light on the passage of the Wagner Act in 1935. See Thomas Ferguson, "Party Realignment and American Industrial Structure: The Investment Theory of Political Parties in Historical Perspective," *Research in Political Economy* 6 (1983): 59–61 (quote p. 61).

70. Ferguson, "From Normalcy to New Deal," p. 88; Alfred L. Bernheim and Dorothy Van Doren, eds., *Labor and the Government: An Investigation of the Role of the Government in Labor Relations* (New York: McGraw-Hill, 1935), pp. vii–viii, 363–73. See also the testimony of the Fund's William H. Davis in Senate Committee on Education and Labor, *Hearings on S. 1958*, pp. 704–23.

71. Ferguson, "From Normalcy to New Deal," p. 69 n. 53; Gerald W. Johnson, *Liberal's Progress* (New York: Coward-McCann, 1948), p. 243. Ferguson's own footnote ("From Normalcy to New Deal," p. 88 n. 105) suggests some autonomy for the Twentieth Century Fund: he says that in internal debates over the Fund's proposals, AFL attorney Charlton Ogburn "won out" over business executives who sought an unfair labor practices section for unions.

72. Bernheim and Van Doren, eds., *Labor and the Government*, p. 75; Nelson, "Company Union Movement," pp. 339–40.

73. Edward A. Filene, *Speaking of Change: A Selection of Speeches and Articles* (New York: Former Associates of Edward A. Filene, 1939), pp. 275–80.

74. Ferguson, "From Normalcy to New Deal," p. 88; Vittoz, *New Deal Labor Policy*, pp. 149–50.

75. Representative William P. Connery, House sponsor of the Wagner bill, recalled during the hearings a bet with Swope, who thought workers would endorse the company union in the G.E. representation election. The company union was rejected by a two-to-one margin. House Committee on Labor, *Hearings on H.R. 6288*, 74th Cong., 1st sess., 1935, p. 62. Vittoz, *New Deal Labor Policy*, p. 150, suggests that Swope "never felt constrained to dissociate himself, either publicly or privately" from the BAC position and "appears to have remained aloof from the controversy."

76. Vittoz, *New Deal Labor Policy*, p. 149.

77. Gross, *Making*, p. 138 n. 141.

78. Senate Committee on Education and Labor, *Hearings on S. 1958*, pp. 212–18.

79. Ibid., pp. 237–40, 477–89, 515–23 (machinery); pp. 276–83, 631–52 (publishing); pp. 346–52, 589–92 (furniture); pp. 359–86 (steel); pp. 469–71 (rubber); pp. 489–500 (meat packing); pp. 515–23 (electric); pp. 526–29 (food distribution); pp. 593–613 (automobiles); pp. 613–18, 624–31 (mining); pp. 667–80, 741–42 (petroleum); pp. 680–96 (textiles); pp. 696–99 (chemicals); pp. 743–45, 751–52 (construction).

80. Ibid., pp. 226–30, 366–70, 515–23, 743–45.

81. Ibid., pp. 462–66 (Harriman), 240–64, 840–69 (Emery).

82. Ibid., p. 278.

83. Ibid., pp. 283–99, 303–7, 335–43, 386–434, 455–62, 472–77, 537–66, 575–80, 652–62.

84. G. William Domhoff, "The Wagner Act and Theories of the State: A New Analysis Based on Class-Segment Theory," *Political Power and Social Theory* 6 (1987): 167.

85. Ibid., pp. 166–67, treats the BAC as the organ of corporate moderates. For an earlier example of this interpretation, see Barton J. Bernstein, "The New Deal: The Conservative Achievements of Liberal Reform" in Bernstein, ed., *Towards a New Past: Dissenting Essays in American History* (New York: Vintage, 1969), p. 275. The BAC's creation as a New Deal support organization and its breakup are discussed in Kim McQuaid, "The Frustration of Business Revival during the Early New Deal," *Historian* 41: 682–704 (August 1979).

86. Vittoz, *New Deal Labor Policy*, p. 150; Domhoff, "Wagner Act," p. 167.

87. Domhoff, "Wagner Act," p. 166.

88. Vittoz, *New Deal Labor Policy*, pp. 11–12; Daniel Nelson, "Managers and Nonunion Workers in the Rubber Industry: Union Avoidance Strategies in the 1930s," *Industrial and Labor Relations Review* 43(1): 43 (October 1989). Philip Burch, Jr., suggests another reason why Ferguson's sectoral distinctions are not always useful in understanding capitalist divisions: major financiers have often linked firms in different sectors by holding positions in them simultaneously. "The Alignment of Economic Forces Involved in Three Key Presidential Elections: 1896, 1912, and 1932," *Research in Political Economy* 11 (1988): 176 n. 7.

89. Michael Goldfield, "Worker Insurgency, Radical Organization, and New Deal Labor Legislation," *American Political Science Review* 83(4): 1274 (December 1989). See also Frances Fox Piven and Richard A. Cloward, *Poor People's Movements: Why They Succeed, How They Fail* (New York: Vintage Books, 1979), pp. 96–180.

90. Goldfield, "Worker Insurgency," pp. 1274–75.

91. Bernstein, *New Deal Collective Bargaining Policy*, p. 90. The text of the act is given in his appendix, pp. 153–60.

92. This often ignored thrust of the Wagner Act receives extensive attention in Casebeer's interview with Keyserling, though the interviewer seems more insistent about its importance than the interviewee. Casebeer, "Holder of the Pen," pp. 291–92, 308–10, 316–17.

After the *Schechter* decision, the preamble was redrafted to give greater emphasis to the impact of labor disputes, since the NRA's macroeconomic impact had not convinced the Supreme Court to uphold it. See Gross, *Making*, p. 144.

93. Goldfield dismisses the drop from 1934 to 1935 as "seasonal," which is odd since the comparison is based on annual data. "Worker Insurgency," p. 1280 n. 29.

94. *New York Times*, May 21, 1935. Strike data shows that Perkins was correct and that the 1934 strike wave was also less threatening than those to come:

Year	Strikes	Participants (thousands)	Volume
1919	3,630	—	—
1934	1,856	1,480	486.2
1935	2,014	1,102	371.9
1937	4,740	1,950	616.5
1946	4,985	4,600	2,099.5

In historical context, then, strike rates did not go from "ionospheric" in 1934 to "stratospheric" in 1935, as Ferguson suggests ("From Normalcy to New Deal," p. 88 n. 102). For sources, see Figure 3. Data on participants and worker days lost, used to calculate strike volume, are not available for 1919.

95. Senate Committee on Education and Labor, *Hearings on S. 1958*, pp. 276–83, 343–46, 587–88, 667–80.

96. Ibid., p. 262.

97. Ibid., pp. 598–613, 680–96, 741–42.

98. Casebeer, "Holder of the Pen," pp. 353–54.

99. Ibid., p. 319.

100. John Franklin Carter [Unofficial Observer], *The New Dealers* (New York: Simon & Schuster, 1934), p. 56.

101. Tomlins, *State and the Unions*, pp. 118–19; Huthmacher, *Senator Robert F. Wagner*, pp. 160–61, 163, 190–91.

102. Kristi Andersen, *The Creation of a Democratic Majority, 1928–1936* (Chicago: University of Chicago Press, 1979).

103. Congressional Quarterly, Inc., *Congressional Quarterly's Guide to Congress*, 2d ed. (Washington, D.C.: Congressional Quarterly, 1976), pp. 49–50.

104. Arthur M. Schlesinger, Jr., *The Politics of Upheaval* (Boston: Houghton Mifflin, 1960), pp. 422–23; Murray Edelman, "New Deal Sensitivity to Labor Interests," in Derber and Young, eds., *Labor and the New Deal*, pp. 185–89.

105. A version of this argument is made in David Jerome Shyrock, "Business Performance and Public Policy: The Formation of the Revenue Act of 1935 and the National Labor Relations Act" (Honors thesis, Harvard College, 1980), pp. 67–69, 88–89.

106. Only twice in Roosevelt's twelve-plus years did Congress override his veto on an important bill. Both overrides came after the election of 1942, when his congressional majority was at its narrowest. David McKay, "Presidential Strategy and the Veto Power: A Reappraisal," *Political Science Quarterly* 104(3): 453–54 (Fall 1989).

107. Huthmacher, *Senator Robert F. Wagner*, pp. 190, 198.

108. Ohl, *Hugh S. Johnson*, chap. 13.

109. Thomas E. Vadey, *The Wayward Liberal: A Political Biography of Donald Richberg* (Lexington: University Press of Kentucky, 1970), p. 150; Irons, *New Deal Lawyers*, p. 231; Bernstein, *New Deal Collective Bargaining Policy*, pp. 118–19. Keyserling described both Johnson and Richberg as "violently opposed" to the Wagner Act. Casebeer, "Holder of the Pen," p. 313.

110. Philip H. Burch, Jr., "The NAM as an Interest Group," *Politics and Society* 4(1): 101–3 (Fall 1973).

111. General background on the split between Roosevelt and business comes from Schlesinger, *Politics of Upheaval*, pp. 264–67, 270–74; James McGregor Burns, *Roosevelt: The Lion and the Fox* (New York: Harcourt, Brace & World, 1956), pp. 219–20, 224–26; Timothy George Massad, "Disruption, Organization, and Reform: A Critique of Piven and Cloward" (Honors thesis, Harvard College, 1978), pp. 92–93; Hawley, *New Deal*, pp. 151–58.

112. The importance to this result of the NLRB's litigation strategy, designed to assure that the strongest possible case was the one that reached the Court, is stressed by Irons, *New Deal Lawyers*, pp. 226–89, and by Gross, *Making*, pp. 173–230.

113. The NLRB's vested interest in labor organization is discussed in Edelman, "New Deal Sensitivity to Labor Interests," pp. 170–72. The development of the NLRB's institutional capacities is discussed in vol. 2 of James A. Gross's study, *The Reshaping of the National Labor Relations Board: National Labor Policy in Transition, 1937–47* (Albany: State University of New York Press, 1981).

114. Beth A. Rubin, Larry J. Griffin, and Michael Wallace, " 'Provided Only That Their Voice Was Strong': Insurgency and Organization from NRA to Taft-Hartley," *Work and Occupations* 10(3): 333–37 (August 1983). The authors found a significant, positive association between unionization and militance for the period 1937–1946. Regression estimates indicated only unstable effects for 1902–1932 and none for 1947–1977.

115. Karl E. Klare, "Judicial Deradicalization of the Wagner Act and the Origins of Modern Legal Consciousness, 1937–1941," *Minnesota Law Review* 62 (1977–78): 265–67, 293–325; Raymond L. Hogler, "Labor History and Critical Labor Law: An Interdisciplinary Approach to Workers' Control," *Labor History* 30(2): 184–86 (Spring 1989); Wythe Holt, "The New American Labor Law History," *Labor History* 30(2): 287–88 (Spring 1989). Keyserling said that the Wagner Act was not intended to impose any limits on the right to strike or the scope of collective bargaining. Casebeer, "Holder of the Pen," pp. 331, 353.

116. Mack C. Shelley II, *The Permanent Majority: The Conservative Coalition in the United States Congress* (University: University of Alabama Press, 1983), p. 151; Gross, *Reshaping*, chaps. 5–12; Tomlins, *State and the Unions*, pp. 210–11; Robin Stryker, "Limits on Technocratization of the Law: The Elimination of the National Labor Relations Board's Division of Economic Research," *American Sociological Review* 54(3): 344–53 (June 1989); idem, "A Tale of Two Agencies: Class, Political-Institutional, and Organizational Factors Affecting State Reliance on Social Science," *Politics and Society* 18(1): 104–5, 109–15, 117–23, 127 (March 1990).

117. Nelson Lichtenstein, *Labor's War at Home: The CIO in World War II* (Cambridge: Cambridge University Press, 1982), pp. 78–80; David Brody, "The New Deal and World War II," in John Braeman, Robert H. Bremner, and Brody, eds., *The New Deal: The National Level* (Columbus: Ohio State University Press, 1975), p. 279; Lynd and Lynd, eds., *Rank and File*, pp. 4, 146.

118. See data presented in note 94.

119. The Taft-Hartley Act's changes to the Wagner Act are summarized in R. Alton Lee, *Truman and Taft-Hartley: A Question of Mandate* (Lexington: University of Kentucky Press, 1966), pp. 75–77.

120. Mike Davis, *Prisoners of the American Dream: Politics and Economy in the History of the US Working Class* (London: Verso, 1986), pp. 111–12.

121. Terry M. Moe, "Interests, Institutions, and Positive Theory: The Politics of the NLRB," *Studies in American Political Development* 2 (1987): 244–71, describes the politics of NLRB moderation and its breakdown.

122. Union density calculated from 1992 data in U.S. Department of Labor, Bureau of Labor Statistics, *Employment and Earnings* 40(1): 172 (January 1993) (civilian labor force), p. 238 (union membership). Of employed wage and salary workers 15.8 percent were union members in 1992; this included 11.5 percent of private nonagricultural workers, 36.7 percent of government workers, and 2.4 percent of agricultural workers.

123. The Wagner Act's prohibition of company unions took on added relevance when the NLRB invoked it against labor-management committees at Electromation, Inc. (December 1992), and Du Pont (May 1993). The NLRB rulings called into question the legality of employee participation programs, such as "quality circles" and "joint production teams," which had been widely adopted by large corporations and had been encouraged by the Reagan, Bush, and Clinton administrations. See Gregory J. Kamer, Scott M. Abbot, and Lisa G. Salevitz, "The New Legal Challenge to Employee Participation," *Labor Law Journal* 45(1): 41–48 (January 1994); Raymond L. Hogler, "Employee Involvement and *Electromation, Inc.*: An Analysis and a Proposal for Statutory Change," *Labor Law Journal* 44(5): 261–74 (May 1993); Stephen I. Schlossberg and Miriam Birgit Reinhart, "Electromation and the Future of Labor-Management Cooperation in the U.S.," *Labor Law Journal* 43(9): 608–20 (September 1992); Joy K. Reynolds, "A Perspective on the *Electromation* Case from the U.S. Department of Labor," *Labor Law Journal* 43(6): 397–402 (June 1992).

124. For example, Troy, *Trade Union Membership*, p. 3; U.S. Department of Commerce, Bureau of the Census, *Historical Statistics of the United States, Colonial Times to 1970*, Bicentennial ed. (Washington, D.C.: U.S. Government Printing Office, 1975), 1:178.

125. U.S. Department of Labor, Bureau of Labor Statistics, *Employment and Earnings* 41(1): 249 (January 1994).

126. Social Security coverage was not extended to most agricultural workers until 1954. In 1966, amendments to the Fair Labor Standards Act placed 40 to 50 percent of agricultural workers under the minimum wage, initially set below the rate for other workers. Agricultural workers are still exempt from maximum hours and overtime provisions and remain outside the protections of the National Labor Relations Act. Kenneth Finegold, "Agriculture and the Politics of U.S. Social Provision: Social Insurance and Food Stamps," in Margaret Weir, Ann Shola Orloff, and Theda Skocpol, eds., *The Politics of Social Policy in the United States* (Princeton: Princeton University Press, 1988), pp. 199–234; Bruce Gardner, "What Have Minimum Wages Done in Agriculture," in Simon Rottenberg, ed., *The Economics of Legal Minimum Wages* (Washington,

D.C.: American Enterprise Institute, 1981), pp. 215–16; Linda C. Majka and Theo J. Majka, *Farm Workers, Agribusiness, and the State* (Philadelphia: Temple University Press, 1982), pp. 94–95, 108, 260.

127. Max J. Pfeffer, "Social Origins of Three Systems of Farm Production in the United States," *Rural Sociology* 48(4): 542–50 (Winter 1983); Carey McWilliams, *Factories in the Field: The Story of Migratory Farm Labor in California* (Boston: Little, Brown, 1939), pp. 103–4; Merle Weiner, "Cheap Food, Cheap Labor: California Agriculture in the 1930's," *Insurgent Sociologist* 8(2–3): 184 (Fall 1978).

128. Majka and Majka, *Farmworkers, Agribusiness, and the State*, pp. 71–72, 106; McWilliams, *Factories in the Field*, pp. 305–6.

129. Edwin G. Nourse, Joseph S. Davis, and John D. Black, *Three Years of the Agricultural Adjustment Administration* (Washington, D.C.: Brookings Institution, 1937), pp. 349–53; Clarke A. Chambers, *California Farm Organizations: A Historical Study of the Grange, Farm Bureau, and Associated Farmers, 1929–1941* (Berkeley and Los Angeles: University of California Press, 1952), pp. 31–32; Sidney C. Sufrin, "Labor Organization in Agricultural America, 1930–35," *American Journal of Sociology* 43(4): 550–53 (January 1938); Weiner, "Cheap Food, Cheap Labor," p. 185; Majka and Majka, *Farm Workers, Agribusiness, and the State*, p. 108.

130. J. Craig Jenkins, *The Politics of Insurgency: The Farm Worker Movement in the 1960s* (New York: Columbia University Press, 1985), p. 46; Edwin G. Nourse, *Marketing Agreements under the AAA* (Washington, D.C.: Brookings Institution, 1935), pp. 126–37, 148–93; "Coöperation at a Profit," *Fortune* 14(1): 92 (July 1936); Nourse, Davis, and Black, *Three Years*, p. 350. The Jones-Costigan Sugar Act of 1934 and its successor, the Sugar Act of 1937, made sugar beets an exception by including a minimum-wage rate in their provisions. See Nourse, Davis, and Black, *Three Years*, pp. 108, 318, 350; McWilliams, *Factories in the Field*, p. 277; Murray R. Benedict, *Farm Policies of the United States, 1790–1950* (New York: Twentieth Century Fund, 1953), pp. 309, 355–56, 370.

131. Majka and Majka, *Farmworkers, Agribusiness, and the State*, p. 129; Chambers, *California Farm Organizations*, p. 73. California cotton production had expanded rapidly during the 1920s. See Majka and Majka, *Farmworkers, Agribusiness, and the State*, pp. 77–78; McWilliams, *Factories in the Field*, pp. 193–96.

132. Sufrin, "Labor Organization," pp. 547–48, 554–55, 558; McWilliams, *Factories in the Field*, p. 211; Daniel, *Bitter Harvest*, pp. 177, 191.

133. Jenkins, *Politics of Insurgency*, pp. 73–75; Weiner, "Cheap Food, Cheap Labor," p. 189.

134. Paul Scharrenberg, quoted in Daniel, *Bitter Harvest*, p. 274.

135. Daniel, *Bitter Harvest*, pp. 105–257.

136. Ibid., pp. 277–81; Majka and Majka, *Farmworkers, Agribusiness, and the State*, pp. 93–96, 126–35.

137. Daniel, *Bitter Harvest*, pp. 119–26, 138, 195–202, 228–31, 251–54; Chambers, *California Farm Organizations*, pp. 39–52, 79–81; Majka and Majka,

Farmworkers, Agribusiness, and the State, pp. 87–93; Jerold S. Auerbach, *Labor and Liberty: The La Follette Committee and the New Deal* (Indianapolis: Bobbs-Merrill, 1966), pp. 184–94; Frank Stokes, "Let the Mexicans Organize!", *Nation*, December 19, 1936, pp. 731–32.

138. Dorothy Healey and Maurice Isserman, *Dorothy Healey Remembers: A Life in the American Communist Party* (New York: Oxford University Press, 1990), p. 71.

139. Daniel, *Bitter Harvest*, pp. 175–77, 204–21.

140. Ibid., pp. 240–49.

141. Ibid., pp. 239, 243, 247. In the 1960s and 1970s, the Teamsters performed a similar function for growers confronting a threat from the United Farm Workers. See Majka and Majka, *Farmworkers, Agribusiness, and the State*, pp. 178–79, 200–207, 211–24; Jenkins, *Politics of Insurgency*, pp. 177–202.

142. Majka and Majka, *Farmworkers, Agribusiness, and the State*, pp. 63, 71–72.

143. Ibid., pp. 131–32; McWilliams, *Education*, p. 76.

144. Majka and Majka, *Farmworkers, Agribusiness, and the State*, pp. 121–23.

145. Daniel, *Bitter Harvest*, pp. 235–36, 259–61; G. William Domhoff, *The Power Elite and the State: How Policy is Made in America* (New York: Aldine de Gruyter, 1990), pp. 97–98; idem, "Class, Power, and Parties in the New Deal: A Critique of Skocpol's State Autonomy Theory," *Berkeley Journal of Sociology* 36 (1991): 34–35.

146. Auerbach, *Labor and Liberty*, pp. 180–81; Majka and Majka, *Farmworkers, Agribusiness, and the State*, pp. 123–25.

147. Stokes, "Let the Mexicans Organize!", p. 732.

148. Charles S. Johnson, Edwin R. Embree, and W. W. Alexander, *The Collapse of Cotton Tenancy: Summary of Field Studies and Statistical Surveys, 1933–35* (Chapel Hill: University of North Carolina Press, 1935), pp. 2–5, 10–11.

149. Ibid., pp. 6–33; Pfeffer, "Social Origins," pp. 550–54; Henry I. Richards, *Cotton and the AAA* (Washington, D.C.: Brookings Institution, 1936), pp. 135–36; Donald H. Grubbs, *Cry from the Cotton: The Southern Tenant Farmers' Union and the New Deal* (Chapel Hill: University of North Carolina Press, 1971), pp. 8–12; Susan Archer Mann, *Agrarian Capitalism in Theory and Practice* (Chapel Hill: University of North Carolina Press, 1990), pp. 75–94; David Eugene Conrad, *The Forgotten Farmers: The Story of Sharecroppers in the New Deal* (Urbana: University of Illinois Press, 1965), pp. 1–18; Lee J. Alston and Joseph P. Ferrie, "Labor Costs, Paternalism, and Loyalty in Southern Agriculture: A Constraint on the Growth of the Welfare State," *Journal of Economic History* 45 (1): 95–96, 98–104 (March 1985); idem, "Resisting the Welfare State: Southern Opposition to the Farm Security Administration," in Robert Higgs, ed., *The Emergence of the Modern Political Economy* (Greenwich, Conn.: JAI Press, 1985), pp. 84–90. The southern system of cotton tenancy is vividly described (and photographed) in James Agee and Walker Evans, *Let Us Now Praise Famous Men* (1941; reprint, Boston: Houghton Mifflin, 1988). See esp. pp. 115–21, 319–48, 454–58.

150. Grubbs, *Cry from the Cotton*, pp. 19–26; Johnson, Embree, and Alex-

ander, *Collapse of Cotton Tenancy*, pp. 47–57; Conrad, *Forgotten Farmers*, pp. 37–82; Mann, *Agrarian Capitalism*, pp. 100–103; Richards, *Cotton and the AAA*, pp. 138–62; Pete Daniel, *Breaking the Land: The Transformation of Cotton, Tobacco, and Rice Cultures since 1880* (Urbana: University of Illinois Press, 1985), pp. 94–109, 168–73; Warren C. Whatley, "Labor for the Picking: The New Deal in the South," *Journal of Economic History* 43(4): 913–29 (December 1983); Jack Temple Kirby, "The Transformation of Southern Plantations, c. 1920–1960," *Agricultural History* 57(3): 265–70 (July 1983).

151. Daniel, *Breaking the Land*, pp. 174–83; Kirby, "Transformation of Southern Plantations," pp. 259, 265, 270–76; Mann, *Agrarian Capitalism*, pp. 103–27; Gilbert C. Fite, *Cotton Fields No More: Southern Agriculture, 1865–1980* (Lexington: University Press of Kentucky, 1984), p. 153.

152. Grubbs, *Cry from the Cotton*, pp. 27–29, 62–87; Conrad, *Forgotten Farmers*, pp. 83–104, 154–76; H. L. Mitchell, *Mean Things Happening in This Land* (Montclair, N.J.: Allanheld, Osmun, 1979), chaps. 3–6.

153. Conrad, *Forgotten Farmers*, pp. 106–12; Grubbs, *Cry from the Cotton*, pp. 30–31; Irons, *New Deal Lawyers*, pp. 119–28.

154. Conrad, *Forgotten Farmers*, pp. 105, 114–16; Jess Gilbert and Carolyn Howe, "Beyond 'State vs. Society': Theories of the State and New Deal Agricultural Policies," *American Sociological Review* 56(2): 211 (April 1991).

155. Quoted in Richards, *Cotton and the AAA*, pp. 140–41.

156. Quoted in Lawrence J. Nelson, "The Art of the Possible: Another Look at the 'Purge' of the AAA Liberals in 1935," *Agricultural History* 57(4): 434 n. 65 (October 1983).

157. Grubbs, *Cry from the Cotton*, pp. 41–47; Conrad, *Forgotten Farmers*, pp. 141–45.

158. Conrad, *Forgotten Farmers*, pp. 136–53; Grubbs, *Cry from the Cotton*, pp. 33–61; Nelson, "Art of the Possible," pp. 416–17, 420–23, 426–31; Irons, *New Deal Lawyers*, pp. 156–79. Irons, *New Deal Lawyers*, pp. 179–80, suggests that the Norcross case gave Davis an opportunity to remove officials who had antagonized him on an entirely different matter, the dispute over how far processors would have to open their books to comply with marketing agreements. The ultimate decision, however, was Wallace's.

159. Conrad, *Forgotten Farmers*, pp. 11, 95.

160. Quoted in Nelson, "Art of the Possible," p. 434. Robinson, from Arkansas, was Senate Majority Leader; Smith, from South Carolina, chaired the Senate Agriculture and Forestry Committee; and Harrison, from Mississippi, chaired the Senate Finance Committee.

161. Richard Lowitt, "Henry A. Wallace and the 1935 Purge in the Department of Agriculture," *Agricultural History* 53(3): 619 (quote), 614 (July 1979).

162. On the Resettlement Administration and the FSA, see ibid., p. 617; Harold L. Ickes, *The Secret Diary of Harold Ickes: The First Thousand Days, 1933–1936* (New York: Simon & Schuster, 1953), pp. 292–93, 302–3; Sidney Baldwin, *Poverty and Politics: The Rise and Decline of the Farm Security Administration* (Chapel Hill: University of North Carolina Press, 1968); Jess Gilbert and Steve Brown, "Alternative Land Reform Proposals in the 1930s: The Nashville

Agrarians and the Southern Tenant Farmers' Union," *Agricultural History* 55(4): 360–67 (October 1981); Grubbs, *Cry from the Cotton*, pp. 136–61; Alston and Ferrie, "Resisting the Welfare State," pp. 91–114; Majka and Majka, *Farmworkers, Agribusiness, and the State*, pp. 108–12; Daniel, *Bitter Harvest*, pp. 270, 282.

163. Roosevelt's skill at handling proffered resignations is noted in Charles E. Jacob, *Leadership in the New Deal: The Administrative Challenge* (Englewood Cliffs, N.J.: Prentice-Hall, 1967), pp. 28–29.

164. J. Joseph Huthmacher, "Urban Liberalism and the Age of Reform," *Mississippi Valley Historical Review* 49(2): 231–41 (September 1962); John D. Buenker, *Urban Liberalism and Progressive Reform* (New York: Norton, 1973).

165. Some historians have argued that Smith's opposition to the New Deal was inconsistent with his progressive record as Governor of New York and attributed it to personal bitterness against Roosevelt. Other historians, however, emphasize the continuity of Smith's positions in the 1920s and the 1930s. For examples of the first view, see Buenker, *Urban Liberalism and Progressive Reform*, p. 233; Schlesinger, *Politics of Upheaval*, pp. 517–20; Paula Eldot, *Governor Alfred E. Smith: The Politician as Reformer* (New York: Garland, 1983), pp. 406–9, 508 n. 87. For examples of the second view, see David Burner, *The Politics of Provincialism: The Democratic Party in Transition, 1918–1932* (Cambridge: Harvard University Press, 1986), pp. 179–216; Samuel B. Hand, "Al Smith, Franklin D. Roosevelt, and the New Deal: Some Comments on Perspective," *Historian* 27(3): 366–81 (May 1965); Jordan A. Schwarz, "Al Smith in the Thirties," *New York History* 45(4): 316–30 (October 1964). Smith adapted progressivism to the needs of the urban working class; a larger question than his personal motivations is the relationship of progressivism to the New Deal. Otis L. Graham, Jr., *An Encore for Reform: The Old Progressives and the New Deal* (New York: Oxford University Press, 1967), shows that the responses of former progressives to the New Deal were varied but mostly negative.

Part 2. Dialogues with Alternative Theoretical Approaches

1. Harry Eckstein, "Case Study and Theory in Political Science," in Fred I. Greenstein and Nelson W. Polsby, eds., *Handbook of Political Science*, vol. 7 (Reading, Mass.: Addison-Wesley, 1975), p. 109. Eckstein mentions his own study of democratic stability as an example. Theodore J. Lowi's frequently cited "American Business, Public Policy, Case Studies, and Political Theory," *World Politics* 16(4): 677–715 (July 1964), is another study that systematically evaluates the correspondence between existing theories of politics and case studies, using the findings of earlier works as evidence to support Lowi's own higher-level theory of policy arenas. See also J. Allen Whitt, "Toward a Class-Dialectical Model of Power: An Empirical Assessment of Three Competing Models of Political Power," *American Sociological Review* 44(1): 97–98 (February 1979).

2. Arthur L. Stinchcombe, *Constructing Social Theories* (New York: Harcourt, Brace & World, 1968), p. 107.

3. Stephen D. Krasner, "Sovereignty: An Institutional Perspective," *Comparative Political Studies* 21(1): 72–74 (April 1988).

4. Max Weber, *Economy and Society*, 3 vols., eds. Guenther Roth and Claus Wittich (New York: Bedminister Press, 1968), 1:56.

5. E. E. Schattschneider, *Party Government* (New York: Rinehart & Co., 1942), p. 35.

Chapter 6. Pluralism and Elite Theories

1. Examples of book-length journalism with a pluralist emphasis on interest-group politics include Hedrick Smith, *The Power Game: How Washington Works* (New York: Random House, 1988); Ethan Bronner, *Battle for Justice: How the Bork Nomination Shook America* (New York: Norton, 1989); Mark Green with Michael Waldman, *Who Runs Congress?*, 4th ed. (New York: Dell, 1984); David Rapp, *How the U.S. Got into Agriculture: And Why It Can't Get Out* (Washington, D.C.: Congressional Quarterly, 1988); William Greider, *The Education of David Stockman and Other Americans* (New York: E. P. Dutton, 1982). T. R. Reid, *Congressional Odyssey: The Saga of a Senate Bill* (San Francisco: W. H. Freeman, 1980), and Jeffrey H. Birnbaum and Alan S. Murray, *Showdown at Gucci Gulch: Lawmakers, Lobbyists, and the Unlikely Triumph of Tax Reform* (New York: Random House, 1987), portray the imposition of waterway user charges in 1978 and the 1986 tax reform, respectively, as exceptional cases in which the public good was served despite pressures from powerful interest groups.

2. Examples of the Chicago School approach include George J. Stigler, *The Citizen and the State: Essays on Regulation* (Chicago: University of Chicago Press, 1975); Sam Peltzman, "Toward a More General Theory of Regulation," *Journal of Law and Regulation* 19(2): 211–44 (August 1976); Gary S. Becker, "A Theory of Competition among Pressure Groups for Political Influence," *Quarterly Journal of Economics* 98(3): 371–400 (August 1983). Terry M. Moe, "Interests, Institutions, and Positive Theory: The Politics of the NLRB," *Studies in American Political Development* 2 (1987): 237, notes the similarity of Chicago School analysis to pluralism.

3. Theodore J. Lowi, *The End of Liberalism: The Second Republic of the United States*, 2d ed. (New York: Norton, 1979), pp. 31–41, 67. Donald R. Brand depicts Lowi as pluralist in his description of the American political process, though antipluralist in his evaluation of its outcomes. Donald R. Brand, "Three Generations of Pluralism: Continuity and Change," *Political Science Reviewer* 15 (Fall 1985): 110, 132–33.

4. David B. Truman, *The Governmental Process*, 2d ed. (New York: Knopf, 1971), esp. pp. xli, 507–12, 520; Robert A. Dahl, *Pluralist Democracy in the United States: Conflict and Consent* (Chicago: Rand McNally, 1967), pp. 325–26, 377–79, 386; Arnold M. Rose, *The Power Structure: Political Process in American Society* (New York: Oxford University Press, 1967), pp. 3, 492.

5. Earl Latham, *The Group Basis of Politics: A Study in Basing-Point Legislation* (Ithaca, N.Y.: Cornell University Press, 1952), pp. viii (quote), 35–40, 223–25; Truman, *Governmental Process*, pp. 262–87, 437–98.

6. Latham, *Group Basis of Politics*, p. 37.

7. Truman, *Governmental Process*, p. 48. Latham, less stridently, describes

groups as the means through which social values cherished by individuals are realized. See Latham, *Group Basis of Politics*, pp. 1, 3–4, 13, 28.

8. Truman, *Governmental Process*, pp. 48–52.

9. Latham, *Group Basis of Politics*, p. 12.

10. Dahl, *Pluralist Democracy*, pp. 338–70, 440–44; Truman, *Governmental Process*, pp. 165–67; Rose, *Power Structure*, p. 63.

11. Truman, *Governmental Process*, pp. 52–62; Dahl, *Pluralist Democracy*, pp. 263–68; Rose, *Power Structure*, pp. 7, 244, 404–5, 483, 487–88; Latham, *Group Basis of Politics*, p. 33.

12. Truman, *Governmental Process*, esp. pp. 506–7.

13. Rose, *Power Structure*, pp. 55–56, 59, 69–73, 89, 102–109, 400–401, 454, 484–87, 491–92; Dahl, *Pluralist Democracy*, pp. 403, 428.

14. Arthur M. Schlesinger, Jr., *The Coming of the New Deal* (Boston: Houghton Mifflin, 1958), pp. 91–92, 95.

15. Louis Galambos, *Competition and Cooperation: The Emergence of a National Trade Association* (Baltimore: Johns Hopkins Press, 1966), chaps. 4–5; Ellis W. Hawley, "Herbert Hoover, the Commerce Secretariat, and the Vision of an 'Associative State,' 1921–1928," *Journal of American History* 61(1): 125–32, 136–37 (June 1974); idem, "Herbert Hoover and American Corporatism, 1929–1933," in Martin L. Fausold and George T. Mazuzan, eds., *The Hoover Presidency: A Reappraisal* (Albany: State University of New York Press, 1974), pp. 101–119. For statistics on waves of foundings of associations by U.S. capitalists, see Philippe C. Schmitter and Donald R. Brand, "Organizing Capitalists in the United States: The Advantages and Disadvantages of Exceptionalism" (Paper presented at the Annual Meeting of the American Political Science Association, Washington, D.C., September 1979).

16. Leo Troy, *Trade Union Membership, 1897–1962* (New York: Columbia University Press for National Bureau of Economic Research, 1965), p. 4; Larry J. Griffin, Michael E. Wallace, and Beth A. Rubin, "Capitalist Resistance to the Organization of Labor Before the New Deal: Why? How? Success?" *American Sociological Review* 51(2): 147–67 (April 1986).

17. Ellis W. Hawley, *The New Deal and the Problem of Monopoly: A Study in Economic Ambivalence* (Princeton: Princeton University Press, 1966), p. 42.

18. Truman, *Governmental Process*, pp. 37, 264–70, 321; Latham, *Group Basis of Politics*, pp. 221–22.

19. Truman, *Governmental Process*, p. 286.

20. Christiana McFadyen Campbell, *The Farm Bureau and the New Deal* (Urbana: University of Illinois Press, 1962), pp. 57, 65–66; John L. Shover, *Cornbelt Rebellion: The Farmers' Holiday Association* (Urbana: University of Illinois Press, 1965).

21. Theodore Lowi, "How the Farmers Get What They Want," *The Reporter*, July 21, 1964, pp. 34–37.

22. Latham, *Group Basis of Politics*, p. 32.

23. Gilbert C. Fite, "Farmer Opinion and the Agricultural Adjustment Act," *Mississippi Valley Historical Review* 48(4): 656–73 (March 1962). See also Van L. Perkins, *Crisis in Agriculture: The Agricultural Adjustment Administration*

and the New Deal (Berkeley and Los Angeles: University of California Press, 1969), pp. 66–69.

24. Truman, *Governmental Process*, pp. 437, 455. See also Latham, *Group Basis of Politics*, pp. 43–49.

25. Brand, "Three Generations of Pluralism," p. 133.

26. Lowi, *End of Liberalism*, p. 67.

27. Truman, *Governmental Process*, pp. 452, 462; Latham, *Group Basis of Politics*, pp. 35 n. 36, 71–72. Lowi compares other programs with the NRA as the paradigm of producer self-government and would revive the rule, stated in the *Schechter* decision invalidating the NIRA, that Congress may not grant unrestricted authority to the executive branch. See Lowi, *End of Liberalism*, pp. 71, 79, 118, 300–301, and idem, *The Politics of Disorder* (New York: Basic Books, 1971), pp. 67, 75. Donald R. Brand, *Corporatism and the Rule of Law: A Study of the National Recovery Administration* (Ithaca, N.Y.: Cornell University Press, 1988), pp. 1–30, insightfully examines Lowi's treatment of the NRA and its implications for his larger theory.

28. Truman, *Governmental Process*, p. 462; Lowi, *End of Liberalism*, pp. 71, 73.

29. Gilbert C. Fite, *George N. Peek and the Fight for Farm Parity* (Norman: University of Oklahoma Press, 1954), pp. 243–66.

30. Edwin G. Nourse, Joseph S. Davis, and John D. Black, *Three Years of the Agricultural Adjustment Administration* (Washington, D.C.: Brookings Institution, 1937), pp. 255–68.

31. Anthony J. Badger, *Prosperity Road: The New Deal, Tobacco, and North Carolina* (Chapel Hill: University of North Carolina Press, 1980), p. 211.

32. Truman, *Governmental Process*, p. xlvii.

33. Ibid., pp. 66–74, 84, 181 (quote p. 73).

34. Dahl, *Pluralist Democracy*, pp. 293, 435–36, 448–49; Rose, *Power Structure*, pp. 122, 127, 490.

35. Truman, *Governmental Process*, p. 73.

36. Ibid., pp. 511–12.

37. Ibid., p. 511.

38. Latham, *Group Basis of Politics*, pp. 31–32 (quote p. 32).

39. Truman, *Governmental Process*, pp. 507–8, 519; Dahl, *Pluralist Democracy*, pp. 22–24, 326–29.

40. David Eugene Conrad, *The Forgotten Farmers: The Story of Sharecroppers in the New Deal* (Urbana: University of Illinois Press, 1965), pp. 147–53, 206–7; Peter H. Irons, *The New Deal Lawyers* (Princeton: Princeton University Press, 1982), chap. 8; Sidney Baldwin, *Poverty and Politics: The Rise and Decline of the Farm Security Administration* (Chapel Hill: University of North Carolina Press, 1968), pp. 405–14. Tellingly, Truman's discussion of the decline of the FSA emphasizes legislators' fear that established administrative relationships would become unsettled and deemphasizes the conflicting class interests involved. *Governmental Process*, pp. 473–75.

41. Charles E. Lindblom, *Politics and Markets: The World's Political-Economic Systems* (New York: Basic Books, 1977), p. 172.

42. Ibid., p. 173.

43. Ibid., p. 119.

44. Ibid., p. 189. Cf. Samuel Bowles and Herbert Gintis, "The Crisis of Liberal Democratic Capitalism: The Case of the United States," *Politics and Society* 11(1): 51–52 (1982); Claus Offe, *Contradictions of the Welfare State* (Cambridge: MIT Press, 1984), p. 179.

45. David Marsh, "Interest Group Activity and Structural Power: Lindblom's *Politics and Markets*," *West European Politics* 6(2): 12–13 (April 1983).

46. G. William Domhoff, *Who Rules America Now? A Vision for the '80s* (Englewood Cliffs, N.J.: Prentice-Hall, 1983), p. 1.

47. C. Wright Mills, *The Power Elite* (New York: Oxford University Press, 1956), includes all three groups. Closer to the Marxist conception are G. William Domhoff, who excludes labor leaders and argues that the military is controlled by the same upper class as other institutions, and Philip H. Burch, Jr., who stresses appointees' business backgrounds as "probably much more important than the appointees' distant social origins." See G. William Domhoff, *The Powers That Be: Processes of Ruling-Class Domination in America* (New York: Random House, 1978), p. 15; idem, *Who Rules America?* (Englewood-Cliffs, N.J., 1967), pp. 115–26; idem, "Where Do Government Experts Come From? The CEA and the Policy-Planning Network," in G. William Domhoff and Thomas R. Dye, eds., *Power Elites and Organizations* (Newbury Park, Calif.: Sage Publications, 1987), p. 190; Philip H. Burch, Jr., *Elites in American History*, 3 vols. (New York: Holmes & Meier, 1981), 1:23.

48. Among Domhoff's many works, those most relevant to the New Deal include *Who Rules America Now?*; *The Higher Circles: The Governing Class in America* (New York: Random House, 1970); "Corporate-Liberal Theory and the Social Security Act: A Chapter in the Sociology of Knowledge," *Politics and Society* 15(3): 297–330 (1986–87); "The Wagner Act and Theories of the State: A New Analysis Based on Class-Segment Theory," *Political Power and Social Theory* 6 (1987): 159–85; *The Power Elite and the State: How Policy Is Made in America* (New York: Aldine de Gruyter, 1990); "Class, Power, and Parties in the New Deal: A Critique of Skocpol's State Autonomy Theory," *Berkeley Journal of Sociology* 36 (1991): 1–49.

Ferguson's most relevant works include "Party Realignment and American Industrial Structure: The Investment Theory of Political Parties in Historical Perspective," *Research in Political Economy* 6 (1983): 1–82; "From Normalcy to New Deal: Industrial Structure, Party Competition, and American Public Policy in the Great Depression," *International Organization* 38(1): 41–64 (Winter 1984); "Elites and Elections, Or What Have They Done to You Lately?" in Benjamin Ginsberg and Alan Stone, eds., *Do Elections Matter?* (Armonk, N.Y.: M. E. Sharpe, 1986), pp. 164–88; Ferguson and Joel Rogers, *Right Turn* (New York: Hill and Wang, 1986). Domhoff, *Power Elite and the State*, pp. 225–55, is a critique of Ferguson and Rogers's treatment of campaign finance in *Right Turn*.

Burch discusses the New Deal in *Elites in American History*, 3:13–68, and in "The Alignment of Economic Forces Involved in Three Key Presidential Elections: 1896, 1912, and 1932," *Research in Political Economy* 11 (1988): 156–75. His analytical framework is explained in *Elites in American History* 1:1–44.

49. Barton J. Bernstein, "The New Deal: The Conservative Achievements of Liberal Reform," in Bernstein, ed., *Towards a New Past: Dissenting Essays in American History* (New York: Vintage, 1969), pp. 263–88; Ronald Radosh, "The Myth of the New Deal," in Radosh and Murray N. Rothbard, eds., *A New History of Leviathan: Essays on the Rise of the Corporate State* (New York: Dutton, 1972), pp. 146–87; Kim McQuaid, *Big Business and Presidential Power: From FDR to Reagan* (New York: William Morrow, 1982), pp. 18–61.

50. Radosh, "Myth of the New Deal," pp. 157–58, 175–76, 187; Ferguson, "From Normalcy to New Deal," pp. 49–55, 66; McQuaid, *Big Business and Presidential Power*, p. 53; Domhoff, "Wagner Act," p. 178; idem, *Power Elite and the State*, p. 98; idem, "Class, Power, and Parties," p. 36.

51. Radosh, "Myth of the New Deal," p. 186.

52. Ferguson, "Party Realignment," pp. 6–7, 11–12, 31–63; idem, "From Normalcy to New Deal," pp. 80–83; Ferguson and Rogers, *Right Turn*, pp. 46–48. See also Burch, "Alignment of Economic Forces," pp. 157–61. Ferguson's conception of political contributors as investors leads him to reject both the Downsian model of party competition (since parties maximize resources rather than votes) and conventional realignment schemes (since the real source of change is investor behavior rather than voter attitudes). Ferguson, "Party Realignment," pp. 4–6, 18–20; idem, "Elites and Elections," pp. 168–83; Ferguson and Rogers, *Right Turn*, pp. 40, 43–46.

53. G. William Domhoff, *Fat Cats and Democrats: The Role of the Big Rich in the Party of the Common Man* (Englewood Cliffs, N.J.: Prentice-Hall, 1972), p. 13; idem, *Power Elite and the State*, pp. 232–35, 246.

54. Frank J. Sorauf, *Money in American Elections* (Glenview, Ill.: Scott, Foresman, 1988), pp. 298–307, summarizes empirical findings about the influence of money on electoral outcomes. Elitist approaches do not convey the complexities of this relationship, which varies between incumbent and challenger as well as by level of election. The New Deal presidential elections, in which the Republicans always outspent the Democrats, demonstrate the most basic point, that the candidate spending the most does not necessarily win. In 1932, Republican financial advantages were overwhelmed by voters' desire to punish Hoover for the Depression. In 1936, Labor's Non-Partisan League gave the Democrats a countervailing organizational force. See Louise Overacker, "Campaign Funds in a Depression Year," *American Political Science Review* 27(6): 770 (October 1933); Alexander Heard, *The Costs of Democracy* (Chapel Hill: University of North Carolina Press, 1960), pp. 18, 169; Philip Taft, *Organized Labor in American History* (New York: Harper & Row, 1964), pp. 607–9.

55. On retrospective voting, see V. O. Key, Jr., *The Responsible Electorate: Rationality in Presidential Voting, 1936–1960* (Cambridge: Harvard University Press, 1966); Morris P. Fiorina, *Retrospective Voting in American National Elections* (New Haven: Yale University Press, 1981).

56. Domhoff, *Power Elite and the State*, p. 230.

57. Domhoff, *Who Rules America?*, pp. 5–10; idem, "Where Do Government Experts Come From?" pp. 189–94; idem, *Who Rules America Now?*, pp. 92–98; idem, *Power Elite and the State*, pp. 48–52, 57–58, 71, 77–78, 92–96, 114–15,

119, 183–85, 199–200, 202; idem, "Class, Power, and Parties," pp. 8–14, 24–25; idem, "Corporate-Liberal Theory and the Social Security Act," pp. 313–15; idem, "Wagner Act," pp. 161, 171.

58. The elite origins of the NRA are discussed in Domhoff, *Higher Circles*, p. 234; Radosh, "Myth of the New Deal," pp. 159–73; Ferguson, "From Normalcy to New Deal," pp. 84–85; Burch, "Alignment of Economic Forces," pp. 168–69; idem, *Elites in American History* 3:35–39; Bernstein, "New Deal," pp. 268–69; McQuaid, *Big Business and Presidential Power*, pp. 21–23, 26–29.

59. The drafting of the NIRA is described in Schlesinger, *Coming of the New Deal*, pp. 94–98; Hawley, *New Deal*, pp. 21–25; Robert F. Himmelberg, *The Origins of the National Recovery Administration: Business, Government, and the Trade Association Issue, 1921–1933* (New York: Fordham University Press, 1976), pp. 196–212. David Loth, *Swope of G.E.: The Story of Gerard Swope and General Electric in American Business* (New York: Simon & Schuster, 1958), p. 223, suggests that Hugh Johnson asked Swope to help him with the final draft.

60. Hawley, *New Deal*, p. 21.

61. William R. Johnson, "National Farm Organizations and the Reshaping of Agricultural Policy in 1932," *Agricultural History* 37(1): 41–42 (January 1963); Campbell, *Farm Bureau and the New Deal*, pp. 52–54; Edward L. Schapsmeier and Frederick H. Schapsmeier, *Henry A. Wallace of Iowa: The Agrarian Years, 1910–1940* (Ames: Iowa State University Press, 1968), pp. 168–70; Henry A. Wallace, *New Frontiers* (New York: Reynal & Hitchcock, 1934), pp. 162–63.

62. William D. Rowley, *M. L. Wilson and the Campaign for the Domestic Allotment* (Lincoln: University of Nebraska Press, 1970), pp. 105–6, 135, 139–40, 154; Richard S. Kirkendall, *Social Scientists and Farm Politics in the Age of Roosevelt* (Columbia: University of Missouri Press, 1966), pp. 33–36.

63. Rowley, *M. L. Wilson*, pp. 154–55; Kirkendall, *Social Scientists and Farm Politics*, pp. 37–39.

64. Jordan A. Schwarz, *The Speculator: Bernard M. Baruch in Washington, 1917–1965* (Chapel Hill: University of North Carolina Press, 1981), pp. 235–41, 279–86. Roosevelt distrusted Baruch, who had worked against his nomination, but Baruch still had enough influence, through his financial contributions and his ties to congressional Democrats, that Johnson and Peek were appointed to head the NRA and the AAA. See pp. 266–70, 282; see also Burch, "Alignment of Economic Forces," pp. 169–70; idem, *Elites in American History* 3:60 n. 75; 3:62 n. 86.

65. David E. Hamilton, *From New Day to New Deal: American Farm Policy from Hoover to Roosevelt, 1928–1933* (Chapel Hill: University of North Carolina Press, 1991), suggests that Ezekiel deserves more credit for the AAA and Black less than most historians have given them. See pp. 186–89 and pp. 297–98 n. 31.

66. Burch, "Alignment of Economic Forces," p. 167, describes Tugwell as "non-elite."

67. Ferguson, "From Normalcy to New Deal," p. 82; Domhoff, "Class, Power, and Parties," pp. 9–13. See also Rowley, *M. L. Wilson*, pp. 31, 122, 140; Elliot A. Rosen, *Hoover, Roosevelt, and the Brains Trust: From Depression to New Deal* (New York: Columbia University Press, 1977), pp. 178, 180. Ferguson,

"From Normalcy to New Deal," p. 55 n. 30, comments that "the politics of farm policy in the New Deal has received more attention than it deserves," even though agricultural support was crucial to Roosevelt's nomination and election and though agricultural recovery was widely seen as a prerequisite for a general economic revival.

68. "Spillman, William Jasper," in Dumas Malone, ed., *Dictionary of American Biography* 9 (New York: Scribner's, 1935–1936), pp. 458–59; Grant McConnell, *The Decline of Agrarian Democracy* (Berkeley and Los Angeles: University of California Press, 1953), p. 71; Rowley, *M. L. Wilson*, pp. 33–38.

69. Martin Bulmer and Joan Bulmer, "Philanthropy and Social Science in the 1920s: Beardsley Ruml and the Laura Spelman Rockefeller Memorial, 1922–29," *Minerva* 19(1): 379–81, 396, 401–2, 406 (Spring 1981). During his time at the Memorial, Ruml played an important role in the creation of modern social science. He later helped convince Roosevelt to accept deficit spending and invented income tax withholding.

70. Kirkendall, *Social Scientists and Farm Politics*, pp. 63–64; Theodore Saloutos, *The American Farmer and the New Deal* (Ames: Iowa State University Press, 1982), pp. 58, 62; Badger, *Prosperity Road*, p. 45; Henry C. Taylor and Anne Dewees Taylor, *The Story of Agricultural Economics in the United States, 1840–1932: Men—Services—Ideas* (Ames: Iowa State College Press, 1952), pp. 440–41.

71. McQuaid, *Big Business and Presidential Power*, pp. 30–33.

72. Ferguson, "From Normalcy to New Deal," p. 85.

73. Ibid., p. 55 n. 30.

74. Henry C. Taylor, *Agricultural Economics* (New York: Macmillan, 1923), pp. 73–76; Nourse, Davis, and Black, *Three Years*, p. 106; Richard Franklin Bensel, *Sectionalism and American Political Development, 1880–1980* (Madison: University of Wisconsin Press, 1984), p. 140.

75. Wallace, *New Frontiers*, p. 163.

76. Domhoff, "Wagner Act," p. 166. This argument is more fully presented in Michael Goldfield, "Worker Insurgency, Radical Organization, and New Deal Labor Legislation," *American Political Science Review* 83(4): 1262–63 (December 1989). Domhoff cites an earlier, unpublished version of Goldfield's article. See also Domhoff, "Class, Power, and Parties," p. 19.

77. Domhoff, *Higher Circles*, pp. 234–49; Radosh, "Myth of the New Deal," pp. 173–85; Ferguson, "From Normalcy to New Deal," p. 88.

78. Stanley Vittoz, *New Deal Labor Policy and the American Industrial Economy* (Chapel Hill: University of North Carolina Press, 1987), pp. 149–50.

79. Senate Committee on Education and Labor, *Hearings on S. 1958*, 74th Cong., 1st sess., 1935, pp. 462–66.

80. Domhoff, "Wagner Act," pp. 177–81; idem, *Power Elite and the State*, pp. 97–98; idem, "Class, Power, and Parties," p. 35.

81. McQuaid, *Big Business and Presidential Power*, pp. 43–48.

82. Burch, *Elites in American History* 3:42–44, 52.

83. Bulmer and Bulmer, "Philanthropy and Social Science," pp. 391–92; Baldwin, *Poverty and Politics*, p. 127; Kirkendall, *Social Scientists and Farm Poli-*

tics, pp. 109–10; Guy Benton Johnson and Guion Griffis Johnson, *Research in Service to Society: The First Fifty Years of the Institute for Research in Social Science at the University of North Carolina* (Chapel Hill: University of North Carolina Press, 1980), pp. 14–18, 101–15, 218–22.

84. Louise Overacker, *Money in Elections* (New York: Macmillan, 1932), pp. 162–64; idem, "Campaign Funds in a Depression Year," pp. 776–77; idem, "Campaign Funds in the Presidential Election of 1936," *American Political Science Review* 31(3): 473, 484–85, 487 (June 1937). Overacker's data on banker and broker contributions over five thousand dollars to the two parties' national committees are given below, with the Democratic proportion of contributions to both parties:

Year	Democratic	Republican	Democratic %
1928	$526,290	$853,421	38.1
1932	$301,100	$335,605	47.3
1936	$ 42,000	$578,910	6.8

See also Michael Patrick Allen, "Capitalist Response to State Intervention: Theories of the State and Political Finance in the New Deal," *American Sociological Review* 56(5): 687 (October 1991); Michael J. Webber, "Business, the Democratic Party, and the New Deal: An Empirical Critique of Thomas Ferguson's 'Investment Theory of Politics,'" *Sociological Perspectives* 34(4): 476, 483–85 (Winter 1991); Thomas Ferguson, "Industrial Structure and Party Competition in the New Deal: A Reply to Webber," *Sociological Perspectives* 34(4): 509–11, 513–14 (Winter 1991).

85. The five Rockefellers were John D.; John D., Jr.; Mrs. John D., Jr.; John D., III; and Lawrence S. Their contributions to the Republicans totaled $130,000. Overacker, "Campaign Funds in the Presidential Election of 1936," pp. 493–94. In 1932, the Republicans received funds from the Rockefeller family and from J. P. Morgan and Company. See idem, "Campaign Funds in a Depression Year," p. 779. Ferguson comments in a footnote that "the complex positions of some large interests (such as the Rockefellers) cannot be discussed here for reasons of space." Ferguson, "From Normalcy to New Deal," p. 92 n. 112.

Chapter 7. Marxist Approaches to Politics and the State

1. See Nicos Poulantzas, *State, Power, Socialism* (London: NLB, 1978), p. 20; Bob Jessop, *The Capitalist State: Marxist Theories and Methods* (New York: New York University Press, 1982), pp. 1, 29–31; Ralph Miliband, *Class Power and State Power: Political Essays* (London: Verso, 1983), pp. 3–4, 9; Martin Carnoy, *The State and Political Theory* (Princeton: Princeton University Press, 1984), p. 45; and Axel van den Berg, *The Immanent Utopia: From Marxism on the State to the State of Marxism* (Princeton: Princeton University Press, 1988), pp. 14, 31–32, 41–42. Each of these authors warns against trying to distill any single theory of politics or the state from Marx's work. In contrast, Hal Draper, *Karl Marx's Theory of Revolution* (New York: Monthly Review Press, 1977), attributes to

Marx and Engels a cohesive "general theory of the state," in which an instrumental relation is the norm but exceptional conditions, such as those of France in 1848, bring forth exceptional kinds of states.

2. "Instrumentalism," "Structuralism," and "Class Struggle" were popularized as labels for sets of Marxist approaches by David A. Gold, Clarence Y. H. Lo, and Erik Olin Wright, "Recent Developments in Marxist Theories of the Capitalist State," *Monthly Review* 27(5): 9–43 (October 1975), and idem, "Recent Developments in Marxist Theories of the Capitalist State," *Monthly Review* 27(6): 36–51 (November 1975). Bob Jessop suggests an alternative classification of Marxist approaches as employing the methods of "subsumption," "derivation," or "articulation." See Jessop, *Capitalist State*, esp. pp. xii, 71–74, 82–83, 213–20.

3. Karl Marx, *Capital: A Critique of Political Economy* (New York: Vintage, 1977), p. 929.

4. Karl Marx and Frederick Engels, *Manifesto of the Communist Party*, in Marx and Engels, *Collected Works* (London: Lawrence & Wishart, 1976), 6:486. This is the wording of the 1888 Authorized English Translation by Engels and Samuel Moore. Hal Draper, *The Annotated Communist Manifesto*, 2d ed. (Berkeley: Center for Socialist History, 1984), pp. 13, 106, suggests "The modern state power is only a committee that manages the common affairs of the whole bourgeois class" as closer to the meaning of the original German.

5. Frederick Engels, *The Origin of the Family, Private Property, and the State*, in Marx and Engels, *Collected Works* (London: Lawrence & Wishart, 1990), 26:271.

6. This point is made by several authors: Poulantzas, *State, Power, Socialism*, p. 129; Jessop, *Capitalist State*, p. 14; Miliband, *Class Power and State Power*, p. 9; Simon Clarke, "Marxism, Sociology, and Poulantzas's Theory of the State," *Capital and Class* 2 (1977): 2; Philip Resnick, *The Masks of Proteus: Canadian Reflections on the State* (Montreal: McGill–Queen's University Press, 1990), p. 113. Jessop, *Capitalist State*, pp. 32–77, is a critical review of "stamocap" theory.

7. George Wolfskill and John A. Hudson, *All But the People: Franklin D. Roosevelt and His Critics, 1933–39* (New York: Macmillan, 1969), pp. 143–49, 152–62; William E. Leuchtenburg, *Franklin D. Roosevelt and the New Deal, 1932–1940* (New York: Harper & Row, 1963), pp. 176–77. In the 1936 election, Roosevelt's business support came from outsiders: firms from the South or West or new industries. Since this was the most class-polarized of the New Deal elections, these out-groups can be seen as his core business support. See Leuchtenburg, *Franklin D. Roosevelt*, pp. 189–90.

8. Ralph Miliband, *The State in Capitalist Society* (New York: Basic Books, 1969), p. 102. Similarly, see Nikolai Sivachev, "The Rise of Statism in 1930s America: A Soviet View of the Social and Political Effects of the New Deal," *Labor History* 24(4): 509 (Fall 1983).

9. Joseph P. Kennedy, *I'm for Roosevelt* (New York: Reynal & Hitchcock, 1936), pp. 7–8. Most of this book was ghostwritten by Arthur Krock, but Kennedy stated the same view in his speeches and interviews at that time. See

William E. Leuchtenburg, *In the Shadow of FDR: From Harry Truman to Ronald Reagan*, rev. ed. (Ithaca, N.Y.: Cornell University Press, 1983), p. 68; David E. Koskoff, *Joseph P. Kennedy: A Life and Times* (Englewood Cliffs, N.J.: Prentice-Hall, 1974), pp. 82–85.

10. Frederick Engels, *Anti-Dühring*, in Marx and Engels, *Collected Works* (London: Lawrence & Wishart, 1987), 25:266. The concept of the state as "ideal collective capitalist," adapted from Engels, is fundamental to the German "capital logic" school. See Elmer Altvater, "Some Problems of State Interventionism: The 'Particularization' of the State in Bourgeois Society," in John Holloway and Sol Picciotto, eds., *State and Capital: A Marxist Debate* (London: Edward Arnold, 1978), pp. 42, 185–86 n. 7. Jessop, *Capitalist State*, pp. 78–141, is a critical review of the capital logic approach.

11. Karl Marx, *The Eighteenth Brumaire of Louis Bonaparte*, in Marx and Engels, *Collected Works* (London: Lawrence & Wishart, 1979), 11:186.

12. Ibid., 11:194–95.

13. Karl Marx, *The Civil War in France* in Marx and Engels, *Collected Works* (London: Lawrence & Wishart, 1986), 22:330.

14. Draper, *Marx's Theory of Revolution*, 1:410–38, 464–83.

15. Antonio Gramsci, *Selections from the Prison Notebooks* (New York: International Publishers, 1971), pp. 219–23.

16. Nicos Poulantzas, *Political Power and Social Classes* (London: New Left Books, 1973), p. 259.

17. Ibid., p. 279. Emphasis in original.

18. Ibid., pp. 287, 298.

19. Ibid., pp. 289, 299–300; Nicos Poulantzas, "The Problem of the Capitalist State," *New Left Review* 58:74 (November–December 1969).

20. Poulantzas, *Political Power and Social Classes*, p. 257.

21. Ibid., pp. 319–21.

22. Ibid., p. 288.

23. Poulantzas, "Problem of the Capitalist State," p. 73. Emphasis in original.

24. Cf. John Mollenkopf, "Theories of the State and Power Research," *Insurgent Sociologist* 5(3): 257–58 (Spring 1975); van den Berg, *Immanent Utopia*, p. 363.

25. Arthur L. Stinchcombe, *Constructing Social Theories* (New York: Harcourt, Brace & World, 1968), p. 58. For Poulantzas's criticisms of various theories as functionalist, see *Political Power and Social Classes*, pp. 40, 105, 110–11, 198–99, 264–65, 267–68, 327–28, 342–44.

26. Stinchcombe, *Constructing Social Theories*, pp. 59, 83; Clarke, "Marxism, Sociology and Poulantzas's Theory of the State," pp. 9, 17–20, 25; G. A. Cohen, *Karl Marx's Theory of History: A Defence* (Princeton: Princeton University Press, 1978), pp. 289–96.

27. Poulantzas, *State, Power, Socialism*, p. 136.

28. Ibid., pp. 38–39, 53, 140–43, 154–55.

29. Ibid., pp. 32, 53–61 (quote p. 61).

30. Ibid., pp. 45, 138.

31. Ibid., pp. 130, 197 (emphasis in original). Similarly, in "The Capitalist

State: A Reply to Miliband and Laclau" (*New Left Review* 95:72 [January–February 1976]), Poulantzas suggests, "The (capitalist) State, in the long run, can only correspond to the political interests of the dominant class or classes. . . . Since he is not some incorrigible Fabian, [Miliband] of course knows this already."

32. Bob Jessop, *Nicos Poulantzas: Marxist Theory and Political Strategy* (New York: St. Martin's Press, 1985), pp. 22, 115–17, 120–22, 327–29; Poulantzas, *State, Power, Socialism*, pp. 13, 163–64, 172–73. Poulantzas, "The Capitalist State," is a transitional work. See esp. pp. 73–74.

33. Poulantzas, *Political Power and Social Classes*, pp. 25, 257, 264, 334; idem, *State, Power, Socialism*, pp. 129–31.

34. Poulantzas, *Political Power and Social Classes*, pp. 257, 271–72, 286–87, 354–55; idem, *State, Power, Socialism*, pp. 13, 190–94.

35. Poulantzas, *Political Power and Social Classes*, pp. 190–94; idem, *State, Power, Socialism*, pp. 184–86, 189.

36. Poulantzas, *State, Power, Socialism*, pp. 132, 135–36.

37. Jessop, *Nicos Poulantzas*, pp. 135–36, 142–44.

38. Poulantzas, *Political Power and Social Classes*, p. 272; idem, *State, Power, Socialism*, pp. 208–9; idem, *Fascism and Dictatorship* (London: NLB, 1974), pp. 58–59, n. 5, and p. 96. The index entries in *Political Power and Social Classes*, p. 365, and *Fascism and Dictatorship*, p. 365, mistakenly refer to *Theodore* Roosevelt.

39. Poulantzas, *Political Power and Social Classes*, pp. 320–21.

40. Rhonda F. Levine, *Class Struggle and the New Deal: Industrial Labor, Industrial Capital, and the State* (Lawrence: University Press of Kansas, 1988), pp. 11–12; idem, "Bringing Classes Back In: State Theory and Theories of the State," in Rhonda F. Levine and Jerry Lembcke, eds., *Recapturing Marxism: An Appraisal of Recent Trends in Sociological Theory* (New York: Praeger, 1987), pp. 102–3.

41. Jess Gilbert and Carolyn Howe, "Beyond 'State vs. Society': Theories of the State and New Deal Agricultural Policies," *American Sociological Review* 56(2): 204–7, 218 (April 1991).

42. Steve McClellan, "Theorizing New Deal Farm Policy: Broad Constraints of Capital Accumulation and the Creation of a Hegemonic Relation," in William H. Friedland, Lawrence Busch, Frederick H. Buttel, and Alan P. Rudy, eds., *Towards a New Political Economy of Agriculture* (Boulder: Westview Press, 1991), pp. 216–20.

43. Poulantzas, *Political Power and Social Classes*, p. 282.

44. Levine, *Class Struggle and the New Deal*, pp. 71–79 (quote p. 79); idem, "Bringing Classes Back In," p. 109; Ellis W. Hawley, *The New Deal and the Problem of Monopoly: A Study in Economic Ambivalence* (Princeton: Princeton University Press, 1966), pp. 31–34; Leverett S. Lyon et al., *The National Recovery Administration: An Analysis and Appraisal* (Washington, D.C.: Brookings Institution, 1935), pp. 8–26.

45. Levine, *Class Struggle and the New Deal*, pp. 2, 43, 46. Cf. Ellis W. Hawley, "Herbert Hoover, the Commerce Secretariat, and the Vision of an 'Associative State,' 1921–1928," *Journal of American History* 61(1): 101–19 (June 1974);

idem, "Herbert Hoover and American Corporatism, 1929–1933," in Martin L. Fausold and George T. Mazuzan, eds., *The Hoover Presidency: A Reappraisal* (Albany: State University of New York Press, 1974).

46. Levine, *Class Struggle and the New Deal*, p. 63. On the basis of a memo from Adolph Berle to Roosevelt, Levine draws the conclusion that "by August 1932 it had become quite clear that the strategy of the Roosevelt election campaign was going to focus on some sort of industrial-stabilization program" (p. 67). This demonstrates the dangers of identifying Roosevelt's intentions with any single one of the diverse views that, with his encouragement, competed within his campaign and, later, within his administration. See Frank Freidel, *Franklin D. Roosevelt: The Triumph* (Boston: Little, Brown, 1956), p. 318; Arthur M. Schlesinger, Jr., *The Crisis of the Old Order* (Boston: Houghton Mifflin, 1957), pp. 413–22, 423–28; idem, *Coming of the New Deal*, pp. 522–36.

47. See, for example, Roy V. Peel and Thomas C. Donnelly, *The 1932 Campaign: An Analysis* (New York: Farrar & Rinehart, 1935), pp. 124, 128; Freidel, *Triumph*, pp. 323, 361–64; Schlesinger, *Coming of the New Deal*, pp. 420, 433; Leuchtenburg, *Franklin D. Roosevelt*, p. 9.

48. Grant McConnell, *The Decline of Agrarian Democracy* (Berkeley and Los Angeles: University of California Press, 1953), pp. 63–68; Christiana McFadyen Campbell, *The Farm Bureau and the New Deal* (Urbana: University of Illinois Press, 1962), pp. 35–41; Robert L. Tontz, "Memberships of General Farmers' Organizations, 1874–1960," *Agricultural History* 38(3): 145–47 (July 1964); David E. Hamilton, *From New Day to New Deal: American Farm Policy from Hoover to Roosevelt, 1928–1933* (Chapel Hill: University of North Carolina Press, 1991), pp. 94, 106.

49. Gilbert and Howe, "Beyond 'State vs. Society,' " pp. 205–9.

50. Gladys Baker, *The County Agent* (Chicago: University of Chicago Press, 1939), pp. xv–xvi, 92, 98–101, 212–13; Charles M. Hardin, *The Politics of Agriculture: Soil Conservation and the Struggle for Power in Rural America* (Glencoe, Ill.: Free Press, 1952), pp. 46–47; Jim Hightower, *Hard Tomatoes, Hard Times: A Report of the Agribusiness Accountability Project on the Failure of America's Land Grant College Complex* (Cambridge, Mass.: Schenkman, 1973), pp. 118, 120, 125–26.

51. Hightower, *Hard Tomatoes, Hard Times*, pp. 25–64; Jack Kloppenburg, Jr., and Frederick H. Buttel, "Two Blades of Grass: The Contradictions of Agricultural Research as State Intervention," *Research in Political Sociology* 3 (1987): 117–19; Jack Ralph Kloppenburg, Jr., *First the Seed: The Political Economy of Plant Biotechnology, 1492–2000* (Cambridge: Cambridge University Press, 1988), pp. 4–6, 12, 17, 35, 39, 58–59, 75, 84–87.

52. Willard W. Cochrane, *The Development of American Agriculture: A Historical Analysis* (Minneapolis: University of Minnesota Press, 1979), pp. 387–95; Frederick H. Buttel, "Agricultural Research and Farm Structural Change: Bovine Growth Hormone and Beyond," *Agriculture and Human Values* 3(4): 92 (Fall 1986).

53. Harry C. McDean, "Professionalism, Policy, and Farm Economists in the Early Bureau of Agricultural Economics," *Agricultural History* 57(1): 64–82

(January 1983); Tom G. Hall, "Professionalism, Policy, and Farm Economists: Comment," *Agricultural History* 57(1): 83–89 (January 1983); Lloyd S. Tenny, "The Bureau of Agricultural Economics—The Early Years," *Journal of Farm Economics* 29(4): 1020 (November 1947); John D. Black, "The Bureau of Agricultural Economics—The Years in Between," *Journal of Farm Economics* 29(4): 1029 (November 1947).

54. Tenny, "Bureau of Agricultural Economics," p. 1025; Henry C. Taylor and Anne Dewees Taylor, *The Story of Agricultural Economics in the United States, 1840–1932: Men—Services—Ideas* (Ames: Iowa State College Press, 1952), pp. 453–54, 456; Charles M. Hardin, "The Bureau of Agricultural Economics under Fire: A Study in Valuation Conflicts," *Journal of Farm Economics* 28(3): 639 (August 1946).

55. Richard S. Kirkendall, *Social Scientists and Farm Politics in the Age of Roosevelt* (Columbia: University of Missouri Press, 1966), pp. 222–25, 227–30, 234–54 (quote p. 246); Gladys L. Baker and Wayne D. Rasmussen, "Economic Research in the Department of Agriculture: A Historical Perspective," *Agricultural Economics Research* 27(3–4): 61–62 (July–October 1975); Hardin, "Bureau of Agricultural Economics," pp. 651–55, 660–64.

56. Baker and Rasmussen, "Economic Research," pp. 62, 67. On Whitten's representation of cotton planters, see Nick Kotz, *Let Them Eat Promises: The Politics of Hunger in America* (Englewood Cliffs, N.J.: Prentice-Hall, 1969), pp. 84–102.

57. Gilbert and Howe, "Beyond 'State vs. Society,' " pp. 209–10; Harold F. Breimyer, "Conceptualization and Climate for New Deal Farm Laws of the 1930s," *American Journal of Agricultural Economics* 65(5): 1155 (December 1983). For similar views of the efficacy of protest in other New Deal contexts, see Frances Fox Piven and Richard A. Cloward, *Poor People's Movements: Why They Succeed, How They Fail* (New York: Vintage, 1979), pp. 41–180; Michael Goldfield, "Worker Insurgency, Radical Organization, and New Deal Labor Legislation," *American Political Science Review* 83(4): 1270–77 (December 1989).

58. This paragraph and the next draw upon John L. Shover, *Cornbelt Rebellion: The Farmers' Holiday Association* (Urbana: University of Illinois Press, 1965).

59. Shover, *Cornbelt Rebellion*, p. 202. Breimyer, "Conceptualization and Climate," p. 1155, refers to Reno as the "civil-disobedience father of the New Deal farm laws."

60. Stephen Skowronek, *Building a New American State: The Expansion of National Administrative Capabilities* (Cambridge: Cambridge University Press, 1982); Levine, *Class Struggle and the New Deal*, p. 161.

61. Robert D. Cuff, *The War Industries Board: Business-Government Relations during World War I* (Baltimore: Johns Hopkins University Press, 1973), pp. 3–5, 11–12, 259–76; Paul A. C. Koistinen, "The 'Industrial-Military Complex' in Historical Perspective: World War I," *Business History Review* 41(4): 391–94, 397–98, 402–3 (Winter 1967); idem, *The Military-Industrial Complex: A Historical Perspective* (New York: Praeger, 1980), pp. 11–12, 117–22; William E. Leuchtenburg, "The New Deal and the Analogue of War," in John Braeman, Robert H.

Bremner, and Everett Walters, eds., *Change and Continuity in Twentieth-Century America* (New York: Harper & Row, 1966), pp. 90–91, 106, 117–18, 134.

62. Lloyd Milton Short, *The Development of National Administrative Organization in the United States* (Baltimore: Johns Hopkins Press, 1923), pp. 402–5, 406–9; Carroll H. Wooddy, *The Growth of the Federal Government, 1915–1932* (New York: McGraw-Hill, 1934), pp. 166–67, 176–78; Hawley, " 'Associative State,' " pp. 119–26, 131, 138–39.

63. John Kennedy Ohl, *Hugh S. Johnson and the New Deal* (DeKalb: Northern Illinois University Press, 1985), pp. 106–8, 112–15, 133–36, 171–74; Lyon et al., *National Recovery Administration*, pp. 48–53; Louis Galambos, *Competition and Cooperation: The Emergence of a National Trade Association* (Baltimore: Johns Hopkins Press, 1966), pp. 209, 227.

64. Ohl, *Hugh S. Johnson*, pp. 107, 111–12; Schlesinger, *Coming of the New Deal*, pp. 103–9; Herbert Stein, *The Fiscal Revolution in America* (Chicago: University of Chicago Press, 1969), pp. 53–54.

65. Breimyer, "Conceptualization and Climate," p. 1155. Taylor's pioneering textbook warned against "sterile" theories that were not empirically tested, and it encouraged a wide variety of research methods for keeping theories "in harmony with the facts." Henry C. Taylor, *Agricultural Economics* (New York: Macmillan, 1923), pp. 405–6. On the biases of the agricultural education movement, see Gilbert and Howe, "Beyond 'State vs. Society,' " p. 208.

66. Lauren Soth, "Agricultural Economists and Public Policy," in Richard H. Day, ed. *Economic Analysis and Agricultural Policy* (Ames: Iowa State University Press, 1982), pp. 46–47, 51.

67. Karl A. Fox and D. Gale Johnson, "Editors' Introduction," *Readings in the Economics of Agriculture* (Homewood, Ill.: Richard D. Irwin, Inc. for the American Economics Association, 1969), pp. xiv–xv.

68. Short, *Development of National Administrative Organization*, pp. 393–94; Wooddy, *Growth of the Federal Government*, pp. 277–78.

69. Gilbert and Howe, "Beyond 'State vs. Society,' " p. 211.

70. Kloppenburg, *First the Seed*, p. 10.

71. Gilbert C. Fite, *George N. Peek and the Fight for Farm Parity* (Norman: University of Oklahoma Press, 1954), pp. 243–66; Kirkendall, *Social Scientists and Farm Politics*, p. 68.

72. McClellan, "Theorizing New Deal Farm Policy," pp. 221, 224–25.

73. For example, Don Paarlberg, "Tarnished Gold: Fifty Years of New Deal Farm Programs," in Robert Eden, ed., *The New Deal and Its Legacy: Critique and Reappraisal* (New York: Greenwood Press, 1989), pp. 42–43; E. C. Pasour, Jr., *Agriculture and the State: Market Processes and Bureaucracy* (New York: Holmes & Meier, 1990), pp. 245–48.

74. Richard C. Wilcock, "Industrial Management's Policies Toward Unionism," in Milton Derber and Edwin Young, eds., *Labor and the New Deal* (Madison: University of Wisconsin Press, 1957), pp. 288–91; Irving Bernstein, *Turbulent Years: A History of the American Worker, 1933–41* (Boston: Houghton Mifflin, 1970), pp. 38–40; idem, *The New Deal Collective Bargaining Policy* (Berkeley and Los Angeles: University of California Press, 1950), pp. 92, 94, 112–13.

75. See van den Berg, *Immanent Utopia*, p. 362.

76. Levine, *Class Struggle and the New Deal*, pp. 65, 82, 86; idem, "Bringing Classes Back In," pp. 109–10.

77. Levine, *Class Struggle and the New Deal*, pp. 6, 147.

78. Ibid., p. 90.

79. Ibid., pp. 10, 15, 46 (quote), 161; idem, "Bringing Classes Back In," p. 100.

80. John D. Hicks, *Republican Ascendancy, 1921–1933* (New York: Harper & Brothers, 1960), pp. 26, 106–7; Ronald Frederick King, "From Redistributive to Hegemonic Logic: The Transformation of American Tax Politics, 1894–1963," *Politics and Society* 12(1): 22–31, 50 (1983).

81. Levine, *Class Struggle and the New Deal*, p. 171. On the Depression as an organic crisis and its resolution through structural transformation, see ibid., pp. 4, 10, 48, 136, 153, 172; idem, "Bringing Classes Back In", p. 101.

82. Levine, *Class Struggle and the New Deal*, pp. 15–16, 151, 157, 175. The concept of an "unequal structure of representation" comes from Rianne Mahon, "Canadian Public Policy: The Unequal Structure of Representation," in Leo Panitch, ed., *The Canadian State: Political Economy and Political Power* (Toronto: University of Toronto Press, 1977), pp. 165–98.

83. Levine, *Class Struggle and the New Deal*, pp. 17, 108, 158–60, 171; idem, "Bringing Classes Back In," p. 112.

84. Levine, *Class Struggle and the New Deal*, p. 15.

85. Mike Davis, *Prisoners of the American Dream: Politics and Economy in the History of the U.S. Working Class* (London: Verso, 1986), pp. 111–12; James A. Gross, *The Reshaping of the National Labor Relations Board: National Labor Policy in Transition, 1937–47* (Albany: State University of New York Press, 1981), chaps. 5–12; David Brody, "The New Deal and World War II," in John Braeman, Robert H. Bremner, and Brody, eds., *The New Deal: The National Level* (Columbus: Ohio State University Press, 1975), p. 279; R. Alton Lee, *Truman and Taft-Hartley: A Question of Mandate* (Lexington: University of Kentucky Press, 1966), pp. 75–77; Karl E. Klare, "Judicial Deradicalization of the Wagner Act and the Origins of Modern Legal Consciousness, 1937–1941," *Minnesota Law Review* 62 (1977–78): 265–67, 293–325.

86. Beth A. Rubin, Larry J. Griffin, and Michael Wallace, " 'Provided Only That Their Voice Was Strong': Insurgency and Organization from NRA to Taft-Hartley," *Work and Occupations* 10(3): 333–37 (August 1983); Christopher L. Tomlins, "AFL Unions in the 1930s: Their Performance in Historical Perspective," *Journal of American History* 75(4): 1021–24, 1039–41 (March 1979); Harvey Klehr, *The Heyday of American Communism: The Depression Decade* (New York: Basic Books, 1984), pp. 366–67.

87. Richard Polenberg, *Reorganizing Roosevelt's Government: The Controversy over Executive Reorganization, 1936–1939* (Cambridge: Harvard University Press, 1966), pp. 21, 185–88; Peri E. Arnold, *Making the Managerial Presidency: Comprehensive Reorganization Planning, 1905–1980* (Princeton: Princeton University Press, 1986), pp. 114–15; Sidney M. Milkis and Michael Nelson, *The American Presidency: Origins and Development, 1776–1993*, 2d ed. (Washington, D.C.: CQ Press, 1994), pp. 287–88; Sidney M. Milkis, *The President and the Parties: The*

Transformation of the American Party System since the New Deal (New York: Oxford University Press, 1993), pp. 104–34.

88. Erwin C. Hargrove, *The Power of the Modern Presidency* (New York: Alfred A. Knopf, 1974), pp. 81–86; James L. Sundquist, *The Decline and Resurgence of Congress* (Washington, D.C.: Brookings Institution, 1981), pp. 35, 59–60; John Hart, *The Presidential Branch* (New York: Pergamon, 1987), pp. 3–4, 27–30, 41–48, 96–124; Alfred Dick Sander, *A Staff for the President: The Executive Office, 1921–1952* (New York: Greenwood, 1989), pp. 4–6, 95, 375–76; Richard P. Nathan, *The Plot That Failed: Nixon and the Administrative Presidency* (New York: John Wiley & Sons, 1975), pp. 45–49, 68–69, 82–84; Milkis and Nelson, *American Presidency*, pp. 288, 301–3, 340; Milkis, *President and the Parties*, pp. 159–61, 221–22, 230–32.

89. Murray R. Benedict, *Farm Policies of the United States, 1790–1850* (New York: Twentieth Century Fund, 1953), pp. 307–8; Edwin G. Nourse, Joseph S. Davis, and John D. Black, *Three Years of the Agricultural Adjustment Administration* (Washington, D.C.: Brookings Institution, 1937), pp. 86–87, 102, 115–50.

90. Pete Daniel, "The New Deal, Southern Agriculture, and Economic Change," in James C. Cobb and Michael V. Namorato, eds., *New Deal and the South* (Jackson: University Press of Mississippi, 1984), p. 60.

91. Nourse, Davis, and Black, *Three Years*, pp. 340–49; David Eugene Conrad, *The Forgotten Farmers: The Story of Sharecroppers in the New Deal* (Urbana: University of Illinois Press, 1965); Donald H. Grubbs, *Cry from the Cotton: The Southern Tenant Farmers' Union and the New Deal* (Chapel Hill: University of North Carolina Press, 1971); Lawrence J. Nelson, "The Art of the Possible: Another Look at the 'Purge' of the AAA Liberals in 1935," *Agricultural History* 57(4): 416–35 (October 1983); Richard Lowitt, "Henry A. Wallace and the 1935 Purge in the Department of Agriculture," *Agricultural History* 53(3): 607–21 (July 1979); Janet Poppendieck, *Breadlines Knee-Deep in Wheat: Food Assistance in the Great Depression* (New Brunswick, N.J.: Rutgers University Press, 1986), pp. 100–102, 187–89; Warren C. Whatley, "Labor for the Picking: the New Deal in the South," *Journal of Economic History* 43(4): 905–29 (December 1983).

92. The STFU, Rex Tugwell, and H. C. Nixon of the Nashville Agrarians intellectual movement all criticized this limitation while supporting the Bankhead-Jones Farm Tenant Act that created the FSA. See Sidney Baldwin, *Poverty and Politics: The Rise and Decline of the Farm Security Administration* (Chapel Hill: University of North Carolina Press, 1968), pp. 163–64, 174, 189–90; McClellan, "Theorizing New Deal Farm Policy," p. 227; Benedict, *Farm Policies of the United States*, p. 359; McConnell, *Decline of Agrarian Democracy*, pp. 84–96; Lee J. Alston and Joseph P. Ferrie, "Resisting the Welfare State: Southern Opposition to the Farm Security Administration," in Robert Higgs, ed., *The Emergence of the Modern Political Economy* (Greenwich, Conn.: JAI Press, 1985), pp. 93–95; Jess Gilbert and Steve Brown, "Alternative Land Reform Proposals in the 1930s: The Nashville Agrarians and the Southern Tenant Farmers' Union," *Agricultural History* 55(4): 360–65 (October 1981).

93. McClellan, "Theorizing New Deal Farm Policy," pp. 225–27 (quote p. 227).

94. Philip H. Burch, Jr., "The NAM as an Interest Group," *Politics and Society* 4(1): 101–3, 110–14 (Fall 1973).

95. Gilbert and Howe, "Beyond 'State vs. Society,' " pp. 206–7, 210, 212, 214–17.

96. Some of the points that follow were suggested by comparisons in Göran Therborn, "Why Some Classes Are More Successful Than Others," *New Left Review* 138 (March–April 1983): 48.

97. Following Claus Offe and Helmut Wiesenthal, Howe and Jerry Lembcke distinguish between business organizations, whose capacity for collective action depends on their members' "willingness to pay," and working-class organizations, whose capacity for collective action depends on their members' "willingness to act." The history of the Farm Bureau places it squarely in the former category. See Claus Offe, *Disorganized Capitalism* (Cambridge: MIT Press, 1985), p. 185; Jerry Lembcke and Carolyn Howe, "Organizational Structure and the Logic of Collective Action in Unions," *Current Perspectives in Social Theory* 7 (1986): 1–2; Jerry Lembcke, *Capitalist Development and Class Capacities: Marxist Theory and Union Organization* (New York: Greenwood, 1988), pp. 41–42; Carolyn Howe, "Farmers' Movements and the Changing Structure of Agriculture," in A. Eugene Havens, with Gregory Hooks, Patrick H. Mooney, and Max J. Pfeffer, eds., *Studies in the Transformation of U.S. Agriculture* (Boulder: Westview, 1986), pp. 132–33, 136.

98. Campbell, *Farm Bureau and the New Deal*, pp. 88–89, 95, 100, 102; Nourse, Davis, and Black, *Three Years*, p. 266.

99. On the "Second New Deal" and its end, see Basil Rauch, *The History of the New Deal* (New York: Creative Age, 1944), pp. 156–90, 317–26.

100. Baldwin, *Poverty and Politics*, pp. 341–44, 348–52, 356, 384–85, 410–11; McConnell, *Decline of Agrarian Democracy*, pp. 97–111; Alston and Ferrie, "Resisting the Welfare State," pp. 112, 117 n. 22.

101. Gregory Hooks, "From an Autonomous to a Captured State Agency: The Decline of the New Deal in Agriculture," *American Sociological Review* 55(1): 37–40 (February 1990).

102. Poulantzas, *State, Power, Socialism*, p. 25.

103. Paul Cammack, "Review Article: Bringing the State Back In?" *British Journal of Political Science* 19(2): 275–76 (April 1989).

104. The quote is from van den Berg, *Immanent Utopia*, p. 491. For a non-Marxist defense of this kind of intellectual eclecticism, see Stinchcombe, *Constructing Social Theories*, p. 4.

105. Fred Block, *Revising State Theory: Essays in Politics and Postindustrialism* (Philadelphia: Temple University Press, 1987), pp. 51–68. This chapter of Block's book was first published as "The Ruling Class Does Not Rule: Notes on the Marxist Theory of the State," *Socialist Revolution* 33 (May–June 1977): 6–28. Block labels himself a "Post-Marxist" in *Revising State Theory*, p. 35.

106. Block, *Revising State Theory*, p. 66.

107. Ibid., pp. 66, 88.

108. For applications of Block's model to non-U.S. cases, see his 1980 es-

say, "Beyond Relative Autonomy: State Managers as Historical Subjects," reprinted in *Revising State Theory*, pp. 81–96.

109. Ibid., pp. 64, 66.

110. Ibid., pp. 62, 66–67.

111. Ibid., pp. 19, 24–25.

112. Philip Selznick, *Leadership in Administration: A Sociological Interpretation* (New York: Harper & Row, 1957), pp. 62–63, 65–89; James Q. Wilson, *Bureaucracy: What Government Agencies Do and Why They Do It* (New York: Basic Books, 1989), pp. 27, 30–49, 92, 109–10, 246.

113. Douglas A. Hibbs, Jr., *The American Political Economy: Macroeconomics and Electoral Politics* (Cambridge: Harvard University Press, 1987), pp. 213–32, 244–54, 294–96, 325–26.

Chapter 8. Rational Choice: Actors and Institutions

1. Jon Elster's introduction to Elster, ed., *Rational Choice* (Oxford: Basil Blackwell, 1986), pp. 1–33, is a good overview.

2. Morris P. Fiorina, *Retrospective Voting in American National Elections* (New Haven: Yale University Press, 1981), p. 199.

3. The label of new institutionalism can be applied equally well to approaches entirely outside rational choice, including the historical institutionalism of this book. James G. March and Johan P. Olsen, in "The New Institutionalism: Organizational Factors in Political Life," [*American Political Science Review* 78(3): 734–49 (September 1984)], survey a broad range of works; only a minority are within the rational choice tradition.

4. Morris P. Fiorina, "Legislative Choice of Regulatory Forms: Legal Process or Administrative Process?" *Public Choice* 39 (1982): 33–66; William H. Riker, *The Art of Political Manipulation* (New Haven: Yale University Press, 1986); Gerald Gamm and Kenneth Shepsle, "Emergence of Legislative Institutions: Standing Committees in the House and Senate, 1810–1825," *Legislative Studies Quarterly* 14(1): 39–66 (February 1989).

5. Terry M. Moe, who criticizes this excessive focus on Congress, treats it as an unfortunate accident of intellectual development rather than an inevitable consequence of the limitations of the theory. Moe suggests that it is possible—and desirable—to construct a rational choice model of the bureaucracy that is not so Congress-centered. Terry M. Moe, "Interests, Institutions, and Positive Theory: The Politics of the NLRB," *Studies in American Political Development* 2 (1987): 278, 280–81, 298; idem, "An Assessment of the Positive Theory of 'Congressional Dominance,'" *Legislative Studies Quarterly* 12(4): 475–520 (November 1987). See also Morris S. Ogul and Bert A. Rockman, "Overseeing Oversight: New Departures and Old Problems," *Legislative Studies Quarterly* 15(1): 9–12 (February 1990); James Q. Wilson, *Bureaucracy: What Government Agencies Do and Why They Do It* (New York: Basic Books, 1989), pp. 254–56.

6. Anthony Downs, *An Economic Theory of Democracy* (New York: Harper & Row, 1957), p. 28.

7. Recent spatial modeling has abandoned Downs's assumption of uni-dimensionality for a more realistic multidimensional conception. Voters and candidates are still treated as rational actors, and centrism is still predicted as the normal outcome of electoral competition. See James M. Enelow and Melvin J. Hinich, *The Spatial Theory of Voting: An Introduction* (Cambridge: Cambridge University Press, 1984), esp. pp. 221–22.

8. Civil servants in the Nixon administration, particularly in the social service agencies, had more liberal attitudes than the president. Joel D. Aber-bach and Bert A. Rockman, "Clashing Beliefs within the Executive Branch: The Nixon Administration Bureaucracy," *American Political Science Review* 70(2): 456–68 (June 1976). Ronald Reagan told a sympathetic reporter, "You know, just between us, one of the hardest things in a government this size—no matter what our people way on top are trying to do—is to know that down there, un-derneath, is that permanent structure that is resisting everything you're do-ing." Quoted in Donald Lambro, *Washington—City of Scandals: Investigating Congress and Other Big Spenders* (Boston: Little, Brown, 1984), p. 252.

9. William A. Niskanen, Jr., *Bureaucracy and Representative Government* (Chicago: Aldine-Atherton, 1971). Downs's own work on bureaucracy also as-sumes that bureaucrats are utility maximizers but distinguishes five types of bureaucrats with nine different motives. His predictions about bureau behav-ior thus depend on sociological statements about the relationships of goals, or-ganizations, roles, and personalities, rather than on deductions from a unitary economic model. Anthony Downs, *Inside Bureaucracy* (Boston: Little, Brown, 1967), esp. pp. 79–91.

10. Niskanen, *Bureaucracy and Representative Government*, p. 30.

11. Ibid., pp. 169–80.

12. On Social Security, see Martha Derthick, *Policymaking for Social Security* (Washington, D.C.: Brookings Institution, 1979), esp. pp. 144–56. On the NLRB, see Moe, "Interests, Institutions, and Positive Theory," pp. 241–62.

13. David Burner, *The Politics of Provincialism: The Democratic Party in Tran-sition, 1918–1932* (Cambridge: Harvard University Press, 1986); James L. Sund-quist, *Dynamics of the Party System: Alignment and Realignment of Political Parties in the United States*, rev. ed. (Washington, D.C.: Brookings Institution, 1983), pp. 182–97.

14. James Q. Wilson has argued, however, that increased funding is not the dominant goal of American bureaucrats. "There is little doubt," he says, "that, other things being equal, bureau chiefs would like more money and no doubt at all that they feel their authority is not adequate to their responsibili-ties. But . . . when confronted with a choice, many if not most bureaus prefer greater autonomy to greater resources." Expansion into new realms of author-ity, which threatens a bureau's autonomy to carry out its existing tasks at the same time that it promises enlarged resources, is often opposed by bureau-cratic leadership: "having a monopoly position on even a small piece of turf is better than having a competitive position on a large one." James Q. Wilson, *The Investigators: Managing FBI and Narcotics Agents* (New York: Basic Books, 1978), pp. 165, 170. See also idem, *Bureaucracy*, pp. 118–19, 179–81.

15. These omissions are particularly evident in Niskanen's discussion of multiservice bureaus, which apparently have no preferences about what they actually do. See Niskanen, *Bureaucracy and Representative Government*, pp. 106–12.

16. Kenneth J. Arrow, *Social Choice and Individual Values*, 2d. ed. (New York: John Wiley & Sons, 1963).

17. Congressional rules are manipulated in the cases of Chauncey DePew's opposition to the Seventeenth Amendment for direct election of senators (*Art of Political Manipulation*, chap. 2), and Adam Clayton Powell's amendment to the education bill (chap. 11). The stratagem discussed in chap. 9 ("How to Win on a Roll Call by Not Voting") depends on a peculiar rule of Virginia's state senate. The importance of party alignment is illustrated by Riker's foremost example of heresthetical genius, Lincoln's question to Douglas whether the people of a territory could lawfully exclude slavery (chap. 1). Asking this question was an effective maneuver because the Democratic party was organized as a cross-sectional coalition, and any possible answer by Douglas would alienate either the northern or the southern wing of the party. Another example of the role of party was the revolt against Joseph Cannon as Speaker of the House, successful because the minority Democrats held enough seats to form a winning coalition with insurgent Republicans (chap. 12). Riker also takes as given particular systems of racial and class subordination, as in his discussions of slavery in the Roman Empire (chap. 7) and at the Constitutional Convention (chap. 8). In addition to *Art of Political Manipulation*, see William H. Riker, "Implications from the Disequilibrium of Majority Rule for the Study of Institutions," *American Political Science Review* 74(2): 432–46 (June 1980); idem, "The Heresthetics of Constitution-Making: The Presidency in 1787, with Comments on Determinism and Rational Choice," *American Political Science Review* 78(1): 1–16 (March 1984); idem, *Liberalism Against Populism: A Confrontation between the Theory of Democracy and the Theory of Social Choice* (San Francisco: W. H. Freeman, 1982), pp. 115–36.

18. Kenneth A. Shepsle, "Institutional Equilibrium and Equilibrium Institutions," in Herbert F. Weisberg, ed., *Political Science: The Science of Politics* (New York: Agathon, 1986), p. 52. See also idem, "Studying Institutions: Some Lessons from the Rational Choice Approach," *Journal of Theoretical Politics* 1(2): 131–47 (April 1989).

19. Shepsle, "Institutional Equilibrium and Equilibrium Institutions," pp. 72–74; Kenneth A. Shepsle and Barry R. Weingast, "The Institutional Foundations of Committee Power," *American Political Science Review* 81(1): 85–104 (March 1987); Gamm and Shepsle, "Emergence of Legislative Institutions," pp. 52, 58; Barry R. Weingast and William J. Marshall, "The Industrial Organization of Congress; or, Why Legislatures, Like Firms, Are Not Organized as Markets," *Journal of Political Economy* 96(1): 132–63 (February 1988).

20. Particularly stimulating examples include Edward C. Banfield, *Here the People Rule: Selected Essays* (New York: Plenum Press, 1985), pp. 317–39; Amitai Etzioni, "Rationality is Anti-Entropic," *Journal of Economic Psychology* 7(1): 17–36 (March 1986); Paula England, "A Feminist Critique of Rational-

Choice Theories: Implications for Sociology," *American Sociologist* 20(1): 14–28 (Spring 1989); Jürg Steiner, "Rational Choice Theories and Politics: A Research Agenda and a Moral Question," *PS* 23(1): 46–50 (March 1990).

21. Stanley Kelley, Jr., foreword to the paperbound edition of *An Economic Theory of Democracy*, by Anthony Downs (New York: Harper & Row, 1957), p. x.

22. Riker, "Heresthetics of Constitution-Making," p. 15.

23. Shepsle, "Studying Institutions," p. 145.

24. James G. March and Johan P. Olsen, *Rediscovering Institutions: The Organizational Basis of Politics* (New York: Free Press, 1989), p. 8.

25. Among the most important works on this topic are Gerald H. Kramer, "Short-Term Fluctuations in U.S. Voting Behavior, 1896–1964," *American Political Science Review* 65(1): 131–43 (March 1971); Howard S. Bloom and H. Douglas Price, "Voter Response to Short-Run Economic Conditions: The Asymmetric Effect of Prosperity and Recession," *American Political Science Review* 69(4): 1240–54 (December 1975); Edward R. Tufte, *Political Control of the Economy* (Princeton: Princeton University Press, 1978); Douglas A. Hibbs, Jr., *The American Political Economy: Macroeconomics and Electoral Politics* (Cambridge: Harvard University Press, 1987).

26. Richard F. Fenno, Jr., *Home Style: House Members in Their Districts* (Boston: Little, Brown, 1978), pp. 215, 217, 242–43; Ogul and Rockman, "Overseeing Oversight," pp. 16–18.

27. March and Olsen, *Rediscovering Institutions*, pp. 54–55. Similarly, see Arthur L. Stinchcombe, *Constructing Social Theories* (New York: Harcourt, Brace & World, 1968), p. 92.

28. A. Cash Koeniger, "Carter Glass and the National Recovery Administration," *South Atlantic Quarterly* 74(3): 362 (Summer 1975).

29. For examples, see Fiorina, "Legislative Choice of Regulatory Forms," pp. 33–66; Mathew D. McCubbins and Talbot Page, "A Theory of Congressional Delegation," and Randall L. Calvert, Mark J. Moran, and Barry R. Weingast, "Congressional Influence over Policy Making: The Case of the FTC," both in Mathew D. McCubbins and Terry Sullivan, eds., *Congress: Structure and Policy* (Cambridge: Cambridge University Press, 1987); Mathew D. McCubbins and Thomas Schwartz, "Congressional Oversight Overlooked: Police Patrols versus Fire Alarms," *American Journal of Political Science* 28(1): 165–79 (February 1984); Barry R. Weingast, "The Congressional-Bureaucratic System: A Principal Agent Perspective (with Applications to the SEC)," *Public Choice* 44:147–91 (1984).

30. Peter Irons, *The New Deal Lawyers* (Princeton: Princeton University Press, 1982), p. 297.

31. John Mark Hansen, *Gaining Access: Congress and the Farm Lobby, 1919–1981* (Chicago: University of Chicago Press, 1991). Idem, "Choosing Sides: The Creation of an Agricultural Policy Network in Congress, 1919–1932," *Studies in American Political Development* 2 (1987): 183–229, presents an earlier version of Hansen's analysis of pre-New Deal farm policy.

32. Hansen, *Gaining Access*, p. 25.

33. Ibid., p. 78.

34. Ibid., pp. 64–67; Gilbert C. Fite, *George N. Peek and the Fight for Farm Parity* (Norman: University of Oklahoma Press, 1954), esp. pp. 151–202; Christiana McFadyen Campbell, *The Farm Bureau and the New Deal* (Urbana: University of Illinois Press, 1962), pp. 35–40; Richard Franklin Bensel, *Sectionalism and American Political Development: 1880–1980* (Madison: University of Wisconsin Press, 1984), pp. 139–47.

35. William R. Johnson, "National Farm Organizations and the Reshaping of Agricultural Policy in 1932," *Agricultural History* 37(1): 35–37 (January 1963).

36. Irvin M. May, Jr., *Marvin Jones: The Public Life of an Agrarian Advocate* (College Station: Texas A&M University Press, 1980), pp. 89–91; Johnson, "National Farm Organizations," pp. 37–39.

37. William D. Rowley, *M. L. Wilson and the Campaign for the Domestic Allotment* (Lincoln: University of Nebraska Press, 1970), pp. 150–52; Richard S. Kirkendall, *Social Scientists and Farm Politics in the Age of Roosevelt* (Columbia: University of Missouri Press, 1966), pp. 41–50; Johnson, "National Farm Organizations," pp. 39–42; Campbell, *Farm Bureau and the New Deal*, pp. 52–57; Gilbert C. Fite, "John A. Simpson: The Southwest's Militant Farm Leader," *Mississippi Valley Historical Review* 35(4): 577–78 (March 1949).

38. Van L. Perkins, *Crisis in Agriculture: The Agricultural Adjustment Administration and the New Deal, 1933* (Berkeley and Los Angeles: University of California Press, 1969), pp. 36–38.

39. Hansen, *Gaining Access*, p. 80.

40. John L. Shover, "Populism in the Nineteen-Thirties: The Battle for the AAA," *Agricultural History* 39(1): 19 (January 1965). Hansen's methodology for analysis of committee hearings (his main source of evidence) is explained in *Gaining Access*, pp. 23–24.

41. Shover, "Populism in the Nineteen-Thirties," p. 24.

42. May, *Marvin Jones*, pp. 102–3.

43. Johnson, "National Farm Organizations," p. 39; Campbell, *Farm Bureau and the New Deal*, p. 49.

44. George H. Gallup, *The Gallup Poll: Public Opinion 1935–1971* (New York: Random House, 1972), 3 vols., 1:9. Overall, 59 percent of the public opposed the AAA; the only region where a majority favored the program was the South.

45. Sylvia Snowiss, "Presidential Leadership of Congress: An Analysis of Roosevelt's First Hundred Days," *Polity* 1(1): 67–71 (1971).

46. In the concluding chapter of his book, Hansen acknowledges that interest groups and political parties are not always "fundamentally at odds, fundamentally in competition for the attention of elected officials. . . . On occasion, interest groups line up with political parties, and on such occasions, interest groups lag behind political parties in their claims on lawmakers' allegiances." He suggests such "party dominance" is rare and specifically mentions New Deal agricultural policy as a case where parties and interest groups *did* compete. Hansen, *Gaining Access*, pp. 226, 223.

47. Robert F. Himmelberg, *The Origins of the National Recovery Administration: Business, Government, and the Trade Association Issue, 1921–1933* (New York:

Fordham University Press, 1976), pp. 183–89, 196–212; Louis Galambos, *Competition and Cooperation: The Emergence of a National Trade Association* (Baltimore: Johns Hopkins Press, 1966), pp. 176–202.

48. The discussion of the origins of the industrial recovery program in this and the next paragraph draw on Himmelberg, *Origins*, pp. 196–206; Ellis W. Hawley, *The New Deal and the Problem of Monopoly: A Study in Economic Ambivalence* (Princeton: Princeton University Press, 1966), pp. 21–26; J. Joseph Huthmacher, *Senator Robert F. Wagner and the Rise of Urban Liberalism* (New York: Atheneum, 1968), pp. 137–51.

49. William E. Leuchtenburg, "The New Deal and the Analogue of War," in John Braeman, Robert H. Bremner, and Everett Walters, eds., *Change and Continuity in Twentieth-Century America* (New York: Harper & Row, 1966), pp. 112–13, 117–23, 127–30; John Kennedy Ohl, *Hugh S. Johnson and the New Deal* (DeKalb: Northern Illinois University Press, 1985), pp. 98–99. The importance of the World War I analogy bears out Deborah A. Stone's emphasis on the ways metaphor can shape public policy; compare Stone's *Policy Paradox and Political Reason* (Glenview, Ill.: Scott, Foresman, 1988), pp. 117–23, with the more rationalistic model of Fiorina, "Legislative Choice of Regulatory Forms," pp. 46–52.

50. Fiorina, "Legislative Choice of Regulatory Forms," p. 40 n. 11; Gamm and Shepsle, "Emergence of Legislative Institutions," pp. 40–41.

51. Edwin G. Nourse, Joseph S. Davis, and John D. Black, *Three Years of the Agricultural Adjustment Administration* (Washington, D.C.: Brookings Institution, 1937), pp. 260–67. Hansen's claim that "Roosevelt reached deep into the farm relief lobby to staff" the AAA emphasizes the interest group connections of AAA officials at the expense of their institutional backgrounds. Hansen, *Gaining Access*, p. 79.

52. Nourse, Davis, and Black, *Three Years*, p. 246. One warning that production control would be impossible to administer came in a January 9, 1933, *Chicago Tribune* editorial that said determination of individual farmers' allotments, as required under the bill introduced by Senator Peter Norbeck during the lame-duck session, was beyond the capacity of any secretary of agriculture. According to the *Tribune*, "A man who combined the integrity of George Washington, the energy of Theodore Roosevelt, and the administrative ability of Alexander Hamilton couldn't handle so prodigious a task." Quoted in Gilbert Courtland Fite, *Peter Norbeck: Prairie Statesman* (Columbia: University of Missouri Press, 1948), p. 167.

53. Margaret Levi, *Of Rule and Revenue* (Berkeley and Los Angeles: University of California Press, 1988), pp. 52–70.

54. Nourse, Davis, and Black, *Three Years*, pp. 38–40, 68–77, 146–50, 255–63.

55. For price and production levels of key commodities, see Table 3. Nourse, Davis, and Black suggest overall participation rates of about 50 percent of corn acreage, 75 percent of hogs raised, 75 percent of cotton acreage, and 75 to 95 percent of acreage for the various types of tobacco. Participation was much higher in regions of concentrated production: over 89 percent of

wheat acreage came under contract in Kansas, Montana, and the Dakotas, while the program covered 93 percent of corn acreage in Iowa and 98 percent of corn acreage in South Dakota. Nourse, Davis, and Black, *Three Years*, pp. 119–20.

56. Leverett S. Lyon et al., *The National Recovery Administration: An Analysis and Appraisal* (Washington, D.C.: Brookings Institution, 1935), p. 136.

57. Ibid., pp. 136, 276.

58. Ohl, *Hugh S. Johnson*, pp. 138–45. The Philadelphia National Football League team provides one vestige of Johnson's efforts: created in 1933, it was named the Eagles after the NRA symbol.

59. Walter Lippmann, *The Essential Lippmann: A Political Philosophy for Liberal Democracy*, eds. Clinton Rossiter and James Lare (New York: Random House, 1963), pp. 478–79. This passage was originally published in October 1933.

60. Lyon et al., *National Recovery Administration*, pp. 141, 266–72.

61. Stephen D. Krasner, "Sovereignty: An Institutional Perspective," *Comparative Political Studies* 21(1): 71 (April 1988).

62. Robert H. Bates, *Essays on the Political Economy of Rural Africa* (Cambridge: Cambridge University Press, 1983), pp. 118–33, is particularly clear in discussing the significance of "meaningful patterns of party competition" (p. 131) and the implications of a rational choice approach for patterns and consequences of public policy.

63. Huthmacher, *Senator Robert F. Wagner*, pp. 27–37, depicts Wagner's politics as part of a pattern of social reformism by Tammany Hall (Manhattan's Democratic machine) and notes that other politicians exposed to the same influences did not become reformers.

64. Sidney Baldwin, *Poverty and Politics: The Rise and Decline of the Farm Security Administration* (Chapel Hill: University of North Carolina Press, 1968), pp. 136–38; May, *Marvin Jones*, p. 127.

65. Fenno, *Home Style*, p. 219.

66. Copeland's political career and his anti–New Deal conservatism are discussed in James T. Patterson, *Congressional Conservatism and the New Deal: The Growth of the Conservative Coalition in Congress, 1933–1939* (Lexington: University of Kentucky Press, 1967), pp. 46–47.

67. Koeniger, "Carter Glass," pp. 356, 362.

68. Daniel R. Fusfeld, *The Economic Thought of Franklin D. Roosevelt and the Origins of the New Deal* (New York: Columbia University Press, 1956), pp. 154–65, 244–46.

69. David Plotke, "The Wagner Act, Again: Politics and Labor, 1935–37," *Studies in American Political Development* 3 (1989): 114.

70. Frank Freidel, *Franklin D. Roosevelt: The Triumph* (Boston: Little, Brown, 1956), pp. 275–290, 370; Roy V. Peel and Thomas C. Donnelly, *The 1932 Campaign: An Analysis* (New York: Farrar & Rinehart, 1935), pp. 216–20.

71. Arthur M. Schlesinger, Jr., *The Politics of Upheaval* (Boston: Houghton Mifflin, 1960), pp. 422–23; Murray Edelman, "New Deal Sensitivity to Labor

Interests," in Milton Derber and Edwin Young, eds., *Labor and the New Deal* (Madison: University of Wisconsin Press, 1957), pp. 185–89. The two key labor issues of 1934 on which Roosevelt equivocated were representation in the automobile industry and Wagner's Labor Disputes Bill, creating a more effective administrative apparatus.

72. J. David Greenstone, *Labor in American Politics* (Chicago: University of Chicago Press, Phoenix Books, 1977), p. 48; Sundquist, *Dynamics of the Party System*, pp. 214–28.

73. Quoted in Baldwin, *Poverty and Politics*, p. 141.

74. David Eugene Conrad, *The Forgotten Farmers: The Story of Sharecroppers in the New Deal* (Urbana: University of Illinois Press, 1965); Donald H. Grubbs, *Cry from the Cotton: The Southern Tenant Farmers' Union and the New Deal* (Chapel Hill: University of North Carolina Press, 1971).

75. Baldwin, *Politics and Poverty*, p. 299.

76. Lawrence J. Nelson, "The Art of the Possible: Another Look at the 'Purge' of the AAA Liberals in 1935," *Agricultural History* 57(4): 426, 433–34 (October 1983).

77. Fiorina, "Legislative Choice of Regulatory Forms," p. 41.

78. Examples include Kenneth A. Shepsle and Barry R. Weingast, "Political Solutions to Market Problems," *American Political Science Review* 78(2): 417–34 (June 1984); Morris P. Fiorina, *Congress: Keystone of the Washington Establishment*, 2d ed. (New Haven: Yale University Press, 1989), esp. chap. 8; Peter Van Doren, "Should Congress Listen to Economists?" *Journal of Politics* 51(2): 319–36 (May 1989); Bates, *Essays on the Political Economy of Rural Africa*, chap. 5.

79. Riker, *Art of Political Manipulation*, chap. 7; Levi, *Of Rule and Revenue*, chap. 4.

80. "To the extent that a theory fails to specify major conditions defining its applicability, it is inadequate theory." George D. Greenberg, Jeffrey A. Miller, Lawrence B. Mohr, and Bruce C. Vladeck, "Developing Public Policy Theory: Perspectives from Empirical Research," *American Political Science Review* 71(4): 1543 (December 1977).

81. Cf. Peter Hall, *Governing the Economy: The Politics of State Intervention in Britain and France* (New York: Oxford University Press, 1986), p. 11; Ogul and Rockman, "Overseeing Oversight," pp. 20–22.

82. "There is nothing in principle wrong with functional explanations, though to identify a function something serves is not necessarily to provide one." G. A. Cohen, *Karl Marx's Theory of History: A Defence* (Princeton: Princeton University Press, 1978), pp. 282–83.

83. Stinchcombe, *Constructing Social Theories*, p. 85. Cf. Cohen, *Karl Marx's Theory of History*, pp. 259–64.

84. This reconstruction follows the logic of functional explanation outlined in Stinchcombe, *Constructing Social Theories*, pp. 87–88.

85. Krasner, "Sovereignty," p. 83. See also idem, "Approaches to the State: Alternative Conceptions and Historical Dynamics," *Comparative Politics* 16(2): 240–43 (June 1984); March and Olsen, *Rediscovering Institutions*, p. 56; Sidney

Verba, "Sequences and Development," in Leonard Binder et al., *Crises and Sequences in Political Development* (Princeton: Princeton University Press, 1971), pp. 307–8.

86. March and Olsen, *Rediscovering Institutions*, p. 34.

87. Downs, *Economic Theory of Democracy*, pp. 117–18, 139; David B. Truman, *The Governmental Process*, 2d ed. (New York: Knopf, 1971), pp. 271–73.

88. Thomas Ferguson, "From Normalcy to New Deal: Industrial Structure, Party Competition, and American Public Policy in the Great Depression," *International Organization* 38(1): 48–61 (Winter 1984); idem, "Elites and Elections; or, What Have They Done to You Lately?" in Benjamin Ginsberg and Alan Stone, eds., *Do Elections Matter?* (Armonk, N.Y.: M. E. Sharpe, 1986), pp. 179–80; G. William Domhoff, *The Power Elite and the State: How Policy is Made in America* (New York: Aldine de Gruyter, 1990), p. 225; idem, *The Higher Circles: The Governing Class in America* (New York: Random House, 1970), pp. 315, 344–46, 349–53; Karl Marx, *The Eighteenth Brumaire of Louis Bonaparte*, in Marx and Engels, *Collected Works* (London: Lawrence & Wishart, 1979), 11:112–13, 119–20, 127–28; Rhonda F. Levine, *Class Struggle and the New Deal: Industrial Labor, Industrial Capital, and the State* (Lawrence: University Press of Kansas, 1988), pp. 42–43, 62–63, 151, 158–60, 172–73. Electorally competitive socialist or communist parties, when not excessively reformist, do provide a real choice in many countries, but of course this is not the case in the United States.

89. Alan Ware, *Citizens, Parties, and the State: A Reappraisal* (Cambridge: Polity Press, 1987), pp. 73–77 (quote p. 73).

90. Quoted in William E. Leuchtenburg, *Franklin D. Roosevelt and the New Deal, 1932–1940* (New York: Harper & Row, 1963), p. 196.

91. Nancy J. Weiss, *Farewell to the Party of Lincoln: Black Politics in the Age of FDR* (Princeton: Princeton University Press, 1983), pp. 29–32, 205–35, 296–301; James Q. Wilson, introduction to Harold F. Gosnell, *Negro Politicians: The Rise of Negro Politics in Chicago* (Chicago: University of Chicago Press, 1967), p. viii.

92. March and Olsen, *Rediscovering Institutions*, pp. 55–56.

Chapter 9. Conclusion: The New Deal and the Next Deal

1. "The impact of previous policy itself," Hugh Heclo suggests, should be an important political variable in policy studies; "what is normally considered the dependent variable (policy output) is also an independent variable (in an ongoing process in which everything becomes an intervening variable)." Hugh Heclo, *Modern Social Politics in Britain and Sweden* (New Haven: Yale University Press, 1974), p. 315.

2. Richard E. Neustadt and Ernest R. May, *Thinking in Time: The Uses of History for Decision Makers* (New York: Free Press, 1986), pp. xiii, 32–57, 136–37; Ernest R. May, *"Lessons" of the Past: The Use and Misuse of History in American Foreign Policy* (New York: Oxford University Press, 1973), pp. ix–xii, 18, 51, 84–86, 112–21, 178–79; Yuen Foong Khong, *Analogies at War: Korea, Munich, Dien Bien Phu, and the Vietnam Decisions of 1965* (Princeton: Princeton University Press, 1992), pp. 3–46, 251–63; Robert Jervis, *Perception and Misperception in*

International Politics (Princeton: Princeton University Press, 1976), pp. 217–82; Yaacov Y. I. Vertzberger, "Foreign Policy Decisionmakers as Practical-Intuitive Historians: Applied History and Its Shortcomings," *International Studies Quarterly* 30(2): 223–47 (June 1986); Otis L. Graham, Jr., *Losing Time: The Industrial Policy Debate* (Cambridge: Harvard University Press, 1992), pp. 248–49; Deborah A. Stone, *Policy Paradox and Policy Reason* (Glenview, Ill.: Scott, Foresman, 1988), pp. 147–65; Stephen Vaughn, ed., *The Vital Past: Writings on the Use of History* (Athens: University of Georgia Press, 1985), p. 294. See also, in *Vital Past*, George O. Kent, "Clio the Tyrant: Historical Analogies and the Meaning of History," pp. 303–4; Arthur M. Schlesinger, Jr., "The Inscrutability of History," pp. 317–18; Lester D. Stephens, "Lessons, Analogies, and Prediction," pp. 327–28; David F. Trask, "A Reflection on Historians and Policymakers," pp. 360, 364; and Otis L. Graham, "Uses and Misuses of History: Roles in Policymaking," pp. 371–72; and see David Hackett Fischer, *Historians' Fallacies: Toward a Logic of Historical Thought* (New York: Harper & Row, 1970), pp. 166–67.

3. Heclo, *Modern Social Politics*, p. 315.

4. William E. Leuchtenburg, "The New Deal and the Analogue of War," in John Braeman, Robert H. Bremner, and Everett Walters, eds., *Change and Continuity in Twentieth-Century America* (New York: Harper & Row, 1966), pp. 117–18, 120–22.

5. Graham, *Losing Time*, p. 114.

6. Neustadt and May, *Thinking in Time*, pp. 89–90, 235, 273.

7. Cf. Jervis, *Perception and Misperception*, pp. 227–29.

8. W. Brian Arthur, "Competing Technologies, Increasing Returns, and Lock-In by Historical Events," *Economic Journal* 99(1): 127 (March 1989). See also Paul A. David, "Clio and the Economics of QWERTY," *American Economic Review* 75(2): 332–37 (May 1985), and, for political applications, Stephen D. Krasner, "Sovereignty: An Institutional Perspective," *Comparative Political Studies* 21(1): 83–85 (April 1988); and Terry Lynn Karl, "Dilemmas of Democratization in Latin America," *Comparative Politics* 23(1): 7–8 (October 1990). David Hackett Fischer warns against "the idea that big effects must have big causes, or that big events must have big consequences." *Historians' Fallacies*, p. 177, and see also p. 167; Jervis, *Perception and Misperception*, pp. 230, 281.

9. R. D. Norton, "Industrial Policy and American Renewal," *Journal of Economic Literature* 24(1): 5–9 (March 1986), compares industrial policy proponents with the stagnationists of the 1930s.

10. J. George Frederick, ed., *The Swope Plan* (New York: Business Bourse, 1931); Felix G. Rohatyn, *The Twenty-Year Century: Essays on Economics and Public Finance* (New York: Random House, 1983). Rohatyn's book is prefaced with a quote from Franklin Roosevelt. For a harsh comment on "business statesmen" such as Swope and Rohatyn, see Eugene Bardach, "Implementing Industrial Policy," in Chalmers Johnson, ed., *The Industrial Policy Debate* (San Francisco: ICS Press, 1984), p. 113.

11. For overviews, see Norton, "Industrial Policy and American Renewal," pp. 33–36; Graham, *Losing Time*; Paul Peretz, ed., *The Politics of American Economic Policy Making* (Armonk, N.Y.: M. E. Sharpe, 1987), pp. 105–6, 127.

12. Lester C. Thurow, *The Zero-Sum Society: Distribution and the Possibilities for Economic Change* (New York: Basic Books, 1980); idem, *The Zero-Sum Solution: Building a World-Class American Economy* (New York: Simon & Schuster, 1985); Ira C. Magaziner and Robert B. Reich, *Minding America's Business: The Decline and Rise of the American Economy* (New York: Harcourt Brace Jovanovich, 1982); Robert B. Reich, *The Next American Frontier* (New York: Times Books, 1983); Business Week Team, *The Reindustrialization of America* (New York: McGraw-Hill, 1982). This last title was an expanded version of a special issue of *Business Week* dated June 30, 1980.

13. Graham, *Losing Time*, p. 99.

14. On the National Industrial Recovery Board, see Leverett S. Lyon et al., *The National Recovery Administration: An Analysis and Appraisal* (Washington, D.C.: Brookings Institution, 1935), pp. 43–45, 75–77, 168–70; Ellis W. Hawley, *The New Deal and the Problem of Monopoly: A Study in Economic Ambivalence* (Princeton: Princeton University Press, 1966), pp. 106–10.

15. George Gilder, "A Supply-Side Economics of the Left," *Public Interest* 72: 29–43 (Summer 1983). As secretary of the treasury, Andrew Mellon succeeded in forcing down the high tax rates imposed during World War I. See Ronald Frederick King, "From Redistributive to Hegemonic Logic: The Transformation of American Tax Politics, 1894–1963," *Politics and Society* 12(1): 19–31 (1983). Graham, *Losing Time*, p. 58, notes that industrial policy and supply-side economics "were the two broad economic reform ideas to emerge from a decade of intensifying trade and regional problems that eluded traditional Keynesian manipulation."

16. Gar Alperovitz and Jeff Faux, *Rebuilding America* (New York: Pantheon, 1984), pp. 49–67; Samuel Bowles, David M. Gordon, and Thomas E. Weisskopf, *Beyond the Wasteland: A Democratic Alternative to Economic Decline* (Garden City, N.Y.: Anchor, 1984), pp. 208–26; Martin Carnoy, Derek Shearer, and Russell Rumberger, *A New Social Contract: The Economy and Government after Reagan* (New York: Harper & Row, 1983), pp. 150–95.

17. Charles L. Schultze, "Industrial Policy: A Dissent," *Brookings Review* 2(1): 3–12 (Fall 1983). A more recent article presenting many of the same arguments is Pietro S. Nivola, "More Like Them? The Political Feasibility of Strategic Trade Policy," *Brookings Review* 9(2): 14–21 (Spring 1991). See also Joseph L. Badaracco, Jr., and David B. Yoffie, " 'Industrial Policy': It Can't Happen Here," *Harvard Business Review* 61(5): 97–105 (November/December 1983).

18. Amitai Etzioni, "The MITIzation of America?," *Public Interest* 72 (Summer 1983): 44–51; idem, "Caution: Industrial Policy Is Coming," *Challenge* 35(5): 58–61 (September–October 1992).

19. Graham, *Losing Time*, pp. 49, 114, 124–25, 143, 259; Julian Gresser, *Partners in Prosperity: Strategic Industries for the United States and Japan* (New York: McGraw-Hill, 1984), p. 275.

20. The importance of "business groups" is emphasized by Lester C. Thurow, *Head to Head: The Coming Economic Battle among Japan, Europe, and America* (New York: William Morrow, 1992), pp. 280–90.

21. Hugh Heclo, "Industrial Politics and the Executive Capacities of

Government," in Claude E. Barfield and William A. Schambra, eds., *The Politics of Industrial Policy* (Washington, D.C.: American Enterprise Institute, 1986), p. 303.

22. Kevin P. Phillips, *Staying on Top: The Business Case for a National Industrial Strategy* (New York: Random House, 1984), pp. 84–87; Clyde V. Prestowitz, Jr., *Trading Places: How We Allowed Japan to Take the Lead* (New York: Basic Books, 1988), p. 269; Heclo, "Executive Capacities of Government," pp. 303–4, 307; Graham, *Losing Time*, p. 100.

23. Graham, *Losing Time*, pp. 36, 284.

24. Edwin L. Harper, "Commentaries," in Barfield and Schambra, eds., *Politics of Industrial Policy*, p. 339.

25. Robert B. Reich, "An Industrial Policy of the Right," *Public Interest* 73 (Fall 1983): 12–15; Michael L. Dertouzos, Richard K. Lester, Robert M. Solow, and the MIT Commission on Industrial Productivity, *Made in America: Regaining the Productive Edge* (Cambridge: MIT Press, 1989), pp. 114–16; George C. Lodge, *Perestroika for America: Restructuring U.S. Business-Government Relations for Competitiveness in the World Economy* (Boston: Harvard Business School Press, 1990), pp. 80–100; Graham, *Losing Time*, pp. 183–87, 232–33; David Vogel, "Government-Industry Relations in the United States: An Overview," in Stephen Wilks and Maurice Wright, eds., *Comparative Government-Industry Relations: Western Europe, the United States, and Japan* (Oxford: Clarendon, 1987), pp. 95, 99–103, 112; Gregory Hooks, "The Rise of the Pentagon and U.S. State Building: The Defense Program as Industrial Policy," *American Journal of Sociology* 96(2): 358–404 (September 1990); idem, *Forging the Military-Industrial Complex: World War II's Battle of the Potomac* (Urbana: University of Illinois Press, 1991), pp. 225–76; Jay Stowsky, "From Spin-Off to Spin-On: Redefining the Military's Role in American Technology Development," in Wayne Sandholtz et al., *The Highest Stakes: The Economic Foundations of the Next Security System* (New York: Oxford University Press, 1992), pp. 114–40.

26. Peter K. Eisinger, *The Rise of the Entrepreneurial State: State and Local Economic Development Policy in the United States* (Madison: University of Wisconsin Press, 1988), pp. 15–33; David Osborne, *Laboratories of Democracy* (Boston: Harvard Business School Press, 1990), pp. 27–35; R. Scott Fosler, ed., *The New Economic Role of American States: Strategies in a Competitive World Economy* (New York: Oxford University Press, 1988), pp. 3–5; Graham, *Losing Time*, p. 164; Vogel, "Government-Industry Relations," pp. 93, 109; Mel Dubnick and Lynne Holt, "Industrial Policy and the States," *Publius* 15(1): 119–20, 124–26 (Winter 1985).

27. Steve Smith, quoted in Osborne, *Laboratories of Democracy*, p. 89.

28. Osborne, *Laboratories of Democracy*, p. 259; Eisinger, *Rise of the Entrepreneurial State*, pp. 25–29, 31–32; Fosler, *New Economic Role of American States*, pp. 314–15; Graham, *Losing Time*, p. 204; Bardach, "Implementing Industrial Policy," p. 96; William E. Hudson, "The Feasibility of a Comprehensive U.S. Industrial Policy," *Political Science Quarterly* 100(3): 474 (Fall 1985).

29. *Business Week* Team, *Reindustrialization of America*, pp. 108–11; Reich, *Next American Frontier*, pp. 69–73.

30. Badaracco and Yoffie, " 'Industrial Policy,' " p. 101.

31. Schultze, "Industrial Policy: A Dissent," pp. 7–8; Bardach, "Implementing Industrial Policy," p. 98.

32. Etzioni, "MITIzation of America?", p. 47; Graham, *Losing Time*, p. 238.

33. Etzioni, "MITIzation of America?", p. 49; idem, "Caution: Industrial Policy Is Coming," pp. 59–60; Nivola, "More Like Them?", pp. 20–21; Schultze, "Industrial Policy: A Dissent," pp. 9–10; Badaracco and Yoffie, " 'Industrial Policy,' " pp. 98–99, 103.

34. William E. Leuchtenburg, *Franklin D. Roosevelt and the New Deal, 1932–1940* (New York: Harper Colophon, 1963), pp. 261–63. The NRA's hours provisions first established the five-day work week as the industrial norm.

35. Hudson, "U.S. Industrial Policy," p. 470. See also Terrence C. Casey, "The Clinton Administration and the Industrial Policy Question," *Journal of Social, Political and Economic Studies* 18(1): 55 (Spring 1993).

36. Hawley, *New Deal*, pp. 205–77.

37. Graham K. Wilson, *Business and Politics: A Comparative Introduction* (Chatham, N.J.: Chatham House, 1985), pp. 29–34; Kim McQuaid, *Big Business and Presidential Power: From FDR to Reagan* (New York: William Morrow, 1982), pp. 284–305.

38. Lane Kirkland, "Labor's View of Reindustrializing America," in Michael L. Wachter and Susan M. Wachter, *Toward a New U.S. Industrial Policy?* (Philadelphia: University of Pennsylvania Press, 1983), pp. 30–37.

39. Reich, "Industrial Policy of the Right," pp. 12–17.

40. Graham, *Losing Time*, pp. 35–45; Casey, "Clinton Administration," pp. 46–47.

41. Robert B. Reich, *The Resurgent Liberal (and Other Unfashionable Prophecies)* (New York: Times Books, 1989), p. 255; Etzioni, "MITIzation of America?", pp. 44–46; Bardach, "Implementing Industrial Policy," p. 112; Graham, *Losing Time*, p. 148.

42. Graham, *Losing Time*, pp. 159–67; Reich, *Resurgent Liberal*, pp. 255–57; Casey, "Clinton Administration," pp. 49–51; Gary Hart, "Industrial Policies and the Major U.S. Parties," in Barfield and Schambra, *Politics of Industrial Policy*, pp. 222–27. Magaziner later became director of President Clinton's White House health care reform task force and was one of the key architects of the original Clinton health plan.

43. Graham, *Losing Time*, pp. 207–8, 219–22, 235–37.

44. Osborne's *Laboratories of Democracy* includes chapters on Dukakis's Massachusetts and Clinton's Arkansas. The paperback edition published in 1990 has a foreword by Clinton and a blurb on the cover, "A New Breed of Governor Creates Models for National Growth." Like Reich and Magaziner, Osborne was a Clinton advisor in the 1992 campaign. On industrial policy in the Dukakis campaign, see Graham, *Losing Time*, pp. 229–30. Clinton's campaign proposals are summarized in Bill Clinton and Al Gore, *Putting People First: How We Can All Change America* (New York: Times Books, 1992), esp. pp. 9–13, 143–45.

45. Peter Passell, "High-Tech Industry is Hard to Help," *New York Times*,

February 2, 1993; John Markoff, "Clinton Proposes Changes in Policy to Aid Technology," *New York Times*, February 23, 1993; Edmund L. Andrews, "Military Industry Strives to Preserve Status Quo," *New York Times*, March 12, 1993; Matthew L. Wald, "Government Dream Car," *New York Times*, September 30, 1993; Graeme Browning, "Listen to the City Boys," *National Journal*, January 9, 1993, p. 101.

46. Ross Perot, *United We Stand: How We Can Take Back Our Country* (New York: Hyperion, 1992), pp. 60–62.

47. Thurow, *Zero-Sum Solution*, pp. 270–71. See also Graham, *Losing Time*, pp. 77, 113, 256–57; Vogel, "Government-Industry Relations," pp. 97–98; Paul Lawrence and Davis Dyer, *Renewing American Industry* (New York: Free Press, 1983), pp. 119–45.

48. Willard W. Cochrane, *Farm Prices: Myth and Reality* (Minneapolis: University of Minnesota Press, 1958); Kenneth R. Farrell and C. Ford Runge, "Institutional Innovation and Technical Change in American Agriculture: The Role of the New Deal," *American Journal of Agricultural Economics* 65(5): 1168–73 (December 1983); Wayne D. Rasmussen, "The New Deal Farm Programs: What They Were and Why They Survived," *American Journal of Agricultural Economics* 65(5): 1158–62 (December 1983); Earl O. Heady, "The Agriculture of the U.S.," in *Scientific American, Food and Agriculture* (San Francisco: W. H. Freeman, 1976), pp. 77–84.

49. Jim Hightower, *Hard Tomatoes, Hard Times: A Report of the Agribusiness Accountability Project on the Failure of America's Land Grant College Complex* (Cambridge, Mass.: Schenkman, 1973); Joseph N. Belden, *Dirt Rich, Dirt Poor: America's Food and Farm Crisis* (New York: Routledge & Kegan Paul, 1986); Joel Solkoff, *The Politics of Food* (San Francisco: Sierra Club, 1985); Marty Strange, *Family Farming: A New Economic Vision* (Lincoln: University of Nebraska Press, 1988).

50. Don Paarlberg, "Tarnished Gold: Fifty Years of New Deal Farm Programs," in Robert Eden, ed., *The New Deal and Its Legacy: Critique and Reappraisal* (New York: Greenwood, 1989), pp. 40–41.

51. Don Paarlberg, "Effects of New Deal Farm Programs on the Agricultural Agenda a Half Century Later and Prospect for the Future," *American Journal of Agricultural Economics* 65(5): 1163–67 (December 1983); James Bovard, *The Farm Fiasco* (San Francisco: ICS Press, 1989); Clifton B. Luttrell, *The High Cost of Farm Welfare* (Washington, D.C.: Cato Institute, 1989); Bruce L. Gardner, *The Governing of Agriculture* (Lawrence: University Press of Kansas, 1981); E. C. Pasour, Jr., *Agriculture and the State: Market Processes and Bureaucracy* (New York: Holmes & Meier, 1990).

52. Quoted (approvingly) in Bovard, *Farm Fiasco*, p. 17.

53. Clinton and Gore, *Putting People First*, p. 33.

54. James Bovard, "Wheat and Chaff," *New Republic*, March 15, 1993, p. 18.

55. Willard W. Cochrane and C. Ford Runge, *Reforming Farm Policy: Toward a National Agenda* (Ames: Iowa State University Press, 1992).

56. William P. Browne, *Private Interests, Public Policy, and American Agriculture* (Lawrence: University Press of Kansas, 1988), pp. 17–18, 22–23, 30, 240–41,

249–50; David Rapp, *How the U.S. Got into Agriculture: And Why It Can't Get Out* (Washington, D.C.: Congressional Quarterly, 1988), pp. 63–66.

57. Robert L. Tontz, "Origin of the Base Period Concept of Parity—A Significant Value Judgment in Agricultural Policy," *Agricultural History* 32(1): 174–81 (January 1958); idem, "Legal Parity: Implementation of the Policy of Equality for Agriculture, 1929–1954," *Agricultural History* 29(4): 3–13 (October 1955); Pasour, *Agriculture and the State*, pp. 81–84, 89.

58. Charles L. Schultze, *The Distribution of Farm Subsidies: Who Gets the Benefits?* (Washington, D.C.: Brookings Institution, 1971); Belden, *Dirt Rich, Dirt Poor*, pp. 45–47; Gardner, *Governing of Agriculture*, pp. 74–82.

59. Income rather than price goals and limitations on payments to large producers were two principles of the Brannan Plan, proposed by the Truman administration in 1949 but rejected by a Democratic Congress. See Reo M. Christenson, *The Brannan Plan: Farm Politics and Policy* (Ann Arbor: University of Michigan Press, 1959); Allen J. Matusow, *Farm Policies and Politics in the Truman Years* (New York: Atheneum, 1970), pp. 191–221; Murray R. Benedict, *Farm Policies of the United States, 1790–1950* (New York: Twentieth Century Fund, 1953), pp. 484–90. Christenson, *Brannan Plan*, pp. 145–56, 173–75, argues that one reason for the defeat of the Brannan Plan was the unwillingness of Secretary of Agriculture Charles Brannan to work with the Farm Bureau and the Grange, which became ardent opponents of the proposal. This contrasts with the Roosevelt administration's successful effort to enlist the same two groups in support of production control, which we described in chapter 3.

The 1985 and 1990 farm bills moved toward an income-based policy by reducing price supports while increasing deficiency payments. Payments to any farm were limited to $50,000 from a single commodity program and $250,000 from all government sources, though large farmers found ways to circumvent these caps. See Rapp, *How the U.S. Got into Agriculture*, pp. 17, 39–44; Browne, *Private Interests*, p. 236; George E. Rossmiller and Rachel A. Nugent, "The Effect of the 1990 Farm Bill on Agricultural Trade," *American Journal of Agricultural Economics* 73(3): 905–6 (August 1991); C. Ford Runge, "The 1990 Farm Bill and the Uruguay Round," *American Journal of Agricultural Economics* 73(3): 911–12 (August 1991).

60. Quoted in Theodore Saloutos, *The American Farmer and the New Deal* (Ames: Iowa State University Press, 1982), p. 55. Similarly, see Henry A. Wallace, *America Must Choose* (New York and Boston: Foreign Policy Association and World Peace Foundation, 1934), p. 6.

61. Saloutos, *American Farmer and the New Deal*, pp. 137–49; Edward L. Schapsmeier and Frederick H. Schapsmeier, *Henry A. Wallace of Iowa: The Agrarian Years, 1910–1940* (Ames: Iowa State University Press, 1968), pp. 190–91, 254–56; Charles E. Jacob, *Leadership in the New Deal: The Administrative Challenge* (Englewood Cliffs, N.J.: Prentice-Hall, 1967), p. 18.

62. Paarlberg, "Tarnished Gold," pp. 42–43; idem, "Effects of New Deal Farm Programs," pp. 1165–66; Pasour, *Agriculture and the State*, pp. 159–61, 170–71; Robert L. Paarlberg, "Is There Anything 'American' About American Agricultural Policy?" in Carol S. Kramer, *The Political Economy of U.S. Agricul-*

ture: Challenges for the 1990s (Washington, D.C.: Resources for the Future, 1989), pp. 47–49.

63. Quoted in Van L. Perkins, *Crisis in Agriculture: The Agricultural Adjustment Administration and the New Deal* (Berkeley and Los Angeles: University of California Press, 1969), pp. 84–85. See also O. B. Jesness, "Validity of the Fundamental Assumptions Underlying Agricultural Adjustment," *Journal of Farm Economics* 18(1): 29–30 (February 1936); Bovard, *Farm Fiasco*, pp. 26–27.

64. Edwin G. Nourse, Joseph S. Davis, and John D. Black, *Three Years of the Agricultural Adjustment Administration* (Washington, D.C.: Brookings Institution, 1937), pp. 37–38, 60–66; Murray R. Benedict, *Farm Policies of the United States, 1790–1950* (New York: Twentieth Century Fund, 1953), pp. 303–4, 517.

65. Paarlberg, "Is There Anything 'American' About American Agricultural Policy?", pp. 52–54; Earl O. Heady, *A Primer on Food, Agriculture, and Public Policy* (New York: Random House, 1967), pp. 136–42; Warren C. Whatley, "Labor for the Picking: The New Deal in the South," *Journal of Economic History* 43(4): 912–13 (December 1983).

66. Willard W. Cochrane, *The Development of American Agriculture: A Historical Analysis* (Minneapolis: University of Minnesota Press, 1979), pp. 308–10, 379; Michael Perelman, "Efficiency in Agriculture: The Economics of Energy," in Richard Merrill, ed., *Radical Agriculture* (New York: Harper & Row, 1976), pp. 67, 74; Lawrence and Dyer, *Renewing American Industry*, p. 141.

67. Whatley, "Labor for the Picking"; Jack Temple Kirby, "The Transformation of Southern Plantations, c. 1920–1960," *Agricultural History* 57(3): 257–76 (July 1983); Pete Daniel, *Breaking the Land: The Transformation of Cotton, Tobacco, and Rice Cultures since 1880* (Urbana: University of Illinois Press, 1985), pp. 239–55; Gilbert C. Fite, *Cotton Fields No More: Southern Agriculture, 1865–1980* (Lexington: University Press of Kentucky, 1984), pp. 139–206.

68. Frances Fox Piven and Richard A. Cloward, *Poor People's Movements: Why They Succeed, How They Fail* (New York: Vintage, 1979), pp. 181–263.

69. Henry A. Wallace, "Farm Economists and Agricultural Planning," *Journal of Farm Economics* 18(1): 1 (February 1936).

70. See Schapsmeier and Schapsmeier, *Henry A. Wallace*, pp. 20-21, 27–29.

71. James G. March and Johan P. Olsen, *Rediscovering Institutions: The Organizational Basis of Politics* (New York: Free Press, 1989), pp. 22–24, 160–62.

72. On practices, see Alasdair MacIntyre, *After Virtue*, 2d ed. (Notre Dame, Ind.: University of Notre Dame Press, 1984), pp. 125–26, 187–203; idem, *Whose Justice? Which Rationality?* (Notre Dame, Ind.: University of Notre Dame Press, 1988), pp. 30–46; Robert N. Bellah et al., *Habits of the Heart: Individualism and Commitment in American Life* (Berkeley and Los Angeles: University of California Press, 1985), pp. 119–20, 154, 251–52, 299–300, 335.

Index

Academy of Motion Picture Arts and Sciences, 126
Acreage restrictions, 141, 144–45, 192, 208, 223, 239
Actors' Equity, 126
African-Americans, 144, 147, 149, 221, 239–40, 251n65. *See also* Race
Agricultural Adjustment Act, 9, 13, 36, 54, 61, 64, 82–83, 90, 103–11 *passim*, 160–62, 170, 205, 208, 236–37; Supreme Court vote on (Hoosac Mills case), 3–4, 19, 37, 105, 162; party and sectional voting on, 209–10
Agricultural Adjustment Administration (AAA): origins of, 3–4, 13–17, 66–89, 104–5, 168–69, 183–84; and visions of industrial recovery, 9–10; Program Planning Division, 19, 107; and the U.S. political economy, overview of, 20–23; and party politics, 31–65; and the state, structure of, 31–32, 50–65, 104–14; and the Extension Service, 58; implementation of, 90–114, 161–62, 170–71; and the role of public experts, 91, 105–8; Legal Section, 97, 106, 163; and the strength of the agricultural state, 104–14; Program Planning Division, 105; Division of Production, 106–7, 109; and marketing programs vs. production controls, 108–10; benefit payments, 109–10, 113; processing taxes, 109, 188, 212; reaction to, by farmers' organizations, 110–12; and class relations, 115–50;

acreage restrictions, 141, 144–45, 192, 208, 223, 239; and pluralist theory, 159–63; and elite theory, 169–70; and Marxist theories, 176–99; and rational choice approaches, 204, 209–21; analogies to, and lessons and limitations of, 222, 223–40; and contemporary agricultural policy, 233–40
Agricultural Marketing Act, 16, 79
Agricultural wage laborers, 163, 238; sharecroppers, 21, 24, 35, 50, 113, 144–45; tenant farmers, 21, 24, 35, 50, 113, 145–147; and class conflict, 116, 140–50, 216; migratory, 141–42; and Marxist theories, 188, 192–94; and the Democratic party, 216
Agriculture: and domestic allotment proposals, 14, 106, 183, 208, 241; and export dumping, 16, 17, 104, 207; and the New Deal, overview of, 17–18; and industry, comparison of, 32–38; and the agriculture state, strength of, 104–14; and agricultural adjustment, theory of, 113; and class conflict, 115–17, 140–50; and acreage restrictions, 141, 144–45, 192, 208, 223, 239. *See also* Agricultural Adjustment Act; Agricultural Adjustment Administration (AAA); Production controls
Air traffic controllers, 140
Alabama, 69
Althusser, Louis, 180
Aluminum production, 32